D1118430

CRITICAL
MASS

Studies in International Governance is a research and policy analysis series from the Centre for International Governance Innovation (CIGI) and WLU Press. Titles in the series provide timely consideration of emerging trends and current challenges in the broad field of international governance. Representing diverse perspectives on important global issues, the series will be of interest to students and academics while serving also as a reference tool for policy-makers and experts engaged in policy discussion. To reach the greatest possible audience and ultimately shape the policy dialogue, each volume will be made available both in print through WLU Press and, twelve months after publication, accessible for free online through the IGLOO Network under the Creative Commons License.

CIGI — The Centre for International Governance Innovation / Centre pour l'innovation dans la gouvernance internationale

CRITICAL MASS

The Emergence of Global Civil Society

edited by
James W. St.G. Walker and
Andrew S. Thompson

Wilfrid Laurier University Press

Wilfrid Laurier University Press acknowledges the financial support of the Government of Canada through the Book Publishing Industry Development Program for its publishing activities. Wilfrid Laurier University Press acknowledges the financial support of the Centre for International Governance Innovation. The Centre for International Governance Innovation gratefully acknowledges support for its work program from the Government of Canada and the Government of Ontario.

Library and Archives Canada Cataloguing in Publication

Critical mass : the emergence of global civil society / James W. St.G. Walker and Andrew S. Thompson, editors.

Includes bibliographical references and index.

ISBN 978-1-55458-022-4

1. Civil Society. 2. Globalization. 3. Political participation. 4. World citizenship. I. Walker, James W. St.G., 1940– II. Thompson, Andrew S. (Andrew Stuart), 1975–

Co-published with the Centre for International Governance Innovation.

JF799.C74 2008   323   C2007-903786-0

© 2008 The Centre for International Governance Innovation (CIGI) and Wilfrid Laurier University Press

Cover design by David Drummond.

Text design by P.J. Woodland.

CONTENTS

ⅲ PROBLEMS AND PROSPECTS

LIST OF ACRONYMS

Afrodad	African Forum and Network on Debt and Development
AMARC	World Association of Community Radio Broadcasters
AMR	Annual Ministerial Review
ANND	Arab NGO Network for Development
APRs	African personal representatives
ASEM	Asia–Europe Meetings
ASPBAE	Asian South Pacific Bureau of Adult Education
ATTAC	Association for the Taxation of financial Transactions for the Aid of Citizens
AU	African Union
BOND	British Overseas NGOs for Development
C&G	Citizen and Governance Program(me)
CAFOD	Catholic Agency for Overseas Development
CBFC	Canadian Beijing Facilitating Committee
CCIC	Canadian Council for International Cooperation
CHR	United Nations Commission on Human Rights
CICC	Coalition for an International Criminal Court
CIIR	Catholic Institute for International Relations
CIVICUS	World Alliance for Citizen Participation
CNICC	Canadian Network for an International Criminal Court
CONGO	The Conference of NGOs
CPC	Canadian Preparatory Committee
CRA	Credit Reform Act
CRID	Centre de recherche et d'information pour le développement
CS	Civil Society
CSB	Civil Society Bureau
CSO	Civil Society Organization
CSR	Corporate Social Responsibility
CSTD	Commission on Science and Technology for Development

DCF Development Cooperation Forum
DESA United Nations Department of Economic and Social Affairs
DGG Democratizing Global Governance
DOD Draft Outcome Document
DDR Disarmament, Demobilization and Reintegration Program
EBRD European Bank for Reconstruction and Development
ECB European Central Bank
ECOSOC Economic and Social Council
EDs IMF Executive Directors
EITI Extractive Industries Transparency Initiative
ESAF Enhanced Structural Adjustment Facility
ESCAP United Nations Economic and Social Commission for Asia and the Pacific
Eurodad European Network on Debt and Development
FAO Food and Agriculture Organization
FIM Montreal International Forum; Forum International de Montréal
FSC Forestry Stewardship Council
G8 Group of 8 (heads of government from Canada, France, Germany, Italy, Japan, Russia, the United Kingdom, and the United States.)
G22 Group of 22 (now G20; finance ministers and Central Bank governors from the G8 and Pacific Rim)
GAID Global Alliance for ICT Development
GCAP Global Call to Action against Poverty
GCS Global Civil Society
GCSF Global Civil Society Forum
GCSO Global Civil Society Organizations
GDP Gross Domestic Product
GMOs Genetically Modified Organisms
GNP Gross National Product
GRI Global Reporting Initiative
HIVOS International Humanist Institute for Cooperation with Developing Countries; Humanistisch Instituut voor Ontwikkelingssamenwerking
HLS ECOSOC High-level Segment
IANGO International Advocacy NGOs
IBSA India-Brazil-South Africa Trilateral
ICANN Internet Corporation for Assigned Names and Numbers
ICBL International Campaign to Ban Landmines
ICC International Criminal Court
ICAE International Council for Adult Education
ICT Information and Communication(s) Technologies

ICT4D Information and Communication(s) Technologies for Development
ICVA International Council on Voluntary Agencies
IDA International Development Assistance
IDR Institute for Development Research
IFCB International Forum of Capacity Building
IGOs International Governmental Organizations
ILC International Law Commission
ILO International Labour Organization
IMF International Monetary Fund
INGOs International NGOs
IOE International Organisation of Employers
LIC Low income countries
LMG Like-minded group
MD IMF Managing Director
MDGs Millennium Development Goals
MDRI Multilateral Debt Relief Initiative
MIA Multilateral Investment Agreement
MIC Middle-income countries
MPH Make Poverty History
NAFTA North American Free Trade Agreement
NEPAD New Partnership for Africa's Development
NGO Non-governmental organization
NSC U.S. National Security Council
ODA Official Development Assistance
OECD Organisation for Economic Co-operation and Development
OHCHR Office of the High Commissioner for Human Rights
PAR Participatory Action Research
PDR Policy Development and Review
PoA Plan of Action
PRIA Society for Participatory Research in Asia
PrepCom Preparatory Committee on the Establishment of an International
Criminal Court
PRGF Poverty Reduction and Growth Facility
PRSP Poverty Reduction Strategy Paper
RSPB Royal Society for the Protection of Birds
PWYP Publish What You Pay
SG United Nations Secretary General
SMEs Small and Medium Enterprises
TNCs Trans-national Corporations
UCLG United Cities and Local Governments
UN United Nations

UNCED   United Nations Conference on Environment and Development
UNCTAD   United Nations Conference on Trade and Development
UNDP   United Nations Development Programme
UNFPA   United Nations Population Fund
UNICEF   United Nations Children's Fund
UN-NGLS   United Nations Non-Governmental Liaison Service
VANI   Voluntary Action Network India
WCAR   World Conference against Racism
WEF   World Economic Forum
WFP   United Nations World Food Programme
WSF   World Social Forum
WSIS   World Summit on the Information Society
WSSD   World Summit on Sustainable Development
WWF   World Wildlife Federation
WTO   World Trade Organization

FOREWORD

Critical Mass is the appropriate title for this excellent study of the emergence of global civil society. This book is the fifth in the Studies in International Governance Series, commissioned by the Centre for International Governance Innovation (CIGI). The series emphasizes timeliness, policy relevance, and academic rigour. The editors of the present volume, James Walker and Andrew Thompson, have commissioned work by some of the leading analysts of the emergence of global civil society. Both historians, Walker and Thompson are well aware of the antecedents to global society such as the international movement to ban slavery over two hundred years ago. They recognize, however, that the global scale, the penetration, and the presence and effectiveness of non-governmental organizations (NGOs) have multiplied since the concept of NGOs first emerged as the United Nations System took form in the 1940s. John Clark, one of the authors, suggests that in the post–Cold War period civil society has become "the third superpower," which galvanizes "public opinion in the management of world affairs."

Clark and others acknowledge that many governments and analysts challenge the legitimacy of the claims of civil society because, unlike parliaments, civil society organizations lack a demonstrable mandate. Yet even critics acknowledge the impact of civil society upon global economics and politics. *Critical Mass* demonstrates how the campaign to establish an international criminal court depended not upon leadership by a particular state but upon international networks, legal activists, and international NGOs. Other chapters demonstrate how civil society has gained a place within the deliberations of international financial organizations where the claims of expertise and security had long predominated. Other chapters study the differences between North and South and the Arab World and the West. The final section looks to the future and the possibilities for a charter for a Global Civil Society Forum. The reader understands how global civil society's emergence now represents a major innovation in international governance.

The Centre for International Governance Innovation recognizes the importance of global civil society in its own work. Most of our workshops and conferences, including those whose proceedings are the foundation for the other books in the Studies in International Governance Series, have significant civil society participation. In the past, government officials, retired practitioners, and academics would dominate discussion of important global issues at a think tank. Today, civil society organizations are recognized internationally for their expertise, research ability, and policy relevance. *Critical Mass* illustrates how a transformation has occurred in the work of organizations like CIGI. Moreover, through its IGLOO knowledge network, CIGI is playing a major role in linking together global civil society organizations. With the advanced communication possibilities that IGLOO provides, civil society organizations can achieve even greater range and effectiveness. There is no innovation in governance that will be more meaningful in the twenty-first century.

John English

ACKNOWLEDGEMENTS

Critical Mass: The Emergence of Global Civil Society is one of the outcomes of a conference that took place October 17–19, 2006, in which academics, international civil servants, and civil society activists met at the Centre for International Governance Innovation (CIGI) in Waterloo, Canada, to discuss the feasibility of a proposal to establish a new venue or entity whose primary purpose would be to enhance global civil society input within international governance institutions. This edited collection of essays would not have been possible without the help and assistance of a number of individuals and organizations.

We would like to extend our special thanks to Gordon Smith, Barry Carin, and the rest of the staff at the Centre for Global Studies in Victoria, British Columbia, for their work in organizing and preparing the conference.

To John English, CIGI's Executive Director, and the rest of CIGI's staff for hosting the conference.

To all of the participants of the conference, many of whom have contributed chapters to this volume.

To Brian Henderson and his staff at Wilfrid Laurier University Press for their role in producing the book.

Finally, we would like to express our appreciation to the civil society organizations for allowing their staff to devote time and energy to this project. They include the Arab NGO Network for Development (ANND), the Conference of NGOs (CONGO), the Montreal International Forum (FIM), the New Rules for Global Finance Coalition, and the Society for Participatory Research in Asia (PRIA).

INTRODUCTION

James W. St.G. Walker and
Andrew S. Thompson

"Think globally, act locally" was a popular slogan some thirty years ago, meant to arouse concern and inspire participation. Today we have discovered that global *is* local, and the consequences can sometimes seem threatening. For many citizens of the early twenty-first century, the concept of "globalization" is discouraging rather than inspirational. An increasingly integrated global marketplace can imply the dominance of transnational corporations concerned only for their own profits, ignoring the best interests of local populations. The creation of regulatory bodies designed to facilitate economic globalization means that decisions affecting the daily lives of millions of people are made beyond the bounds of the nation state, and therefore outside the authority of national governments and unaccountable to their voters. A suspected parallel process is cultural homogenization, which could suffocate local traditions and values. And while the influence of nation states seems to decline, new global issues are proliferating: climate change, infectious diseases, violations of human security and human rights, terrorism, nuclear weapons, environmental destruction, and economic inequality. These and similar problems cannot be isolated from each other or solved individually. Locally directed action may be dismissed as futile in the face of such overwhelming and inter-territorial issues, and global action is too complex for fast and ready answers. Climate change, for example, is intimately connected to sustainable development, energy usage, technological innovation, resource management, human rights and freedoms, personal health, power relationships, job security, individual standards of living, and the industrialization of regions long kept on the periphery of the world economy. What is an individual citizen to do?

The chapters in this book identify another phenomenon occurring today that offers not solutions per se but a process for engagement with the most pressing problems of our contemporary world: the emergence of global civil society. In recent years a consciousness of a global civil society has been reaching "critical mass," in the sense of attracting attention and anticipating influence; it is a critical mass too in the sense that it is becoming better informed, and therefore critical, of the liabilities of globalization, and people are massing together in social movements, NGOs, and ad hoc demonstrations to confront some of the most encompassing challenges facing humanity today. Of course "civil society" as a concept has existed for centuries. The ancients wrote of a *societas civilis*, meaning the rule of law and active citizen participation in the public life of their societies; in the late eighteenth century, enlightenment authors distinguished civil society from the state, encouraging the awareness of a citizenry capable of mobilizing to achieve social goals and to counteract despotism and oppression. The campaign to abolish the Atlantic slave trade, launched in the 1780s, is frequently cited as an early example not only of a mass movement for social change but of its application to a transnational problem. A more formal and systematic role for civil society in international affairs accompanied the establishment of the United Nations (UN), when a group of "consultants" from civil society organizations (CSOs) attended the founding San Francisco Conference in 1945 and collaborated in drafting the UN Charter. That charter provided for a continuing relationship between the UN and civil society through the accreditation of certain non-governmental organizations (NGOs) to the Economic and Social Council (ECOSOC). Over the years this relationship strengthened, especially during the leadership of Kofi Annan. In 2003 the Secretary-General established a Panel of Eminent Persons on United Nations–Civil Society Relations, chaired by Fernando Henrique Cardoso. The Cardoso Report, issued in 2004, concluded that "civil society is now so vital to the United Nations that engaging with it well is a necessity, not an option," and it offered a number of reform suggestions toward that objective.[1] Reflecting these solid accomplishments, and other factors to be described in succeeding chapters, there has been a virtual explosion of civil society involvement in global issues. Most noticeably, the number of CSOs dedicated to global concerns has grown exponentially, and they have expanded their scope from aiming at specific targets like slavery or prisoners of conscience to fundamental matters of global governance. The process has been dubbed "globalization from below."[2]

The rapidity and extent of civil society's recent growth on the international scene prompted the Centre for Global Studies (CGS) at the University of Victoria to explore the possibility of establishing some "venue" or "forum" that might coordinate the voices of global civil society in order to enhance their effectiveness, accountability, inclusiveness, and credibility in their negotiations with agencies of international governance. With funding from the Ford Foundation, CGS director Gordon Smith and associate director Barry Carin approached the Centre for International Governance Innovation (CIGI) in Waterloo, Ontario, to co-sponsor and host a small conference where civil society activists, international officials, and academics could probe the usefulness, nature, and possibility of such a coordinating effort and the practical steps that could lead to its implementation. The conference, with a little over thirty participants, convened at CIGI in October 2006.

At the time, the participants thought better of establishing a coordinating body. They did so, in part, because a number of highly effective transnational coalitions and alliances already facilitate NGO/CSO engagement with international governmental organizations (IGOs). Indeed, over the course of the conference, as the participants exchanged ideas, it became increasingly clear that global civil society was having a significant influence on the international system. Although this was not necessarily a new discovery, it also became apparent that civil society actors could learn a great deal from each other. All agreed that many of the ideas, particularly those that pertained to assisting and mobilizing global civil society, deserved further examination.

This book is an attempt to do just that. The aim is to enlarge the debate about global civil society's various roles and activities by bringing a broader audience into the discussion that includes students and academics, NGO/CSO activists and social movement leaders, and policymakers and international civil servants. We hope that it will foster an exchange among these various groups by assessing activist strategies that worked well in the past as well as those that fell short of their intended objectives.

There is a large and growing literature on global civil society and related developments. The "bible" of the entire movement is surely *Global Civil Society* from the London School of Economics, edited by Helmut Anheier, Marlies Glasius, and Mary Kaldor, and published annually since 2001. Some foundational monographs have been produced in the last decade, several journals such as *Global Governance, Human Rights Quarterly, Journal of Civil Society, Journal of Human Rights, Millennium: Journal of International Studies, Social Forces,* and *Third World Quarterly* are among those that regularly carry articles relevant to this topic, and there is an increasing number of edited collections devoted to exploring aspects of the global community and collective action. Readers interested in pursuing the issues raised in the current volume will have a wealth of choices.[3]

Critical Mass: The Emergence of Global Civil Society is obviously not unique as an offering of information and ideas about the exciting movement taking place in today's world to engage citizens in the shaping of our global future. What does make this volume unique, however, is its particular mix of academic and activist perspectives. Our contributors include the leaders of some of the most influential CSOs operating in the field and some of the most respected academic analysts of the global civil society phenomenon. This mixture, as we learned at the Waterloo conference in October 2006, is an extremely fruitful one, capable of generating fresh ideas and insights and innovative directions for future action and scholarship. The essays offered in one volume cannot be genuinely comprehensive, but our selection is intended to represent solid examples of achievement and suggestive discussions of continuing processes. Section 1 contains two articles that explore some of the fundamental questions and theoretical approaches in this field of study. The eight case studies in section 2 provide detailed descriptions of specific projects and campaigns, with a view to illuminating the various ways global CSOs and social movements are affecting the evolution of global civil society. Section 3 concludes the book with three forward-looking essays addressing the prospects for an enhanced engagement between global civil society and the existing instruments of global governance.

"Civil society" is a contended and contentious term, especially when combined with "global." Noting that there is no agreed definition, Mary Kaldor remarks that "its ambiguity is one of its attractions," and in fact "the debate about its meaning is part of what it is about."[4] Is there such a thing as a global civil society? What makes it "global" rather than simply "transnational"? And if it is a recognizable phenomenon, why is it occurring today and what are its characteristics? These are among the intriguing questions addressed in section 1. Both chapters in this section bear dynamic titles, intended to convey the notion of movement and process, the very ideas that characterize the current debate about global civil society.

John Clark's "The Globalization of Civil Society" begins with the subject of civil society and its traditional role in sustaining democracy. In recent years the substance of politics has been globalized, that is, the issues requiring attention are no longer restricted by national boundaries, but the process of political decision making has remained at the national level. This, for Clark, provides the opening for a genuinely global civil society, a "space" where organizations and movements can operate as the "citizen's voice" to monitor transparency, accountability, and equality in transnational deliberations. At the same time, citizens' recognition of the various deficits in the ability of their governments to represent them in global fora encourages them to turn to civil society organizations, where they can actually participate in policy debates and influence not only governments but transnational corporations and trading practices. Writing from his experience as a GCSO administrator and activist, Clark remains optimistic about the opportunities for civil society to become increasingly influential, but he warns that there is a perceptible backlash against GCSOs' interventions and suggests that organizations representing civil society must ensure their own adherence to principles of legitimacy, representativity, and accountability. "Ethical globalization," Clark concludes, is within our grasp, and civil society is poised to offer alternative policies and to change the underlying rules, moving beyond campaigns to stop particular projects or practices in a global manifestation of civil society's democratic function.

Paul van Seters, one of academe's most respected and influential commentators on global civil society, offers a highly sophisticated yet readily accessible discussion of the various ways of "Approaching Global Civil Society," from the perspective of several different disciplines. He lays out the historical currents that have accumulated to produce a conscious community of interests among CSOs and social movements, and he gives the flavour of the theoretical debates by canvassing their chief contributors in history, philosophy, sociology, political science, and international relations. Through an analysis of the leading theoreticians van Seters arrives at an innovative theory of his own, and in its support he marshals evidence from several recent global campaigns, for the Mine Ban Treaty, the International Criminal Court, and Jubilee 2000 for debt relief. Acknowledging that CSOs have a longer history of involvement with transnational issues, van Seters's finely constructed argument demonstrates convincingly that there is something new and promising in contemporary developments and that indeed we can recognize the emergence of a global civil society. This chapter amply rewards a reader's attention and will become a standard citation in future writings on this subject.

Renate Bloem, Isolda Agazzi Ben Attia, and Philippe Dam reflect on the work of the Conference of NGOs (CONGO) in facilitating and strengthening civil society participation at the United Nations. First established in 1948, it is an umbrella organization for local, national, and international NGOs operating within the UN system. Its principal objective is to "democratize global governance," meaning to enhance global civil society engagement at the UN in order that "the governed" can have a say in the shape and direction of decision making at the international level. As the authors note, fulfilling the organization's mandate has not been easy. During the Cold War, ideological rivalry between East and West provided few opportunities for civil society engagement. Although new opportunities emerged in the 1990s following the collapse of the Soviet Union, so too did new challenges. As the number of

NGOs with consultative status increased, coordinating their activities became more difficult (NGOs tend to be fiercely independent), particularly around the various UN world summits in which parallel civil society summits were organized. Despite these challenges, CONGO has, through a variety of techniques, become both adept at encouraging common platforms among NGOs without insisting that they speak with a single "voice," and highly skilled in fostering favourable conditions for NGO–UN dialogue on a wide range of issues. CONGO has been operating in an environment that has often been less than hospitable to greater civil society inclusion in decision-making processes; there is little evidence that this hostility will change anytime soon. As a result, much of the organization's recent activities have focused on securing access for NGOs by codifying their legal status at the UN, depoliticizing the mechanisms for granting consultative status in order that a more diverse range of NGOs can obtain accreditation, promoting greater independence from political authorities for national NGOs, and encouraging multi-stakeholder partnerships between the UN and civil society. Throughout its nearly sixty-year history, CONGO has attempted to create space for NGOs and CSOs to have their voices heard at the UN. In doing so, it has contributed a great deal to a larger, yet arguably elusive, end, namely the realization of "a more just and equitable world where peoples can have a sense of ownership and belonging."

As the chapters in section 1 argue, global civil society is above all a democratic movement dedicated to involving the citizens of this world in the decisions that affect their daily lives. It is, in short, distinguished by the concept of participation. An instructive example of citizen participation is presented by Rajesh Tandon, president of the Society for Participatory Research in Asia (PRIA), whose chapter co-authored with Mohini Kak illustrates the achievements that are possible when civil society is mobilized. PRIA has recently celebrated its twenty-fifth anniversary as an agent for change in India and its South Asian neighbours, proving that with appropriate tactics and goals civil society can be truly inclusive and effectively global in its reach. PRIA goes to the very basis of this concept, gathering the knowledge and experience of ordinary citizens in confronting their problems and utilizing this knowledge to construct a more thorough understanding of the underlying structures and, over time, to design more effective solutions to the problems the citizens have identified. Tandon and Kak describe PRIA's origins and ideology and demonstrate how they have been fulfilled through local action and especially through networking nationally, regionally, and globally. PRIA's energizing influence has extended to the formation of complementary organizations dedicated to capacity building in Asia and, ultimately, to Asian participation in the emerging dialogue on global governance. The quarter-century history of PRIA is virtually the history of civil society in South Asia over that period, and Tandon and Kak close their chapter with some of the most important lessons they have learned from their extensive experience.

Elizabeth Riddell-Dixon assesses the utility of the Canadian government-sponsored mechanisms for consultation with Canadian NGOs that were established in anticipation of the two United Nations World Summits of 1995, the World Summit for Social Development in Copenhagen, Denmark, and the Fourth World Conference on Women held in Beijing, China. In her chapter, she examines both the procedural characteristics of the consultation processes (whether they were transparent, and inclusive, as well as whether the respective organizing committees that facilitated NGO participation were accountable to their constituents) and the degree to which these mechanisms allowed NGOs opportunities to shape and influence government policies. Riddell-Dixon laments that the immediate legacies of consultation processes were mixed, falling short of expectations: while the mechanisms themselves were relatively open, the NGOs that participated did not, in the end, have much sway with the Canadian government. Nonetheless, she contends that the mechanisms were by no means a wasted effort. Rather, they strengthened NGOs in Canada in ways that were not necessarily obvious at the time. For the Canadian NGOs that participated, the consultations allowed them to deepen both their domestic and transnational networks, giving them new allies both at home and abroad. Moreover, the mechanisms provided important learning experiences by enabling them to develop a richer understanding of the UN system and how to manoeuvre within it. Both developments have been invaluable. Since 1995, opposition to NGO involvement at the UN has grown considerably. "In light of these developments," Riddell-Dixon concludes, "the knowledge base of NGOs and their abilities to collaborate transnationally become all the more important."

The Arab NGO Network for Development (ANND) has taken on a challenge of global dimension: to stimulate the participation of civil society in a region where there is not always a tradition or the circumstances favourable for this kind of initiative. Ziad Abdel Samad, ANND executive director, and Kinda Mohamadieh, program manager, offer an intriguing analysis of the activities of their Network in promoting programs for development, trade, and democracy. Typically, they argue, civil society develops at the local level and then, with some organizational experience, moves into transnational issues as opportunities arise. In the Arab world, as they describe it, the process can move in a different direction: civil society can be strengthened through participation in transnational networks and GCS fora, with the experiences and information gained there translated back to local problems and advocacy campaigns. The rich array of transnational coalitions committed to positive social change and economic development is described in this chapter, indicating the opportunities available to Arab and other Southern activists. The ANND goal remains the strengthening of democratic participatory capacity within Arab societies, and although Samad and Mohamadieh honestly lay out the barriers confronted by civil society in their region, the vivid description of their projects presents an inspirational example of how the global movement can interact positively with the aspirations of parts of the global South.

In her chapter, Gina E. Hill examines the efficacy of the tactics employed by the Coalition for an International Criminal Court (CICC), the ad hoc umbrella organization that acted as the liaison between state governments and civil society during the negotiations for the creation of an International Criminal Court in the mid- to late-1990s. Hill argues that what separates the CICC from other NGO coalitions was its ability to foster genuine co-operation between concerned NGOs and like-minded states, as well as among NGOs themselves, many of which came to the negotiations with differing priorities. The CICC was able to do so in part because of the expertise that the NGOs brought to the negotiations and also because of the importance that it placed on facilitating and coordinating civil society activism. In addition to engaging in high-level lobbying of government officials (and in some cases even becoming members of government delegations), the CICC acted as a repository for information about the court and the state of the negotiations, provided logistical and infrastructure support to NGOs that wanted to participate in the coalition, and, with the help of the internet, initiated public awareness campaigns around the world aimed at the general public as well as the media. Through its multi-pronged campaigning, both sympathetic states and the UN came to view the CICC as a legitimate partner in the negotiations, permitting NGOs considerable input during the proceedings. According to Hill, the process that led to the final text of the Rome Statute of the International Criminal Court in July 1998 was as important as the ultimate objective, namely securing agreement on the creation of a strong and independent court; indeed, through a combination of specialized engagement and extensive outreach, the various formal and informal partnerships that the CICC was able to cultivate resulted in a "high-water mark for collaborative efforts."

The complicated operations of international financial institutions are difficult to penetrate and therefore present a barrier for many citizens who might otherwise be inclined to seek reforms in existing global financial arrangements. There could be no better guide through these complexities than Jo Marie Griesgraber of New Rules for Global Finance Coalition, with her impressive personal history of engagement with the giants of international finance. In a chapter that is at once authoritative and accessible, Griesgraber introduces the International Monetary Fund (IMF) and explains how it affects national and international economies and why it is in desperate need of reform. She offers four cases, in three of which she was intimately involved, where civil society organizations attempted to influence the IMF, and an additional case that is still in progress. Her examples range from a world-spanning campaign to have the IMF cancel the debts of the poorest countries, involving rock stars, celebrity endorsements, political lobbying, mass demonstrations, and even a papal blessing, to a strategic strike conducted by experts and Fund insiders in an effort to enforce transparency upon Fund management. Although collateral benefits have accrued from each of the civil society actions, the IMF has been immune to genuine reform. But at this moment, the chapter concludes, global circumstances make the Fund vulnerable to outside pressure as never before in its history. For example, middle-income countries, those who can repay their debts on time, are not going to the Fund for further loans, with the result that Fund profitability is declining dangerously. CSOs, in conjunction with co-operative governments who want the Fund to fulfil its original mandate, have the opportunity at last to influence power relations and decision making at the IMF if the lessons from past campaigns are taken to heart.

Virginia Haufler assesses recent initiatives aimed at pressuring multinational corporations (entities that are often not considered to be part of global civil society and yet are increasingly involved in issues of global governance) that are operating in zones of conflict to engage in socially responsible practices. She begins by charting the origins and evolution of "Corporate Social Responsibility" (CSR), a concept that today has become widely accepted, in part because it offers companies a response to anti-corporate campaigns designed to highlight the private sector's malpractices. But CSR is also a reflection of the changing nature of global governance. With the rise of economic globalization, non-state actors, including corporations, find themselves increasingly drawn into issues of global governance, and, more than ever, are being asked to become partners in their resolution. Haufler then examines the various ways that trade and investment can negatively affect societies that suffer from weak governing institutions; in some cases, corporations have been complicit in human rights violations, while in others their presence has exacerbated violent conflict and made securing a lasting peace more difficult. While innovative steps are being taken at both the national and international levels to change the ways in which corporations do business in these fragile states, such as the UN Global Compact, the Chad–Cameroon Natural Gas Pipeline Project, and the much heralded Kimberly Process, the purpose of which is to halt the trade of blood diamonds, Haufler remains dubious of their effectiveness. None of these steps, she argues, are perfect, and all suffer from "a lack of political commitment and weak institutionalization." Weak national governments and corporate practices that favour short-term gain over long-term stability have meant that substantial progress has been slow in coming. In view of this, she concludes by questioning whether the time has come to create an international regulatory mechanism able to govern how and where corporations can do business.

The Forum International de Montréal/Montreal International Forum (FIM) began its institutional life as an alliance intended to focus attention on the operations of the UN and other multilateral organizations, to monitor and encourage their adherence to their own stated goals. One extremely influential multilateral grouping is the G8, whose annual meetings bring together the heads of the most powerful governments in the industrial world, and whose decisions have a major impact on policies and events in all parts of the globe. In 2002, following mass demonstrations at G8 and other gatherings of world leaders, the G8 were seeking a means of opening a constructive dialogue with civil society representatives. FIM was selected for this role, and at each G8 meeting, beginning at Kananaskis, Canada, in 2002, FIM has coordinated discussions among civil society organizations and G8 officials and occasionally even with government heads. FIM president and CEO Nigel Martin offers a lively and intimate play-by-play account of this engagement, giving readers an almost diary-like description of events told from the civil society perspective. Martin's candid warnings about the risks attending this operation serve as a cautionary tale for any GCSO in its relations with multilateral agencies and with other CSOs. Martin also provides the lessons learned from each annual G8/GCSO meeting, a unique and carefully considered set of insights that will enlighten civil society activists and international officials alike. Over the five meetings he describes, Martin perceives a conceptual evolution, from trying to base FIM's legitimacy on "representativity" to a new understanding that credibility derives from solid background preparation on the issues and a record of performance in marshalling civil society's concerns to the G8. And therein lies what is perhaps the most significant lesson to be learned from FIM's G8 project.

The final three chapters look ahead to the future and the possibilities for new types of interaction between global civil society and international governance institutions. Those by Andrew S. Thompson and Jan Aart Scholte assess the potential benefits of a new Global Civil Society Forum that could act as a nexus between global civil society and international governmental organizations (IGOs). Thompson's chapter considers whether the 2006 International Non-Governmental Organisations' Accountability Charter might act as a possible blueprint for organizers of a new GCSF, who would have to determine the forum's mandate, the criteria for determining its membership, its sources of funding, and its relationship to existing IGOs. He argues that, while the Accountability Charter could serve as a useful beginning point for any discussion of a GCSF, resolving these issues is an "inherently political act," and it is the values and practices that organizers of the forum choose to adopt that will ultimately determine whether global civil society actors, states, and IGOs come to see it as a legitimate and useful body. Scholte's chapter begins with the assertion that intensified globalization has generated a demand for greater citizenship participation in global policy processes, and yet the existing global governance institutions are not well equipped to accommodate this desire for greater inclusion; in theory, a GCSF could help address this deficit. If established, the forum could be a site for global civil society to assemble rather than an instrument to formulate singular policy positions; it would function as a facilitator for a dialogue, not a campaign machine. Its mission would be to promote informed civil society activism and responsive global regulation on the understanding that there are reciprocal benefits from contacts between global civil society associations and global governance institutions. Its explicit function would be to provide channels of dialogue useful to both civil society groups and global governance actors. Scholte then proposes possible "shapes" that the GCSF might take and examines the necessary conditions that would need to be met in order that a forum of this kind could be established. He concludes that a new forum that helps bridge the divide between global civil society and international governance agencies is not out of the realm of possibility.

The final chapter, by Martin Albrow and Fiona Holland, serves as a conclusion both to section 3 and the book as a whole. They abandon the idea of a GCSF in favour of greater democratization of global governance through new media of communication promoting free expression. The two suggest that global democratic governance is an ongoing process rather than an end in itself, the aim of which is to decentralize, not centralize, democratic engagement. This, they argue, is possible through new and innovative forms of communication that articulate the diverse voices that make up global civil society. One example is community radio, which advocates the "right to communicate," local, non-profit ownership, and greater space for minority voices. A second is the Independent Media Center[5] (Indymedia), which democratizes media communications by allowing anyone with the proper equipment to report on world events. A third is the emergence of blogging, culture jamming, and contemporary art. While the content that is disseminated through these media tends to focus on local concerns, there have been examples where these forms of communication have had an effect on global issues. The most notable example of this is the Global Call to Action against Poverty (GCAP), which revealed how "democratic voices and globally networked media" allowed anti-poverty activists to place considerable pressure on the G8 and British government to take action on poverty reduction in Africa. For

Holland and Albrow, democratic global governance (DGG) is an ongoing process. It involves seeking alternative forms of expression, organization, and collective action. Often these are manifested in everyday activities in which democracy is the shared ideal. This, they contend, is in direct contrast to international institutions, which they argue have a "sclerotic" tendency to "fall under oligarchic control." They conclude that the role of global civil society is to resist this temptation towards aggregation, which tends to favour the ruling elite. Rather, its purpose is to ensure that there is always a balance between the ideal of perfect global democracy and a "knowledge society" dominated by the few.

Globalization, accordingly, has a positive and participatory meaning, as witnessed by the resurgence of citizen initiative in confronting the human needs and aspirations that governments and existing international institutions seem unable to address on their own. The "world order" set in place after 1945 is being redesigned, and this time it really is "we the peoples" who are determined to establish conditions for world peace, for universal human rights and equality, for justice and social progress. But if global civil society is to offer genuinely global solutions, one urgent requirement is the engagement of the South in the process, and this is only beginning to take place. Northern CSOs tend to set the agenda and therefore to channel policy directions, just like their governmental and corporate counterparts. The examples of the Arab Non-Governmental Network for Development and the Society for Participatory Research in Asia show that the inclusion of the global South can happen, and is happening, following a somewhat different trajectory from their Northern colleagues, and a recognition of this fact throughout the civil society realm will contribute significantly to its genuinely global character. Indeed, an awareness of what other CSOs are doing, in different cultural and political environments, mobilized for different goals, and following different organizational models, is in itself a major step forward in the quest for new structures of global governance. Such an awareness will include "best practices" as revealed in successful campaigns, as well as lessons learned from campaigns still in progress, and it will be informed and sophisticated by a sense of humankind's historical quest for a just world order.

Critical Mass: The Emergence of Global Civil Society is one attempt to encourage awareness and cross-fertilization among CSO practitioners, international agency officials, and the academics who analyze both the problems and the proffered solutions to issues of global governance. If, as it is argued in several of the following chapters, CSOs gain their credibility from the knowledge they are able to bring to the negotiating table, then more collaboration with institutions of higher learning will not only strengthen their position but improve the analytical capacities of the academics committed to their cause.

Only with confident and informed social movements will the demand for changes in public policy and social relationships meet with success. The question today is not whether new global structures are desirable but what those structures will be like and how they can be achieved. It is the intention of the authors and editors of this book to bring attention to the challenges facing the world in the twenty-first century, to outline the immense gaps that still need to be filled, and to provide inspiration through the case studies showing how ordinary citizens have been able to make a difference. We hope to encourage readers to become engaged, and to indicate some of the ways engagement is possible. "Free and effective societies exist in direct proportion to their degree of citizen participation and influence," it has been written,[6] and this applies to the building of a just international community just as it does to individual nations. Global governance requires global citizenship, and that means all of us.

NOTES

1 United Nations, *We the Peoples: Civil Society, the United Nations and Global Governance, Report of the Panel of Eminent Persons on UN–Civil Society Relations* Report A/58/817 (Cardoso Report) (New York: United Nations, 2004). The panel defined "civil society" as "the associations of citizens (outside their families, friends and businesses) entered into voluntarily to advance their interests, ideas and ideologies. The term does not include profit-making activity (the private sector) or governing (the public sector). Of particular relevance to the United Nations are mass organizations (such as organizations of peasants, women or retired people), trade unions, professional associations, social movements, indigenous people's organizations, religious and spiritual organizations, academe and public benefit non-governmental organizations" (13).

2 For example, Richard Falk, "Resisting Globalization from Above through Globalization from Below," *New Political Economy* 2 (1997): 17–24.

3 Endnote references in subsequent chapters offer an animated guide to much of this literature, including full bibliographic details for the *Global Civil Society* annual publications from the London School of Economics. Among those titles not mentioned, attention might be drawn to these monographs: John Ehrenberg, *Civil Society: The Critical History of an Idea* (New York: New York University Press, 1999); Mary Kaldor, *Global Civil Society: An Answer to War* (Cambridge, UK: Polity Press, 2003); John Keane, *Global Civil Society?* (Cambridge, UK: Cambridge University Press, 2003); Jan Aart Scholte, *Globalization: A Critical Introduction* (New York: Palgrave Macmillan, 2005). Interesting additional examples of edited collections would include Esref Aksu and Joseph A. Camilleri, eds., *Democratizing Global Governance* (New York: Palgrave Macmillan, 2002); Berch Berberoglu, ed., *Globalization and Change: The Transformation of Global Capitalism* (Lanham, MA: Lexington Books, 2005); Raymond Breton and Jeffrey G. Reitz, eds., *Globalization and Society: Processes of Differentiation Examined* (Westport, CT: Praeger, 2003); Steve Chan and James R.

Scarritt, eds., *Coping with Globalization: Cross-national Patterns in Domestic Governance and Policy Performance* (Portland, OR: Frank Cass, 2002); Andrew F. Cooper, John English, and Ramesh Thakur, eds., *Enhancing Global Governance: Towards a New Diplomacy?* (Tokyo: United Nations University Press, 2002); John Eade and Darren J. O'Byrne, eds., *Global Ethics and Civil Society* (Aldershot, UK, and Burlington, VT: Ashgate, 2005); Michael Edwards and John Gaventa, eds., *Global Citizen Action* (Boulder, CO: Lynne Rienner, 2001); Barry Holden, ed., *Global Democracy: Key Debates* (London and New York: Routledge, 2000); Gordon Laxer and Sandra Halperin, *Global Civil Society and Its Limits* (Houndmills, UK and New York: Palgrave Macmillan, 2003); Roland Robertson and Jan Aart Scholte, general editors, *Encyclopedia of Globalization* (4 vols., New York: Routledge, 2007); Lester M. Salamon, Helmut K. Anheier, Regina List, Stefan Toepler, and S. Wojciech Sokolowski, eds., *Global Civil Society: Dimensions of the Nonprofit Sector* (Baltimore: Johns Hopkins Center for Civil Society Studies, 1999) and *Global Civil Society, Vol. 2, Dimensions of the Nonprofit Sector* (Bloomfield, CT: Kumarian Press, 2004); Jan Aart Scholte and Albrecht Schnabel, eds., *Civil Society and Global Finance* (London and New York: Routledge, 2002); P.J. Simmons and Chantal de Jonge Oudraat, eds., *Managing Global Issues* (Washington, DC: Carnegie Endowment for International Peace, 2001); Jackie Smith, Charles Chatfield, and Ron Pagnucco, eds., *Transnational Social Movements and Global Politics: Solidarity beyond the State* (Syracuse, NY: Syracuse University Press, 1997); Thomas G. Weiss and Leon Gordenker, eds., *NGOs, the UN and Global Governance* (New York: St. Martin's Press, 1998); Peter Willetts, ed., *The Conscience of the World: The Influence of NGOs in the UN System* (Washington, DC: Brookings Institution, 1996).

4 Kaldor, *Global Civil Society*, 2.

5 http://www.indymedia.org.

6 Brian O'Connell, *"First Lights": Recollections of the Beginnings and First Years of CIVICUS: World Alliance for Citizen Participation* (Washington, DC: CIVICUS, 2000), 11.

Overview and Theory

1

The Globalization of Civil Society

John D. Clark

CIVIL SOCIETY AND THE DEMOCRATIZATION OF DEMOCRACY

The history of democracy has been about the evolution of mechanisms by which citizens play a role in shaping government policies and holding officials to account. The efficacy of democratic tools, therefore, can be judged by the degree to which they shorten the gulf between citizens and the decisions that affect them. This chapter argues that among the various roles for civil society, one that is coming most rapidly to ascendancy is that of strengthening democracy through advocacy, particularly as international arenas are fast becoming the crucibles in which new policies are forged, and traditional instruments of democracy hold little sway in that realm.

This trend is particularly powerful because of the increasing interconnectedness of the world we live in. An important paradox is unfolding: although a great deal of the *substance* of politics has been globalized (trade, economics, climate change, HIV/AIDS, the SARS pandemic, terrorism, etc.), the *process* of politics has not. Its main institutions—elections, political parties, and parliaments—remain rooted at the national level. Civil society organizations (CSOs), on the other hand, have proved well able to adapt to working in strong global organizations and networks.

Few CSOs, however, carry a popular mandate; in general their spokespeople are not elected by a wide franchise (trade unions are exceptions). Most owe their power base to their credibility with the media and with those in positions to shape policy, and to the widespread support of citizens who care strongly about and will campaign on the subject matter of the organizations. The lack of demonstrable mandates leads many governments and parliamentarians to challenge the legitimacy of their power, implying that they are bogus or anti-democratic. Although there are important issues pertaining to the governance of civil society, such criticisms often reveal a stubborn resistance to recognizing the changing nature of democracy.

The assumption is that democracy means little more than the opportunity of citizens to vote every few years for politicians who sit in assemblies or parliaments representing their constituents' concerns and interests across the spectrum of political matters. This could be called traditional or *representative* democracy. Although it remains important, representative democracy has been greatly eroded in recent years throughout much of the world as citizens are voicing and demonstrating increasing disenchantment with electoral politics. Moreover, the more politically active citizens (a minority, but traditionally those who have driven change in society) are increasingly exercising opportunities to take part in democracy in different ways. Through joining NGOs, pressure groups, social movements, and protests, etc., they are forging *participatory* democracy, by entering directly the debates that most interest them.

It could be argued that participatory democracy is not new but dates back to the earliest democracy of Ancient Greece in which any native-born citizen (except slaves and women) could gather in the forum to speak and vote on any issue that concerned him. This was rule (*kratein*) of the people (*demos*). As city-states grew, such decision making became unwieldy, and the practice of electing delegates to represent a constituency was born.

In traditional democracy we are grouped according to where we live; our neighbourhoods form the constituencies for which we elect our parliamentary representatives. The range of political parties often assumes that our class and income, and the locality where we live, are the determinants of our politics. Participatory democracy is changing the *geography* of politics. It allows us to aggregate differently with others who share our burning concerns wherever they live. In other words, community of *neighbourhood* is being supplemented by community of *interest*, and, thanks to modern information and communications technologies (ICT), such communities can be global as easily as local.

CSOs are not just tools by which citizens advance their direct interests. They are the conduits for ethical arguments. In earlier times, the Church monopolized this role in Western polities. The separation between State and Church has hence been one of the liveliest debates in political theory, although the two institutions often promoted the same vested interests and were led by the same families. Now, ethical challenges to governments and morally argued alternatives have become the preserve of CSOs and independent media as religious organizations become more marginal in most societies.

The collapse of the Berlin Wall ended the superpower rivalry that defined politics for most of the twentieth century, but in its place a different set of three superpowers has emerged. The first is the government and military complex of the United States and its allies. The second is the might of the global corporation. The third is the power of public opinion and civil society. This power is not inevitably a force for good; it can be highly destructive and divisive (for example, when peddled by racists). This chapter centres on the third superpower, and specifically on the role civil society plays in galvanizing that public opinion in the management of world affairs.

GLOBAL CIVIL SOCIETY AND THE ETHICS OF GLOBALIZATION

Civil society is not a new phenomenon. In England, the Peasant Revolt following the passage of the English Statute of Labourers in 1351 was a prototypical example of modern protest. The statute came shortly after the Great Plague, when labour was in short supply and so workers were pressing for higher wages. It put a ceiling on wages and compelled workers to stay with their employers, cruelly blocking the one occasion in which market forces worked in their favour. The revolt forced major concessions until it was brutally put down and its leaders executed.

The Anti-Corn Law League was a more successful civil society campaign. It was founded in 1839 to protest the extortionate price of staple foods due to high import duties and market restrictions designed to protect British landowners. After six years of struggle and bread riots, the government gave way and repealed the Corn Law. It was an early example of a pressure group, and it was established to campaign *for* globalization.

Civil society today cannot be put into any nutshell. In structural forms it ranges from the organized NGOs for public benefit (such as Amnesty International, Oxfam, Greenpeace, and CARE) and associations for member benefits (such as trade unions, consumers' groups, professional associations, and sports clubs) to faith-based organizations, internet-based pressure groups (or what I call "dot-causes"), and anti-war protestors. Its characteristics and impact vary from country to country. As with the private sector and the natural world, diversity is a cornerstone of its strength. A vibrant civil society is packed with organizations and causes competing for the attention of citizens.

Given this diversity, it is dangerous to generalize about the sector or imply homogeneity. For every cause espoused by some CSOs there will be a counter cause waged by others. With that caveat, I'll now risk two generalizations.

First, those CSOs that have learned to organize or network internationally have become especially influential in recent years. Paradoxically, the forces of globalization that are so fiercely resisted by a growing protest movement also afford transnational civil society opportunities to grow immeasurably in strength. The world's first international CSOs were the International Typographical Union (established in 1852), the World Alliance of Young Men's Christian Associations (1855), and the International Committee of the Red Cross (1863). By 1874 there were thirty-two such organizations. According to the Brussels-based Union of International Associations, this number rose gradually to 1,500 in the mid 1950s and then accelerated after 1975 to reach 9,789 in 1981 and 24,797 in 2001. The London School of Economics now publishes a yearbook on this phenomenon (*Global Civil Society*).

Secondly, within this band of international CSOs is located a strong segment of very diverse organizations that critique globalization in different ways. The combined impact has been to outline a common set of values and aims, one that has come to dominate civil society advocacy in international policy debate. This constellation comprises NGOs, unions, protest groups, religious organizations, and others. Very loosely it could be called the "global social justice movement." This isn't a rigorous term because, unlike other social movements, this one isn't a coherent network of people and groups uniting in solidarity around common conditions or common aims. It straddles those seeking specific reforms (for example, regarding Third World debt) to those who want to smash capitalism. Its bonds stem from what its constituents *don't* like, rather than what they call for. However that term is more rigorous than the name many establishment journalists and others know it by: the "anti-globalization movement."

This movement flourishes on the growing malaise with the institutional fabric of democratic political systems, a subject to which we return later. It has also become popular because it has depicted an unethical framework for globalization.

Though some economists maintain otherwise, most now recognize that wealth and income gaps are growing; this is true *within* most countries and also *between* countries. The dissenting view maintains that developing countries as a group have been catching up with the rich countries throughout the 1990s. True, the economic growth of this group exceeded that of developed countries in the 1990s, but two factors must be remembered. The story of growth in developing countries is largely due to China, India, and a few other "tiger economies." By just taking out China, the remaining developing countries are continuing to see a *declining* share of world economy. Secondly, faster growth isn't the same as catching up; it means their economies are *accelerating* faster, not necessarily that they are catching up. It is like saying that a bicycle setting off to catch up with a jetliner at full cruising speed is doing a good job because, for a while, it can accelerate faster than the jet. East Asia, the fastest-growing region, would need to maintain its current rate of growth (or acceleration) for seventy-four years to catch up with the West, and for the first fifty years the absolute wealth gap would continue to rise.

Within most countries, particularly the most market-oriented ones, wealth and income gaps have risen throughout the 1990s. This is largely because new opportunities are leading to the rich getting richer, rather than that the poor are getting absolutely poorer, but signs of political and social tension relate to the economic polarization of society. The richest 20 percent in the world as a whole enjoyed a 12 percent increase in their incomes from 1988 to 1993 while the poorest *half* saw no growth at all and the poorest 5 percent suffered a 25 percent fall.

Our global civil society movement actively publicizes this accelerating economic polarization in today's world and roundly blames globalization and "neo-liberal economic policies" for it. Mainstream economists counter that the problem rests more with the resistance of many developing countries to adopt market mechanisms. True, the countries where the populations have fared worst have been those, such as North Korea, that have stayed outside the global economy. And true, in my view, unshackled global markets do offer powerful opportunities. But the "globo-skeptics" are also right that today's management of globalization compounds economic polarities.

In practice there is not *one* market of international trade but many—different markets for the different factors of production. Some of these are being liberalized to become truly global markets—and the major traders in these markets benefit greatly—but other markets tell an opposite story. The former comprise the markets for high-tech products, for capital, the modern service sector, top management, and highly skilled labour such as ICT specialists; the major sellers in these markets are rich countries and very rich people. The latter comprise raw commodities, labour-intensive goods such as textiles and footwear, and unskilled labour; the major sellers are developing countries and poor people. These markets have not been opened; indeed they are often subject to *tougher* restrictions than before. Liberalizing some markets while retaining or raising barriers in others drives today's polarization. The problem isn't with globalization per se but with *selective* globalization. This is the root of economic injustice.

THE MALAISE WITH DEMOCRATIC POLITICS TODAY

The increasing power of civil society to garner public opinion and shape politics stems not so much from the growing sophistication of CSOs as from increasingly evident flaws in the traditional institutions of democracy, flaws that civil society has done much to expose and contest. We can describe five democratic deficits:

1. *The ideological deficit*: Political parties, especially in rich countries, have become less relevant to the political cleavages that concern most people, especially in rich countries. They remain substantially stuck in old political rivalries of socialist versus capitalist theories of the ownership of the means of production. Increasingly, voters aren't interested in such issues, but in a greater array of issues concerning not just who *owns* the means of production, but *what* is being produced, *how*, who *decides*, how this impacts and shapes society, what are the alternatives, and so on. Pressure groups and social movements are natural leaders in these newer and more diverse debates.

2. *The deficit of integrity*: Parties in much of the world seem increasingly mired in sleaze, nepotism, and corruption, often associated with their fundraising and corporate links. Furthermore, politicians seem increasingly willing to bargain priorities ruthlessly in political coalitions in order to cling onto power for today. But a new generation is emerging that is increasingly cynical about "the best democracy money can buy." CSOs such as campaign reform advocates and Transparency International and investigative journalists are rooting out and pillorying such corruption.

3. *The deficit of representation*: The principle of electing representatives is that citizens can choose among their peers to speak for them in the national political forum. But increasingly, to get into office demands great wealth and powerful contacts. Hence members of Parliament rarely reflect the diversity of the electorate. Only 15 percent worldwide are women; few come from ethnic minorities, from poor, or from working class backgrounds. Voters are increasingly disillusioned that democracy has failed to offer them the chance to be represented by their peers. Reform is largely due to pressure groups outside the parties.

4. *The deficiency of reach*: In the globalizing world, traditional institutions of democracy no longer hold sway over the many decisions affecting everyday life. These are increasingly forged in regional forums (such as the North American Free Trade Agreement (NAFTA) and the European Union), in intergovernmental forums (such as the International Monetary Fund (IMF) or World Trade Organization), and in global corporations. These forums may be accountable to some governments for some things, but they don't regularly come under the purview of national parliaments or other traditional democratic instruments as would forums at the national level, and no supra-national parliaments fill the void. These are issues targeted by the global social justice movement.

5. *The deficiency of sovereignty*: Most national governments experience dwindling autonomy as they become powerless to buck trends set by global powers, particularly in the economic realm. For example, developing countries find that they now have little latitude to set tariffs, exchange rates, or interest rates at levels that differ substantially from what "the market indicates." Similarly they must increasingly conform to "received wisdom" when it comes to currency controls, labour market policies, and taxation regimes. Paradoxically, just as *formal* democracy has spread into new areas of the globe for the first time, substantive democracy—the ability to participate in decisions affecting everyday life—has been eroded by this loss of autonomy of national states.

These deficiencies combine to provoke a widespread public image (perhaps unfair to the many politicians who are committed to international justice issues) that elected representatives are irrelevant to the global debates, are obsessed by Nimbyism and pork-barrel politics. Just as many voters are prioritizing issues, such as global justice and the environment, that are *long-term and global,* they see parliamentarians as consumed by matters that are *short-term and parochial.*

The evidence of the democracy deficits is clear to see. Voter turnouts have fallen in most Western democracies (except Scandinavia). In the United Kingdom and the United States, for example, the turnouts in national elections averaged about 80 percent since the war until the last few years; at the most recent elections they were 59 percent and 51 percent, respectively—even though election-advertising budgets have rocketed. Even in the new democracies of Eastern Europe, turnouts are falling steeply—so too in Mozambique, where only 20 percent voted in the recent election.[1] More marked still is the fall in membership of political parties. In a range of OECD countries (again, not Scandinavia), party membership has declined to between one-half and one-fifth of 1960s levels. The British conservative party dwindled from 2.2 million members to just 350,000 today.[2] In contrast, membership of cause-specific NGOs has risen sharply. In the UK, more people now belong to the Royal Society for the Protection of Birds than to all political parties combined.

People no longer want to belong to political parties, and neither do they trust politicians. And even though they flock to buy branded goods from the large corporations they trust the *products* but not the institutions. A forty-country survey, commissioned by the World Economic Forum in 2002, showed that of seventeen leading institutions of influence in these countries, those *least* trusted were parliaments, large corporations, and the IMF; and those *most* trusted were NGOs and the military.[3]

To summarize: people speak passionately about democracy. Many are prepared to lay down their life to defend it, but fewer than ever can be bothered to use it. We have become cynical in much of the OECD that electoral democracy means little more than the chance to choose every four or five years between one white millionaire or another to run our country. But on the other hand a revolution is under way—a mounting crescendo of diverse voices—as NGOs and pressure groups gain confidence and members. Through active support of specific CSOs, we can engage more directly in policy debates that particularly interest us. And we are all interested in different issues. In participatory democracy, we make our choice by aligning ourselves with the groups that most closely speak for us. CSOs compete for our attention, as do shops in an arcade. Civil society is a veritable marketplace, but not of goods and services. It is a marketplace of *interests*, *ideas*, *and ideologies*. Customers don't trade with cash and shares, but with their support and their time. Those, and media coverage, are the assets prized by policy activists.

CIVILIZING GLOBAL GOVERNANCE

How can CSOs use these assets to win reforms in how globalization is managed, to civilize global governance? The ingredients can be found in the prescriptions that the donor community urge on developing and transition countries for reforming their governments and their institutions. These measures are designed to ensure governments are honest, fair, responsive, efficient, and concentrate on citizens' priorities, and that citizens are well informed about their rights and are politically empowered. These same five pillars of "good governance" apply well to the intergovernmental realm:

Transparency

CSOs are powerful not just as conduits to disseminate information about what intergovernmental agencies, transnational corporations (TNCs), and others are doing (based on their research, evidence gathering and eyewitness experience, anecdotal as this may be). They also inform citizens about how these institutions work and make decisions. During the WTO ministerial talks in Seattle and Doha, for example, millions of people logged onto various websites of dot-causes every day to find out what was going on and what it all meant. CSOs have also campaigned successfully for organizations such as the World Bank to bring into the open swathes of documentation that was previously confidential, and they continuously press for observer access and public minutes for all intergovernmental meetings.

Accountability

By pressing national media and national parliaments around the world to give serious attention to how the IMF, WTO, and other global bureaucracies are behaving and to tackle the excesses of corporate greed and sleaze, CSOs working transnationally are drawing these powerful *global* players into national accountability structures. By setting up their own watchdogs and international campaigns, they are also introducing new, albeit informal and self-appointed, accountability mechanisms. In the absence of regional or global parliaments, these are the only effective international mechanisms for citizen accountability.

Rule of Law

Good governance requires a comprehensive framework of clear and well-understood laws that are predictably applied to protect citizens and all their legitimate interests. But there is little in the way of international law, and even that is generally subservient to national legislatures. Hence only national concerns are well protected by laws; global ones are mostly ignored or are covered by exhortative but toothless treaties. Many global social justice CSOs campaign for globally rigorous laws, regulations, and rules for intergovernmental processes and TNCs. The treaties on climate change, landmines, and whaling are examples of their achievements, as are the International Criminal Court and the Inspection Panels or Ombudsman offices within intergovernmental organizations. The latter afford due process to those who have been disadvantaged by the actions of those organizations.

Citizen's Voice

The right to know what is going on is one thing, but CSOs seek more active citizenship. They want seats in intergovernmental deliberations, public consultations on issues that have societal implications, and participatory approaches in programs and projects. They advocate public and legislative hearings to which CSOs can give evidence. And, through their public campaigns and media coverage, they make sure that citizens' voices are heard (well … a select sample of them).

Level Playing Field

Good governance must embrace equality of opportunity. This entails the right of minorities, not just the elite, to be heard on the global stage. CSOs who reflect those minority views therefore want a right be heard, albeit a "voice, not a vote" in international forums. Global social justice CSOs also campaign for a greater voice for the South in international forums and are increasingly vocal in campaigns to curb the power of the "G1"—the USA.

Civil society, especially when globally networked, is helping to reshape multilateralism. This has been studied by the Panel of Eminent Persons on UN–Civil Society Relations, set up by the UN Secretary General and chaired by President Cardoso.[4]

Today's multilateralism is different from that of thirty years ago. In those days, governments would come together to discuss an emerging issue until there was sufficient consensus for an intergovernmental resolution. Then governments and intergovernmental organizations would work on implementing this agreement. Today, it is increasingly likely that a civil society movement and crescendo of public opinion puts a new issue on the global agenda; next, a few like-minded governments become first among their peers to recognize the power of the case and start pressing for global action. Together with the leading civil society protagonists they form an ad hoc coalition on the issue; this builds public and political support for global action through iterative processes of public debate, policy dialogue, and perhaps pioneering action to demonstrate ways to redress the problem. Such *global policy networks* have shaped responses to issues as diverse as climate change, gender relations, poor-country debt relief, affordable treatment for AIDS, landmines, the trade in small arms, and the campaign for the International Criminal Court.

These shifting informal and opportunistic alliances of governments and non-state actors around specific policy issues constitute an exciting new phenomenon. Even the moves made by a powerful group of developing countries to stand up against the world's strongest trading powers displayed this characteristic. The group grew and shrank as some countries joined and others were pressed by their Northern trading partners to quit. Hence it was variously called the G20, the G21, and even, at one point, the G24. (I hope it will eventually settle on calling itself the G21, not because of the number in the group, but for the new hope Southern unity offers to the twenty-first century.) What was constant, however, was the active support it received from some of the leading NGOs and trade unions attending the WTO Ministerial. The CSOs were clearly giving useful advice to the trade negotiators about latest developments in the meetings and about media strategy. The benefits were mutual; the CSOs also gained credibility by appearing on G21 platforms, and the close links enhanced their "media-worthiness."

As such policy networks are coming to shape the deliberative processes, we are similarly witnessing the increasing importance of partnerships (often including the private sector, civil society, local authorities, and governments) for getting things done. Hence, as concluded the Cardoso panel, civil society has become as much a part of global governance today as governments. To adapt to this new multilateralism, it urged, the Secretary General must con-

tinue to transform the UN's institutional culture from a rather inward-look-
ing institution to an outward-looking, networking organization.

The UN has played a major role in consistently engaging CSOs in its deliberative processes, particularly in the "Big Conferences" of the 1990s. This has
helped shape an emerging set of *cosmopolitan political rules and norms* that tran-
scend national sovereignty and that are enforced (albeit imperfectly) by international institutions, especially in areas of human rights, gender relations, and
the environment. Although some governments resist these trends, the Cardoso
panel concluded that constructive and strategic engagement with civil society is a vital defence against the challenges the UN itself faces today. A UN that
is more attuned to global public opinion, that is strongly connected with leading CSOs, and that is strategic in its ability to broker dialogue with diverse
stakeholders is better able to ensure that the challenges come into the open
and are dispatched and that global governance is strengthened. In short,
there is a symbiosis: civil society is strengthened by opportunities the UN
affords, but this gives new raison d'être that in turn empowers the UN and
makes it seem more relevant.

CIVILIZING TRANSNATIONAL CORPORATIONS

One of the most exciting recent currents in civil society is the myriad of efforts
to inject environmental and social responsibility into transnational corporations. NGOs and think tanks first sat down with corporate chiefs to discuss
the *values of business* and convinced them that they should be in the *business of
values*. Corporate citizenship was born.

Some TNCs are experiencing today what the World Bank did in the 1990s.
They are no longer private entities making decisions in private. A new era of
corporate ethics and citizen accountability means that their CEOs are becoming increasingly answerable to the public. The proliferation of independent
channels of information (from the serious to the scurrilous) enables activists
and the media to probe what TNCs are doing, and make it impossible to trace
leaks, so institutions might just as well learn to be open. Television and jour-
nalism is increasingly penetrating, and senior executives cannot avoid the
cameras. It has become easier for activists to get shareholders, the media,
and others to adopt their campaigns. The more TNCs avoid contact with pressure groups the more it looks like they have something to hide, and so the
greater the risk of street protests.

Since the Nestlé boycott that started in the 1970s, claiming it marketed baby
formula irresponsibly in developing countries, and campaigns against Barclays
Bank and other companies with links to apartheid South Africa, there have
been numerous TNC-focused campaigns. These have attacked companies for

the social impact of their products (e.g., pesticides and baby formula), for their support to immoral regimes (e.g., those trading in Burma), for environmental damage (e.g., tropical hardwood traders and mining firms), for their direct or indirect abuse of intensive standards and human rights (such as sweatshop conditions in Nike's suppliers or Shell's involvement in Ogoniland), for their part in the debt crisis (High Street banks), for forcing the spread of genetically modified crops (Monsanto), and for bio-piracy (e.g., those seeking to patent genes for basmati and jasmine rice). There has also been consumer action on wasteful packaging (McDonalds), animal cruelty (furs and Huntington Life Science), and ozone layer depletion (aerosols and refrigerators).

As Noreena Hertz says, "increasingly the most effective way to be political is not to register one's demands and wants at the ballot box ... but to do so at the supermarket ... All over the developed, democratic world, people are shopping rather than voting ... consumer activism is beginning to enter the mainstream." Such campaigns have hurt the companies, and though some have tended to ignore CSO criticism (notably Exxon/Mobile, the world's largest oil company), most have responded by trying to improve their company's image in various ways.[5]

It is interesting to speculate *why* most TNC chiefs take public pressure so seriously. They are supposed to be concerned solely with making profits, and there is little evidence that these campaigns have any discernable influence on turnover or profit. Though noisy, the proportion of people actually "voting with their purse" is still quite small. Hence the financial performance of a company is in reality largely unaffected by whether the company is gaining a better or worse reputation. But companies *act* as if there is a steep profit–reputation connection. Why do TNCs care so much about NGO campaigns, and why also do they spend such vast sums on corporate public relations rather than product promotion, if the company's reputation is relatively unimportant?

Clearly, image *is* critical in the eyes of TNC chiefs. One major insurance company conducts an annual survey of corporate bosses to find out what they see as their principal risks. Usually issues such as fire, crime, or war top the list. In 2001, however, chief executives ranked "reputational loss" highest.[6] The company accountant or stock market investor might not agree, but that is how top management sees it.

There are three likely explanations for the image-consciousness of CEOs. The first is that they take a long-term perspective. Image loss today will be customer loss tomorrow. In a world where product differentiation is so small, customer loyalty is hard to come by, and once lost it will never be regained. A second explanation stems from the growth in ethical investment. In the US over $1 trillion—one-eighth of all fund investment—is in managed portfolios that use at least one social investment strategy, a thirty-fold increase since 1984.[7] The membership of the US Interfaith Center on Corporate Responsibility includes 275 institutional investors with combined assets of over $110 billion. US foundations have combined assets of $486 billion (not all invested ethically). Ethical investors are now big business, and corporate CEOs are getting this message.

The third explanation—I think the strongest—concerns staff and management morale. People don't like to work for an organization accused of immoral behaviour. It reduces their commitment, and perhaps performance, and leads to unproductive management time going to internal damage limitation and devising public relations responses to public criticisms.

I met the CEO of Nestlé UK in the early 1980s to discuss Oxfam's campaign against baby formula. He was furious about another NGO's postcard campaign directed at top Nestlé managers worldwide, accusing them of killing babies. He said the postcards started pouring in just before a pivotal meeting at Nestlé's Swiss headquarters. Everyone was so outraged, particularly the company president, that the whole meeting was a disaster. The managers were proud of their company and were fed up with constantly having to defend themselves, even to their own staff. Apparently they even contemplated discontinuing baby formula altogether, since it accounted for only a few percent of corporate turnover. He insisted that the boycott had not noticeably affected the company's finances, but they were clearly worried about the image threat. The postcard campaign had hit a mark (but I couldn't fathom why Nestlé didn't more strenuously conform to the international code for marketing baby formula). The issue continues still today. Nestlé is still attacked for its marketing methods, but it has now appointed an independent ombudsman to oversee the implementation of the marketing code.

Large companies are increasingly concerned to address or protect themselves from public criticism. The best approach, many think, is to adopt ethical standards that at least sound convincing so that they can reposition themselves as "corporate citizens." There has been a steep growth in TNC "corporate social responsibility" in all areas from community work to global philanthropy and engagement with the UN; and CEOs are increasingly convinced this is good for business. Many TNCs are drafting and publishing codes of conduct or statements of ethics. Some now have social and environment departments, often hiring former NGO campaigners as advisors. Many subject themselves to social and environmental audits, perhaps using one of a growing array of externally devised accreditation methodologies (such as SA8000, which assesses intensive standards against UN agreements, or Global Reporting Initiative, which initially focused just on environmental issues, but now includes social and economic factors).

Some TNCs have drawn up partnership arrangements with major NGOs, or commission NGOs to assess their operations and provide them feedback. Others seek to carry NGO-devised certification logos on their product labels (certifying the product as being environmentally sound, free from use of child intensive labour, or containing wood only from sustainably managed forests). Similarly, many corporations are keen to join with NGOs and perhaps UN agencies in business–civic partnership or corporate citizenship ventures. Sometimes unexpected partnerships arise. For example, the Environmental Defense Fund in the USA (a fierce environmental campaigner) has helped McDonalds develop a replacement for the non-biodegradable polystyrene burger packaging they used to use. And BP's CEO, acting for the World Business Council for Sustainable Development, made a joint press appeal in 2002 with a spokesman from his traditional enemy, Greenpeace, calling on governments assembling for the Johannesburg Earth Summit to take decisive and globally coordinated action on climate change—pointing out that TNCs want a level and predictable playing field. (Greenpeace pointed out that the last time they had shared a platform with BP was just before they were arrested for chaining themselves to one of the company's North Sea oil platforms.)

One increasingly prominent approach to promoting business ethics is through the demonstration effect of "alternative marketing," in which NGOs provide products they guarantee conform to high social and environmental standards. Sales of "fair trade" products in Europe have been rapidly growing and by 2001 accounted for about $250 million per year. While originally the emphasis was on products imported by NGOs or non-profit companies, now the favoured approach is to source ethically sound producers and encourage mainstream supermarkets or wholesalers to import from these; the product is sold under a Fair Trade logo, licensed by the NGO network, but without it having to make up-front investment for importation. These goods are retailed at only slightly higher prices than commercial competitors yet typically provide the producer twice world market prices, and a higher proportion of this price reaches the actual grower or worker. Ethical trading is an even bigger business in the US than in Europe.

ACTION—AND REACTION: THE BACKLASH AGAINST GLOBAL CIVIL SOCIETY

As we have discussed, global civil society is starting to impact the management of global change. No longer can a group of seven finance ministers spend a weekend in a hotel near the White House, announce a "Washington Consensus" on a monetarist approach to international economics, and escape with little public controversy. And corporate CEOs are routinely challenged to demonstrate corporate social responsibility. Today, citizens everywhere are more economically literate and more politically savvy than before the internet age. They want to know what's going on, what it means to them, and they want to have a say. We're all in the debating chamber now! And with transnational CSOs as the well-trusted crack forces of this new civic consciousness, the potential is almost unlimited. As Jody Williams said on receiving the Nobel Prize on behalf of the International Campaign to Ban Landmines, "Together, we are a superpower!"[8]

Superpowers, however, are inevitably resented. The clear ascendancy of policy-oriented NGOs and interest groups over the last decade has been greeted by increasingly aggressive counter-strategies by governments, intergovernmental agencies and corporations, and by the establishment media. Hence the *Financial Times* journalist Martin Wolf fulminated in 1999 about "the claims of NGOs to represent civil society as a whole, and, as such, to possess legitimacy rivalling—perhaps even exceeding—that of elected governments is outrageous."[9] A year later *The Economist* demanded to know "who elected Oxfam, or, for that matter, the League for a Revolutionary Communist International?... In the West, governments and their agencies are, in the end, accountable to voters. Who holds the activists accountable?"[10] In 2003 the right-wing think tank American Enterprise Institute announced that it was forming, with others, "NGO Watch" to monitor objectionable practices of NGOs.

Whether CSO leaders like it or not, such critics do raise important issues. In their attacks on CSOs, three words come up over and over again: legitimacy, representativity, and accountability. These are presented as the fundamental flaws of civil society, but how fair is this? Let's explore each.

Issues of Legitimacy

Whenever a small pressure group irritates a large bureaucracy the cry goes up: "What's its legitimacy; what right does a one person and a dog outfit have to meddle in the affairs of legitimate companies/governments/bureaucracies?" The answer is very simple. Any group, however small, has a perfect right to speak out on issues that concern it, because that is what freedoms of expression and democracy are all about. These groups are legitimate as long as they are honest and the interests they promote don't harm others. If the CSO is lying or pretending to be other than it really is, it is guilty of deception, but size has nothing to do with legitimacy when it comes to engaging in political debate. Firms, likewise, are no less legitimate because they are small—though you'd be unwise to buy a life insurance policy from a tiny company.

We need a change of mindset. Democracy is strengthened, not weakened, when minority voices can be heard directly. NGOs, unions, protest movements, and intellectuals can join the deliberative process directly. It is no longer necessary to prove that you were elected or have a large constituency before you can speak. Certainly there are pressure groups that punch well above their weight, either because of special authority in their field or their special communication pull. Some manage to get that mass media support on the basis of flimsy but sensationalist evidence, but this is *media* irresponsibility. The solution is to encourage more responsible reportage and more responsible use by politicians and others in the public eye of campaign claims by CSOs. They are often the middlemen between the pressure groups and wide-scale public opinion; they should check the facts and study the underlying motivations before blindly reproducing them. As for customers in other markets, the maxim must be *caveat emptor*.

Issues of Representativity

Whom do CSOs speak for and how they can prove it? Trade unions have mass memberships, and people join because they want a union to represent them. Some NGOs also have mass memberships (such as environmental organizations), churches similarly may have large congregations, but it is less clear that these members feel themselves to be represented by these entities. I am a member of the Royal Society for the Protection of Birds (RSPB) in the UK because I'm a birdwatcher, I want access to RSPB's reserves, and I enjoy its magazine. When RSPB speaks out on conservation issues it does so with great authority, but this stems from its long experience managing sensitive habitats, not its membership. It is unlikely that they could get their members to flood officials with letters, still less turn out at a protest.

Likewise, the suffragettes—a hundred years ago—didn't need to prove (by membership lists or democratic procedures) that they spoke for all women. Representativity isn't simply about speaking *on behalf* of a constituency. It is also about speaking with expertise on an issue—representing the facts—and being able to demonstrate that you have the support of a constituency.

Those wanting to probe the representativity of a development NGO should look less to the number of members it can claim than to the quality of the experience it wields and the degree to which others in the field admire this expertise. They should ask whether the NGO's own programs have been effective, whether it has strong "local knowledge," and whether its working style exposes it to the perspectives of poor people and their delegated representatives. And NGOs should be able to respond well to such inquiries.

Issues of Accountability

Accountability has three dimensions: for what, to whom, and how. For policy-oriented CSOs the "for what" is for ensuring that their messages are honest, accurate, realistic, and serve the goals they claim (whether conservation or poverty reduction); that the solutions they advocate are sustainable, not just short-term expedients; that they aren't purporting to represent anyone without their blessing, and so on.

The "to whom" is problematic. They should certainly not be expected to be accountable to elected governments (as some of their critics infer), any more than private companies or newspaper editors are. Most CSOs engaged in social concerns, such as development NGOs, claim moral accountability to the vulnerable groups they serve, which is good rhetoric but pretty meaningless. In practice, they don't explain to these groups the choice of their strategy; nor indeed do they to their members or supporters. CSOs nominally account to their boards of directors or trustees but in practice this may be superficial. The strongest accountability in practice tends to be to institutional donors: governmental and foundations. These are well placed to ask probing questions. But do they ask the right questions? And should they be the ethical guardians? In practice, few donors delve much beyond routine accounting matters, and if they do, they risk imposing their own values. (He who pays the piper calls the tune!) Even if the scrutiny were both rigorous and objective, it isn't altogether healthy to rely on this type of accountability. Earlier I advocated a *caveat emptor* maxim for drawing on CSO campaigns. This, in my view, is preferable to "*caveat* donor." Questions of civil society accountability ought to rest with the people, not external funders.

Finally, *how* should CSOs be accountable? The imperatives should be to maximize accountability within the constituencies addressed by their advocacy and to get as close to the citizens as possible. All CSOs should open themselves to public scrutiny (including media scrutiny) through full transparency. This is far from the case at present. NGOs are typically coy with internal evaluations and business plans, tending only to disseminate information that puts their organization in a good light.

Since meaningful accountability to the voiceless is a pipe dream, and accountability to funding institutions isn't fully appropriate, increasing attention is being given to mechanisms of self-regulation within the CSOs sector, through politically neutral monitors of NGOs and CSOs' own networks. But this discipline is in its infancy; there is still little tradition of peer review and peer criticism. This will inevitably change. As the sector becomes more powerful in challenging the ethical standards of others, it will find itself increasingly under the moral microscope. When watchdogs have powerful bites they can become a public menace unless well disciplined. This trend should pose no threat to ethical CSOs. Indeed, their prospects could be all the rosier for being contrasted favourably with less scrupulous ones by independent and trustworthy sources.

ENSURING GLOBAL CIVIL SOCIETY IS ETHICAL

The central question is: What are the hallmarks of integrity regarding CSOs seeking to influence political debate? (Even more important, of course, is the integrity of politicians, officials, companies, and others who shape policies.) This is becoming a critically important issue for civil society leaders to tackle as their influence grows, otherwise it will become their Achilles heel. Issues of representativity, accountability, and legitimacy are important, but so too is ensuring a fair representation of voices from the global South, from women, and from minorities, and other factors.

CSOs must also recognize that they are *complements* to traditional democracy, not substitutes for it. It is important not to overstate their potential. They may be more trusted than political parties and governments, but this doesn't mean they are displacing traditional democratic processes; they play different roles. Indeed, to influence policy, they need well-functioning governments and parliamentary processes. Pressure groups usually focus on very specific policy issues. A vibrant civil society will generate a thousand points of pressure, but if you join those points together you don't get an alternative blueprint for governing. We still need state instruments to balance competing demands, fill in the gaps, and construct a coherent, overall policy framework.

CSOs achieve influence by persuading people to use the democracy at their fingertips, not just through their voting choices but as consumers, shareholders, lobbyists, demonstrators, educators of their children, workers, employers, and investors. Civil society is an arena for deliberation of policies and contestation, not decision making on policy matters. While every pressure group has a right to make its case, governments must, in the end, make policy decisions. Civil society can ensure that these decisions are well informed and that weaker voices are not drowned out. Governments have to reach their decisions by weighing together myriad, often-conflicting claims; when they simply appease every powerful vested-interest group, politics becomes atomized and coherence is lost. They must listen to the cacophony but maintain a holistic view, which is difficult.

A GLOBAL CIVIL SOCIETY AGENDA FOR ETHICAL GLOBALIZATION

There is clearly a growing head of steam for a new departure. As the Nobel Prize–winning economist Amartya Sen says, "The real debate on globalization is, ultimately, not about the efficiency of markets, nor about the importance of modern technology. The debate, rather, is about the inequality of power, for which there is much less tolerance now than in the world that emerged at the end of the Second World War."[11] Equity of power, opportunity, and resources is the cornerstone of what could be a different course, that of ethical globalization. Civil society is the driving force, and has growing opportunity. Summits rarely happen these days without some involvement of CSOs, and these are no longer just optional extras after the important delegates leave. Heads of governments are keen to reach out to hear their citizens' voices. The Prime Minister of Belgium, Guy Verhofstadt, for example, convened a special conference in October 2001 to ensure that civil society concerns about globalization were heard. Political leaders increasingly seek to attend (or at least to demonstrate that they are tuned into) the annual World Social Forum, and it has become standard to invite numerous CSO leaders alongside political and corporate chiefs at the World Economic Forum.

The future holds immense opportunities for CSOs to influence international policy and change the path of global change. It may be that in the fullness of time we will see well-respected global democratic institutions that formally connect citizens with the governance of global institutions. Some call for a World Parliament; but this is not a likely scenario any time soon. Some call for a "second chamber" in the UN comprising leading civil society organizations (which the Cardoso panel concluded would be impossible to realize in practice). There are various efforts to form strong regional blocs to offer a counterweight to G8 (or G-1!) power, but few of these so far have achieved much muscle. And there are many ideas for "revitalizing" the United Nations and other intergovernmental organizations. All these ideas are important but show little immediate promise of shortening the distance between citizens and the decisions that are made globally but which affect their locality.

In the meantime, the informal and admittedly self-appointed accountability roles CSOs play in matters of global governance is the only route through which citizens come close to the levers of transnational power. Global civil society, by itself, is not *the* answer; but it is vital to making an answer possible. And this is needed all the more in face of the mounting world polarization triggered by the Iraq war.

Civil society networks are learning to create their own widely used, noncommercial new media channels, to network globally and, equally important, to form novel alliances across sectors: with trade unions, environmental pressure groups, NGOs, human rights activists, social movements, intellectuals, and pop stars all coming together on common platforms. While not presenting a total alternative, this is helping to introduce a set of global political values and norms and a new sense of accountability of those holding public office to a global public. This is opening the door to the possibility that perhaps politics *can* be globalized.

CSOs face tough choices. One way leads to greater confrontation, more aggressive street demonstrations, more youthful hostility vented toward authority, and more polarization and unease in our societies. The other direction, equally challenging, leads to negotiations and working for institutional reform—public and private.

There is no doubt which path will be chosen. Because of its plurality, civil society will surely go *both* ways. Participatory democracy knows many styles of engagement. Hence the future of contention is largely in the hands of the official institutions themselves. The more responsive they are to dialogue, the more confident CSOs will be in constructive engagement. But if they ignore groups who want to engage then those groups will lose prestige and support, leaving street activists the stronger. Conversely, NGOs who get co-opted into policy dialogue that is for show only undermine more radical reform efforts.

I don't attempt any blueprint for action, but I conclude with one observation. Earlier civil society campaigns have been to *stop* things from happening or to *oppose* policies. As the sector becomes more confident, we are starting to see pressure for what *should* be done. This is vital for building consensus about a new way of managing globalization that puts the needs of poor people first. This reflects a maturing of global civil society, a greater willingness to take risks, and a preparedness to engage with "the establishment" and to define what it stands *for*—a compelling vision of Ethical Globalization—not just what it is *against*. It is about "Getting from No."

NOTES

A version of this paper was presented at the Seminar on "Globalization, Identity, Diversity," Forum of Cultures, Barcelona, July 2004. The views expressed here are the author's alone and are based largely on his book *Worlds Apart: Civil Society and the Battle for Ethical Globalization*.

1 International Institute for Democracy and Electoral Assistance. www.idea.int.
2 P. Mair and I. Van Biezen, "Party Members in Twenty European Democracies, 1980–2000," *Party Politics* 7, no. 1 (2001).
3 GlobeScan. www.globescan.com.
4 Cardoso Panel Report, *We the Peoples: Civil Society, the United Nations and Global Governance,* report of the Panel of Eminent Persons on UN–Civil Society Relations (New York: United Nations, 2004).
5 Noreena Hertz, *The Silent Takeover: Global Capitalism and the Death of Democracy* (London: William Heinemann, 2001).
6 *Financial Times,* 27 July 2001.
7 Hertz, *Silent Takeover.*
8 Quoted in Motoko Mekata, "Building Partnerships toward a Common Goal: Experiences of the International Campaign to Ban Landmines," in *The Third Force: The*

Rise of Transnational Civil Society, ed. Ann Florini et al. (Washington, DC: Carnegie Endowment for International Peace, 2000), 174.

9 Martin Wolf, "Trade: Uncivil Society," *Financial Times*, 1 September 1999.

10 "Anti-Capitalist Protests: Angry and Effective," *The Economist*, 23 September 2000.

11 Amartya Sen, "Global Doubts," Commencement Address, Harvard University, 8 June 2000.

2

Approaching Global Civil Society

Paul van Seters

DAVOS V. PORTO ALEGRE

In the last week of January 2001, two distinctively global meetings took place that were closely linked but at the same time worlds apart. One meeting was the World Economic Forum (WEF) in Davos, Switzerland, the gathering place of some two thousand political leaders and captains of industry from all over the globe; the other meeting was the World Social Forum (WSF) in Porto Alegre, Brazil, the rallying point for some fifteen thousand activists from more than a hundred countries. An initiative of the German banker Klaus Schwab, the WEF had been assembling once a year since 1970 in Davos. By 2001, the WEF was widely seen as a mainstay of the global elite and a champion of free-market neoliberalism, i.e., economic globalization. In contrast, the WSF convened for the first time in 2001 and was intended to contribute to the international struggle against neoliberal globalization and its consequences. That is to say, those meeting in Porto Alegre were united first and foremost in their opposition to the views and values held by those meeting in Davos. The name of the WSF, which emphasized a global *social* concern, must be read as a direct criticism of the one-sided *economic* fixation of the WEF.[1]

Davos and Porto Alegre were polar opposites, not only geographically (North v. South) but also ideologically (neoliberalism v. global justice). The idea for an alternative to the WEF had been first discussed at a protest meeting and demonstration in Davos in January 1999. Among the people who were subsequently instrumental in getting the WSF off the ground were Bernard Cassen, senior editor of the French radical monthly *Le Monde diplomatique* and director of ATTAC (Association for the Taxation of financial Transactions for the Aid of Citizens); Oded Grajew, a Brazilian social entrepreneur (Instituto Ethos); and Chico Whitaker, director of the Brazilian Commission for Justice and Peace.[2] For these people, the WEF was the declared enemy, the antithesis of the WSF. The same position was held by José Bové, a French sheep farmer, labour organizer, and committed activist who had gained worldwide notoriety in 1999 by driving his tractor into a newly built McDonald's restaurant in the French town of Millau. Bové was one of the keynote speakers in Porto Alegre in January 2001. Ironically, Bové had also been invited by the organizers in Davos, but he had preferred to attend the meeting in Porto Alegre. According to newspaper reports, Bové said in his speech that he saw the meeting in Porto Alegre as a "symbol for the start of a new social movement."[3] Since then, many commentators have written about the rise of this new global social movement, often referring to it as the harbinger of a "global civil society."[4]

In this chapter, I explore the relationship between this new social movement and global civil society. In subsequent sections, I offer a brief history of the new global social movement, point out the significance of international nongovernmental organizations (INGOs) in this context, provide an outline for a theory of global civil society, deal with various notions of global society, and discuss whether, on the basis of all of this, we are indeed approaching global civil society.

A NEW SOCIAL MOVEMENT

Many of the activists of the new social movement José Bové was talking about in Porto Alegre in January 2001, that is to say many of those present at the first meeting of the World Social Forum, called themselves "antiglobalists." The bearing of that name seemed self-evident: there is such a thing as globalization, in the sense of economic, neoliberal globalization, favoured by the people attending the meetings of the World Economic Forum in Davos; and there are people opposing that kind of globalization because of its supposed bad effects. These latter people then are the antiglobalists. This was also why many commentators early in 2001 used the word antiglobalist when alluding to the first meeting of the World Social Forum in Porto Alegre. Antiglobalist seemed a proper name for this new social movement.

When we focus on antiglobalization thus understood, however, it is clear that what José Bové said in Porto Alegre about the birth of a new social movement was misleading. For one reason, the antiglobalist movement had not started in Porto Alegre in 2001 but rather in Seattle two years earlier. In late November/early December 1999, when the World Trade Organization (WTO) held its biennial Ministerial Conference in Seattle, that event turned into a disaster in at least two ways. Though huge investments had been made to prepare for it, the conference failed to lead to an agreement. But the real disaster was caused by the disruptions of the proceedings by an unexpectedly large crowd of demonstrators and activists. These disruptions soon became known as the "Battle of Seattle," a phrase that can be taken literally. Some fifty thousand people took to the streets of Seattle, blocked WTO conference halls and hotels, and organized demonstrations that directly interfered with conference meetings; a relatively small but highly visible number of the protesters even ended up in ugly fights with Seattle police officers.[5]

The Battle of Seattle was the first time that activists took to a global podium in numbers that large, sabotaged the assembly of an institution they held responsible for the ills of globalization, and became the object of worldwide media attention. It was also the first time the antiglobalist label was employed by the media to refer to these types of activities. Before Seattle 1999, there had been occasional references to a so-called antiglobalization movement, but without exception these had been used to describe the activities of populist politicians like Pat Buchanan in the United States and Jean-Marie Le Pen in France. Criticism of globalization by these populists had manifested itself in the early 1990s, for example in connection with the North American Free Trade Agreement (NAFTA), which became effective on January 1, 1994. In Seattle in 1999, however, antiglobalization clearly acquired an entirely new, much more inclusive meaning.[6]

In the same vein, during the 1990s a variety of historical events already had carried a distinct antiglobalist flavour, such as the Zapatista uprising in Mexico in 1994 (also connected to NAFTA), the worldwide protests against the Multilateral Investment Agreement (MIA) initiated by the Organisation for Economic Cooperation and Development (OECD) in 1995, and the massive demonstration of the Jubilee 2000 campaign at the G8 meeting in Birmingham in 1998 (with eighty thousand demonstrators, Birmingham 1998 outnumbered Seattle 1999).[7] However, because of their specific angle or restricted scope, these events can be considered at most as the precursors of the new antiglobalist movement. Only when the smoke had cleared from the streets of Seattle did the world recognize the new global social movement for what it was: involved in a rainbow of global issues, dealing not only with economic globalization but also engaged in the cultural, social, and political consequences of globalization; drawing its inspiration and support from all over the world; and clearly determined to capture the global stage and to stay there.

Hence it was appropriate that this movement was baptized with a new name on the spot, i.e., while the events of Seattle unfolded. For all of these reasons, Seattle rather than Porto Alegre can claim to be the place of birth of the antiglobalist movement.

In Seattle it was the WTO that was the target of this new and unruly social movement. Subsequently, in 2000 and in 2001, meetings of the World Bank and the IMF in Prague, Quebec, and Barcelona, and meetings of the European political leaders in Nice and Gothenburg were used by the antiglobalists to vent their opposition against the agents of globalization. So the rather colourful "March against Neoliberalism" that opened the WSF in Porto Alegre in February 2001 must be seen in the context of a string of much nastier protests in a host of cities the world over.

If the new social movement that José Bové hoped to inaugurate at the World Social Forum in Porto Alegre has to be understood in this wider context, the Battle of Seattle too must be put in the right perspective. We know that many of the fifty thousand demonstrators and activists in Seattle were representatives of international nongovernmental organizations (INGOs), many of which had been officially invited to attend the WTO Conference and had been accredited even to participate in official conference proceedings.[8] Seattle 1999 then should be seen not only as the battleground where the antiglobalist movement was born but also as an event that signified the growing prominence of international NGOs at meetings of global institutions such as the WTO. Against this background, it is instructive to take a closer look at the role of these INGOs.

INTERNATIONAL NONGOVERNMENTAL ORGANIZATIONS

An estimated 1300 international NGOs were present in November 1999 in Seattle when the WTO held its conference. Of course, this was by no means the first time that INGOs had been involved officially and massively in global events of this sort. In fact, throughout the 1990s a number of conferences organized by the United Nations had carved out this new role for the INGOs.[9] The first, and probably most famous, of these meetings was the UN Conference on Environment and Development held in 1992 in Rio de Janeiro, the first so-called Earth Summit. While INGOs had played a role at international meetings, pushing their cause and lobbying politicians and government officials, for a long time prior to 1992, it was in Rio de Janeiro in 1992, according to many observers, that these social organizations moved for the first time from the backstage and wings of the global theatre to centre stage. Between Rio de Janeiro 1992 and Seattle 1999, there were major UN Conferences in Vienna (on human rights), Bridgetown (on sustainable development of small island developing states), Cairo (on population policy), Copenhagen (on social development), Beijing (on women), and Istanbul (on human settlements). In all these places and conferences, INGOs assumed an increasingly visible and prominent position. To give just one example: in Beijing, some four thousand INGOs were officially accredited.[10]

This last figure well reflects the overwhelming number of international nongovernmental organizations that attend these global conferences, and suggests something about the level or quality of their participation. In this sense, the decade of the 1990s was truly the decade of the INGOs, and it is clear that these major UN conferences have played an important role in what Lester Salamon has called the "associational revolution."[11] According to informed guesses of the World Bank and the Union of International Organizations, in 1900 there existed around two hundred INGOs (well-known examples are the International Red Cross and the Anti-Slavery Society). By 1990 this number had risen to about six thousand (Greenpeace, Amnesty International, Doctors without Borders, etc.). But after 1990 the number of INGOs exploded. In 2000, their number was estimated at 26,000; in 2004, at 47,000.[12] Many of these INGOs are involved in global issues, such as human rights, environmental protection, migration, climate change, child labour, biodiversity, and so on. In the 1990s, the rapidly increasing engagement with global issues of a fast-growing total of INGOs formed, so to speak, the fertile soil out of which, at the end of the decade, the antiglobalist movement emerged. INGOs were instrumental in organizing both the demonstrations and protests of Seattle 1999 and of initiating the WSF in Porto Alegre 2001. The antiglobalist movement therefore has to be understood as an offshoot of this new global political activism of the INGOs—an activism that merits the qualification globalist much more than antiglobalist. But then, what's in a name?

Over the past few years, many commentators have referred to globalism thus understood, i.e., globalism as the sphere of action and influence of international NGOs, as the "global civil society."[13] This raises an interesting question. When we define the global civil society as the practice of INGOs as briefly sketched above, can we then derive a coherent theory of the global civil society from that practice?

FROM CIVIL SOCIETY TO GLOBAL CIVIL SOCIETY

Civil society is one of the most complex and problematic notions in the history of social and political thought. The philosopher Charles Taylor, in a seminal essay originally published in 1990, has argued that the Western idea of civil society in fact is "an amalgam of two rather different traditions," which he calls the "L-stream" and the "M-stream," where "L" stands for Locke, and

"M" for Montesquieu. Although both traditions or streams build on the contrast between "civil society" and "the state," Taylor shows that the two traditions are very different in this respect and that the "society/state distinction" is much more complicated than commonly assumed. "The essential feature of the L-stream," Taylor states, "is the elaboration of a richer view of society as an extrapolitical reality." Central here is "the idea of a nonpolitical dimension to society." In contrast to this, the M-stream provides "the picture of a society defined by its political organization, but where this is constitutionally diverse, distributing power among many independent agencies." In a way, Montesquieu offered an antidote to the threats to freedom inherent in the liberal tradition of Locke. While Tocqueville's concept of civil society clearly belongs in the M-stream, Hegel's approach can best be understood as a combination of the L- and the M-streams.[14]

The sociologist Jeffrey Alexander, in a recent book, distinguishes between three ideal-typical forms of civil society: "civil society I," "civil society II," and "civil society III." CSI is, like an overarching umbrella, associated with the ideas of Harrington and Locke, Ferguson and Smith, Rousseau and Hegel, all the way to Tocqueville. CSII is, under the influence especially of Marx, narrowly and pejoratively associated with market capitalism alone. And CSIII is associated with more recent "social and cultural events [that have] created the circumstances for a renewed intellectual engagement with civil society." Alexander wants us to understand CSIII "as a sphere that can be analytically independent, empirically differentiated, and morally more universalistic [i.e., more so than either CSI or CSII] vis-à-vis the state and the market and ... other spheres as well." CSIII then is conceived "as a solidary sphere, in which a certain kind of universalizing community comes to be culturally defined and to some degree institutionally enforced." This is how, according to Alexander, this might work out: "To the degree that this solidary community exists, it is exhibited and sustained by public opinion, deep cultural codes, distinctive organizations—legal, journalistic and associational—and such historically specific interactional practices as civility, criticism, and mutual respect."[15]

The political scientists Jean Cohen and Andrew Arato conceptualize civil society again differently. In their encyclopedic study of civil society and political theory, they contrast the civil society not only with the market and the state but also with the political society and the economic society.[16] Right at the start, they offer the following "working definition": the civil society is "a sphere of social interaction between economy and state, composed above all of the intimate sphere (especially the family), the sphere of associations (especially voluntary associations), social movements, and forms of public communication."[17] This allows them to present the following picture: "Modern civil society is created through forms of self-constitution and self-mobilization. It is institutionalized and generalized through laws, and especially subjective rights, that stabilize social differentiation. While the self-creative and institutional dimensions can exist separately, in the long run both independent action and institutionalization are necessary for the reproduction of civil society."[18]

Theories of civil society thus typically display highly diverse variations on the society–state distinction. To return to Charles Taylor, he uses this insight to distinguish between three different conceptions of civil society:

> (1) In a minimal sense, civil society exists where there are free associations that are not under tutelage of state power. (2) In a stronger sense, civil society exists where society as a whole can structure itself and coordinate its actions through such free associations. (3) As an alternative or supplement to the second sense, we can speak of civil society wherever the ensemble of associations can significantly determine or inflect the course of state policy.

Obviously, in (1) we recognize the conventional, all too simple contrast between civil society and the state; in (2) we encounter the civil society tradition associated with the name of Locke; and in (3) we meet the civil society tradition that goes back to Montesquieu. For Taylor, the core idea of civil society resides not in (1), but in (2) and (3): "[C]ivil society as contrasted with the state in western political theory incorporated more than [(1)]; it involved (2) and sometimes (3) … We might say that (2) and (3) introduce a public dimension that has been crucial to the concept in the western tradition."[19]

Analogous to Taylor's different conceptions of civil society, I propose to distinguish between (I) a minimal conception of global civil society (there are international nongovernmental organizations as free associations that are not under tutelage of state, international, or global power), (II) a stronger conception of global civil society (the global society as a whole can structure itself and coordinate its actions through such international NGOs), and (III) another conception stronger than (I), as an alternative or supplement to (II) (the ensemble of INGOs can significantly determine or inflect the course of international or global policy). Now turning to the question of whether the current practice of INGOs deserves to be called global civil society, it seems obvious to me that there *does* exist a global civil society in sense (I), but I think it is equally obvious that it is very much a question whether there exists a global civil society in sense (II) or (III). Notice how Taylor's civil society (1), (2), and (3), especially the relationship between (2) and (3), greatly differ from our global civil society (I), (II) and (III). While civil society (2) and (3) may be thought of as more or less continuous with each other—the growth of (2) fostering the development of (3)—the relationship between global civil society (II) and (III) seems to be not like this at all. The progressive career of globalization over the past several decades does not mean that we now know for sure to what extent a global society, in any meaningful sense of the word society, can be imagined, let alone realized.

So the critical question about the global civil society (GCS) is not whether it exists in the minimal sense of GCSI (it does), but whether it exists in the strong(er) sense of GCSII and/or GCSIII. The answer to this is by no means self-evident. In recent years, much has been written on the transnational advocacy networks that INGOs typically form to pursue their goals.[20] These writings, directly or indirectly, invoke the idea of the global civil society. With respect to our critical question, however, that literature has been somewhat evasive. The main focus has been on GCSI, not on GCSII or GCSIII. To the extent that there is any empirical evidence regarding the latter two, it remains impressionistic and does not provide much systematic insight. The obvious thing to call for then, as always, is to engage in more research, especially more empirical research, on whether and how a global society may be emerging, and whether and how the ensemble of international nongovernmental organizations and their networks significantly determines or inflects the course of global governance.

In the next section, we therefore look more closely at some of the most successful examples of INGO networks in recent history and at some recent academic writing that tries to conceptualize the idea of a global society. These examples and concepts may bring us closer to an answer to our question of whether we are indeed approaching global civil society.

GLOBAL SOCIETY

The first example of an extremely well-known, widely celebrated network of INGOs has to do with efforts to prohibit the production and use of landmines. In the 1990s, more than one thousand INGOs became involved in the International Campaign to Ban Landmines (ICBL).[21] The ICBL is an advocacy network composed of human rights, mine clearance, humanitarian, children's, veterans,' medical, development, arms control, religious, environmental, and women's organizations. It was formally launched by six nongovernmental organizations in October 1992. In 1997 the campaign culminated in the signing, by fifty-one countries, of the Ottawa Convention (Convention on the prohibition of the use, stockpiling, production, and transfer of antipersonnel mines and on their destruction, commonly referred to as the Mine Ban Treaty). In the same year ICBL and its coordinator, Jody Williams, from the United States, received the Nobel Peace Prize. Meanwhile more than 150 countries have signed the Mine Ban Treaty. Even some of the major countries that still stay out of the convention (like Japan and the United

States) de facto adhere to the Mine Ban Treaty's norms. The ICBL is still very active, at the moment comprising more than 1,400 INGOs from some ninety countries.

A second example has to do with the INGOs that were involved in establishing the International Criminal Court. In 1995 Bill Pace, director of the World Federalist Movement, and Christopher Hall, legal advisor of Amnesty International, created a new network of INGOs, the Coalition for the International Criminal Court (CICC).[22] The International Criminal Court came into being on July 17, 1998, in Rome, when a huge majority of the 160 countries present approved the Statute of Rome. At that time CICC counted some 800 INGOs, 236 of which had one or more representatives in Rome. The CICC delegation was larger than that of any of the 160 countries. After ratification, the International Criminal Court opened its doors in The Hague on July 1, 2002. Today more than two thousand INGOs participate in CICC.

A third example is Jubilee 2000, the global campaign in the 1990s to cancel the debt of the poorest countries.[23] The campaign was initiated by retired diplomat Bill Peters and retired professor Martin Dent, both from the United Kingdom. In 1996 the campaign was officially launched, directed by Ann Pettifor and supported by a motley coalition of social organizations that soon developed into a global network of INGOs. In a previous section, it was mentioned that the Jubilee 2000 campaign staged a mass demonstration at the G8 meeting in Birmingham in 1998, when eighty thousand demonstrators formed a human chain around the centre of Birmingham. By December 2000, the petition asking the rich countries to cancel the debt had been signed by twenty-four million people from some 170 countries, the first global petition ever. At that point the G7 had cancelled $110 billion of debt of a total of twenty countries. Jubilee 2000 was supported by autonomous groups in more than sixty-five countries and these groups have continued their own campaigns unwearyingly.

What lesson can be drawn from these three examples? Do they suggest that the activities of (networks of) INGOs herald a new era of a truly global society, and hence of a truly global civil society? That is indeed the suggestion from recent theoretical studies from a variety of disciplines. The philosopher Peter Singer published a book in 2002 tellingly entitled *One World: The Ethics of Globalization*.[24] According to Singer, vested academic ethics is highly determined by the borders of national states and the central role of governments therein. Exploring four typical globalization themes (climate change, the role of the World Trade Organization, human rights and humanitarian intervention, and foreign aid), he discusses the ethical consequences of the fact that these national borders, and the state centrism they foster, increasingly blur and that all people on this planet increasingly share one and the same world. He argues that the new global society, which connects people across the globe and makes them interdependent, constitutes the material basis for a new ethic. That new ethic has to accommodate the interests of all persons that live on our planet; he claims that no previous ethic, much rhetoric notwithstanding, has succeeded in this. For that reason he advocates a moral philosophy that is based not on national borders but on the idea of one world. Hence Singer's exercise in philosophy can be read as a theoretical reflection on the globalization of society as such.

Also in 2002, the historian Akira Iriye published a book entitled *Global Community: The Role of International Organizations in the Making of the Contemporary World*.[25] Iriye claims that the "global community" is not just an idea that has been around for a long time but that in today's world it has become a reality. He looks in great detail at the emergence, growth, and activities of international organizations—both governmental and nongovernmental—from the end of the nineteenth century to the present. As the standard academic literature on international relations deals mainly with interstate affairs (politics, war, diplomacy, etc.), he feels justified in focusing on the creative role that international organizations have played in determining the shape of our modern world: "While states have been preoccupied with their own national interests, such as security and prestige, international organizations have been engaged in promoting cultural exchange, offering humanitarian assistance, extending developmental aid, protecting the environment, and championing human rights."[26] By making the world more interdependent and peaceful, he argues, international organizations have directly and importantly contributed to the evolution of the global community and global consciousness. Thus Iriye's historical study adds substance to a theory of the global society.

More recently, in 2004, the sociologist Amitai Etzioni published a book entitled *From Empire to Community: A New Approach to International Relations*.[27] Opposed to both conservative and liberal ways of thinking, Etzioni promotes in this book a public philosophy that he describes as "an international form of communitarianism." He discusses the global normative synthesis of core values that currently evolves out of multiple dialogues between Eastern and Western civilizations. According to him, this reflects a trend that he refers to as the emergence of a "transnational community" or "new global society." Beyond this general trend toward a global normative synthesis, he sees a process enabling people from different regions of the world to achieve shared moral understandings on specific issues: "These issues range from values that drive the movement to ban land mines, to the quest to curb the warming of the Earth, the condemnation of child pornography, and the opposition to invading sovereign countries." A key idea in this context is that of "moral dialogue." In his definition, "[m]oral dialogues occur when a group of people engage in a process of sorting out the values that should guide their lives."[28] In the new global society, moral dialogues are no longer mainly intra-national but increasingly transnational. So Etzioni's new book provides a truly communitarian perspective on the global society.

Also in 2004, the international law scholar Anne-Marie Slaughter published a book entitled *A New World Order*.[29] Current public and academic discussions of globalization, Slaughter argues, have been preoccupied with two major shifts: from national to global and from government to governance. She claims a third shift is much more important: from the unitary state to the disaggregate state. The influence of traditional international organizations created by unitary sovereign states is waning. Substituting for these, a myriad of transnational networks of regulators, judges, and legislators—representing not their national state but their own regulatory agencies, ministries, courts, and legislatures—express the reality of the new decentralized or disaggregate state. Examples of such government networks are the Financial Stability Forum, International Competition Network, World Intellectual Property Organization, Parliamentarians for Global Action, and the Commission on Environmental Cooperation, to name a few. Against this background, her main thesis is that we not just *should* have a new world order, but that we already *do* have one. That is to say, her account of modern global governance is both strongly empirical and strongly normative. Clearly Slaughter's new world order deals with important legal aspects of a theory of the global society.

APPROACHING GLOBAL CIVIL SOCIETY

These practices and these theories offer an intellectual challenge and an urgent message. Perhaps it is not too ambitious to take the arguments of Singer, Iriye, Etzioni, and Slaughter as philosophical, historical, sociological, and legal building blocks for a grander theory of global society.[30] If such a global society is indeed conceivable, INGOs and their networks clearly are part of it. Action such as that undertaken by ICBL, CICC, and Jubilee 2000 contributes to what in a previous section we have called global civil society (III), i.e., when the ensemble of INGOs can significantly determine or inflect the course of international or global policy. To the extent that global society à la Singer, Iriye, Etzioni, and Slaughter takes root, GCSIII may indeed evolve from a possibility into a reality. But then global civil society (II) may turn out to be a realizable option too, i.e., the global society as a whole structuring itself and coordinating its actions through these INGOs. In that case, the global civil society, shifting from GCSIII to GCSII, will have reversed the historical course of the civil society, which went from civil society (2) to civil society (3), if I am reading Taylor correctly.

The significance of Taylor's essay for our theme is not exhausted by this analogy. That is because Taylor's civil society (2) and (3) can serve as signposts to the emergent global civil society in a very different way. Global civil society (II) may be thought of as the realm of economic globalization serving the interests of those present or represented in the World Economic Forum. And global civil society (III) may be conceived as the sphere of social globalization that is characteristic for those participating in and identifying with the World Social Forum. Once more, Davos v. Porto Alegre. GCSII then becomes the world of "globalization from above," while GCSIII, its antipode, provides the stage for "globalization from below."[31] But while these two modes of globalization may historically have begun as radical opposites, Taylor's analysis of the evolution of civil society should teach us that both may be part of a broader current and that, if we are interested in a more sophisticated understanding of global civil society, we should be looking for some kind of combination or balance between the two.

Hence we may conclude that the new global social movement that crystallized in Seattle in 1999 did indeed bring us closer to global civil society. Global civil society *is* approaching. But it is important to realize that this involves not just GCSI, but GCSII and GCSIII as well. Equally important, the latter two are more closely connected than many of the neoliberals and antiglobalists assume. Interestingly enough, some of these insights are reflected in the evolution of the World Economic Forum and the World Social Forum after 2001. In recent years, the WEF has definitely broadened and intensified its concern with a host of global issues.[32] The WSF, which held its seventh annual meeting in 2007, this time in Nairobi, Kenya, has matured and evolved too. In 2001, it may have been mainly anti-Davos; today, it is offering real alternatives through a web of global networks.[33] In the same period, WSF has spawned hundreds of local, national, regional, and thematic social forums. This history is fairly extensively documented in the *Global Civil Society* yearbooks edited at the London School of Economics by Mary Kaldor, Helmut Anheier, and Marlies Glasius.[34]

Reading through these yearbooks, one gets a clear sense that the World Social Forum has become an important vehicle of the global social movement and of the global civil society as such. In this context, it is appropriate to refer to the change of name that occurred after the first WSF in 2001. In the opening section of this chapter, we saw how the WSF was identified with the antiglobalist movement and how this movement derived its name from the Battle of Seattle in 1999. But since 2001, many people, both within and outside of this movement, prefer alternative names. The four most popular ones are (a) different globalization or alterglobalization (from the French *alter mondialisation*) movement; (b) global justice movement; (c) ethical globalization movement;[35] and (d) movement of movements.[36] Should we perhaps understand these names as just alternative approaches to the one and only global civil society?

NOTES

1 John Lloyd, "Attack on Planet Davos," *Financial Times Weekend*, February 24–25, 2001.

2 José Seoane and Emilio Taddei, "From Seattle to Porto Alegre: The Anti-Neoliberal Globalization Movement," *Current Sociology* 50 (2002): 99–122; Marlies Glasius and Jill Timms, "The Role of Social Forums in Global Civil Society: Radical Beacon or Strategic Infrastructure?," in *Global Civil Society 2005/6*, ed. Marlies Glasius, Mary Kaldor, and Helmut Anheier (London: Sage, 2006), 190–238.

3 *NRC Handelsblad*, January 27, 2001.

4 For example, see Marlies Glasius, "Global Civil Society: Theories and Practices," in *Globalization and Its New Divides: Malcontents, Recipes, and Reform*, ed. Paul van Seters, Bas de Gaay Fortman, and Arie de Ruijter (Amsterdam: Dutch University Press, 2003), 193–207.

5 Janet Thomas, *The Battle in Seattle: The Story Behind and Beyond the WTO Demonstrations* (Golden, CO: Fulcrum Publishing, 2000); Eddie Yuen, Daniel Burton Rose, and George Katsiaficas, eds., *The Battle of Seattle: The New Challenge to Capitalist Globalization* (New York: Soft Skull Press, 2002).

6 Ibid.

7 For a comprehensive genealogy of the movement, see Seoane and Taddei, "From Seattle to Porto Alegre."

8 Thomas, *The Battle in Seattle*; Yuen, Rose, and Katsiaficas, *The Battle of Seattle*.

9 See Bas Arts, Math Noortmann, and Bob Reinalda, eds., *Non-State Actors in International Relations* (Aldershot: Ashgate, 2001).

10 "Table 5.1: Major UN conferences and summits of the 1990s," in *Global Civil Society 2005/6*, ed. Glasius, Kaldor, and Anheier, 160–63.

11 Lester M. Salamon, "The Rise of the Nonprofit Sector: A Global 'Associational Revolution,'" *Foreign Affairs* 74, no. 4 (1994): 109–22.

12 Michael Edwards, *Civil Society* (Cambridge: Polity, 2004), 23.

13 See the many contributions in Helmut Anheier, Marlies Glasius, and Mary Kaldor, eds., *Global Civil Society 2001* (Oxford: Oxford University Press, 2001); Marlies Glasius, Mary Kaldor, and Helmut Anheier, eds., *Global Civil Society 2002* (Oxford: Oxford University Press, 2002); Mary Kaldor, Helmut Anheier, and Marlies Glasius, eds., *Global Civil Society 2003* (Oxford: Oxford University Press, 2003); Helmut Anheier, Mary Kaldor, and Marlies Glasius, eds., *Global Civil Society 2004/5* (London: Sage, 2005); Marlies Glasius, Mary Kaldor, and Helmut Anheier, eds., *Global Civil Society 2005/6* (London: Sage, 2006); and Mary Kaldor, Martin Albrow, Helmut Anheier, and Marlies Glasius, eds., *Global Civil Society 2006/7* (London: Sage, 2007).

14 Charles Taylor, "Invoking Civil Society," in *Philosophical Arguments* (Cambridge, MA: Harvard University Press, 1995), 204–24.

15 Jeffrey C. Alexander, *The Civil Sphere* (New York: Oxford University Press, 2006). All quotations here are taken from chap. 2, "Real Civil Societies: Dilemmas of Institutionalization," 23–36.

16 Jean L. Cohen and Andrew Arato, *Civil Society and Political Theory* (Cambridge, MA: MIT Press, 1992).

17 Ibid., ix.

18 Ibid.

19 *Philosophical Arguments*, 206.

20 Margaret E. Keck and Kathryn Sikkink, *Activists beyond Borders: Advocacy Networks in International Politics* (Ithaca, NY: Cornell University Press, 1998); Ann Florini, ed., *The Third Force: The Rise of Transnational Civil Society* (Washington, DC: Carnegie Endowment for International Peace; Tokyo: Japan Center for International Exchange, 2000); John D. Clark, *Worlds Apart: Civil Society and the Battle for Ethical Globalization* (Bloomfield, CT: Kumarian Press, 2003); John D. Clark, ed., *Globalizing Civic Engagement: Civil Society and Transnational Action* (London: Earthscan, 2003); Srilatha Batliwala and L. David Brown, *Transnational Civil Society: An Introduction* (Bloomfield, CT: Kumarian Press, 2006).

21 www.icbl.org.

22 www.iccnow.org.

23 www.jubilee2000uk.org.

24 Peter Singer, *One World: The Ethics of Globalization* (New Haven, CT: Yale University Press, 2002).

25 Akira Iriye, *Global Community: The Role of International Organizations in the Making of the Contemporary World* (Berkeley: University of California Press, 2002).

26 Ibid. The quotation is taken from the book's jacket.

27 Amitai Etzioni, *From Empire to Community: A New Approach to International Relations* (New York: Palgrave Macmillan, 2004).

28 Ibid., 4, 40, 49, 67.

29 Anne-Marie Slaughter, *A New World Order* (Princeton, NJ: Princeton University Press, 2004).

30 This I would think is both more challenging and more promising than the model of a "world culture" that is on display in the well-known work of John Boli and George M. Thomas, eds., *Constructing World Culture: International Organizations since 1875* (Stanford, CA: Stanford University Press, 1999).

31 These phrases were coined by Richard Falk and first aired in Jeremy Brecher, John Brown Childs, and Jill Cutler, eds., *Global Visions: Beyond the New World Order* (Boston: South End Press, 1993). See also Jeremy Brecher, Tim Costello, and Brendan Smith, *Globalization from Below: The Power of Solidarity*, 2nd ed. (Cambridge, MA: South End Press, 2002), 141.

32 See Maggie Brenneke, John Elkington, and Sophia Tickell, *Growing Opportunity: Entrepreneurial Solutions to Insoluble Problems* (London: SustainAbility, 2007). See also www.weforum.org.

33 Immanuel Wallerstein, "The World Social Forum: From Defense to Offense," www.sendika.org, February 9, 2007.

34 See the sources cited in note 13.

35 Clark, *Worlds Apart: Civil Society and the Battle for Ethical Globalization*. Also note the appearance of Realizing Rights: Ethical Globalization Initiative, the INGO founded in 2002 by Mary Robinson, former president of Ireland and former United Nations High Commissioner for Human Rights. See http://www.eginitiative.org.
36 See Tom Mertes, ed., *A Movement of Movements: Is Another World Really Possible?* (London: Verso, 2004), and the various contributions to the special issue of *Development* 48, no. 2 (2005), "The Movement of Movements."

Case Studies

3

The Conference of NGOs (CONGO)

The Story of Strengthening Civil Society
Engagement with the United Nations

Renate Bloem, Isolda Agazzi Ben Attia,
and Philippe Dam

INTRODUCTION

Brief History

The Conference of NGOs in Consultative Relationship with the United Nations (CONGO) was founded in 1948 to safeguard the rights of NGOs in consultative status based upon article 71 of the UN Charter, which provides that the Economic and Social Council (ECOSOC) "May make suitable arrangements for consultation with NGOs which are concerned with matters within its competence." ECOSOC established such arrangements by Resolution 288B (1950); revised it by Resolution 1296 (1968) and then replaced the latter by ECOSOC Resolution 1996/31 (1996). For nearly sixty years, CONGO has actively promoted and facilitated the participation of civil society organizations in the work of the United Nations and its agencies. More recently, CONGO has made a major push to influence and democratize global decision-making processes. Today, CONGO reaches out to NGOs around the world to facilitate and strengthen their efforts to deal more effectively with the important matters treated in United Nations fora. It seeks to strengthen and raise national NGOs' voices at the global as well as the regional levels in support of the consensus reached at the various world conferences and exemplified in the Millennium Summit Declaration and the Development Goals (MDGs).

Membership

With more than five hundred members representing all categories of NGOs (many of which are umbrella organizations themselves), at all levels (locally, nationally, and internationally) and dealing with all major issues, CONGO is indeed a truly global organization and is well recognized as a most effective interface between the UN and NGOs.

Mission

CONGO's main purpose is to be a primary support for civil society represented by informed, empowered, and committed NGOs to fully participate with the UN in decision making and implementation of programs leading to a more just, peaceful, diverse, sustainable, and socially and economically responsible world. CONGO believes that a global civic ethic, based on core values that can unite people of all cultural, political, religious, or philosophical backgrounds should be the bedrock for global governance. Global governance should be underpinned by human rights, gender equality, and true democracy at all levels and ultimately by the rule of enforceable law. The United Nations is the main intergovernmental body and the seat of policy formulation in the areas of economic and social development, peace, and security. In order to give the governed an opportunity to have a say in these processes and their outcomes, it is crucial for NGOs and civil societies to actively participate at all levels of the UN mechanisms. CONGO can provide this access.

Strategy

CONGO's strategic goals are to enhance dialogue to build partnership and synergy; outreach, particularly in the global South; training and capacity building; global communications; and member services. Partners in carrying out that mission are CONGO members, other ECOSOC status NGOs, civil society organizations, other intergovernmental organizations, and the United Nations, in particular its NGO sections of the Department of Economic and Social Affairs (DESA), the Department of Public Information (DPI), and the Non-Governmental Liaison Service (UN-NGLS).

General Assembly

CONGO's General Assembly is the most important organ of the conference and convenes every three years to establish the organization's policy for the following triennium. The Assembly elects the president and twenty member organizations to serve on the board.

CONGO's 22nd General Assembly was held in Geneva, Switzerland, December 4–6, 2003, at the International Labour Organization (ILO) building under the theme "Inclusive Global Governance: Challenges and Opportunities for CONGO in Partnership with the United Nations." The general debate included discussions relating to UN reform and NGOs, a dialogue with members of the UN–Civil Society High-level Panel and a focus on the Millennium Declaration and Development Goals.

Four commissions dealing with peace, security, and disarmament; human rights; sustainable human development and information and communication technologies—all including a gender perspective and ethical values—have deepened the discussion and prepared for a call for action guiding CONGO into the following triennium.

CONGO Committees

CONGO does not take positions on substantive issues. However, it has established NGO committees in Geneva, New York, and Vienna that work on substantive issues in conformity with the objectives of the UN Charter. These range from human rights to development, peace and security, spiritual values, and the status of women. Committees are independent. Their detailed list and activity reports can be found at the CONGO website: http://www.ngocongo.org.

LEGAL BASIS FOR THE CONSULTATION OF NGOS WITHIN THE UN SYSTEM

Before presenting CONGO in more detail, we will briefly expose the legal mechanisms that allow NGOs to participate in the activities of the United Nations. At the UN, national, sub-regional, regional, and international NGOs may be granted consultative status to ECOSOC on the basis of the following two resolutions.

1. Article 71 of the UN Charter

"The Economic and Social Council may make suitable arrangements for consultation with non-governmental organizations which are concerned with matters within its competence. Such arrangements may be made with international organizations and, where appropriate, with national organizations after consultation with the Member of the United Nations concerned."[1] This is where the term "NGO" (as opposed to "association") appeared for the first time in an official text.

ECOSOC resolution 1968/1296 was the first one to be adopted by ECOSOC and to spell out the modalities of NGO accreditation. However, under that resolution, only international NGOs could get the consultative status and their possibilities of participation were still limited.

2. ECOSOC Resolution 1996/31

The resolution opened up the accreditation to national and regional NGOs, provided that "their aims and purposes are in conformity with the spirit, purposes and principles of the UN Charter"[2] and encouraged the accreditation of NGOs from developing countries. In order to get consultative status, an NGO must have an established headquarters, a democratically adopted constitution, an assembly, an executive organ, a representative structure, accountability to its members and authorized representatives to speak in its name at the UN.

The consultative status is granted by the Committee on NGOs,[3] an ECOSOC standing committee made up of 19 member states that meets two to three times a year in New York. However, the consultative status can also be suspended or withdrawn, particularly in the case of "unsubstantiated or politically motivated acts against Member States of the UN incompatible with those purposes and principles."[4] There are three different categories of consultative status: general, special and roster, for a total number of over 3000 NGOs at the time of writing. ECOSOC Resolution 1996/31 also sets the modalities of accreditation to UN conferences of NGOs that are not in consultative status.

THREE GENERATIONS OF UNITED NATIONS–
CIVIL SOCIETY RELATIONS

Even though legally grounded in article 71 of the Charter, the relationship between the UN and NGOs has evolved over the more than sixty years of UN existence. Tony Hill, until recently head of the UN-NGLS, distinguishes three generations of UN–civil society relations.[5]

The First Generation

During the first generation, which lasted roughly from 1945 to the end of the Cold War (1991), NGOs with consultive status with ECOSOC were almost exclusively international. As the Cold War paralyzed the deliberations at the UN, NGOs had little concrete involvement in the activities of the organization at the policy level. Indeed, NGO fora had been organized parallel to international summits, but they were more or less autonomous and had little impact on intergovernmental deliberations. An important exception was during the 1970s and early 1980s, that of NGOs involved in North–South dialogue under the auspices of the United Nations Conference on Trade and Development (UNCTAD) to promote a New International Economic Order. NGOs contributed, however, to some extent to standard-setting in the area of human rights. Altogether, they helped to make concrete the rules of accreditation inscribed in article 71 of the Charter and detailed in ECOSOC Resolution 1968/1296.

The Second Generation

During the 1990s, with the end of the Cold War, the UN organized a series of world summits that initiated new relationships with not only international NGOs but especially national and regional ones from Western and Southern countries and, to a lesser extent, from the former Eastern Bloc. NGOs began to get interested in UN work because several themes that were dealt with during these conferences were not receiving enough attention at the national level, or at least not in a satisfactory way. Contrary to the first type of NGOs, these new national and regional NGOs tried to get directly involved in inter-governmental deliberations and, through lobbying and mobilization, to influence their outcomes. New forms of transnational and international organizations started to emerge, such as the Oxfam family, Third World Network, and the Coalition for the International Criminal Court. Talk began about the emergence of "global civil society," about its participation in international deliberations ("democratization of global governance"), and about the UN as the backbone of the new international architecture. It is also at this time that the private sector started to appear at the UN.

Thus, in 1996 a new ECOSOC resolution redefined UN relations with NGOs, opening up the accreditation to include national NGOs. The number of NGOs requesting consultative status exploded in the following seven years (from 744 in 1992 to almost 2900 in 2006). More than seven hundred NGOs participated in the World Summit on the Information Society. NGOs of the second generation have a more "political" character and they seek to democratize the process of decision making at the global level (global governance). This generation is characterized by the increase in operational relations between the UN agencies, the Secretariat itself, and NGOs. The United Nations Development Programme (UNDP), the UN World Food Programme (WFP), the United Nations Children's Fund (UNICEF), the Food and Agriculture Organization (FAO), the United Nations Population Fund (UNFPA), and other agencies finance projects and programs in developing countries directly through NGOs, contrary to what happened in the past, when funds used to go exclusively to governments. This is especially the case for humanitarian aid and emergency programs.

Toward a Third Generation

Today CONGO is assisting in the emergence of a third generation of UN–civil society relations: coalitions of governments and like-minded CSOs leading to outcomes such as the International Criminal Court or the International Convention to Ban Landmines and various forms of multi-stakeholder partnerships (public–private, such as the Global Compact and the more than two hundred "Track II" partnerships launched in Johannesburg, or in the World Summit on the Information Society processes).

Many NGOs, however, are skeptical of these new forms of partnerships, particularly those involving the private sector.

EVOLUTION OF CONGO'S RELATIONSHIP WITH THE UN

The First Generation

Founded in 1948 to safeguard the rights of NGOs in consultative status, CONGO has been an advocate for civil society since the beginning. While the Cold War was paralyzing the activities of the United Nations and generating endless debates at the General Assembly, CONGO provided a platform where NGOs from East and West could meet and look for common positions. It is interesting to note that, by an unwritten rule, half of the twenty CONGO Board members were NGOs from Western countries and half NGOs from the former socialist bloc.

The Second Generation

At the World Conference on Human Rights, held in Tehran, Iran, in 1968 to celebrate the twentieth anniversary of the Universal Declaration of Human Rights, NGOs were not allowed to participate. In response to this refusal, CONGO organized the first NGO Forum in conjunction with a UN summit, which was convened in Paris, France, not in Tehran. Since then, CONGO has insisted that whenever UN summits are organized, NGOs in consultative status be automatically invited and invitations extended also to NGOs not in status but with relevant expertise on the subject at stake. CONGO was most notably present in Rio de Janeiro, Beijing, Vienna, Durban, Johannesburg, Geneva, and Tunis. In the process toward the World Conference on Human Rights, held in Vienna, Austria (1993), CONGO established an NGO Preparatory Committee but was not sensitive enough to include relevant human rights actors with different regional and diversity issues perspectives. Within the heated debate on cultural relativism that was one of the most salient features of the Summit, CONGO was accused of being insensitive to cultural diversity and trying to impose a single voice on NGOs. Since then, CONGO has strived to adopt a bottom-up, participatory approach that reflects the diversity of sensitivities and opinions of NGOs participating in meetings. It has been careful to present its positions as emanating from a general consensus among NGOs and never pretended to "represent" or even "coordinate" NGOs, less so to speak on their behalf. CONGO rather sees its mission as being the facilitator and creator of space for NGOs to speak with their own voice.

At the World Conference against Racism, in Durban, South Africa (2001), CONGO participated actively in the NGO Forum and was responsible for space allocation and events held in the international tent. During the Government Conference—from the opening of the conference to the last day—CONGO helped organize and chair the morning briefings for NGOs during which space and opportunities were given to different caucuses to express their views and impact on the conference. In briefings after the tumultuous Forum meetings, in which each group focused narrowly on its own cause with the loudest possible voice, efforts were made to reunite, to listen to each other, and to see the larger picture of what the conference was all about. Each morning a different member of the CONGO delegation chaired the briefing and was responsible for the program. Throughout, CONGO's approach to the World Conference had been one of a visionary of tomorrow, of changing mentalities, of recognizing and respecting the "other," of addressing and redressing wrongs of the past in order to meet the wrongs of the present.

After the Rio conference in 1992, the process to the 2nd World Summit on Sustainable Development (WSSD—Johannesburg, South Africa, 2002) was meant to involve civil society "major groups," which included both NGOs and the private sector. The outcome of the WSSD itself was hailed by some as a great success and by others as a great failure, depending on the issue or geographical perspective.[6] The most complex agenda ever dealt with in one conference—social and economic development and environmental protection, all in one basket—made for difficult negotiations. The methods applied with track I (government negotiations) and track II (partnerships with civil society) outcomes were innovative, although suspicious to many NGOs, who feared that governments were trying to shy away from their responsibilities and leave too much to the private sector.

Civil society's impact on the conference was fragmented due to many factors, including long distances between the different venues. CONGO was a member of the international steering committee set up to organize the People's Forum. It tried to be a bridge between NGOs who worked as "major groups" (however limited) at the government convention centre at Sandton and the hundreds of NGOs that had come together at the Global Peoples' Forum at Nasrec. CONGO also negotiated successfully with governments and UN officials during the first days at Sandton to avoid an embarrassing NGO boycott or walk-out after security officials denied access to the convention centre.

The Third Generation

After the adoption of ECOSOC Resolution 1996/31—which opened the consultative status to national and regional NGOs—the number of accredited NGOs exploded, reaching more than 2900 in 2006. This poses an enormous challenge to NGOs in general and to CONGO in particular, which strives to reach a certain degree of coordination for the maximum impact while preserving specificity. NGOs are each unique and do not want to speak with one voice. They have very different constituencies and insist on keeping individual positions. In order to be taken seriously by governments, however, and not to overload an already impressive agenda, they need to rationalize their endeavours. Despite initial mistrust and even open opposition from some large and experienced NGOs, CONGO has successfully advocated among fellow civil society entities for more concerted action that has borne the greatest fruits in the following events:

- the World Summit on the Information Society (WSIS)
- the civil society fora organized in the regions and at UN Headquarters
- the Millennium + 5 process
- human rights activities

THE WORLD SUMMIT ON THE INFORMATION SOCIETY (WSIS)

The World Summit on the Information Society, the last UN global summit to date, constituted an historic breakthrough in UN–NGO relations. For the first time, a Civil Society Bureau was established by civil society constituencies involved in the Summit, as a counterpart to the Governmental Bureau, for the preparation and the holding of the Summit itself. The WSIS process was in that way close to a multi-stakeholder tripartite model and created an exchange platform between governments, civil society, and the private sector. The promotion and the practical application of the multi-stakeholder approach towards an international political process are considered some of the main outcomes of the Summit, providing a strong legitimacy to the WSIS process. During both Phase I and Phase II of the Summit, civil society entities benefited from the most favourable conditions to date for their participation in the decision-making process. These included access to policy documents and to meeting spaces, modalities of interaction during the negotiation process of the outcome document, and the inclusion of marginal groups.

Civil Society Self-organized Structures

A main achievement of civil society entities during the WSIS process, and strongly supported by CONGO, was the establishment of a civil society self-organizing structure. The Civil Society Plenary, fully inclusive and open to participation from all civil society entities accredited to WSIS, was the ultimate decision-making space for civil society and the main organ for common civil society actions and initiatives. More than thirty regional and thematic civil society caucuses and working groups, voluntarily established by groups of NGOs working on the same issue, dealt with the creation of substantive content, the drafting of statements and official joint submissions, and the strengthening of joint lobbying strategies. A Content and Themes group was in charge of coordinating and strategizing among the initiatives of these content-related groupings. This group notably coordinated the drafting of the independent Civil Society Declaration "Shaping Societies for Human Needs" at the end of Phase I and the civil society statement "Much more could have been achieved" at the end of Phase II.

The Civil Society Bureau dealt with procedural issues and organizational arrangements to facilitate civil society contributions to the whole process. It maintained a close relationship and regular interactions with the Intergovernmental Bureau and the WSIS Executive Secretariat. The Civil Society Bureau was composed of twenty members representing various civil society families, and CONGO led a process in which each of the families had to identify a representative to serve on this new Bureau. CONGO also played a moderating function and a leading supporting role in the work of the Civil Society Bureau, servicing its meetings and implementing its initiatives, in particular during Phase II of the Summit. In addition to physical meetings of the preparatory committees (PrepComs), civil society structures established listservs and websites to keep contact and continue the transparent working process CONGO provided between the official meeting periods. Through these listservs, CONGO supplied regular information and reports on the ongoing process and led consultations on procedural and organizational matters.

This bottom-up dynamic within civil society constituencies accredited to the WSIS was one of the greatest successes of their contributions to the Summit. It brought greater visibility to civil society's shared positions and joint actions during the negotiations processes while guaranteeing transparency, diversity, and quality in the civil society contributions to the official process. It also promoted a gathering and information-sharing space, inclusive of all civil society entities, thus encouraging the exchange of experience and ideas and the creation of new networks among civil society participants in the Summit and its preparatory process. Civil society working methods were hailed by most of the governments and NGOs/CSOs as a major step forward. They also caught the attention of the media and were widely reported on in the press.

The WSIS experience of working together despite the diversity of civil society entities and their sometimes opposing interests brought to CONGO a new vision of its role within civil society processes. The modern nature of the issues addressed by the Summit and the development of Information and Communications Technologies (ICT) based on working methods at the global level contributed to offering CONGO a better understanding of the challenges and opportunities facing civil society at large, even beyond WSIS. The WSIS process will certainly impact on how CONGO will approach multilateral processes within the UN and on how CONGO will promote the construction of common understanding and consensus building among NGOs.

WSIS Phase I, Geneva Summit, Switzerland, December 8–12, 2003

CONGO played an important and central role throughout the preparatory process of the Summit: Renate Bloem, president of CONGO, has served on the Civil Society Bureau since its creation during PrepCom-2, in 2003, to ensure the effective inclusion of civil society in the negotiation process. The secretariat and servicing activities of the Civil Society Bureau were provided by the Civil Society Division of the WSIS Executive Secretariat. On the more technical side, Rik Panganiban, CONGO Communications Coordinator, organized the WSIS Civil Society News Centre, a website publicizing the most current news and views from civil society organizations involved in the WSIS. The CS News Centre fed information and analysis of the negotiations to civil society groups around the world and published their views and proposals.

During the first phase of the Summit itself, the News Centre was hosted on the WSIS-online website,[7] significantly increasing the visibility of civil society's proposals and perspectives. CONGO also organized several parallel events on critical issues, including the eradication of poverty, human rights, interfaith dialogue, and combatting HIV/AIDS using entertainment media.[8] These events served to highlight their relation to the information society, bringing together key actors in civil society, UN agencies, and governments to discuss these issues. CONGO also sponsored a booth at the Information and Communication(s) Technologies for Development (ICT4D) exhibition, making publications and information from CONGO and members of CONGO available to the wider public. Finally, the president also spoke on behalf of civil society at a welcome ceremony sponsored by the Swiss government, and Isolda Agazzi, senior program officer, spoke at a side-event about the NGOs' contribution to the implementation of the Millennium Development Goals (MDGs).

WSIS Phase II, Tunis Summit, Tunisia, November 16–18, 2005

CONGO continued to play a strong facilitating role for the 606 registered NGO entities (more than 6000 civil society participants). A reform of the working methods of the Civil Society Bureau (CSB) in December 2004 entrusted CONGO with the role of performing the support and servicing activities of the CSB until the holding of the Tunis Summit. CONGO committed its staff to ensure that adequate facilities be available for civil society during the summit, including access to meeting rooms, office spaces, computers, internet, printers, and photocopiers.

CONGO regularly met throughout the process with the top-level staff of the WSIS Executive Secretariat and maintained relationships with the chairperson of the Intergovernmental Bureau, with a view to reporting back and consulting with the wider civil society constituency. CONGO also managed room requests, the establishment of speakers' lists, the attribution of fellowships during PrepCom-2 and PrepCom-3, and the preparations for the Summit Opening meetings in Tunis. In addition to organizing well-attended orientation sessions at the beginning of each meeting of the preparatory committees, CONGO staff also prepared a detailed orientation kit in collaboration with UN-NGLS with some financial support from the International Humanist Institute for Cooperation with Developing Countries (Humanistisch Instituut voor Ontwikkelingssamenwerking)(HIVOS). A first version of this fifty-page document was circulated to civil society participants during PrepCom-3 in September 2005, and a revised and updated version, and a French version, was made available on the occasion of the Tunis Summit.

As mandated by the Civil Society Bureau, CONGO was also responsible for managing sensitive issues for civil society constituencies. This included the establishment of a close dialogue between NGOs and the WSIS Executive Secretariat on the modalities of implementation of the Summit Host Country Agreement. There were tensions between human rights NGOs and the Tunisian Government, and the issue of human rights violations, particularly the lack of freedom of expression in the host country, accompanied civil society interactions for the entire WSIS process. CONGO's attempts to dialogue with, as well as to challenge, Tunisian high government officials were not successful, and a hoped-for lessening of restrictions did not occur. While the summit itself was well organized, and no incidents occurred on the summit's premises, repression outside to prevent meetings in support of Tunisian independent civil society continued. CONGO also supported and organized much of the media coverage of civil society participation in the Summit.

Lastly, CONGO facilitated the achievement by civil society of a broad consensus for an independent civil society statement and the CONGO president gave the statement during the first plenary session. CONGO also organized a parallel event, "Civil Society Best Practices to Bridge the Digital Divide," featuring high-level UN officials and members of grassroots organizations as speakers.

WSIS Follow-up

The Tunis outcome had left CONGO with a complex follow-up structure. It had created the Internet Governance Forum, and had asked ECOSOC to oversee the overall follow-up within the UN system. It entrusted relevant UN agencies and organizations to facilitate the multi-stakeholder thematic implementation at the international level. For this to happen, ECOSOC was asked to review and strengthen its existing Commission on Science and Technology for Development (CSTD) with an additional new mandate of WSIS follow-up (this would mean, among other things, enlarging the commission), taking into account the multi-stakeholder approach. More recently the Secretary General established the Global Alliance for ICT and Development (GAID), an open multi-stakeholder mechanism for advancing the UN development agenda, including the MDGs, through ICTs.

ECOSOC and the CSTD

A series of open consultations between February and May 2006, convened by the ECOSOC president, paved the way for the negotiations on ECOSOC's review of the CSTD. CONGO pleaded to open the CSTD process to more stakeholders, in particular to WSIS-accredited entities, including those not holding ECOSOC status (only 10 percent of all civil society participants in the WSIS had ECOSOC status). In parallel, CONGO held informal talks with the executive director of the WSIS Secretariat and with the United Nations Conference on Trade and Development (UNCTAD) providing the Secretariat to the CSTD, to explore their support and identify future opportunities for NGO participation.

A negotiation team of the Working Group of ECOSOC, chaired by Ambassador Janis Karklins, met in parallel to the annual ECOSOC Substantial Session held in July 2006. CONGO advocated to ensure that civil society representatives could observe and contribute to the negotiations in an open and transparent way until a consensus could be achieved. Even though the wording of the consensus text is rather weak, it does not contain provisions against civil society inclusion. The CSTD reform therefore paves the way for a follow-up process in an intergovernmental body using the multi-stakeholder approach. The final agreed-on text also includes very positive provisions including interim modalities for the participation of WSIS-accredited civil society entities in the next two sessions of the CSTD. This commission will therefore be one of the first intergovernmental bodies in which a multi-stakeholder model might be implemented. The CSTD held the first session after its review in May 2007.

Global Alliance for ICT and Development (GAID)

GAID is conceived as an open multi-stakeholder forum composed of representatives of governments, UN agencies, civil society, and the private sector, with a small secretariat in the United Nations Department of Economic and Social Affairs (DESA), New York. Membership is open to all. GAID is governed by a Strategy Council, a small Steering Committee, to which the president of

CONGO has been appointed, and is assisted by a High-level Advisory Group and a Champion's Network.[9]

The Global Alliance represents an innovative multi-stakeholder model, working in an inclusive, dynamic, and bottom-up manner, opening great opportunities for the commitment of civil society actors and other stakeholders in the use of ICTs in the achievement of the MDGs. CONGO will continue to play a leading role in supporting the strengthening of the Global Alliance and the achievement of its goals and to mobilize the involvement of civil society actors in its activities.

THE CIVIL SOCIETY FORA IN THE REGIONS AND AT UN HEADQUARTERS

Reaching out to the people in the regions is one of CONGO's most important strategic activities. The UN and its agenda do not stop in New York or Geneva. The UN goals need to get to the people on the ground, who must be allowed to express their views which, in turn, need to be channelled to international decision makers. CONGO has organized major civil society gatherings in the regions, targeting both NGOs in consultative status and those not familiar with the UN system. With the general aim of democratizing global governance and contributing to achieving the MDGs, these fora have been tailored to regional realities and local needs and organized with local counterpart NGOs. Two fora were held in Africa, two in Asia, and one in Latin America.

African Regional Consultation, Kampala, Uganda, 1998

The African Regional Consultation of NGOs, held in Kampala, Uganda, in 1998 was the first of CONGO's outreach activities. In response to key interests stated by African NGOs consulted by CONGO, four development themes were selected: "health and reproductive health," "human rights and gender equality," "peace and conflict resolution," and "democracy and good governance." The discussion cut across thematic boundaries and revealed, among many other things, the dynamism of women's contributions to and the centrality of women's concerns for the future of African societies. For each thematic area the consultation also revealed much about the difficulties African NGOs encounter in the context in which they have to operate.

African Civil Society Forum, Addis Ababa, Ethiopia, 2007

The theme of the African Civil Society Forum organized by CONGO with its partners in Addis Ababa, Ethiopia, in March 2007 was "Democratizing Governance at the Regional and Global Level to Achieve the MDGs." The forum targeted more than 250 participants and addressed the following issues:

"peace and human security," "governance and human rights," and "development: trade, finance, debt relief, and investment." The forum closed with the adoption of a final declaration that contains recommendations for the African Union, civil society, and the United Nations, relating to these issues as well as to gender mainstreaming, ICT development, and HIV/AIDs.

Asian Civil Society Forum, Bangkok, Thailand, 2002

The Asian Civil Society Forum was held in Bangkok, Thailand, in December 2002 at the United Nations Economic and Social Commission for Asia and the Pacific (ESCAP), under the theme UN/NGO Partnerships for Democratic Governance: Building Capacities and Networks for Human Rights and Sustainable Development. Its objectives were:

- to promote co-operation and solidarity among NGOs in Asia engaged in advocacy activities at the UN;
- to raise the awareness of Asian NGOs about the MDGs and to assess their contribution to their implementation;
- to facilitate proactive dialogue and debate among NGOs on the issues concerning UN/NGO partnership for democratic governance at all levels;
- to provide NGOs with practical and innovative training about advocacy at the UN;
- to assess the impact and implementation of UN conferences in Asia, such as the UN Millennium Summit 2000, the World Conference against Racism (WCAR) 2001, and the World Summit on Sustainable Development (WSSD) 2002; and
- to develop NGOs' strategies to ensure that governments' pledges made at the UN conferences are fully implemented.[10]

The Forum was a success, gathering a total of 572 participants from thirty-three countries, which exceeded by far everyone's optimistic expectations. Given the particular situation in Afghanistan and the urgent need to strengthen an emergent civil society, four Afghan NGO representatives attended the Forum. It is worth noting that most NGOs had come by their own means (CONGO was able to fund 148 participants), which is proof not only of their interest in the issues but also of the timeliness of the Forum. Participation was balanced in terms of geographical spread and gender, even though some countries came with relatively larger delegations such as those from India, Korea, the Philippines, and other places with a strong and vibrant civil society.

Another interesting point is that most of the NGOs represented were not accredited to the UN—hence not CONGO members. Also, many of them were participating in an international conference of this kind for the first time. Judging from the scope and nature of the organizations represented, the target of reaching out to grassroots organizations that are active, especially at the local and national levels, seems to have been achieved. This meant, however, that most of the participants had not done much advocacy work within the UN system. Therefore the forum, to a large extent, provided the much-needed opportunity for exposure to and learning about the workings of the UN in relation to the many global issues expressed at the local and most basic level in society. At the end of the forum, many participants expressed serious interest in developing international advocacy work with a focus on the UN.

NGO Forum to the ECOSOC High-level Segment on Rural Development, Geneva, Switzerland, 2003

CONGO had been asked by the ECOSOC Secretariat to organize for the third consecutive year an NGO forum preceding the High-level Segment (HLS) of ECOSOC's Substantive Session. The theme of the forum, and of the HLS, was "Promoting an integrated approach to rural development in developing countries for poverty eradication and sustainable development." The forum took place in the Palais des Nations, Geneva, Switzerland, on June 27, 2003.

The purpose of the forum was to bring to the attention of the HLS the recommendations of NGOs for input into the debate and the Ministerial Declaration. Altogether, the forum gathered about one hundred participants, among which many were members of NGOs in consultative status with ECOSOC—and hence already used to the functioning of UN mechanisms and aware of the advocacy activity of NGOs. Half of the participants represented NGOs without consultative status and no previous UN exposure. The program was clustered around five thematic subjects focusing on rural areas: poverty eradication, agricultural development and food security, the promotion of health, water and sanitation, participation and decentralization, and the promotion of women and gender equality. Speakers were selected by applying the criteria of geographical and gender balance and on the basis of their experience in working in rural development. The panellists were asked to present concrete recommendations, which were then summed up by the general rapporteur of the session. These recommendations were subsequently developed into a declaration, which the CONGO president presented to the ECOSOC HLS. The declaration was well received by the audience, which—it is worth stressing—applauded the concerns and aspirations of NGOs.

Latin America and Caribbean Seminar, Santiago de Chile, 2004

CONGO organized a seminar for Latin America and the Caribbean under the theme "Partnerships for a New Era: Achieving the Millennium Development Goals" in Santiago de Chile June 1–4, 2004. The seminar was attended by some 130 participants, representing 120 local, national, and regional NGOs from thirteen countries.

Although achieving the MDGs by 2015 is considered by many to be an impossible and unrealistic target, in the second report released by the UN Secretary General on the Implementation of the Millennium Declaration (September 2003) predictions were mixed; for Latin America and the Caribbean, however, the prospects were quite good, and improvements in most of the indicators had been witnessed in the region between 1990 and 2000.

The Latin American seminar represented one more step on the way from commitment to implementation, and it constituted a momentum in the awareness-raising of NGOs and civil society organizations in Latin America: all the people in that region—and all over the world—should now be aware that their governments have committed themselves to halve poverty, reduce child mortality, empower women, and achieve universal primary education. Although these are basic economic and social rights embedded in the International Covenant on Economic, Social and Cultural Rights, the MDGs give them a new perspective: they put a timeframe on these commitments, they set precise indicators, and their achievement is constantly monitored by the UN. The seminar was held to learn more about the MDGs and about the best way for NGOs to contribute to their achievement. It produced a very concrete Plan of Action (PoA) that was seen as a strong commitment to lobby the governments of the region, in co-operation with the UN agencies, to increase their efforts to reach the MDGs.

The Santiago PoA is very explicit in requesting governments to include the MDGs in their plans, underlying that "the best results were achieved in those countries whose presidents have done so."[11] It also underlines the need to foster good governance at the national level—transparency, accountability, participation, and decentralization—by requesting governments to:

1. Clearly say which governmental body is responsible for implementing which MDG;
2. Establish a decentralized agenda for the attainment of the MDGs;
3. Disseminate the MDG reports to all levels of society, notably by including the media. (The need for joining forces between civil society organizations and the media to educate and raise the awareness of public opinion cannot be underlined strongly enough; the PoA states that "the power of information helps to demand accountability from governments");
4. Involve NGOs in designing policies to achieve the MDGs and in reporting on their implementation. CSOs in the region do not want only to provide vague monitoring; they also want to be actively involved in the elaboration

of pertinent indicators for reporting on the MDGs and stress the need to "get each country to redefine and construct its indicators, as the 48 indicators were defined at the global level with no participation of the regions or civil society"; and

5. Include the private sector in order to find sufficient resources to achieve the MDGs.[12]

Latin American NGOs also advocated for a "change in mentality" that would help bring about changes in international bodies. These NGOs want to become the protagonists of their own development and "stop being poor and dependent on the rich." They stress the importance of sustaining initially the investment from rich countries in the area of research and development, with the aim of replacing these funds progressively with state and private sector investment. Knowledge—human intelligence—is seen as having the highest economic and social value. In general, the PoA underlines the importance of tailoring the MDGs to the needs of local communities, specific socio-economic groups and cultural realities.

Civil Society Forum to the ECOSOC High-level Segment on Employment and Decent Work, Geneva, Switzerland, 2006

The ECOSOC Substantive Session's HLS 2006 dealt with "Employment and Decent Work." The objective of the forum was to produce recommendations that would be discussed interactively with dignitaries and, ideally, included in the Ministerial Declaration. It was imperative to give a concerted view on the issue, because many civil society activists believe that globalization requires an appropriate international framework to help implement the Millennium Declaration, including the MDGs. They also wanted to see incorporated in such a framework the respect for human rights and more particularly the core labour rights. CONGO considered that ECOSOC—mandated by the High-level Meeting of the General Assembly (September 2005) to act as the coordinating body for development policies at the international level—should boldly take up its strengthened mandate and strive for a consensus on how best to guarantee these rights.

The forum gathered 306 participants, representing eighty civil society organizations from over fifty countries. They participated in the following six clusters:

1. Globalization and its impact on decent work, both in developing and developed countries (with a special focus on labour migration);
2. Creating an enabling environment at the national level conducive for growth and employment creation (with a special focus on the informal sector);

3. Employment for women, youth, and the elderly;
4. Human rights and employment for vulnerable groups: indigenous peoples, people with disabilities, and people living in post-crisis situations;
5. Employment in the rural and urban areas; and
6. New forms of employment (including e-employment).

Every cluster included speakers and workshop conveners from all over the world, chosen on the basis of geographical, thematic, and gender balance. It is worth noting that African civil society organizations had expressed their strong interest to participate in the forum. CONGO particularly encouraged them, since Africa is the continent that lags the furthest behind in achieving the MDGs. Every cluster was divided into workshops on specific issues identified according to previously expressed interests. Every workshop was expected to produce recommendations. These were then channelled and synthesized into cluster recommendations to be debated and adopted by the plenary. The final outcome recommendations were presented at the HLS and discussed with HLS dignitaries and representatives of international organizations during an interactive luncheon on July 5, 2006.

Cluster 1 dealt with globalization issues and discussed how to achieve policy coherence among international financial institutions, the World Trade Organization (WTO) and the International Labour Organization (ILO). Tackling the issues of decent work and economic growth, migration, decent work, and development, the cluster emphasized that migration is the product of the globalization that has failed to achieve its goals: full employment and decent work.

Cluster 2 debated working environments at the national level and featured a workshop on quality public services, with a special focus on the universal access to energy as a key factor for development. Among issues worth mentioning were social dialogue and alliance building, the presentation of country experiences and study cases, labour standards, and the role of the ILO in promoting these key concepts.

Cluster 3 looked at the issue of decent work from a gender perspective, with an emphasis on discrimination against women (particularly in Eastern Europe) and on "women in development." The cluster's main theme invited participants to equally consider major topics, including equality of opportunity for women, education issues, trafficking, the fight against poverty in Africa, youth employment, and child labour.

Cluster 4 centred its debate on vulnerable groups, with presentations by NGOs from war-torn countries and indigenous and marginalized people. Another workshop was devoted to the issue of HIV/AIDS and decent work, particularly in Africa.

Cluster 5 addressed the theme of employment in rural and urban areas, discussing the informal economy and the role of decentralized co-operation and local authorities in employment creation.

Cluster 6 dealt with the new forms of employment, focusing on the use of ICTs and e-employment to provide youth, women, and deprived populations with decent work.

The recommendations emanating from the different clusters were amended and adopted by the plenary of the forum and discussed during an interactive luncheon with dignitaries and UN officials.

THE MILLENNIUM + 5 PROCESS

One of the most important roles held by NGOs is that of a "watchdog"; they remind governments of the commitments taken at international conferences, e.g., to ratify treaties and try to monitor their implementation. The Millennium Assembly and the MDGs are a case in point in this regard. In May 2000, the Millennium Forum in New York gathered NGO representatives from all over the world to elaborate a declaration and an action plan that largely influenced the adoption of the official declaration by governments in September of the same year. This Declaration, in turn, resulted in the adoption of the MDGs, eight goals with objectives and indicators that crystallize the engagements taken during the 1990s in terms of poverty eradication, heath, education, gender, environment, and international partnerships.[13]

On June 23–24, 2005, the General Assembly held its first ever hearings with representatives of civil society and the private sector in preparation for the High-level Summit to be held September 14–16, 2005. The purpose of the hearings was to listen to the voices of two hundred organizations—and one thousand observers—on the four clusters of the Secretary General's report "In Larger Freedom": freedom to live in dignity (human rights), freedom from want (MDGs), freedom from fear (security), and United Nations reform.[14] The outcome of the hearings was supposed to feed into the Draft Outcome Document (DOD) of the 60th General Assembly session's Summit, also known as the "Millennium + 5 Summit," that would assess the implementation of the Millennium Declaration and the MDGs five years after their adoption and eventually endorse the ambitious reform proposals of the Secretary General.

Despite the informality of the event, the hearings were defined as a "historic moment," since never before had the General Assembly directly consulted CSOs and the private sector. Hearings were chaired by the General Assembly President, Ambassador Yang Ping, opened by Deputy Secretary General Louise Fréchette, closed by Secretary General Kofi Annan, and witnessed the participation of numerous member states. Renate Bloem, president of CONGO, had the honour of making a statement at the opening session of the hearings.

The first session dealt with the freedom to live in dignity—namely, human rights. Generally speaking, NGOs concurred with the Secretary General on the principle that human rights must become the foundation of the UN system and be given the same institutional position as security and development. The proposal to create a standing Human Rights Council and to elevate it to one of the principal organs of the UN was welcomed by many. Most also supported the idea that members should be elected by two-thirds of the General Assembly on the basis of a real commitment to the promotion and protection of human rights. Speakers insisted that NGOs be ensured at least the same level of participation in the council that they presently have in the Commission on Human Rights. Due consideration should be given to equitable geographic distribution and the council should be able to alert the Security Council when urgent action is needed. Consensus was also reached on the need to strengthen the Office of the High Commissioner for Human Rights (OHCHR), both by increasing its financial resources (to be doubled within five years) and diversifying its staff. Rights of vulnerable groups, particularly women, children, youth, and indigenous peoples, should be included when taking action on human rights. Several NGOs regretted that the DOD did not adequately reflect the question of women's human rights, at a time when an issue such as violence against women should become a top priority of the international community.

The sessions on freedom from want (MDGs) conveyed the general dissatisfaction of NGOs with the prevailing approach to development that is centred on markets and not on human beings. NGOs advocated for a paradigm shift from a neo-liberal approach to a human-rights-based approach to development, arguing that strengthening the markets, liberalizing trade, and producing goods primarily for export had proved to be "disastrous." Several speakers criticized the MDGs for "relying on the discredited notion that economic growth can reduce poverty."

More specifically, during the session on MDGs 1–7, speakers insisted on the interconnectivity of all MDGs, indicating these must complement one another and cannot be treated separately. They argued that poverty can be eliminated only with the true participation of the poor and called for the inclusion of particular groups in the development and implementation of strategies to achieve the MDGs, especially indigenous peoples and youth. Women are an essential component of this participation effort, and the DOD was blamed again for the disappointing way it treats women's rights, particularly since the core actions for achieving the equality of rights for women are well known.[15] Local communities and grassroots organizations are other key stakeholders, and it was recommended that 25 percent of national MDG-related budgets be allocated to community-based projects and indigenous people to speed up implementation.

Regarding other specific MDGs, NGOs insisted on the importance of environmental sustainability for the realization of the MDGs, pointing to the need to increase agricultural productivity as one of the essential elements to achieve it; they proposed that the DOD call for universal access to health care services and called for a substantial increase of resources to fight HIV/AIDS to at least $22 billion by 2007; regarding education, they asked for the elimination of school fees and other barriers that limit the access to education.

The session on MDG 8 witnessed other strong calls by NGOs to resist the economic paradigm of "marketization" and a policy framework that privileges the market over the state, giving "priority to profits over the needs of the people." Several speakers accused MDG 8 of being "full of contradictions," including the assumption that trade liberalization can solve the problem of poverty. Speakers instead proposed "fair trade," the benefits of which are worth twenty times what aid can do. There was a vibrant call for the UN reform process to strengthen ECOSOC, so that the World Bank, the International Monetary Fund, and the WTO policies get in tune with UN values. Emphasizing the fact that "social progress" has slowed since 1999, it was noted that Official Development Assistance (ODA) must be increased without "cheap accounting tricks." It was pointed out that thirty-six years had passed since countries committed themselves to the 0.7 percent Gross National Income (GNI) target of ODA, a target that is far from having been met and an anniversary that nobody would dare to celebrate.

Insisting on the local ownership of national development strategies and on the need "not to impose global economic policies on individual countries" (a reference to the "policy space" of the São Paolo Consensus), it was said that "Africa has to take its fate in its own hands, with development coming from within and not from without." Economic growth is not a solution in itself because the origin of poverty lies in income distribution. Hence assistance should not be given to countries that don't practise democracy, since civilian populations need to know where the money is going.

Some speakers also challenged the importance given by member states and the private sector to foreign direct investment, arguing that it often did not benefit the poor. They stressed the importance of corporate social responsibility of transnational corporations and insisted on the need to protect workers' rights, along the ILO's four dimensions of decent work.[16] On the issue of debt, there was a strong call for immediate and wide-ranging debt relief.

The session on freedom from fear and conflict prevention witnessed an enthusiastic endorsement of the Secretary General's call for the establishment of a Peacebuilding Commission to help countries in the transition from war to a lasting peace. NGOs stressed that sustainable security is based on human security, not on state security, and hence the need to shift from reaction to prevention of armed conflicts. Women, youth, and disabled people are key stakeholders in any conflict prevention strategy and in any peacebuilding measure. Following the Secretary General's proposal, NGOs endorsed the idea that when prevention fails, the UN has a responsibility to protect the populations, particularly the most vulnerable, including women, children, refugees, and aboriginal people.

During the session on freedom from fear and peace and security, some speakers argued that a non-representative Security Council is a threat to international peace and security, hence the need to democratize the international peace and security system. Stressing the responsibility of arms-exporting states, speakers proposed to adopt a binding instrument on the regulation of small arms, which would regulate the arms trade. As the exploitation by multinational corporations of mineral resources is often the cause of armed conflicts, the need to recognize the right of indigenous peoples to self-determination was underlined. Women were once more at the heart of concerns, since they and girls are hidden victims of armed conflicts, and prostitution and trafficking represent acts of violence against them.

The session on strengthening the UN centred on the idea that "people, not power, must regain the priority they deserve by taking back the UN." Strong support was expressed again for a Human Rights Council and for a strengthened ECOSOC that would become a high-level development forum. It was argued that "for the UN reform to be effective there must be a reinvention of the World Bank and the WTO and a coordination mechanism with enforceable power over all intergovernmental organizations." The wish was expressed to end the veto in the Security Council. Finally, and once more, it was argued that gender equality must be endorsed by the UN, by nominating more women in visible roles.

HUMAN RIGHTS

The issue of human rights is probably the one in which NGOs have become the most involved at the United Nations. The Commission on Human Rights (replaced in 2006 by the Human Rights Council) was the ECOSOC subsidiary organ to which NGOs had gained the greatest access. Thanks to the lobbying of NGOs—and of CONGO in particular—this practice continues at the Human Rights Council. This is certainly due to the intrinsic nature of human rights, the initial affirmation of which aimed to guarantee the freedom of the individual from the absolute power of the State.

The paradox of human rights lies precisely in the fact that these rights are set by states to self-restrain their sovereignty toward the individual. Hence their protection would make no sense if NGOs—or associations of individuals—did not have the chance to denounce their violations by the same states.

Since the number of NGOs in consultative status is increasing steadily, so are NGOs participating in the Commission/Council. Participation constitutes a great challenge for NGOs: they must organize themselves in order not to present repetitive statements to the plenary. During the 61st session of the Commission on Human Rights (CHR) (2005), 261 NGOs participated, represented by a total of 1,946 individuals.

But concretely, what do NGOs do at the HR Commission/Council?

1. NGOs can present written statements (351 in 2005) and/or oral ones (473), the latter being limited to six for each NGO for the duration of the session with a speaking time of three minutes. In order to avoid repetitions and to have more speaking time, NGOs are encouraged to present joint statements (eighty-four this year). This is the typical "advocacy" activity of NGOs in international fora.

2. NGOs can lobby national delegations to present or co-sponsor a given resolution. The real impact of this lobbying activity depends on the receptivity of member states, some of which are known for being more "NGO-friendly" than others.

3. In addition to making statements in plenary, NGOs have the possibility to organize parallel events, which generally take place during the lunch break and which have reached the record number of 153 in 2005.

The main challenge for CONGO at the Human Rights Commission/Council is to guarantee some kind of coordination among NGOs, most notably by encouraging the delivery of quality rather than of quantity involvement.

CONGO also facilitates the participation of newcomers at the Commission/Council, mainly national NGOs from the regions. CONGO routinely organizes training sessions on UN mechanisms, briefings and debriefings, and consultations for concerted input by NGOs. CONGO also liaises with the Bureau and other Commission/Council organs to guarantee the best possibilities for NGOs to speak. One of the greatest challenge for NGOs in the human rights field are the GONGOs—Government-Organized NGOs or NGOs that are not genuinely independent but are controlled in one way or another by states. These NGOs are more and more numerous. Many have obtained ECOSOC consultative status through the UN Committee on NGOs (consisting of nineteen governments, including China, Cuba, Pakistan, India), who often see them as their allies when it comes to their own human rights record. Once having consultative status, these NGOs have the right to speak and can water down other relevant human rights testimonies.

The Commission on Human Rights

The Commission on Human Rights, created in 1946, had become the main body within the UN system and at the universal level, dealing with the promotion and protection of human rights. The Commission was a subsidiary organ of ECOSOC and comprised fifty-three member states elected by ECOSOC for a period of three years. It met every year in Geneva for six weeks, and its sessions were attended by governmental delegates, NGOs, national institutions, and independent experts.

However, Secretary General Kofi Annan, in his report "In Larger Freedom: Towards Development, Security and Human Rights for All," released in March 2005,[17] proposed to replace the Commission with a Human Rights Council. In this report, which came out, whether hazardously or not, in the midst of the 61st session of the Commission on Human Rights (CHR), Kofi Annan recognized the unique contribution of the Commission to the development and codification of international human rights law and its "close engagement with hundreds of civil society organizations," which "provides an opportunity for working with civil society that does not exist elsewhere."[18] However, he also bluntly acknowledged a situation that NGOs had been denouncing for years, namely that the Commission had lost credibility and professionalism and, even worse, that "states had sought membership to the Commission to protect themselves against criticism or to criticize others."

In order to obviate this contradictory situation, and in his quest to elevate human rights to one of the three main pillars of the organization—along with peace and security and development—the Secretary General suggested replacing the Commission with a smaller, standing Human Rights Council. It would become a principal organ of the UN—like the Security Council and the ECOSOC—or, alternatively, a subsidiary organ of the General Assembly whose members would be elected by the GA by a two-thirds majority. Additionally, and maybe most importantly, "those elected to the Council should abide by the highest human rights standards."

This proposal put NGOs in a conflicted and somewhat embarrassing situation. Though they generally favoured reforming the discredited Commission, there was a fear that, with the new council, NGOs could lose the rights and privileges acquired at the Commission and fought for over more than fifty years. After Kofi Annan personally presented his reform proposal in Geneva, the Commission devoted an informal session to discussing the issue, and NGOs delivered three joint statements that all expressed this concern.[19] On March 15, 2006, the General Assembly Resolution A/60/251 establishing the Human Rights Council was adopted in New York after several delays. During the month of March CONGO organized NGO strategy meetings in order to discuss how to approach the final days and agenda of the last session of the Commission. The Commission had started its work on March 13 only to adopt a motion to suspend its work. NGOs had wanted the Commission to end in dignity and approve in its last session two long-awaited standards-setting instruments: the Convention on Enforced Disappearances and the Declaration on the Rights of Indigenous Peoples. However, governments could not find consensus on any substantive issue and decided after a long struggle to end the Commission in a one-day procedural session. Space would be given to one NGO to speak for all, to recall the history of the Commission from an NGO perspective. CONGO called another strategy meeting on March 24 during which it was decided not to accept this top-down decision of one for all NGO voice, but rather to read a short non-statement that this was unacceptable given the diversity and history of NGOs in the Commission. On March 27, 2006, the Commission thus ended its 62nd session and with it sixty years of human rights history in what NGOs called "a shameful funeral way."

The Way to the New Human Rights Council

With this chapter closed, the attitude changed, both at the level of governments and with NGOs. The focus was now to look forward toward the creation of the Human Rights Council with considerable expectations. General Assembly president Jan Eliasson had sent his vice-president, Ambassador Ricardo Arias, to discuss with the Geneva community ways for a smooth transition. CONGO arranged an NGO meeting with him for more in-depth discussions of NGOs' prospects. Many governments held informal meetings that were open to NGOs. At the same time the OHCHR, as Secretariat for the Council, held numerous consultations with NGOs on procedure, substance, and NGO participation in the Council. As the election of members to the Council was approaching, set for May 9 at the General Assembly in New York, many governments were actually lobbying with NGOs to show their best face. There was almost no day in April and early May that did not see a meeting or consultation in which CONGO was not involved. The CONGO president was invited to speak at the opening session of the Committee on NGOs on May 10 in New York. She used this opportunity to arrange an early appointment with General Assembly president Eliasson on May 9 to brief him on the ongoing positive consultations in Geneva. He invited her then to attend the election on the same day of the forty-seven members of the Council. This was the largest election ever held, with all 191 member states participating. Each elected member drew lots for one, two, or three years.

Soon thereafter, on May 19, the chair-designate, Ambassador Luis Alfonso De Alba from Mexico, was elected for the first session of the Council. He helped significantly with creating a climate of transparency and dialogue, systematically holding consultations with all actors, including NGOs, to prepare the agenda and methods of work for the first session of the Council, to be held June 19–30. He had invited the NGO community to provide him with three to five individuals or organizations to speak during the official inaugural section. CONGO then started a difficult but dignified process with many NGOs through which they identified five speakers from different regions who were all known as human rights defenders. One of them, Shirin Ebadi from Iran, could in the end not make it. The others were Arnold Tsunga (Zimbabwe), Nataša Kandić (Serbia), Sunila Abyesekera (Sri Lanka), and Marta Ocampo de Vásquez (Argentina). When taking the floor, they echoed the vision of many NGOs and profoundly moved participants during the first session's ceremonial part. The High Commissioner called CONGO in the evening to thank the speakers for their contributions and CONGO for the process of identifying them. Prior to the first session, on June 12, CONGO invited some key ambassadors and NGOs for an informal discussion over coffee on how to address some upcoming difficult issues. This was a first attempt from CONGO's side to help enhance the spirit of dialogue among and with governments and NGOs. Detailed information on the human rights process, including reports on the transitional period, the first session of the Council and the president's various letters to the chair, De Alba, may be found on CONGO's website under human rights and resources.[20]

After the sessions of the new Council in 2006 and 2007, the institution-building phase has not yet been entirely finalized.

LESSONS LEARNED

The experiences acquired by CONGO during its almost sixty years of existence—and more particularly since 2000, when the conference has been strengthened with a professional staff and could expand its activities substantially—allow us to identify several lessons learned.

The current system of global governance needs to be democratized

The international system is increasingly susceptible to the phenomenon of eroding state sovereignty, while at the same time the role of multilateral organizations in international decision making is expanding. In this context, there is pressure from civil society groups, NGOs, and the private sector to further democratize the global decision-making processes by incorporating more thoroughly the voice of civil and non-institutional stakeholders in the shaping of global governance.

The current system of global governance is considered by many as undemocratic. More and more decisions are made by international organizations

without the participation of people's representatives, be it elected national parliaments or civil society organizations. The demand for enhanced participation
in international decision-making processes is particularly supported by NGO
representatives within the United Nations system and by some international
law experts. This is reflected in the Cardoso Panel on UN–Civil Society Relations. The UN is engaged in an internal reform process aimed at reinforcing
its political legitimacy. In this context, former Secretary General Kofi Annan,
in his report "In Larger Freedom," acknowledged the need for the increased
participation of civil society in the activities of the United Nations, on the
basis of the recommendations of the Cardoso Panel on UN–Civil Society Relations.[21] The 2005–2006 president of the UN General Assembly, Jan Eliasson,
expressed the same concern. In light of this reform focus, and in accordance
with the rules of the international system, it appears that the best method of
reinforcing NGO participation in global decision-making processes is at the UN
level. In other words, the improvement of global governance implies the
broadening of decision-making processes within the UN system.

The civil society fora organized by CONGO in the regions and at UN Headquarters aim to democratize global governance by empowering NGOs to participate more effectively in international decision-making processes. Within
the UN system, NGOs can be consulted by ECOSOC, but not by the more
political organs like the General Assembly and, above all, the Security Council.[22] Nor can NGOs bring a claim before the International Court of Justice.
Among the UN agencies, NGOs are often kept apart from the negotiations and
decisions taken by the World Bank and the International Monetary Fund
that have an impact on the lives of billions of people around the world.
CONGO's activities concentrate predominantly on the ECOSOC. However,
CONGO had the privilege of addressing the opening session of the first ever
hearings of the General Assembly with civil society, expressing the wish that
the address would become the first of a long series. Since then, the hearings
have been institutionalized and take place every year on different subjects,
such as, in 2006, on migration.

Concerning the World Bank and the IMF, even though CONGO does not
work directly with these financial institutions, CONGO has expressed several
times the wish that the activities of these organizations be supervised and coordinated by ECOSOC. CONGO looks forward to the enhanced role attributed
to the Council by the UN reform, more particularly to the Annual Ministerial Review (AMR) and the biannual Development Cooperation Forum (DCF).
In June 2007, CONGO organized a civil society forum aimed at giving a concerted input by NGOs into these new ECOSOC mechanisms and contributing
to the countdown to 2015 of the Millennium Development Goals. The forum
is expected to be an annual event.

The current status of NGOs within the international system needs to be enhanced

The growing importance of NGOs in the international scene has not been adequately reflected in international law or in the formal structure of international institutions. NGOs do not have international legal personality—the single exception being Convention 124 of the Council of Europe, entitled "Recognition of the legal personality of international NGOs" (thus far ratified by only nine states). Hence there is a widening gap between their international responsibilities and activism and their legal standing in terms of international rights and duties. Additionally, it needs to be underlined that every UN subsidiary organ and agency has its own accreditation mechanisms with NGOs and that these are very diverse.

Within the UN system, national, regional, and international NGOs may be granted consultative status to ECOSOC, according to article 71 of the UN Charter and to ECOSOC resolution 1996/31. NGOs "in status" can be consulted by the Council or by any of its functional commissions (such as the former Commission on Human Rights) on matters falling within their competence. This means that NGOs can be "consulted," while decision-making power lies exclusively with states. Hence NGOs can influence decision-making processes mainly by the following means:

- Advocacy, by presenting to the sub-groups and to the plenary statements with their positions on particular issues;
- Lobbying, by trying to approach and influence individual delegations and "sympathetic" governments for the inclusion of particular provisions into a draft text under negotiation; and
- Provision of expert advice and testimony, scientific, technological, or professional.

Despite limitations, the advocacy activity undertaken by NGOs is of capital importance. Thanks to the persuasiveness of NGOs, progressive commitments have been taken by governments in the form of both non-binding and binding instruments of international law. It is significant to recall the outcome documents of world conferences such as the Rio Conference on Environment and Development (1992), the Copenhagen Conference on Social Development (1995), the Beijing Conference on Women (1995), or the General Assembly resolution containing the Millennium Declaration (2000). From a conventional perspective, one could barely have expected the surprisingly rapid entry into force of the Rome Statute of the International Criminal Court, which can be attributed largely to the campaign for the ICC launched by NGOs worldwide, as well as the adoption of the International Convention to Ban Landmines and the almost universal ratification of the Convention on the

Rights of the Child, both of which can be attributed to the persuasive action of civil society organizations worldwide.

However, there are built-in limits to the impact of this advocacy activity. A striking example can be drawn from the hearings held by the General Assembly in June 2005 in preparation for the September High-level Summit. On this occasion NGOs contributed valuable input that was incorporated to a large extent in the intermediate Draft Outcome Document prepared by the president of the General Assembly. Unfortunately, much of the text had to be deleted after the hearings. Even though some parts of the original text were retained throughout the negotiations, the final Outcome Document is considered by many civil society organizations highly unsatisfactory because, for example, of its complete silence on disarmament and proliferation, its vague commitments on aid and the MDGs, its poor reference to women's rights, its complete failure to address the reform of the Security Council.

However, CONGO promotes the idea that, even though NGOs cannot contribute to the "decision making," they certainly give invaluable input into the process of "decision shaping" by governments. The influence of NGO statements and lobbying on governments' decisions is unquestionable and is growing, at least among "sympathetic" governments. On the other hand, it must certainly be underlined that the number of countries skeptical or even hostile toward NGOs is still significant.

The granting of the consultative status needs to be de-politicized

Since 1946, consultative status with ECOSOC has been granted on the basis of a screening by the Committee on NGOs, an ECOSOC Standing Committee now made up of nineteen member states, many of which are deficient in promoting a genuine culture of civil society, democracy, and human rights. The granting of this status is often highly political and, in the case of national NGOs, it can even be subject to the approval of the concerned UN member state. Hence NGOs that are not legally recognized in their home country, or NGOs that are too critical of their own government in autocratic states have little chance of getting consultative status, whereas GONGOs (government-organized NGOs) tend to obtain it very easily. Among the over 3000 NGOs currently in consultative status, quite a few are not independent NGOs. It is a serious problem that has been acknowledged by the Cardoso Panel on UN–Civil Society Relations and by the Secretary General himself. If NGOs have long recognized the disturbing interferences of the GONGOs— most particularly at the former Commission on Human Rights, where they provide wrong information on governmental policies and "dilute" the voices of the victims—it is difficult to de facto sideline them without violating the legitimate right to freedom of expression of any organization. Some NGOs—

including CONGO—have tried to tackle the issue, but for the time being no real progress has been made in this respect.[23]

However, the problem needs to be addressed. It was evident during the recent second phase of the World Summit on the Information Society that it was impossible for independent Tunisian NGOs to obtain accreditation to the summit in their own name. Accreditation was also refused for Human Rights in China—an NGO that has never been accredited to a UN Summit because of its role in denouncing human rights violations perpetrated by China.

Beyond these examples, problems also arise in relation to how inclusion or exclusion from accreditation impacts upon the representation of particular minority groups in intergovernmental decision-making fora (for example, NGOs focused on sexual orientation issues, or those accused by their national governments of being terrorists due to their political stance). CONGO has pleaded before the Committee on NGOs for the widest possible inclusion of NGOs representing different sensitivities and for freedom of expression.

NGOs need to question themselves on their legitimacy and independence

The quest for a renewed status for NGOs should thus address the questions of responsibility and accountability of NGOs. It should also examine the problem of their representativity, which is in turn linked to their legitimacy.[24]

Another problematic issue relates to the degree of NGO independence in relation to political authorities and governments, particularly in the case of national (contrasting with international) NGOs. This is one of the lessons drawn from the Tunis World Information Summit on Civil Society, where debates were submerged by an impressive number of Tunisian pro-governmental NGOs, which hindered Tunisian human rights defenders and independent civil society organizations in their quest to express themselves. This is just one of many examples that one could point to where so-called GONGOs distort the representation of civil society. The Tunis Summit was nonetheless an opportunity for independent NGOs (i.e., those not associated with governments or private interests) to express their concerns to the UN Secretary General. They insisted on the need "to revise the UN rules for civil society accreditation to ECOSOC and to UN conferences in order to end the exclusion of civil society organizations on the basis of a decision of an individual government with no right of appeal to any independent commission."[25] This concern has been echoed by a delegation of members of the European Parliament at a meeting organized in Tunis. The European Union had supported the accreditation of "Human Rights in China" at the WSIS and also supported the holding of the "Citizens Summit," which was cancelled by the Tunisian authorities. During the WSIS preparation and the Tunis Summit itself, CONGO tried to play the particularly uncomfortable role of mediator between the freedom of expression of NGOs, particularly human rights groups, and its limited interpretation by the host government.

Multi-stakeholder partnerships may be the way forward

One of the most recent evolutions in terms of UN–civil society relations was represented by the World Summit on the Information Society, the second phase of which took place in Tunis in November 2005. Maybe because of the complexity and the technical character of the issues at stake—bridging the digital divide and reforming the system of internet governance—this recent world summit went the furthest in implementing the "multi-stakeholder approach" warmly called for by the Cardoso Panel on UN–Civil Society Relations. As already largely discussed, CONGO made an important contribution to the building of these civil society structures during the WSIS preparatory process and during the summits themselves.

CONCLUSION

CONGO has been in existence for almost sixty years now. It has accompanied and pushed for a stronger involvement of NGOs and CSOs in the UN activities and in the democratization of global governance. Despite CONGO's efforts, the world we are currently living in is not particularly favourable to civil society and, despite rhetoric, to a stronger involvement of non-state actors in multilateral affairs. However, this will have to change if the international community intends to respond successfully to the threats of the new millennium, most notably the most crucial one of world poverty. CONGO will certainly continue its fight for a more just and equitable world where peoples can have a sense of ownership and belonging.

NOTES

1 For article 71 of the UN Charter: United Nations Charter, San Fransisco, June 26, 1945, http://www.un.org/aboutun/charter/.
2 For ECOSOC Resolution 1996/31: "The aims and purposes of the organization shall be in conformity with the spirit, purposes and principles of the Charter of the United Nations." ECOSOC Res. 1996/31, part 1, paragraph 2, July 25, 1996, http://www.un.org/documents/ecosoc/res/1996/eres1996-31.htm.
3 Currently the Committee on NGOs' members are Angola, Burundi, China, Colombia, Cuba, Dominica, Egypt, Guinea, India, Israel, Pakistan, Peru, Qatar, Romania, Russian Federation, Sudan, Turkey, UK, and USA.
4 ECOSOC Res. 1996/31, part 1, paragraph 2, July 25, 1996, http://www.un.org/documents/ecosoc/res/1996/eres1996-31.htm.

5   Tony Hill, *Three Generations of UN–CS Relations,* Padova, Italy, 2004—paper written for a seminar on global civil society.

6   See http://www.johannesburgsummit.za.

7   See http://www.wsis-online.net/csnews.

8   One of CONGO's board members used entertainment such as soap operas in television, radio, and other traditional communication devices to transfer vital messages all over the world in order to reach a wide range of social sectors, including rural areas often not reached or targeted by more sophisticated means of transmission.

9   The Champions Network is a group of activists, experts, and practitioners promoting development through the use of information and communication technologies.

10 http://www.ngocongo.org/index.php?what=resources&id=156.

11 Seminario de América Latina y El Caribe: "Asociación para una Nueva Era: Cumpliendo con los Objetivos de Desarrollo del Milenio," Plan de Acción para América Latina y el Caribe sobre el Complimiento de los Objetivos de Desarrollo del Milenio, page 4, http://www.ngocongo.org/files/lacplandeaccion.doc.

12 Idem.

13 http://www.un.org/millenniumgoals.

14 Kofi Annan, "In Larger Freedom: Towards Security, Development and Human Rights for All," Report of the Secretary General of the United Nations for decision by Heads of State and Government in September 2005, http://www.un.org/largerfreedom/.

15 These are education; universal access to reproductive information and assistance; reduction of labour-intensive, time-consuming tasks for women; improving inheritance rights; closing gender gaps in earning; increasing women's participation in government; and fighting violence against women.

16 Employment, basic rights at work, social protection, and social dialogue.

17 "In Larger Freedom."

18 "In Larger Freedom," par. 181.

19 See http://www.ngochr.org/view/index.php?basic_entity=DOCUMENT&list_ids=522.

20 http://www.ngocongo.org/index.php?what=resources&id=10136.

21 "In Larger Freedom."

22 While some limited access to these fora (or the formal participants in these fora) exist, full access is limited and NGO participation is usually informal and ad hoc.

23 Isolda Agazzi, "NGOs and GONGOs in the Context of the UN-CHR," 2004, website http://www.ngochr.org/view/index.php?basic_entity=DOCUMENT&list_ids=130.

24 Is their legitimacy bound to the causes they are defending? Are those NGOs democratic in their internal organization? Is it important that they are? Where are their funds coming from? What relevance does this have in relation to their legitimacy?

25 See http://www.citizens-summit.org/Letter-SecGen-241105.shtml.

4

Amplifying Voices from the Global South

Globalizing Civil Society

Rajesh Tandon and
Mohini Kak

INTRODUCTION

The twenty-first-century world is a world with porous boundaries, where very little remains limited within the national or local frame. Local issues and priorities, like that of water and sanitation, are no longer local but are determined by global policies and priorities. Our goals of development are no longer ours, but instead are clearly outlined for us by multilateral institutions in the form of Millennium Development Goals, Kyoto Environmental norms, etc. It is the concerns and the needs of the most marginalized that these global goals seek to address. Yet who determines these goals? Is it the "developed" North or the "underdeveloped" South?

Thirty years ago, the answer would have been an emphatic "developed" North. Within the developed North, what mattered were the views and priorities of the governments. Today, the situation has changed. Governments of southern countries (especially bigger ones, like "Chindia," or India-Brazil-South Africa Trilateral [IBSA], or G22 at Cancun) have begun to speak out and emphasize their views too.

Civil society has also emerged as a growing voice on the global arena. It is the voice of non-state actors—the people's voice. Northern civil society organizations have occupied much of the global space over these decades. During the past fifteen years or so, Southern civil society has also begun to be visible and audible at the global arena.

The growth of Southern civil society as a credible and influential actor in the development sector, both nationally and globally, has been a journey of challenges, influenced by a range of individual and collective endeavours and emergent politico-economic conditions. Addressing all such influences is not only difficult but perhaps beyond the scope of this chapter. The chapter does, however, seek to look at the development of Southern civil society from the eyes of an institution, Participatory Research In Asia (PRIA), with a twenty-five-year history of engaging with civil society. It looks at how its belief in the tenet "knowledge is power" provided a depth and a direction to its efforts at amplifying the voices of the marginalized from the South in the global debates on development.

This chapter is divided into four sections. The first examines the role of participatory research in the development of PRIA. The second section looks at PRIA's involvement in the growth of the civil society movement and at networks in India and internationally, and the third section focuses on civil society voices in global governance today. Finally, some lessons learned during this journey are shared.

HISTORY OF A MOVEMENT: PARTICIPATORY RESEARCH AND PRIA

What people in this movement share is a commitment to working with those women and men in our different societies whose voices are not heard. They share a belief in the fundamental intelligence of everyone and the right of all to make history and to create knowledge. No matter how compelling, abstract theories are not sufficient to transform the world without the involvement of the vast majority of working people.[1]

Every movement has a history, a motivation, an angst that stirs action for change. The movement of participatory research had similar trajectories. Within that movement, the birth of the Society for Participatory Research in Asia (PRIA) was no different. Stirred by the emerging discourse on participatory research in the 1970s, its founding members joined the debates motivated by the possibilities that participatory research offered as a methodology of social change.

The movement for participatory research was a movement for equality and for a voice. It was a movement and ideology that captured the imagination of young scholars and practitioners around the world in the 1970s. Participatory research believed in the power of people's knowledge—the knowledge of communities, the knowledge of farmers, tribals, workers—the knowledge of the common man or woman.

The existing academic regime at the time, with its stress on scientism (objectivity and neutrality) had dispossessed people's knowledge of all credibility. It had robbed people of self-belief—belief in their capacity and knowl-edge gained from years of experience of living and struggling. For example, the voices of the farmers were made irrelevant in assessing the quality and credibility of new seeds; doctors' views on the health of industrial workers were more relevant than the experiences of the workers themselves; the gov-ernment agency was more proficient in determining tribal rights than the tribals themselves. Participatory research thus sought to wrest the power of knowledge from the hands of the academic and policy elites back into the pub-lic domain, into the hands of the creators and generators of knowledge—the people.

The challenge for participatory research, however, was not only "whose knowledge matters" but also "how to make knowledge matter." Knowledge alone held no relevance if it did not transform social conditions. Thus, partic-ipatory research strove "to play a liberating role in the learning process by pro-moting the development of a critical understanding of social problems, their structural causes and possibilities of overcoming them."[2] In other words, par-ticipatory research aimed at bringing about a conscientisation that gave mar-ginalized peoples the capacity to challenge unjust social, political, and insti-tutional structures.

It was this philosophy of participatory research that formed the soul of PRIA. Although formally instituted in February 1982, its amoebic shape emerged in 1978 when its founding member took on the role of Asian node for the International Participatory Research Network. As the node for the Asian region, PRIA (in its prenatal avatar) organized a number of meetings and experience-sharing workshops on participatory research in India and its neighbouring countries. Being a member of ASPBAE (Asian South Pacific Bureau of Adult Education, a regional association of adult education practi-tioners) facilitated the organization of these meetings and resulted in the initiation of an informal network of organizations interested in the possibil-ities of participatory research.

The International Participatory Research Network

Young adult educators from the International Council for Adult Education (ICAE) Movement motivated by the ideas and practices of Paulo Friere and Myles Horton were interested in exploring and developing the idea of partic-ipatory research as a new empowering approach toward participation. In response to the realization that people in many countries were thinking along similar lines, Budd Hall compiled a special issue of the ICAE Journal *Conver-gence* titled "Participatory Research." The overwhelming response to the pub-lication led to the idea of initiating an international network of participatory research.

"The adult education community and related community development and activists bought out all the copies of the journal for the first time in the history of the journal. Requests for copies poured in from all over the world and the small item in my lead article inviting persons who were interested in exchanging information about their activities went from a trickle to a stream to a river. It was clear to me that many people in the majority world and people working with or for marginalised persons in the rich countries were actively engaged in research projects which were very different from the standards of the day in most of the universities of the world."[3]

Further exploration of the idea at the 1st World Assembly of the ICAE in Dar es Salaam, 1976, and the Cartagena Conference of April 1977 on "Action Research," organized by Orlando Fals Borda, gave impetus to this movement, and by September 1977 an informal meeting in Aurora, Ontario, gave birth to the an international network of participatory research. By 1978 there were five nodes in the network: Toronto, New Delhi, Tanzania, Netherlands, and Venezuela.

In 1980, PRIA founder (Dr. Rajesh Tandon) took on the responsibility of International Coordinator of this network.

In these initial years PRIA not only promoted its ideology of "knowledge is power" but added to the development of participatory research as a concept. The rural context of Asian development and the largely unorganized nature of the marginalized—landless, etc.—meant participatory research efforts in Asia required corresponding efforts at organization building. The existence of traditional discrimination hierarchies also required stronger efforts at challenging oppressive social and political structures.[4] It was through these and more experiences specific to the Asian socio-economic and political context that PRIA emerged as a leading ideologue on participatory research globally and regionally.

Networking as a Vehicle for Collective Solidarity

Although the teachings of Paulo Friere, Myles Horton, Budd Hall, Orlando Fals Borda, and others had given birth to the concept of participatory action research (PAR), it was the adoption of a concerted strategy of networking that gave participatory research its global outreach. The establishment of strong regional networks not only ensured the strengthening of local voices but also provided a channel whereby local voices could reach out to the global fora.

The creation of regional networks of participatory research in 1978 had been a starting point, but as the concept of participatory research developed, global acceptance of the idea of "peoples' knowledge" became essential. Only the united voices of civil society actors supported by visible successes of the tools of participatory research could bring about this acceptance. And it was toward this end that PRIA as the Asia regional node and as international coordinator of the Participatory Research Network worked during the 1980s. This was an important strategic decision, as a hindsight, though global networks were rare thirty years ago.

PRIA promoted the practice of experience sharing both through the organization of formal workshops and through the dissemination of informational material for activist practitioners, thereby developing a loose network of a large number of practitioners. It also initiated a series of capacity-building initiatives for field-based development workers of voluntary organizations, promoting the practice of participatory research to enhance the depth and effectivity of their programs.

The strength of this network gained visibility at the 1985 International Conference on Adult Education held in Paris, where the ICAE recommendation on the "Right to Learn" was accepted as the declaration of the conference. The "Right to Learn" not only accepted learning as a means of empowerment but also granted legitimacy to local practices—a starting point for global recognition of the relevance of local knowledge and practice.

The 1985 conference also held great significance because it was the first time that Non-Governmental Organizations (NGOs) had been invited to such an intergovernmental meeting and asked to address the plenary and present statements on agenda items.

"Through the strong presence of so many women and men associated with its member national and regional organisations, the ICAE was widely acknowledged as proof of the importance, value and maturity of the non governmental sector. The value of a strong international network was clearly demonstrated."[5]

Thus, by the late 1980s civil society had started gaining credibility and visibility in international development forums, propagating the bottom-up perspective of combatting social and economic development issues. Although a great success for civil society actors, it also posed a great challenge. Recognition as the "third sector" meant an increased space for participation and an increased responsibility to ably fulfil the role. From being a small localized player, civil society had gained recognition as an important national and international player.

Recognizing this challenge, PRIA turned its focus to creating a network of civil society organizations (CSOs) aimed at influencing policies and debates defining and outlining the nature and scope of civil society—globally and nationally.

RECOVERING CIVIL SOCIETY IN THE 1990S

Strengthening Civil Society: Local and Global

Civil society was growing; it was a new emerging force, as yet sparsely under-stood and surrounded by conservative beliefs about its capacities. Rather than have the state and market actors define and limit its role, civil society needed to define itself. It was this role that PRIA took upon itself in the early 1990s.

The emergence of an open market economy, the rise of liberalization, and the growing emphasis on civil society by multilateral institutions led to a ver-itable "associational revolution" in the Asian region in the 1990s. While the number of civil society organizations grew, corresponding reform of legal and institutional structures within the government accommodating and respond-ing to this rise of the "third sector" did not take place. For example, in India, the law governing the registration of societies dated back to 1860. The exis-tence of such a dated act was not only an indication of the non-acknowl-edgement of the diverse and changing nature of new civil society organizations but also a disincentive for the growth of civil society.

In response to this need of constructing an enabling environment for civil society in India, PRIA, along with a number of civil society leaders, decided to create a national forum for the protection, enrichment and growth of vol-untarism in India, giving birth to a Voluntary Action Network India (VANI) in 1988.[6] As a loose network of member organizations spanning the entire length and breadth of the country, VANI took on the mandate of promoting a collective voice for the voluntary sector. Providing leadership to VANI in its initial years, PRIA built on its existing participatory research network to include smaller local organizations and worked toward developing a com-mon framework and agenda of actions that incorporated the shared demands of diverse civil society organizations.

The network took on broader issues concerning the voluntary sector in India as a whole, such as initiating a debate on structural adjustment and the role of civil society therein and advocacy for the simplification of acts, rules, and regulations governing the voluntary sector, etc.

An important aspect driving these efforts was the need to provide increas-ing credibility to Indian and southern civil society. Although civil society in the South was increasing numerically, its significance in terms of influence was overshadowed by its northern counterparts which were better organized, more resourced, and highly articulate. Two sets of challenges were faced by these emerging civil society organizations in the southern countries of Asia, Africa, and Latin America. The first related to the weak capacities of the actors in the areas of intellectual material, institutional capacities, or local CSOs. PRIA began to play the role of a support organization for the civil society sector, first in India and then beyond. In partnership with IDR (Institute for Development Research, Boston), it promoted a South Asian, Asian-wide, and international network of support organizations dedicated to the mission of empowering local CSOs through enhancing their capacities for people-centred developments.

The second challenge facing southern CSOs was the lack of enabling regulatory frameworks in many southern countries. Old archaic structures existed in some (like former colonies of Britain); many others had no such frameworks (like Vietnam). Most governments of these southern countries had a "suspicious" orientation toward CSOs engaged in social mobilization and community empowerment. It was, therefore, necessary to create a modern framework of regulation for GO–NGO relations. Building on its earlier work that examined such relations in many countries,[7] PRIA supported the efforts of the Commonwealth Foundation to develop such a framework. This document, "Guidelines for Global Policy and Practice," was released by the Commonwealth Foundation in 1996.

Strengthening civil society voices from the South required more than focused efforts at the national level. Thus, parallel to the national efforts in creating VANI, a network was initiated to advocate on issues concerning the voluntary sector in international fora. In 1991 this idea of bringing together non-profit organizations on a global stage was floated by an international group of civic leaders and activists, an idea that materialized in the shape of CIVICUS: World Alliance for Citizen Participation, with PRIA as one of its founding members. It was one of the "first major attempts to establish a worldwide framework specifically geared to the promotion of civil society ... a bold new idea."[8]

Aimed at strengthening civil society through providing it with visibility, encouraging partnership and voluntarism, and engaging with multilateral and other major international agencies, CIVICUS's multi-sectoral approach gave it strength and an unprecedented global outreach.

By bringing together actors from different sectors on a common platform— NGOs, donors, foundations, and corporate grant makers—CIVICUS tapped the unexplored opportunities of multi-sector dialogue and co-operation. It also increased the outreach and influence of civil society through the creation of horizontal platforms of engagement and dialogue between the donors and the donees. Sharing between sectors increased the capacity of CSOs, motivating them to explore innovative forms of interaction with business and governments.

Sleeping with the Bear

Rooted in the perspectives of social transformation from below, civil society was still hesitant to engage with global multilateral institutions and governments. Entering into dialogue with the "power holders" was seen as the first step toward co-opting—or in other words "selling out"—the voices of the marginalized. The role of civil society was seen as an external pressure group demanding accountability from such global institutions and questioning unequal power structures. Change was thus asserted from the outside not from within, and entering into direct relationship with such global multilateral institutions with the government was seen as a compromise of civil society values and traditions. This was particularly the case for such international financial institutions like the World Bank and International Monetary Fund in the early 1990, as they were seen to be the "villains" of the poor.

Yet, engagement was necessary to ensure long-lasting change. With the formation of a World Bank NGO working group in 1981, multilaterals had provided a foothold to civil society; it was up to civil society to carve out a space and leave a mark. Though civil society had been successful in establishing the identity of the group as an autonomous body within the World Bank, its influence in policy decisions was limited. By the late 1980s, participation had become the keyword and the World Bank was exploring strategies for the adoption of participation in its policy planning and operations. Its participation report was released in 1994, and, encouraged by the seriousness of the WB toward its adoption, the NGO working group activated a subgroup on participation in 1995 "to monitor and influence effective implementation of World Bank policy on participation and promote a wider and deeper involvement of civil society in the Bank's participatory development efforts."[9]

Gauging the relevance and possible impact of the participation subgroup on the Bank's long-term policy of participation in its programs, PRIA accepted the responsibility of chair of the World Bank-NGO Working Group–Subgroup on Participation in 1995 (despite facing flak for selling out to the enemy).

Its unique contribution as member and chair of this group came from its underlying philosophy of participatory research—the focus on the decentralized nature of engagement through the involvement of local and regional CSOs and the emphasis on capacity building of all primary stakeholders on the processes of participation.

For the first time, regional meetings were held to involve smaller national and local NGOs in the dialogue and decision-making process.

"The decentralised meetings enabled a more narrow geographic focus and gave more Southern NGOs the opportunity to participate in their region, to learn more about the Bank and its activities in their countries and to become advocates for issues of greatest concern to them."[10]

Capacity building too began to be seen as an integral part of promoting participatory approaches—with the World Bank beginning to stress its inclusion in its country programs.

The participation subgroup, though limited by its mandate to influencing World Bank policies, envisioned its efforts as setting a trend for other multi-laterals to follow. Through its efforts, issues related to the participation of the poor in large-scale development projects and policy formulation became a global agenda.

Enhancing Capacities: Civil Society as Catalyst of Change

While strengthening civil society voices through the formation of united platforms of action was one side of the equation, enhancing the capacity of local and national regional CSOs of southern countries was the other. Most NGOs engaged in the promotion of development initiatives worked at the grassroots. Their primary mode of functioning was service delivery and social mobilization—empowering the poor and marginalized through the delivery of a range of services, including health, education, and income generation through micro-credit enterprises. The local nature of their pursuits kept them largely outside of global occurrences and priorities until they were forced by circumstances to face up to the changing contexts and challenges.

The wave of democratization and liberalization in the 1990s shifted the focus of most governments and multilateral institutions toward democratization, decentralization, and accountable governance. This meant changing socio-economic and political structures within the State and a re-examination of the roles and relevance of civil society actors in society.

"These shifts in roles, functions and expectations are necessitating renewed and comprehensive attention toward strengthening capacities of all these categories of actors to prepare themselves to be relevant and effective in the new millennium."[11]

It required a redefinition of roles and linkages with respect to the community, other civil society actors, media, government, and private sector, etc. In 1996, to address this challenge of ensuring an effective and efficient civil society with the capacity to learn and adapt to the changing contexts, PRIA along with other Southern NGOs proposed the formation of an interagency group for the capacity building of Southern NGOs. This proposal laid the foundation for the formation of the International Forum of Capacity Building (IFCB) in 1998 with PRIA as its first global secretariat.

PRIA played the role of a catalyst and leader of this multi-layered, multi-party coalition focused on the specific capacity-building needs of civil society organizations of the South. Capacity-building interventions were not new, but up to that point had largely followed universal prescriptions set down by agencies of the North who financed these initiatives. Improving the effectiveness of program delivery through better organizational management had been their prime agenda. Capacity building for enhancing sustainability was ignored; at the same time it assumed great significance for SNGOs in the context of changing conditions and new challenges.

The declining role of the State meant the need to increase efforts to ensure service provision for the most marginalized; the increasing global nature of policy formulation meant the need for civil society to enhance their strength through knowledge and synthesis of experiences, such as implementing micro-projects to influence macro social and economic policies. It also meant the need for the engagement of multiple stakeholders—beyond the community and the state to include the media, academia, and the private sector.

The new priorities for southern civil society, thus, were (1) greater systematization of program planning and implementation, (2) institutional development focusing on networking, building partnerships, and alliances, (3) the use of information technology, (4) policy advocacy with enhanced skills of research and documentation with the focus of linking micro experiences to macro policy reform, and (5) last and most importantly resource mobilization and financial sustainability.[12]

The IFCB's capacity-building endeavours from a "southern" perspective complemented the ongoing efforts at networking—national and international. It made more effective the voices from the underdeveloped regions of the world. New leadership and capacity emerged, with many CSOs taking on larger roles and making an impact on the global development scene.

CITIZENS AND GLOBAL GOVERNANCE

"It is a truism that the state exists to promote the well-being of its citizens. However, it is only now becoming accepted that the only true definition of well-being can come from citizens themselves, because it is they who have to live with their problems, their needs, their hopes and their aspirations."[13]

By the late 1990s, civil society, largely represented by NGOs, had become an integral part of the development discourse and widely recognized by the State as the most credible medium of bringing the voices of the marginalized to the fore. However, in all debates and contestations aimed at defining the roles and purposes of civil society, the most essential component of civil society was left out—the citizens. With enhanced capacities and strong networks, civil society was more focused on deepening and changing the nature of its engagement with the State rather than using its newly developed capacities for empowering citizens to raise their own voices and engage directly with governance.

"In the discourse, the basic building blocks of civil society—citizens—have largely remained invisible. Neither governments nor other civil society intermediaries can assume the voices of these citizens. They themselves must be listened to."[14]

It was this realization that motivated PRIA as a partner of the Common-wealth Foundation to play a key role in the formulation of its Citizens and Gov-ernance (C&G) Program. With a strong belief in participatory research, PRIA's mission had always been the empowerment of citizens by enhancing their belief in their own knowledge and capacities. Through the C&G Program, PRIA created the opportunity of promoting the idea of citizen-centred devel-opment, where citizens, and not simply civil society organizations, were the key actors.

Focus on citizens meant deepening the level of interventions and more comprehensive efforts at linking the local to the global. This depth of focus was becoming more and more essential in light of the increasing globalization of issues in the new millennium. It necessitated the participation and involve-ment of citizens not simply as "users and beneficiaries" but as active players and "contributors" in the development process. With the role of the state declining in the new liberalized era, it was essential for citizens to be empow-ered and create spaces, ensuring that their voices have an impact.

The Citizens and Governance Program, through voicing the views of the people from across forty-seven countries of the Commonwealth, brought the focus back to the people and led to an increase in efforts by civil society organ-izations and state actors to promote citizen participation in governance at the national level. The study laid the foundations for the above program by highlighting the almost universal nature of concerns held by citizens across the Commonwealth. The study also focused on the need to shift the roles of intermediary NGOs toward supporting and enabling ordinary citizens to get involved in public spheres, public issues, and public institutions. While civil society influence had grown globally, its influence on UN agencies and other multilaterals was still largely limited to big international conferences that invited civil society involvement, debates, and suggestions on specific issues. This engagement was sporadic and far from achieving the level of influence required for focused advocacy. There was no mechanism in place that could ably demand accountability from these institutions that formed and influenced global–national policies.

In an attempt to address this lacuna, the Forum International Montreal (FIM) was formed in 1998 by a number of civil society activists and leaders. It was formed with the specific goal of "improving the influence of interna-tional civil society on the United Nations and the multilateral system."[15] PRIA, with its vast experience of engagement with international multilat-eral institutions, became an integral part of this forum.

Its interest in promoting multilateral democracy gained initial recogni-tion in 2002, when it took on the focused project of engaging with the G8—a body infamous for its lack of public accountability yet with undeniable global influence. It sought to transform engagement with this highly influential body from a sporadic demonstration-based engagement to a serious dialogue-based interface. Through its efforts, it sought to "demonstrate to the G8 organisers the value of open and frank dialogue with international civil society."[16] While most host G8 country governments have been consulting with their own civil society, there had been no attempt to dialogue with civil society from the South.

Although no formal space has as yet been created for civil society–G8 dialogue, a norm has definitely been established whereby dialogue with southern civil society on specific issues forms part of the G8 agenda.

Likewise, PRIA supported efforts by FIM, CIVICUS, and other global networks and platforms of civil society to enable the voices of southern CSOs to be heard directly and concretely. In this regard, it has facilitated workshops and conferences that aim at democratizing global governance through southern civil society engagements. These attempts have been made in the past five years in "global" venues like New York, London, Paris, Geneva, and Montreal; they have also been made at "local" venues (with global frameworks of reality) like Delhi, Sao Paolo, Nairobi, Manila, and Hong Kong. PRIA's commitment to supporting the voice of civil society from the South has been widely manifested and appreciated in these fora.

EMERGING LESSONS

PRIA's journey—twenty-five years and more—is ongoing. New experiences and situations are creating new possibilities. It is important, however, to look back over the past thirty years and draw some lessons from the journey so far. Some of these are enumerated here.

1. Clarity of perspectives, values, and purposes is essential to sustain any impact. PRIA's perspective of participatory research—local knowledge and participation—continued to inform its efforts in supporting its mission of "amplifying voices from the south." Despite many opportunities to become the "sole spokesperson" for southern civil society voice, PRIA resisted this role and enabled many others to join together to gain a collective voice.

2. Thirty years ago, "globalizing civil society" was not even on the horizon; no donors, NGOs, governments, or academics could imagine this possibility. PRIA joined a few other like-minded civil society actors from other countries who were beginning to see the value of a "southern-led" international network. Network of Participatory Research provided the first such opportunity. Building alliances of associations with like-minded others was important for PRIA then too. The networking approach to building

global visibility is radically different from the managerial approach to creating multinationals.

3. PRIA's credibility in global fora was maintained primarily because of its national and local roots. PRIA's work with countries, CSOs, trade unions, and governments in India—on participation, empowerment, and governance—gave it practical insights and helped shape its analysis of global forces and institutions. But acting simultaneously in local and global spaces is neither easy nor sustainable. Important choices had to be made to remain rooted in local actions, even when global actions were most crucial and demanding.

4. "Amplifying southern voices" also implies dealing with unequal North–South relations of power. Such unequal relations of power exist everywhere. Their local/national manifestation is far less complex to deal with than international manifestations. Some of these northern civil society actors (who were also donors of many southern CSOs) felt challenged and threatened in the process. Funding relations distorted several opportunities for global co-operation among CSOs from the North and the South.

5. Finally, it is important to acknowledge that leadership is crucial in such transformative interventions. Leadership of ideas, perspectives, and values plays a significant role in building global coalitions. Leadership rooted in southern contexts gains its inspiration and maintains its accountability from that southern context. Local practice empowers leadership for global actions.

NOTES

1   PRIA, "Participatory Research: An Introduction," New Delhi: PRIA, 1982, 1.
2   Ibid., 3.
3   Budd L. Hall, "Looking Back, Looking Forward: Reflections on the Origins of the International Participatory Research Network and the Participatory Research Group in Toronto, Canada," Paper prepared for the Participatory Research: Strategies for Empowerment Workshop, April 16–18, 1998, in PRIA, New Delhi.
4   Rajesh Tandon, "Issues and Experiences in Participatory Research in Asia," Paper presented during the Adult Education Research Seminar held at Kungalv, Sweden, June 25–27, 1979.
5   International Council for Adult Education, "The Right to Learn: Participation of ICAE and member organisations in the 1985 UNESCO International Conference on Adult Education in Paris," Toronto: ICAE, 1985, 1.
6   VANI—www.vaniindia.org.
7   PRIA, "GO–NGO Relations: A Source of Life or Kiss of Death," New Delhi: PRIA, 1989.
8   CIVICUS, *Citizens: Strengthening Global Civil Society*, Washington: CIVICUS: World Alliance for Citizen Participation, 1994, ix.

9 Carolyn Long, *Participation of the Poor in Development Initiatives: Taking Their Rightful Place*, London: IDR and Earthscan Publications, 2001, 41.

10 Ibid., 42.

11 IFCB, "Future Capacity Building of Southern NGOs," International Conference, May 6–8, 1998, Brussels, Prepared by the Global Secretariat IFCB, New Delhi: PRIA, 1998, 3.

12 PRIA, "Capacity Building of Southern NGOs," *Global Alliance News*, 1/5, June 1997, 5–6.

13 The Commonwealth Foundation, Foreword. www.commonwealthfoundation.com.

14 Ibid., 19.

15 FIM. www.fimcivilsociety.org. See chapter 10, Nigel T. Martin, "The FIM G8 Project, 2002–2006: A Case Analysis of a Project to Initiate Civil Society Engagement with the G8."

16 Nigel Martin, "Not Representative but Still Legitimate: FIM and the G8," *Global Alliance News*, 10/2, June 2005, 17.

5

Facilitating NGO Participation

*An Assessment of Canadian Government-Sponsored
Mechanisms for the Copenhagen Summit for
Social Development and the Beijing
Conference on Women*

Elizabeth Riddell-Dixon

INTRODUCTION

Democratic global governance requires that the voices of civil society be heard
at all levels—the local, subnational, national, regional, multilateral, and international. The term "civil society" refers to those engaged in activities that
"involve no quest for public office (so excluding political parties) and no pursuit of pecuniary gain (so excluding firms and the commercial mass media)."[1]
Civil society encompasses a wide range of actors, both individuals and groups,
from the amorphous and unstructured pressures, such as student uprisings
and food riots, to the well-organized, structured groups.

The current democratic deficit in global governance and the potential role
for civil society in helping to address these deficiencies are well documented.[2]
The tough question to answer is: how can civil society participate more fully
so as to enhance democratic global governance? Establishing strategies for civil
society, in all its diversity, to participate is a herculean task. As one step in that
process, this chapter examines two cases in which mechanisms were established in Canada to facilitate the participation of non-governmental organizations (NGOs) within the foreign policy-making process, and draws lessons
from these experiences. As such, it addresses two questions. First, to what
extent did the government-sponsored mechanisms established to facilitate
NGO participation for the Copenhagen Summit for Social Development and
the Beijing Conference on Women, respectively, realize process objectives and

influence objectives?[3] Process goals are measured in terms of the extent to which the mechanisms produced processes that were transparent, inclusive, and accountable. Influence goals are assessed in terms of the extent to which the mechanisms offered NGOs opportunities for meaningful participation (i.e., participation that was taken seriously by government officials and that offered real opportunities for exerting influence). Of the many ways in which NGOs can exert influence in the policy-making process, three are particularly salient to this study: helping to determine the issues on the political agenda; establishing parameters within which decision makers have to operate, thereby limiting the range of policy options considered; and influencing the content of policies.

The analysis focuses on NGOs—although they are only one subset of civil society—because they have far greater chances of exerting influence on the behaviour of states and international organizations than do amorphous and unstructured pressures. Nonetheless, the literature on Canadian foreign policy concludes that NGOs—the best-organized components of civil society—exert relatively little influence in the policy-making process.[4] What influence were the NGOs able to exert in the two cases? What lessons can be learned from them?

The cases offer interesting points of comparison because they took place during the same time period and involved similar, and in fact overlapping, sets of government and NGO actors. There were, however, some profound differences in the ways in which the NGO coordinating committees were struck and in the effectiveness of their respective operations. Members of the Canadian Beijing Facilitating Committee (hereafter the Beijing Facilitating Committee) were democratically elected by women's groups from across Canada. In contrast, executives from the leading NGOs in the fields of domestic poverty and international development assistance created the Canadian NGO Organizing Committee for the World Summit for Social Development (hereafter the Copenhagen Organizing Committee) and assumed leadership roles. There were advantages and disadvantages to each selection process. The process of creating the Beijing Facilitating Committee was more democratic, but most of its members had no UN experience and, hence, their operations were less effective than would have been the case had they had expertise in preparing for international negotiations. The Copenhagen Organizing Committee had highly experienced leaders, but it was somewhat autocratic in its operations.

The chapter begins with brief overviews of the government-sponsored mechanisms established for the Copenhagen Summit and Beijing Conference. The utility of each set of mechanisms is then assessed in terms of its success in realizing process and influence goals. After examining the extent to which they facilitated meaningful participation in agenda setting, parameter setting, and policy setting, the longer term consequences of these mechanisms are considered. The chapter concludes that the mechanisms did result in processes that were more transparent, inclusive, and accountable. Although they did little to realize the influence goals, the mechanisms have had important longer-term benefits for Canadian NGOs in terms of the quality and quantity of co-operation now taking place among them, their transnational networks, their knowledge of global politics, their institutionalization, and the sophistication of their lobbying techniques.

THE GOVERNMENT-SPONSORED MECHANISMS

Copenhagen Summit for Social Development

The Copenhagen Summit for Social Development was the first global summit on poverty. It met from March 6 to 12, 1995, to address three core issues: the alleviation and reduction of poverty; the expansion of productive employment; and the enhancement of social integration, especially of those groups that are most marginalized and disadvantaged. These issues were intrinsically important to domestic anti-poverty groups and international development groups as well as to organizations representing labour, Aboriginal peoples, and women, and those concerned with environmental protection and human rights. The summit's discussions were premised on the idea that the growing gulf between rich and poor, both within national boundaries and among countries, was not only morally wrong but posed a threat to peace and stability around the globe. The *Programme of Action* adopted at the summit serves as a valuable tool for NGOs to use in their campaigns to hold state governments responsible to the commitments they made in Copenhagen.

In October 1993, senior executives of the Canadian Committee of the International Council on Social Welfare, Canadian Council on Social Development, and Canadian Council for International Co-operation organized a meeting to which they invited the leaders of fifty-six Canadian NGOs to discuss preparations for the summit. Those invited included international development, anti-poverty, and environmental groups, business organizations, labour unions, and associations representing specific categories of people, such as indigenous peoples, women, children, youth, seniors, immigrants, visible minorities, and people with disabilities. As a result, some twenty-five groups met to establish the Copenhagen Organizing Committee and to prepare a proposal requesting federal government funding to facilitate NGO preparations for the summit. They also formed a steering committee, the Administrative Team, to oversee the management and administration of the Copenhagen Organizing Committee's work.[5]

The Copenhagen Organizing Committee got off to an effective start, largely because key members of its Administrative Team had extensive experience with UN negotiations and with lobbying the federal government to affect policy outcomes; hence, they understood the type of preparations that were required. Early in the process, they secured government funding to hire a coordinator to prepare a comprehensive proposal to submit to government.

The proposal contained many provisions that were highly advantageous to the Copenhagen Organizing Committee; hence, securing ministerial approval of these provisions was an early and extremely important success for the committee. The provisions included:

- government funding for one (subsequently two) full-time staff member (coordinator);
- a modest operating budget, which included funds to enable the Copenhagen Organizing Committee to communicate with its members and to hold national consultations with interested groups and individuals across the country;
- a commitment on the part of government officials to hold regular meetings with Copenhagen Organizing Committee representatives prior to and following each set of international negotiations;
- access for the Copenhagen Organizing Committee to all documentation, including the Canadian government's positions as well as UN documents and government publications;
- two places on each Canadian delegation for the Copenhagen Organizing Committee's nominees; one of which was to be filled by an NGO representative with international expertise, while the other was to go to someone knowledgeable about poverty in Canada;
- additional places on the Canadian delegation for indigenous peoples, organized labour, and youth;[6]
- funds to allow some NGO representatives to attend the preparatory meetings as well as the Summit; and
- assurance that the selection of those to be funded would be made by the Copenhagen Organizing Committee's Administrative Team from a list of those nominated by Canadian NGOs.[7]

In short, government approval of the proposal ensured that the Copenhagen Organizing Committee had some full-time staff, an operating budget, access to documents critical to its work, regular meetings with government officials, two places on Canada's delegations to the international negotiations, and the right to determine which Canadian NGOs would receive government funds to attend these negotiations. In addition to this governmental support, the Copenhagen Organizing Committee received some significant contributions-in-kind from several of its key member organizations. For example, the United Nations Association in Canada provided space for the Copenhagen Organizing Committee's headquarters and two staff members; the Red Cross provided meeting rooms on several occasions and other infrastructure support; and the Canadian Council for International Co-operation donated some staff time. The Copenhagen Organizing Committee had the advantage of being backed by several prominent Ottawa-based NGOs, which had established generally collegial relations with government officials.

The Beijing Conference on Women

The Beijing Conference on Women—the largest conference in UN history—made significant advances in providing strategies for overcoming major obstacles to the advancement of women. The *Platform for Action* adopted in Beijing outlines strategies in twelve interconnected critical areas: poverty, decision making, education, human rights, health, media, violence, environment, armed conflict, protection of the girl child, economics, and mechanisms for the advancement of women. The advances made include the reaffirmation that rape is a war crime, the delineation of state responsibilities to eliminate violence against women, and the affirmation of sexual and reproductive rights for women. In light of the range of issues on the agenda, it was not surprising that the Beijing conference attracted a lot of interest from diverse NGOs, including labour, development, human rights, peace, women's, indigenous, and environmental groups.

Plans for a Canadian NGO facilitating committee developed out of a conference organized in March 1993 by the Manitoba UN End of the Decade Committee. The latter was the only Canadian group meeting annually to assess Canada's progress in achieving its commitments to women's human rights. A steering committee, which was established at the Manitoba UN End of the Decade Committee's 1993 conference, drafted a proposal in consultation with the Women's Program[8] and Status of Women Canada, for establishing government-sponsored mechanisms to facilitate NGO preparations for the Beijing Conference on Women. The proposal received government approval and two mechanisms were established: the Beijing Facilitating Committee, and the Canadian Preparatory Committee. The specific mandate of the former was as follows:

- The role of the Canadian Beijing Facilitating Committee (CBFC) is to facilitate Canadian Women's NGOs' participation in the Beijing process;
- The CBFC will work through its seats on the Canadian Preparatory Committee (CPC) to lobby on behalf of women's groups in terms of process, access, and representation. In this capacity, it will bring Canadian women's voices to the CPC and will strive to influence the government's preparations.

- Through the secretariat in Ottawa, the CBFC will serve as a clearinghouse for information in preparation for Beijing. The CBFC newsletter will play a crucial role in this networking. As well, the CBFC will be compiling a list of Canadians who will be going to New York and Beijing.[9]

Thus, the Beijing Facilitating Committee was responsible for distributing information relating to the Beijing Conference, facilitating the participation of Canadian NGOs, and lobbying on their behalf.

The Canadian Preparatory Committee was established to facilitate consultations between members of NGOs and the federal Interdepartmental Committee on the World Conference on Women, during the preparation of Canada's positions on documents pertaining to the UN Conference on Women. The Canadian Preparatory Committee began meeting in December 1993. In 1994 it met after each of the major international negotiations pertaining to the Beijing Conference, and by 1995 it was meeting prior to, as well as following, each of the international negotiating sessions.

Thus, the main impetus for facilitating NGO preparations for the Copenhagen Summit for Social Development and the Beijing Conference on Women came from the NGOs themselves. Nonetheless, the government was willing to provide funding to facilitate NGO participation and to guarantee the NGOs regular access to the government decision makers responsible for formulating Canada's positions for the international negotiations. How effective were these mechanisms in realizing process and influence goals?

PROCESS GOALS

The key question here is did the government-sponsored mechanisms result in a process that was transparent, inclusive, and accountable?

Transparent

The term implies that operations are easily seen through and clearly visible. Procedures need to be open to public scrutiny so that any corruption or abuses of power will be apparent to those who care to look. Measures to enhance transparency include holding open meetings, and making information freely available.

Although the procedures used to create each set of mechanisms were fairly open, those used in establishing the Beijing Facilitating Committee were most transparent. The Copenhagen Organizing Committee was established by the executives of the leading NGOs in the fields of domestic poverty and international development assistance. Membership in the Beijing Facilitating Committee was decided by a remarkably democratic process. Two thousand women's groups from across the country were asked to nominate potential candidates. From these nominations, national women's groups elected six representatives of national groups; provincial/regional groups elected six representatives from their ranks; and groups representing specific constituencies, such as indigenous women, lesbians, visible minorities, and immigrant women, elected eight representatives.

Both government officials and NGO representatives sat on the Canadian Preparatory Committee. The government members came from the four key bodies represented on the interdepartmental committee: Status of Women Canada, Department of Foreign Affairs and International Trade, Canadian International Development Agency, and the Women's Program.[10] NGO membership comprised six representatives selected by the Beijing Facilitating Committee as well as eight members chosen by government officials to represent development, labour, and human rights groups. The decision to expand the NGO membership to include labour, development, and human rights groups was made to ensure that a broad spectrum of Canadian society was represented on the committee and to provide access to groups that clearly had specific interests related to the Platform for Action. But the decision to include them may also have been prompted by the fact that these groups enjoyed better working relations with their respective departments than those that existed between the women's groups and Status of Women. Clearly a process in which government officials selected the majority of the NGO members on the Canadian Preparatory Committee did not enhance transparency.

In terms of their operations, both the Copenhagen Organizing Committee and Beijing Facilitating Committee contributed significantly to making the process more transparent. They kept the attentive public informed of salient developments on an ongoing basis. They produced informative newsletters, which they circulated, along with relevant government and UN documents and briefing kits, to all who expressed an interest in being on their distribution lists. The lists themselves reflected considerable regional, linguistic, and racial diversity. Through their distribution lists, the committees also conveyed information about their own operating procedures and ongoing advice for those interested in getting more actively involved. Thus, the creation and operation of the mechanisms reflected large degrees of transparency.

Inclusive

The term implies that all will be afforded equal opportunities to participate. The discussion thus focuses on an examination of the extent to which those involved represented at least key sectors of the attentive public, and to which they were able to actively participate. Again the assessment is largely positive: the mechanisms permitted a far larger and more diverse range of groups to participate, and they enabled the NGOs to produce more comprehensive responses to the conference/summit documents than would have been possible without government funding.

Membership in the Copenhagen Organizing Committee was open to anyone who expressed an interest in belonging. It included domestic anti-poverty groups and groups promoting international development. It comprised not only those working in these two fields of endeavour but also those with first-hand experience living in poverty. The structure of the Copenhagen Organizing Committee reflected the principal duality of its members' interests: it had two co-chairs and two coordinators to ensure that both fields of expertise were represented and accorded equal importance.

There was, however, tension between some francophone groups in Quebec and the Copenhagen Organizing Committee. Although the latter enjoyed good relations with several Quebec NGOs, including Solidarité populaire du Québec and Association québecoise des organismes de coopération internationaux, other francophone groups in Quebec wanted to conduct their preparations independently. At the same time that the founders of the Organizing Committee were holding their first meeting, Réseau Québécoise de sensibilisation sur le développement social convened a meeting of twelve Quebec groups to discuss their preparations for the Summit. These Quebec NGOs wanted a share of the government funds allotted to NGO preparations that was proportional to the population of their province. The Canadian International Development Agency did offer to fund the Quebec groups, but overall the Canadian government preferred to fund one NGO preparatory process because the separation of civil society into two language groups was too political. There were, moreover, the logistical problems of having to deal with two NGO committees instead of just one. In the end, the Copenhagen Organizing Committee also urged the government to provide separate funding for the Quebec groups and Human Resources Development provided such funding prior to PrepCom III.[11] Nonetheless, the ongoing tension between the Copenhagen Organizing Committee and some key Quebec groups not only consumed time and energy but weakened the Committee's claim to be speaking for NGOs from across the country.

The Copenhagen Organizing Committee held meetings every two months, which all member groups were welcome to attend. On paper, therefore, the process was inclusive, since all were invited to participate. There were, however, practical barriers to participation, since the groups had to cover their own travel expenses. As a result, most of the groups that attended were from Ottawa, Toronto, and Montreal.

The election process ensured that the members of the Beijing Facilitating Committee represented a wide range of women's groups. On its distribution

list were women's, indigenous, peace, human rights, development, and environmental groups as well as those devoted to promoting the rights of lesbians, children, the disabled, women of colour, and seniors. They included Eng-
lish-speaking groups, and francophone associations from Quebec and other
parts of the country. In ideological terms, the vast majority of the participants were feminist in orientation. Several prominent right-wing groups,
including REAL Women, contacted government officials on numerous occasions and were on the Beijing Facilitating Committee's distribution list. It is
not surprising, however, that they did not exercise leadership roles in the
government-sponsored mechanisms, since the Beijing Facilitating Committee's
membership was elected and the right-wing groups comprised a very small
minority of those participating. Out of deference to the country's bilingual her-
itage, the Beijing Facilitating Committee elected two co-chairs, an Anglo-
phone and a Francophone.

Although the Beijing Facilitating Committee remained the key NGO facilitating body and its members included representatives of Quebec groups,
twenty-three other women's groups from the province formed a Quebec
Preparatory Committee for Beijing in the autumn of 1994. While most of the
government funding was channelled through the Beijing Facilitating Committee, some funds were given directly to the Quebec Preparatory Committee
for Beijing.

As was the case with the Copenhagen Organizing Committee, the government did not pay travel expenses for NGO representatives on the Canadian
Preparatory Committee. For this reason, and because many of the groups had
offices in the capital, most of the groups represented were Ottawa-based.

Both the Copenhagen Organizing Committee and Beijing Facilitating Committee made strong efforts not only to keep the attentive public informed
but also to actively involve a wide range of NGOs from across Canada in the
development of the NGO responses to the conference and summit documents.
There was, however, a significant difference. In the case of the Copenhagen
Organizing Committee, the coordinator, in consultation with the Administrative Team, retained control of the drafting process, while the Beijing process
involved much more direct participation by women's groups across the country, and was, therefore, more democratic.

Beginning with PrepCom II, the Copenhagen Organizing Committee produced composite line-by-line analyses of the draft Copenhagen *Programme of
Action* prior to each set of international negotiations. In preparing its texts, the
Copenhagen Organizing Committee conferred with the Canadian Labour
Congress, academics, and Aboriginal and youth groups, each of which was
asked to critique the sections of the text that corresponded to its particular
areas of expertise. In preparing its analyses for PrepCom III and the Summit,

the Copenhagen Organizing Committee also drew on the information and insights gained from holding consultations with NGOs in every province and territory in Canada to hear their views on the issues in the Copenhagen *Programme of Action*. These consultations were important on at least three scores. First, they were useful tools in consciousness-raising about the Summit. Second, the reports of each of the consultations provided valuable background material to use in drafting the Copenhagen Organizing Committee's composite NGO texts. Third, conducting such consultations enhanced the legitimacy and credibility of the Copenhagen Organizing Committee's claim to be representing the views of groups concerned with poverty in Canada and with international development. The committee's coordinator sent her draft texts to the NGOs on the list for their responses. Their comments were used in revising the final NGO texts before they were presented to government.

The Beijing Facilitating Committee went further and involved women's groups directly in the drafting of its composite texts. Instead of having a central committee or key organizer write the document, the Beijing Facilitating Committee allocated responsibility for drafting responses to one or two of the twelve critical areas of concern in the *Platform for Action* to lead groups with expertise in respective area(s). In preparing their respective sections, the lead groups consulted widely. As a result, thousands of women had input. The lead groups' reports were compiled into a composite text, which was submitted to the government within one month of the Beijing Facilitating Committee having received the UN document.

The composite texts prepared by the Copenhagen Organizing Committee and Beijing Facilitating Committee assisted them in presenting their priorities and positions to government officials at home and at the international negotiations, and facilitated assuming leadership roles in the international NGO caucuses. Without government funding, it would not have been possible for such geographically dispersed and diverse groups to have worked together to develop composite texts.

Accountable

Being accountable means having to answer for one's actions and being held responsible for them. The leaders of the Copenhagen Organizing Committee and Beijing Facilitating Committee, and the NGO representatives on the Canadian Preparatory Committee were expected to be responsible to their constituencies. In the case of the Copenhagen Organizing Committee, this meant being accountable to domestic anti-poverty groups and Canadian international development groups. The members of the Beijing Facilitating Committee were to be responsible to the women's community, which had elected them. Likewise, the NGO representatives on the Canadian Preparatory Committee were expected to convey the views of the NGO community at the meetings with government officials and to report back to their constituencies, which they did. The NGO representatives on all three bodies deserve credit for keeping their attentive publics apprised of relevant developments and for conveying the views of their members to government.

INFLUENCE OBJECTIVES

This section addresses the question: did the government-sponsored mechanisms affect the policy-making process and its outcomes in either of the two cases. The extent to which they facilitated meaningful participation during their life spans is discussed in the context of agenda setting, parameter setting, and policy setting.[12] The longer-term implications are discussed in the subsequent section.

Agenda Setting

This form of influence involves persuading government officials to give serious attention to particular issues. Agenda setting was not evident in either of our cases. The agendas for the Beijing Conference on Women and Copenhagen Summit for Social Development were established through intergovernmental negotiations that took place before the mechanisms to facilitate NGO involvement came into existence. As a result, the Canadian NGOs played no role in establishing the initial content of the UN-generated documents. Likewise, Canada's broad objectives for the Summit and Conference were established by government officials very early in the process, before NGOs became actively involved. Hence, NGO involvement came too late to affect the national or the international agendas.

Parameter Setting

This type of influence involves establishing boundaries within which policymakers must operate. It encompasses positive limits (i.e., issues that must be considered) and negative restrictions (i.e., precluding particular options). Parameter setting was evident in each case, especially when the mechanisms were being established. Although the impetus for establishing the mechanisms came from the NGO communities, there was an existing recognition inside government that some form of government support for NGO participation was required. The Liberal government had come to power in 1993 with a promise to democratize the Canadian foreign policy-making process;[13] hence, government support for NGO participation was expected inside and outside government circles.

The culture within the women's movement also established parameters in the sense that women's groups expected the process of choosing members for the Beijing Facilitating Committee to be democratic. In response to this expectation, elections were held. Likewise, Canadian women's groups expected the Beijing Facilitating Committee to have its headquarters within the women's movement and their wishes were respected. For logistical and financial reasons, it was based in Ottawa. The Canadian Research Institute for the Advancement of Women—a national organization that encourages and promotes research conducted by and for women in Canada—was the only Ottawa-based group to offer space and some staff time; hence it became the headquarters for the Beijing Facilitating Committee.

While NGOs, particularly the women's groups, exerted some influence over the parameters for establishing the mechanisms, it is more difficult to assess the extent to which NGO pressure affected the issues that had to be included and options that could not be considered, as the vast majority of groups in both cases favoured the general direction of government policy. For example, in the case of the Beijing Conference, almost all the NGOs—like the government negotiators—took a feminist approach and thus advocated equal rights for women in all spheres of life. As a result, they supported moving the agenda ahead in all the twelve key areas in the Beijing *Platform for Action*. Similarly, in the case of the Copenhagen Summit, the domestic anti-poverty groups and international development groups—like the officials in Human Resources Development, the Canadian International Development Agency, and the Department of Foreign Affairs and International Trade—advocated positions aimed at reducing poverty at home and abroad. The main difference in each case was that the NGOs wanted to go further and faster than the government.

There was, however, a graphic example of NGOs failing to establish parameters. On February 27, 1995, just a week before the start of the Summit, Canada's Finance Minister, Paul Martin, Jr., presented the federal budget, which slashed every area of spending on social development, including cutting Canada's foreign aid budget by 20 percent over three years, reducing payments to the provinces for health, education, and welfare by seven billion dollars over two years, drastically reducing funding for Canadian NGOs, and disbanding the Advisory Council on the Status of Women. Such measures were an anathema to the vast majority of groups involved with the Copenhagen Summit and Beijing Conference. The government's fiscal priorities clearly trumped issues vital to the well being of Canadian NGOs and their objectives. On such critical matters, the NGOs were unable to establish parameters to protect their interests.

The 1995 budget was the catalyst that resulted in the undermining of the positive relations that had existed throughout the preparatory process between government officials and the Copenhagen Organizing Committee. At the

Summit, angry Canadian NGO representatives denounced the budget for making a mockery of Canada's commitments to social development. After the Summit, the Copenhagen Organizing Committee sought government funding for follow-up work, but the proposal was rejected for two reasons. First, the 1995 federal budget, with its prescriptions for massive cuts to social spending and to NGO funding, limited the prospects of securing follow-up funding. Second, the Minister of Human Resources Development had been alienated by the highly confrontational meeting with the Canadian NGOs in Copenhagen. In the case of the Beijing process, the 1995 budget served to further undermine relations between women's groups and the federal government on the eve of PrepCom III, which was held in March of that year.

Policy Setting

Influencing the specific content of policies is the traditional measure of success for NGOs themselves, as well as for practitioners and scholars. The government-sponsored mechanisms resulted in the NGOs being better positioned to lobby the government by guaranteeing access to government decision makers and facilitating the formulation of joint NGO positions and lobbying strategies. Nonetheless, the findings of these two cases regarding NGO influence over government positions are similar to those of the literature on Canadian foreign policy. Government officials exercised a large degree of autonomy in establishing the direction and substance of Canada's positions for the Copenhagen Summit and Beijing Conference. In each case, Canada's broad positions were formulated by public servants in the core departments before the NGOs even presented their texts to government. Nonetheless, the Copenhagen Organizing Committee was able to exert some influence over the priority allocated to issues and over the specific wording of positions during the preparatory phase. The evening before the formal intergovernmental negotiations began at PrepCom II, members of the Copenhagen Organizing Committee met in small groups with government negotiators to work on a line-by-line analysis of particular sections of the official text. For example, representatives of NGOs concerned with international development worked with the government negotiator(s) responsible for such issues, while those concerned with education met with the government officials negotiating provisions in this area. According to the coordinator of the Copenhagen Organizing Committee, government officials and NGO representatives were able to agree on the wording for about 90 percent of the text.[14] The strategy worked well; hence it was replicated at PrepCom III, where government officials and members of the NGO community again met in small groups to discuss wording for particular sets of issues. For the NGO representatives, this collaboration had two very positive outcomes: they were able to have some input into Canada's positions, and the process fostered constructive relations with the government negotiators.

While the government-sponsored mechanism established for the Copenhagen Summit for Social Development did afford NGOs some meaningful participation in the policy-making process during the preparatory phases, in the sense that they had some influence over the wording of specific Canadian positions, the Beijing Facilitating Committee and Canadian Preparatory Committee exerted very little influence over the direction and substance of Canada's positions at any point in the Beijing process. Of the NGO members on the Canadian Preparatory Committee whom I interviewed, none thought that they had exerted any significant influence over the direction or substance of the instructions to the Canadian delegation. The Canadian Preparatory Committee functioned primarily as a venue through which government officials could provide information to the NGOs. It was not a forum where the two sets of actors came together to establish joint positions. Why was the Copenhagen Organizing Committee able to exert more influence over policy setting than was the Beijing Facilitating Committee?

The main reason was that the lead groups in the Copenhagen Organizing Committee enjoyed better long-standing relations with the key departments formulating Canada's positions than did Canadian women's groups. Before preparations for the Summit began, both Human Resources Development and the Canadian International Development Agency already enjoyed constructive relations with domestic anti-poverty and international development groups, respectively. In contrast, women's groups began the process with a serious handicap: relations between them and the federal government had been deteriorating since the late 1980s, as a series of government policies had undermined the gains that feminist groups had worked so hard to achieve. Thus, well before the time preparations for the Beijing Conference on Women began, relations between the government and women's groups were strained. The tension was reflected in the composition and functioning of the Canadian Preparatory Committee. There government officials not only selected the majority of the non-state members but they also called and chaired its meetings and set its agendas. In sharp contrast, Copenhagen Organizing Committee staff members and government officials collaborated in setting the agendas for their meetings and the sessions were co-chaired by a government official and the chair of the Copenhagen Organizing Committee.

The Copenhagen Organizing Committee also benefited from having leaders with UN experience. Its co-chairs and coordinators understood the issues, they knew the environment in which they were operating, and they presented substantial, user-friendly briefs to government. For example, prior to the Summit, the Copenhagen Organizing Committee presented Bracket Analysis: *Declaration and Plan of Action*, which identified key paragraphs in the text considered in need of amendment, outlined the issue at stake, proposed alternate wording and/or deletions, and explained the proposed changes.

The Beijing Facilitating Committee's briefs were less well focused and user-friendly than those produced by the Copenhagen Organizing Committee. The former failed to establish priorities early in the process or to develop a conceptual framework for assessing the evolving international texts. Although the members of the Beijing Facilitating Committee had extensive expertise in women's issues, most had no previous UN experience. To conduct effective line-by-line analysis, one needs to know UN language, rules, procedures, and structures, all of which comprise the parameters within which government delegates and all participants must function. Over time, the Beijing Facilitating Committee's texts became more focused and more effectively presented, but the Committee never achieved the desired goal of producing a concise, well-organized line-by-line analysis for key priorities in the *Platform for Action*.

More than a decade has now passed since the government-sponsored mechanisms to facilitate NGO participation for the Copenhagen Summit for Social Development and the Beijing Conference on Women were functioning. Hence, one has a vantage point from which to assess the extent to which the experience of participating in these mechanisms enhanced NGO efficacy in the longer term.

ASSESSING THE LEGACY OF THE GOVERNMENT-SPONSORED MECHANISMS

The most important contributions of the government-sponsored mechanisms have been their long term benefits for Canadian NGOs. In making this assertion, one must recognize that many of the NGOs that were active in these two studies also participated in other UN conferences and summits held in the 1990s: hence it is impossible to assess the longer-term effects of the Copenhagen Organizing Committee and Beijing Facilitating Committee on NGO efficacy in isolation from what happened apropos the other major UN negotiations on social and economic issues. What one can say with certainty is that the government-sponsored mechanisms did enhance NGO efficacy in a number of ways, as discussed below.

Networks among Canadian NGOs Were Expanded and Strengthened

The mechanisms promoted networking among a large number of diverse associations, many of which had never worked with each other previously. The

Beijing Facilitating Committee helped to strengthen the linkages among women's groups sharing common goals, while the Canadian Preparatory Committee brought women's organizations together with NGOs focusing on other issues, including development, labour, and human rights. Following the Beijing Conference on Women, the Canadian Research Institute for the Advancement of Women, which had served as the secretariat for the Beijing Facilitating Committee, organized a meeting to explore the possibility of creating a women's umbrella group to continue the work started in Beijing. From this initiative, the Feminist Alliance for International Action was born. Its leaders were drawn extensively from those who had participated on the Beijing Facilitating Committee and its members from some fifty women's groups from across the country. It receives program funding from the Status of Women Canada and works in partnership with groups, such as Amnesty International, the Canada Assembly of First Nations, and the National Anti-Poverty Organization.

Relations between Status of Women and women's groups have become more collegial than they were prior to the Beijing process. The Feminist Alliance for International Action lobbied the Foreign Affairs Standing Committee to have the government revoke its September 2006 decision to make massive cuts to the Status of Women budget. The existence of good relations between Canadian women's groups and Status of Women is recognized internationally as exemplified by the fact that foreign NGOs, which find their own governments unreceptive, often contact Canadian NGOs, knowing that the latter will pass on information to the Canadian delegation. This practice is mutually beneficial. It provides the Canadian negotiators with useful information, and it gives foreign NGOs a chance to have some access—albeit indirect access—to government actors.

The Copenhagen Organizing Committee promoted collaboration between international development and domestic anti-poverty groups, both in Ottawa and, through its cross-country consultations, at the grassroots level. Unlike the Feminist Alliance for International Action, the Copenhagen Organizing Committee was unable to get ongoing federal funding for its follow-up work; hence, it has had to rely heavily on collaborations with international NGO networks.

Transnational NGO Networks Were Expanded and Strengthened

Strong transnational NGO networks developed from connections made while attending the international negotiations. The Beijing NGO Forum was particularly important in this process, as it was the largest such gathering ever held, attracting thirty thousand participants. Attending such venues served to diminish the North–South divide. For example, the global dimensions of problems such as trafficking in women became apparent, as did the need for multilateral approaches.

The Copenhagen Summit encouraged groups to move beyond debates over whether Southern poverty constitutes a more serious problem than does the plight of the poor in Northern countries. Both are now recognized as being important, and the advantages of collaboration among Northern and Southern NGOs are understood.

The issues on the Beijing and Copenhagen agendas are global and complex; hence, they require a level of research and collaboration that no one group can do all alone. At Copenhagen, an international coalition of NGOs established the Social Watch Coordinating Committee to ensure that the link between Northern and Southern poverty is maintained and that the norms enshrined in the Summit document are implemented. The Canadian Centre for Policy Alternatives and the North–South Institute constitute the Canadian chapter of Social Watch. The Feminist Alliance for International Action works closely with women's groups, such as the United States–based Center for Women's Global Leadership.

NGOs Gained Knowledge of UN Procedures and Language

Participating in the Copenhagen and Beijing processes enabled NGOs (especially women's groups and anti-poverty groups, many of which did not have previous experience in the global arena) to learn how to participate effectively at the international level. They gained deeper knowledge of the workings of the UN and of strategies for lobbying the Canadian government regarding international negotiations. As a result, there are now more experienced and more diverse constituencies to monitor government progress in meeting the commitments it made in both Copenhagen and Beijing. The Copenhagen Organizing Committee was particularly effective in accelerating the learning curve by providing briefings for NGO representatives before they left for the international negotiations and, once there, by holding daily organizational sessions to coordinate the NGOs' efforts.

NGOs Learned How to Use International Instruments to Advance Domestic Agendas

Through their analyses of the conference and summit documents, Canadian NGOs learned about the content of these texts and their potential utility as resources for advancing domestic agendas. In 1998, when Canada's compliance with its legal obligations under the Covenant on Economic, Social and Cultural Rights was being reviewed, a coalition of Canadian NGOs (e.g., women's, indigenous, legal, anti-poverty, and housing groups) travelled to Geneva to provide their own critiques of their government's record to the UN treaty body. The NGOs pointed out that many of the provisions in the 1995 budget had been inconsistent with Canada's obligations under the Covenant. The treaty body produced a report highly critical of Canada. It is doubtful that the treaty body would have been able to include the level of specificity in its criticism without input from Canadian NGOs.

NGO Participation Became More Institutionalized

The establishment of the Copenhagen Organizing Committee and Beijing Facilitating Committee served to recognize NGOs as legitimate representatives of particular social interests, which in turn increased the pressure on political authorities to continue meaningful dialogue with them. This has been particularly evident with women's groups. Since Beijing, the Canadian government has included two NGO representatives on its delegations to the annual meetings of the UN Commission on the Status of Women. Likewise, government funding was provided to assist women's groups to attend the Beijing +10 conference in New York. In each case, the selection of NGOs was made by the Feminist Alliance for International Action (i.e., in accordance with the expectations that such decision should be made within the women's movement). The practice of government negotiators providing daily briefings to NGOs has continued and it is now expected not only by Canadian NGOs but also by other countries and foreign NGOs.

Relations between former Copenhagen Organizing Committee participants and government departments continue on a more ad hoc basis than is the case with the former members of the Beijing Facilitating Committee. No government funding was provided to assist Canadian NGOs in coordinating their participation for the Copenhagen +5 conference in 2000. There were, however, some NGO representatives on the Canadian delegation and daily briefings were provided by the Canadian negotiators.

The 1995 federal budget served much more as a catalyst to undermine relations between the NGOs and government officials in the case of the Copenhagen Summit than the Beijing Conference for two reasons: the timing and the targeting of the NGO criticism. The budget was announced just before the Summit; hence, that was the time when there was greatest venting of frustrations. At Copenhagen, over three hundred NGO representatives attended a two-hour meeting with Lloyd Axworthy, in which the former lambasted the latter for the budgetary cuts. Targeting Axworthy was somewhat unfair since he had a record of being more receptive to NGO participation in the policy-making process than had most of his cabinet colleagues. Furthermore, he had worked to make positive changes in Human Resources Development, and his department was badly undercut by the 1995 federal budget. On the other hand, the NGOs were angry and Axworthy was the senior government representative at the Summit. Thereafter, Minister Axworthy was much less receptive to NGO requests for funding. The Beijing Facilitating Committee established constructive working relations with Status of Women Canada that were not marred by nasty public confrontations. As a result, the Women's Program was willing to continue providing funding, first to the Beijing Facilitating Committee and then to the Feminist Alliance for International Action.

CONCLUSION

In closing, the government-sponsored mechanisms were more effective in achieving process goals than in realizing influence goals. Each enhanced the transparency, inclusiveness, and accountability of the process. They did not assist the NGOs in having issues included on the agenda. This was largely due to timing: decisions as to which items would be included on the agenda were made before the mechanisms were functioning. The political climate at the time, as well as NGO demands, did establish parameters, in terms of ensuring that government support of NGO participation was forthcoming. There were, however, major limits to NGO efficacy in parameter setting, as exemplified by the passing of the 1995 budget.

In addition to allowing large numbers of NGOs to have input, the mechanisms facilitated doing much more in-depth analysis of the negotiating documents and producing more comprehensive composite texts to present to government officials and to use at the international negotiations than would otherwise have been possible.

In terms of policy setting, neither set of mechanisms enabled the NGOs to affect the direction, broad objectives, or content of Canada's positions, although the Copenhagen Organizing Committee did exert some minor influence over the allocation of priorities and specific wording. The Copenhagen Organizing Committee's relative success in policy setting during the preparatory phases is explained by two factors. Its leaders had previous experience with United Nations negotiations; hence they knew what preparations were necessary for effectively lobbying at home and in the global arena. In contrast, few members of the Beijing Facilitating Committee had this type of prior experience to guide them. More importantly, the Copenhagen Organizing Committee had the advantage of pre-existing constructive relations with key government departments. Furthermore, its leadership succeeded in maintaining constructive relations until the 1995 budget was announced.

The government-sponsored mechanisms established to facilitate NGO participation for the Copenhagen Summit for Social Development and the Beijing Conference on Women have resulted in major long-term benefits for Canadian NGOs. These gains can be measured in terms of experience and knowledge gained and in terms of the strengthening of domestic and international NGO networks.

Since 1995, there have been some developments in the international environment that have assisted NGOs. In particular, UN information and documents are more readily available. In other ways, however, the environment has become less friendly to their participation. Overall, states are less welcoming of NGO input within the UN system. The rules governing NGO participation are unclear; hence they are frequently negotiated for each forum and sometimes for each session. This uncertainty of access impedes the work of NGOs. In light of these developments, the knowledge base of NGOs and their abilities to collaborate transnationally become all the more important.

NOTES

1 Jan Aart Scholte, "Civil Society and Democracy in Global Governance," *Global Governance* 8, no. 3 (2002): 283.
2 Scholte, "Civil Society and Democracy in Global Governance," 281–304; Elizabeth Riddell-Dixon, "Social Movements and the United Nations" *International Social Science Journal* 144 (June 1995): 325–42; and John Trent, "The Reform of International Institutions: Lessons from Their Origins and Develoment," Paper Presented to the Annual Conference of the Academic Council on the United Nations System, Ottawa, June 17, 2005.
3 The discussion of these two mechanisms draws on Elizabeth Riddell-Dixon, "Democratizing Canadian Foreign Policy? NGO Participation for the Copenhagen Summit for Social Development and the Beijing Conference on Women," *Canadian Foreign Policy* 11, no. 3 (2004): 99–118; and, in the case of the mechanisms for the Conference on Women, it also draws on Elizabeth Riddell-Dixon, *Canada and the Beijing Conference on Women: Governmental Politics and NGO Participation* (Vancouver: University of British Columbia Press, 2001). Research for the earlier works as well as for this chapter relied heavily on interviews with a wide range of government and NGO representatives, to whom I extend my heartfelt thanks.
4 Most scholars share the view that government officials enjoy a large degree of autonomy from civil society in the formulation and implementation of Canada's foreign policies. See Mark Neufeld, "Democratization in/of Canadian Foreign Policy: Critical Reflections," *Studies in Political Economy* 58 (Spring 1999): 97–119; Kim Richard Nossal, "Analysing the Domestic Sources of Canadian Foreign Policy," *International Journal* 39, no. 1 (1983–1984): 1–22, and "The Democratization of Canadian Foreign Policy: The Elusive Ideal," in *Democracy and Foreign Policy: Canada among Nations 1995*, ed. Maxwell A. Cameron and Maureen Appel Molot (Ottawa: Carleton University Press, 1995); Cranford Pratt, "Dominant Class Theory and Canadian Foreign Policy: The Case of the Counterconsensus," *International Journal* 39, no. 1 (1983–1984): 99–135; and "Competing Perspectives on Canadian Development Assistance Policies," *International Journal* 51, no. 2 (1996): 235–58; and Sandra Whitworth, "Women, and Gender, in the Foreign Policy Review Process,"

in *Democracy and Foreign Policy: Canada among Nations 1995*, ed. Cameron and Molot.

5 Membership of the Administrative Team comprised one representative from each of the following: Action Canada Network, Campaign 2000, Canadian Council for International Co-operation, Canadian Council on Social Development, Canadian Ethnocultural Council, Canadian Red Cross, International Council on Social Welfare, National Anti-Poverty Organization, and United Nations Association in Canada.

6 Although the Copenhagen Organizing Committee did not claim to speak for these groups, it recognized the importance of having their voices heard.

7 Canadian NGO Organizing Committee for the World Summit for Social Development, "World Summit on Social Development: Proposal for Canadian Civil Society Participation," February 1994.

8 The Women's Program is "the primary government source of financial and advisory assistance to women's groups and other voluntary organizations working to improve the status of women," in Secretary of State, "The Women's Program and the Role of Women's Voluntary Organization in Promoting Change" (Ottawa: Government of Canada, 1985).

9 *Onward to Beijing: For Equality, Development and Peace* (Newsletter of the Canadian Beijing Facilitating Committee) 1, no. 2 (December 1994): 23.

10 The Women's Program was first part of the Department of Secretary of State, then part of Human Resources Development, and subsequently moved to Status of Women Canada on April 1, 1995.

11 Four sets of preparatory negotiations were convened at the UN headquarters in New York prior to the Summit. In drafting the Beijing *Platform for Action*, the UN Commission on the Status of Women convened three preparatory meetings, as well as intersessional working groups, and five days of informal consultations.

12 The terms are drawn from Denis Stairs, "Public Opinion and External Affairs: Reflections on the Domestication of Canadian Foreign Policy," *International Journal* 22 (Winter 1977–1978): 130–36.

13 Liberal Party of Canada, *Creating Opportunity: The Liberal Plan for Canada*, Ottawa, 1993, 109.

14 Interview with Peggy Teagle, executive coordinator, Canadian Consortium for International Social Development and former coordinator for the Canadian NGO Organizing Committee for the World Summit for Social Development in Ottawa, February 25, 1998.

6

The Arab NGO Network for Development

A Case Study on Interaction between Emerging
Regional Networking and Global Civil Society

Ziad Abdel Samad and
Kinda Mohamadieh

FORMATION OF CONCEPTIONS BEHIND GLOBAL CIVIL SOCIETY

With the rise of the debates and studies around global civil society, certain basic assumptions have been made to explain this phenomenon, which is becoming influential but also controversial. Many have described the formation, role, and impact of this global force and aim to explore its potential as a tool for mass mobilization and awareness, a space for exchange and elaboration of alternatives, and an agent for democratic change.

Among other definitions, "global civil society is claimed to be the international transnational analogue of that which is called civil society in a settled domestic democratic society."[1] Civil society institutions that are part of the social fabric of such a society are able to play the role of single-minded, advocacy organizations with an axe to grind and a social mission to accomplish.[2]

In this line of thought, it can be noted that the progress of democratic systems and spaces has definitely had a part in enhancing the role of civil society organizations. The flourishing of the global civil society concept and its realization are often linked to the democratization of the international system. Indeed, in the 2004/5 edition of *Global Civil Society*, Anderson and Reiff went on to challenge the whole ideological rhetoric surrounding global civil society based on the claim that global civil society is stuck in a system that lacks democratic spaces.[3]

In addition, one of the main discourses explaining global civil society cites the rise of processes of economic globalization with all its institutions, legislations, and transnational business bodies. In this context, global civil society is seen as a rising force to protect the rights and interests of the world's peoples against the narrow interests of the international business community. It is worth noting that civil society has taken on different roles and types of mobilizations in this area. Protests and mass mobilization are the most visible strategies, seen especially when the street protests in Seattle and other cities contributed to the collapse of the multilateral negotiations in the World Trade Organization (WTO). But spaces for civil society participation are becoming increasingly available in international institutions, events, and meetings. Civil society groups are increasingly taking on a consultative role with international institutions and are becoming more capable of addressing the details of highly complicated negotiations schemes and are even presenting and advising governments on alternative scenarios. The challenges remain in how to make these spaces opportunities to influence economic globalization.

In this context, global democratic governance is one of the main objectives and struggles of global civil society. Democratic governance is essential to the enhancement of sustainable development, social justice, and global peace. Global civil society actors struggle for democratic governance, which is based on fair and democratic participatory processes in the decision making of global institutions and the implementation of their strategies, policies, and decisions. Yet democratic participatory processes necessitate equal and independent participation of national governments and civil society actors at the global level. Hence, global civil society has a role in supporting national civil society in assuring that national governments' participation reflects national interests.

Based on the above, this chapter relates some of these assumptions to the reality of civil society organizations in the Arab region, in a quest to explain where Arab civil society groups stand in a rising global civil society. This in turn leads to an explanation of the complexities and challenges that a regional networking process faces in the Arab region.

CIVIL SOCIETY IN THE ARAB REGION: WHERE DOES IT STAND FROM THE EMERGENCE OF GLOBAL CIVIL SOCIETY?

This section sheds light on some obstacles and missing factors facing the emergence of a prosperous civil society in the Arab region, the latter being an added value to global civil society processes. Among these obstacles are the following:

- the emergence and predominance of the strong state;
- the limited space available for the emergence of civil society;
- the nature of the priority challenges for civil society in the Arab region;
- the kind of linkages to the international system and global governance dynamics;
- the structural and contextual complexities of the role of Arab civil society groups;
- lack of common platforms; and
- the emergence and predominance of the strong state in a democracy deficit.

The democracy deficit in the Arab states has set high limitations on the progress of the role of civil society organizations, which have been struggling for their right to association and existence instead of developing an advocacy role for social change and the development of rights-based policies. Moreover, the breakdown of the labour and popular movements, due to the economic decay abundant in the region, deprived all secular and progressive trends of the broad social support needed to construct vibrant and effective civil societies.[4] This has contributed to the isolation of groups in the region from processes at the international level.

It is worth noting that states in the Arab region are the result of a struggle against the colonial system that replaced the Ottoman Empire after World War I. This struggle took place during the period between WWI and WWII, leading to the creation of several independent states. This process was paralleled by the emergence of the new state of Israel. This reality, which has caused instability, has had negative consequences on the region as a whole. Indeed, instead of launching efforts to empower the newly emerging nation states and invest in development and social and economic justice, the main agenda of emerging Arab states was national liberation and "the mission" to end the occupation of Palestine. Accordingly, there was justification for the rule of "the strong state"; this situation led to the emergence of one-party regimes, and in many cases totalitarian and dictatorship regimes, where the militarization of the state and "security" in its very narrow understanding dominated.

These emerging states largely restricted the role of local societies and forbade the emergence of independent civil society institutions, leading to limitations on the forms of democratic participation. To a certain extent, Arab societies supported these regimes with the assumption that this was the way to achieve the people's aspirations for economic growth, development, and national liberation. Yet, the more the prevalent model of the Arab states failed in meeting the challenges—whether in accomplishing national liberation by ending the occupation of Palestine or in achieving economic and social justice and development—the more they tended to limit freedoms and restrict democracy. (This was the case in several countries such as Tunisia, Algeria, Libya, Egypt, Sudan, Jordan, Syria, Iraq, and Yemen.)

Where democracy is lacking, there is a need for a more active role of civil society in the struggle to open more space for participation, change, and respect for diversity and human rights. Consequently, the lack of democracy per se is an important agenda for civil society to struggle against. Furthermore, the struggle for democracy encompasses a wider agenda, including social and economic along with political and cultural challenges. Claiming space for participation brings with it the test of presenting alternative visions and perspectives for change, challenging civil society to elaborate alternatives or at least features for alternative policies and strategies.

Moreover, the lack of democratic practices in Arab societies can be linked to the threats to national identity, deriving from:

- on one hand, foreign occupation in Palestine and parts of other countries such as Syria, Egypt, Lebanon, and the West Bank and Gaza since 1967; and the lack of security due to the fear of the Israeli expansionist tendencies, and
- on the other hand, the call for a pan-Arab nationalism superseding the identification with a nation-state.

These two factors constituted a permanent feeling of threat to national security and the national sovereignty of the Arab states.

When analyzing the state of democracy in the region, it is also important to take into consideration the rise of "Islam as a solution." Establishing Islamic regimes was denounced by the ruling elites and the popular mass due to the mistrust in the nature of the Islamic movements (Political Islam) and their objectives in the region. Consequently, Islam and democracy came to be seen as two antagonistic paradigms.

All of the above-mentioned factors can also explain why the space for tolerance and respect for differences and diversity remains highly limited and tension-filled, while clashes and even civil wars are prevalent in many Arab countries.

Space for the Emergence of Civil Society

The theories of global civil society assume that civil society becomes the advocate for the people of the world in the time when transnational forces, whether economic or other, are taking advantage of the current erosion of national sovereignty and while global governance processes are still weak.[5] This approach assumes availability of space for civil society's role to rise while there is lack of state power on certain policy-making areas. However, in most of the Arab region, the role of the state has dominated policy making, and the issues behind sovereignty have been used at their worst,[6] often exploited to protect regimes that oppress their own people.

Earlier, the link between the tendency toward strengthening the power of the state and limiting the spaces for freedom and democracy was high-lighted. Empowering the state in the Arab region became a way to protect the narrow interests of the ruling elites instead of achieving the goals of sustainable development and social justice. The main agenda of these elites became their own safety, security, and control over power, instead of national security. This was always paralleled with a strong repression of civil society. In this context, the prevailing focus of civil society remained accommodating—not challenging—the regimes in their struggle against foreign threats and those deriving from the emergence of religious tendencies, more specifically the Islamic movements.

Consequently, the space available for civil society organizations in the Arab region is questionable; are civil society groups proactive in enhancing and gaining more space and influence in their societies, or are they simply operating in the spaces made available to them by national governments? In light of this, are civil society groups moving away from being mechanisms of enhancing democracy and democratic governance to becoming an elitist force that is more accommodating to the states' agenda than fighting for the priorities and justice of local communities?

Moreover, national sovereignty as it is understood by the ruling regimes in the Arab region led governments to accuse civil society organizations benefiting from foreign financial support of threatening national sovereignty. In this regard, the dominance of faith-based donations, mainly directed to charitable programs and organizations, weakened them and forced them to look for financial support and aid from foreign donors. In addition, the lack of grants provided by the public institutions to civil society groups also contributed to their weakness.

Weak civil society that is reliant on foreign aid will be more exposed to the threats of adopting and implementing the agenda of foreign donors, which are not necessarily in compliance with the national agenda and priorities. This might be due to the lack of experience and knowledge about local sensitivities, traditions, and realities. The danger of civil society organizations from Southern and former communist-ruled countries becoming monopolized by Western-styled and Western-funded NGOs has been debated in several articles.[7] However, an aware and capable civil society empowered by a clear vision and concrete mission, strategies, and policies, with internal good governance, will be able to preserve its focus on local priorities and resist any kind of foreign agenda.

Priority Challenges for Civil Society in the Arab Region

Arab governments have often tried to keep their people concerned with struggles around sovereignty and identity, keeping social and economic concerns a secondary priority. Although these concerns have been shaping the international system, they have not been a priority to governments and peoples of the region as a whole. This is clearly reflected in the reports published by the international institutions, mainly the World Bank and the United Nations Development Programme.[8]

Choices facing local civil society organizations have become highly provocative; they question identity, in its national, pan-Arab, and even Islamic dimensions. Other related strategic options in the region include choices regarding the role of the state and the relation between the public and the private sectors in light of the transition from closed economies to open market economies. In addition there are queries about the objectives of foreign investments and their contribution to the development process within the context of dominant rental and cliental economic models in most of the Arab countries.

Moreover, although transnational economic powers have been invading the region as in other developing countries, civil society organizations in the Arab region are still not taking any significant role within the global movement against this invasion. Here, the lack of linkages between political, economic, social, and cultural agendas in the region, and the dominance of the political discourse within the framework of a weak political movement, contributed to the weakening of the role of civil society organizations.

In this context, issues of peace and security remain the central challenges for the Arab civil society organizations. They often dominate other threats considered priority issues in other regions and which form the basic grounds for common fights and missions that bring global civil society together.

The Palestinian–Israeli conflict, which is at the core of peace, security, and stability concerns in the region, has become an identity-forming issue and a religious challenge. Political motives, particularly those related to the Palestinian national struggle, provided the main impetus for mobilization in the Arab region of the anti-globalization movement and accordingly of global civil society.[9]

Moreover, the Iraqi problem has increasingly become a conflict with a global dimension since the early 1990s, with the beginning of the sanctions imposed by the United Nations on the country. Decades of sanctions preceded the invasion of Iraq in 2003 and its occupation, which in turn became a source of an internal conflict threatening the stability of the whole region. This case was also another main topic raised by the Arab civil society and reflects the unfairness, bias, and double standards of the international community when it comes to its role in the region.

In fact, the participation of Arab organizations in the World Social Forums (WSF) is more focused on the Palestinian, and most recently the Iraqi causes, than any other issues; it is the issue they find themselves most concerned with and the easiest through which they can relate with organizations from other regions.

Linkages to the International System and Global Governance Dynamics

People in the region have been frustrated with the current international order and double standards in the implementation of international laws, and see no space or capability in investing toward the change of this system. Accordingly, perceptions of global civil society in the Arab region are influenced by a sense of alienation that is rooted in the Arab relationships with the present international system.[10]

The invasion of Iraq raised another dimension of the problem related to the ability of foreign interference to change the reality in the region. This issue was always a subject of an internal debate among civil society. The challenge deriving from this dilemma was mainly about the need to use foreign support to change dictator regimes controlling societies while still being able to conserve local agendas and priorities.

The global community has rushed to push initiatives concerning political changes in the region in response to the rise of violent tendencies in several Arab countries, which have been linked to the rise of terrorism globally. However, the main reason for these violent tendencies is directly related to peace and security, the double standards in implementing international laws, and the degraded social and economic realities. The international community interfered through launching the so-called "war on terror" as a strategic military choice, marginalizing other types of interventions tackling the root causes of terrorism. This in turn strengthened violent tendencies and marginalized the capacities of local societies, particularly civil society organizations and social movements, and limited their potential to be effective actors in deterring violence.

Structural and Contextual Complexities in the Role of Civil Society Groups in the Arab Region

Civil society in the Arab region is referred to as the "indigenous sector."[11] The use of this terminology reflects the nature of societal relations, which are dominated by tribal, clan, family, and religious ties and links. In several Arab countries, these relations are more important than the relation of the citizen to the state.[12] Besides being a main contributor to the production of "social capital"—those bonds of trust and reciprocity that have been found to be critical preconditions for democracy and economic growth[13]—civil society organizations are also a result of a healthy relationship among communities and between them and the state. In the Arab societies, there is a weakness of the notion of citizenship, which reflects itself in a distorted relation between state and citizen.

Moreover, the inconsistency of development processes and lack of development policies in the Arab countries, in addition to the impact of war and instability on those processes, is a challenge facing the consistency of the work of civil society organizations in the region.

Accordingly, we witness that the third sector (civil society) in the region is dominated by welfare and charitable understandings and is mainly involved in service provision, social assistance, and welfare. The focus on service provision and the lack of a developed role in advocacy limits the capacities of civil society organizations in the region to take part in social change and policy-influencing dynamics.

This could explain why many global campaigns often lack contacts and effective counterparts in the Arab region. The sector suffers increasingly from limitations put on non-governmental organizations, the lack of emergence of effective social movements—including peasants', students', and women's movements—and the neutralization of the role of unions, which are being co-opted by the government.

In addition, the lack of a democratic culture among civil society organizations themselves, due to structural problems in the emergence, vision, and mission of these groups, forms an obstacle for their civic efforts toward bringing greater democracy and participation to society at large.[14]

Common Issues, Debatable Conceptions, and Lack of Common Platforms

A growing global civil society is built on common interests, fights, goals, and messages in addition to global forums at which leaders develop shared social agendas. Yet in the Arab region, civil society has had difficulty creating national and regional common platforms, which necessarily limits their ability to take an active part in global platforms.

Among other issues, religion is a dividing issue among civil society in the region. Since the failure of the liberal and socialist projects in the last century to gain independence and to establish the modern nation-state in the Arab region, religious tendencies and movements have risen as alternative providers of change and social justice. Yet the role of religion and its relation with the state and civil society remain an issue of debate and often division. This is a major debate in the current spheres of civil society institutions and is increasingly creating an obstacle for the emergence of a more coherent and effective role for civil society institutions in the Arab region.

In the Arab region, religious tendencies are diversified, with a wide range of agendas. Some of them recognize the democratic political processes as ways for change. Even though many of them are involved in the political process in several countries of the region, they do not hide their willingness to establish the Islamic system as a solution. Thus, they struggle for the Islamic system, which is not seen by many other actors in civil society organizations as a democratic system leading to constructive and substantial participation. Moreover, many people with these tendencies believe that violence is a way for change, which can explain the military clashes and conflicts in several countries (Saudi Arabia, Algeria, Sudan, Somalia, Iraq, and most recently in Morocco and Tunisia).

On the issue of democracy, many with nationalistic tendencies, some of them with leftist backgrounds, are not convinced of the Western model of democracy that is currently being pushed into the region through various reform initiatives. These stands lead them to reject any form of partnership and coordination with foreign actors, including civil society groups. It also leads them to accuse any local calls for modernization and democracy of holding foreign agendas and supporting foreign interferences. Although these nationalistic forces are secular, they do not mind partnering with the existing Islamic groups in their struggle against what they refer to as "colonial and hegemonic western tendencies." It is worth noting that both Islamic and nationalistic tendencies are the dominant forces among Arab civil society.

This was obvious throughout the experience and efforts to organize the Arab Social Forum. In fact these efforts were strongly restricted due to the above-mentioned antagonistic and complicated relationships among civil society. Diversity could be a factor of strength and richness to the process of organizing the social forum, yet the lack of experience and mainly the lack of tolerance among Arab civil society organizations was behind the inability to manage these differences. The inability to accept differences and to launch a public debate about strategic choices is a factor preventing the strengthening of social capital and the rise of social movements in many Arab countries.

In the new paradigm of global civil society, the religious dimensions are discussed as genuine variables. The fact that religious actors are present in the global arena including the World Social Forum confirms that the "religious" can no longer remain rigidly contrasted with the "civil."[15]

An important area for future examination would be how different global agents negotiate across the secular–religious divide and how they achieve an overlapping consensus.[16] Together with clashes in cultural understandings and perceptions, these questions and divides are increasing worldwide. However, does this negatively impact the rise of the processes of global civil society or does it strengthen it? Answers to this question could shed light on commonalities and differences among trends of global and Arab civil societies.

At the global level, there is a claim that assumes that civil society organizations in the Arab region lack common interests and threats with international groups, thus causing a limited participation of the former in global civil society dynamics. However, the anti-war movement rallied behind causes that originate from the struggle of peoples of the region, whether in Iraq, Palestine, or Sudan. Considering that, we ought to question whether Arab civil society groups' role, contribution, and leadership in this movement were limited due to the lack of common interests or due to other structural limitations stemming from the nature of the civil society groups themselves, including their vision, policies, strategies, and work mechanisms.

This leads to another very important question regarding the relation between resistance, armed struggle, and the anti-war movement. This question is not only shaping the global anti-war movement but it is strongly dividing Arab civil society. It is worth noting in this regard that the resistance against foreign occupation is legitimate and approved as a non-contested right of people to self-determination. But the question is what do we understand by foreign occupation? Is the Israeli presence in the West Bank and Gaza considered foreign occupation, but not in the 1948 territories? What concept can be used to justify this reason? Is it the United Nations General Assembly Resolution 181 issued on November 29, 1947? Can the Palestinians recognize the state of Israel without being recognized by Israel as an independent and sovereign state themselves? Are the multinational forces in Afghanistan not considered as foreign occupation because their presence was justified by a UN Security Council resolution, which deprives the Afghan people of their right to resist? Isn't the presence of the American army and its allies in Iraq foreign occupation? Does the struggle against foreign occupation justify targeting civilians and civil objectives? Does fighting foreign occupation justify targeting all political and economic interests around the world (for example, the 9/11 attacks and others in Saudi Arabia, Egypt, Madrid, London, and elsewhere)? All these are questions that often divide civil society in the Arab region.

We can conclude that a combination of factors influence the prosperity of civil society in the Arab region as a force that can actively be part in a rising global process;[17] this includes the lack of democracy, the lack of an adequate legal framework, restrictions imposed by the ruling regimes and the highly centralized systems, in addition to restrictions stemming from cultural and social realities. Moreover, the very low indicators of development, the prevalence of illiteracy, and the limitations and lack of communication contribute to the weakening of civil society and the lack of progress on developing and empowering its role for change.

The above-mentioned challenges highly affect the environment where the Arab NGO Network for Development (ANND) operates. The following section outlines the main strategies that ANND is undertaking to face these challenges and to enable civil society to improve its role and increase its impact in the regional and global policy-making scene.

THE EXPERIENCE OF ANND: NETWORKING IN THE ARAB REGION

The previous section underlined how a combination of factors hinder Arab civil society organizations from joining the rising trends of global civil society, from developing goals, building networks, and proposing strategies for common work among organizations in the Arab region. This reality reflects itself in the daily work of any networking initiative that emerges in the region.

Often Arab groups lack a coherent and organized participation in international affairs and summits; this often results from the following three reasons:

1. The numbers of participants are limited; this is due to many factors, including limited financial capacities, limited interests, and lack of experience and knowledge.
2. Competition often deters coordination among groups, which is due to the antagonistic positions on several issues in addition to the lack of tolerance and the lack of democratic culture and practices.
3. Their positions remain passive, with no clear, targeted, and aggressive change agenda.

This reality clearly reflects itself in the limited numbers of Arab organizations in consultative status with international agencies, such as the United Nations Economic and Social Council among others.

In fact, the initiative behind the establishment of the ANND was taken in light of the preparations for the 1995 Summit on Social Development. Given the lack of coordination among Arab groups participating in the Summit, and the inability to take active stands in regard to the agenda of the Summit, a group of Lebanese and Tunisian organizations initiated a coordination process that ended up with a consensus on the need for a consistent coordination body to emerge in the region.[18]

ANND is a regional network that aims to enhance the voice of Arab civil society organizations at the international fora, strengthening the mobilization of civil society both regionally and internationally, thus presenting more space for coalition building and coordination, such as is the case through the WSF and the Euro-Mediterranean Civil Forum. In general, it can be noted that additional spaces for civil society to influence policy making have been created through the increasing attention toward the Arab region, specifically those concerning issues of democracy and reforms and human rights, including the rights of women, the participation of civil society, and solidarity campaigns especially with Iraq and Palestine. In this context, ANND perceives that the increase of spaces with the rise of global civil society could offer a brilliant opportunity for the voicing of Arab protests against injustices seen to be inflicted upon the Arab region by the present international system.[19]

ANND thus uses such opportunities to empower and enhance the participation of Arab civil society organizations. This is done not only by supporting their participation in global fora, but also by bringing global civil society to the region through organizing various kinds of events and mobilizations. For example, ANND organized the Global Forum on Globalization and Trade in 2001 in preparation for the fourth WTO Ministerial Meeting held in Doha, the General Assembly of the Social Watch in 2003, and the Global Meeting of the Global Call to Action against Poverty in 2006. In addition, ANND supported the organization of the Moroccan Social Forum in Rabat, Morocco in 2004. ANND was also involved in the organization of several regional preparatory meetings for international events such as the World Summit on Sustainable Development (WSSD) and the World Summit on the Information Society (WSIS) among others.

All these events and occasions contributed to enhancing and empowering the participation of civil society organizations from the Arab region in the global arena.

Cases of ANND's Involvements at the Global Level

ANND is benefiting from its active participation in global networks, which opens opportunities to exchange experiences and expand the learning processes. ANND is a proactive member of several international networks, where it aims at shedding light and bringing attention to the challenges in the Arab region, with a particular focus on the role of civil society and the difficulties it faces.

ANND is strategically involved in Social Watch, a global network advocating for issues related to development and for monitoring the implementation of the UN commitments and goals. ANND actively contributes to the yearly report issued by Social Watch, both at the national and global levels. ANND also translates the global report into Arabic in order to make the information available and to encourage civil society groups to use it as a tool for advocacy campaigns. The process of preparing national reports and the dissemination of the global report in the different countries of the region is a tool to engage additional groups and to raise their awareness on developmental issues and challenges.

ANND is also a member of CIVICUS: World Alliance for Citizen Participation, which contributes to the empowerment of civil society by working on the

Civil Society Index and the Civil Society Watch Report. ANND sees in these programs important tools to strengthen Arab civil society and support their struggle for their rights and freedoms. Enhancing the participation of additional Arab groups in the world assemblies organized by CIVICUS is another strategy adopted by ANND to strengthen the global engagement of the Arab civil society.

The WSF is another space where ANND carries the challenges of the Arab region and Arab civil society, and shares it with other partners and colleagues from around the world. The WSF can also be a forum for mobilizing more solidarity and a very important learning process to bring about knowledge and sharing of experiences.

As mentioned above, ANND succeeded in organizing a Global Forum on Globalization and Trade in 2001, with the support of the Our World Is Not for Sale, which is a global network that challenges trade and investment paradigms that threaten the interests of the people and the environment. This forum contributed to enhance the debate around the World Trade Organization and other trade agreements in the Arab region and increased the engagement of civil society organizations with this highly important and challenging topic. ANND is still active in this network and tries to create an interactive debate on trade issues among Arab civil society in a process of advocacy and lobbying on the Arab governments.

ANND also acts as a regional focal point for the Global Call to Action against Poverty (GCAP). It succeeded to mobilize civil society in several countries and supported the establishment of national coalitions actively working on issues related to poverty eradication strategies. Two GCAP regional meetings (May 2005 in Cairo and August 2006 in Khartoum) and another GCAP global meeting (March 2006 in Beirut) were organized by ANND. These meetings contributed to enhancing the participation of organizations in the Call to Action and highlighted the potential power of civil society in the Arab region.

An additional role of ANND is participation in the Millennium Campaign by promoting the Millennium Development Goals and involving Arab civil society groups in the efforts to monitor and push for the achievement of these goals. Civil society in the Arab region is a potential partner to meet the challenges of development, but this needs the empowerment of civil society organizations and the elaboration of a civil society agenda. This is what ANND is trying to contribute to, through the participation in the GCAP and the Millennium Campaign.

The Euro-Mediterranean NGO Platform is another venue where ANND contributed to enhance and expand the participation of civil society organizations from several Arab countries. There is now an ongoing active debate tackling the New European Neighborhood Policy through the Euro-Med NGO platforms initiated in various countries of the Mediterranean. The three dimensions of Barcelona process[20]—(1) political (peace and security and democracy and human rights), (2) economic (bilateral agreements and free trade zone), and (3) cultural (cultural exchange and dialogue)—make the Euro-Mediterranean partnership an opportunity for the Arab civil society, particularly in the involved country, to work on a comprehensive agenda in relation to the interlink among these three challenging dimensions. ANND thus sees the Euro-Mediterranean NGO Platform as a space for a real exchange among societies on concrete issues and topics. Through its engagement in the platform, ANND aims to promote the participation of Arab civil society and facilitating the shaping of the future of the partnership.

ANND consistently works on developing an interactive website that can contribute to providing Arab civil society with the needed resources and information, a website that facilitates the exchange of ideas and experiences among various civil society groups within and outside the region. ANND perceives a necessity in using all available resources, including information and communication technologies, to improve the performance and productivity of civil society. This can help the latter to enrich its experience and improve the outreach to groups with minimum time and efforts. It also contributes to elaborating a strategy for the use of information and communication technologies for the purposes of development.

Analyzing the Obstacles: Where Do They Lie?

The lack of national governmental policies in many areas in the first place, and the lack of trust in the ability to affect policies due to undemocratic political systems and regimes, led civil society organizations in the Arab region to distrust advocacy and policy-oriented work and invest in direct service provision, where outcomes tend to be more tangible on the quantitative side.

On the other hand, there has been a strong polarization of perspectives on key issues within the Arab societies, especially concerning issues of reform and democratization and the role of religion. An emerging paradox is evident with the accusations against local civil society groups of holding foreign agendas when they struggle for more space, for an effective political participation, and for reforms and human rights. Democracy and human rights are even seen by some civil society groups as a product of globalization and therefore are rejected. Accordingly, the severe opposition in perspectives on these issues, especially the factor of foreign interference and the position held due to dealing with resistance and occupation, as explained earlier in the chapter, increase the division between organizations and limit co-operation and partnerships.

This reality feeds into increasing the artificial space available for civil society mobilization in the region. States put limitations on the space available to public participation and make it look very formal, and civil society organizations often take positions that do not support an increase in dialogue and negotiations, putting more pressures on democratic debates.[21] This is mainly the result of the mistrust between the state and the society and the fear of civil society organizations of being co-opted and thus losing their independence and freedom to manoeuvre.

In many countries, engaging civil society in negotiations and dialogue with the government is highly criticized and seen as a co-option and dominance by the government over the society. In many other countries, the rejection of participation is from both sides; the government wants to set the frames and the rules of the participation, and the civil society organizations in turn negatively respond to this participation. This raises another question about the understanding of the role of civil society organizations and the ways of achieving effective engagement leading to positive change.

The main need in this regard is that of elaborating clear visions and propositions for alternatives by civil society. This will be followed by the creation of national coalitions able to conduct internal open debate on various issues and topics leading to the elaboration of an alternative agenda. Then advocacy campaigns and lobbying can be organized using different means and tools, including negotiations, active participation, and engagement with governments.

Accordingly, the main concern revolves around the ability of civil society organizations in the Arab region to actually engage in suggesting alternatives, especially when they are faced with such limited space to manoeuvre and work on the national as well as regional levels. In this regard, it is important to see the rise of global civil society as an additional support and space for their causes.

The more internet use and information sharing, in addition to spillover from issues of the Arab region onto international politics, the more civil society groups from the region will address global linkages of issues they work on and link up with other actors at the global level.

And with the realization of new threats as priority areas, new trends of work and networking will be emerging. Moreover, the more civil society organizations in the Arab region realize certain international threats as priorities over regional and national problems, the more common platforms and strategies will be shared with global civil society. In this process, it is important to work toward limiting the tendency for competition while enhancing the culture of partnership, networking, and fostering complementarities.

This interaction between civil society in the Arab region and that at the global level contributes to enlarging the former's vision on various issues and facilitating the adoption of a more comprehensive approach to face the challenges and the threats to the region.

CONCLUSION

The rise of a more elaborated role for global civil society promotes democracy, good governance, and social justice in the current global system and among its institutions. The development of global civil society dynamics is linked to the elaboration of common platforms in the face of common threats and challenges. But it is also directly related to availability of (1) more democratic spaces for the rise of global civil society dynamics, (2) more exchange between the actors of these dynamics, and (3) more dialogue and tolerance among these actors.

This chapter assumes that civil society must originally gain a place at the national level in order to secure adequate national representation and engage with the main national challenges. This is a necessary process toward developing a role in global issues and addressing challenges through global channels.

The chapter has explored the challenges and obstacles preventing Arab civil society from being active and effective at the national level, and accordingly limiting its participation at the global level as an effective partner within a global civil society movement.

Accordingly, in order to empower civil society to move toward engaging in a proactive agenda with a clear perspective for change, networking experiences in the Arab region need to address the objective and subjective challenges that civil society faces.

Together, civil society groups should challenge the space available to them and not accommodate to it. They should address a comprehensive reform agenda that includes political as well as economic, social, and cultural reforms. Networking initiatives emerging in the region should courageously address the need to open spaces for dialogue among civil society groups on challenging and debatable issues in the region, including the notion of sovereignty and identity, the centrality of peace and security and its relation to socio-economic challenges, the notion of citizenship, the role of religion, and the relation of the state and civil society.

The coming together of Arab organizations through networking processes should help to enhance their role beyond service provision and toward advocacy and policy-oriented work. It should also support a more constructive engagement and dialogue with governments and international institutions.

Under these directions, ANND has focused on an advocacy strategy around social and economic rights. It is committed to working on governance issues and following up on the implementation of related declarations and commitments of Arab governments at the UN summits. In addition, ANND works toward active engagement with regional and international institutions influencing socio-economic rights.

In this context, ANND consistently invests in the creation of national and regional civil society coalitions that engage in advocacy campaigns. In the quest to strengthen this campaigning, ANND seeks to make available opportunities for developing resources and information that promotes dialogue and debate. It perceives a necessity in investing in civil society resource centres and think tanks in the Arab region, which could further contribute to exchanging and engaging with various global processes, networks, and institutions.

NOTES

1   Kenneth Anderson and David Reiff, "Global Civil Society: A Skeptical View," in *Global Civil Society 2004/5*, ed. Helmut K. Anheier, Mary Kaldor and Marlies Glasius. (London: Sage Publications, 2004), 29.

2   Ibid.

3   Ibid.

4   Mohamad Sayed-Said, "Global Civil Society: An Arab Perspective," in *Global Civil Society 2004/5*, 69.

5   Anderson and Reiff, "A Skeptical View," 29.

6   Ibid., 27.

7   Jan Aart Scholte, "Civil Society and Democracy in Global Governance," Working Paper No. 65/01, Centre for the Study of Globalisation and Regionalisation, University of Warwick, January 2001.

8   See the Arab Human Development Reports, http://hdr.undp.org/.

9   Sayed-Said, "An Arab Perspective," 60–76.

10 Ibid.

11 Amani Kandil, "Status of the Third Sector in the Arab Region," in *Citizens: Strengthening Global Civil Society*, ed. Miguel Darcy de Oliveira and Rajesh Tandon (Washington, DC: CIVICUS, 1994), 107–44.

12 Ziad Abdel Samad, "Civil Society in the Arab Region: Its Necessary Role and the Obstacles to Fulfillment," unpublished conference paper, "Strengthening Civil Society in the Arab Region: Models for Legal Reform," Washington, DC: International Center for Non-Profit Law, 2006.

13 Lester M. Salamon, S. Wojciech Sokolowski, and Regina List, "Global Civil Society: An Overview," in *Global Civil Society, Vol. 2: Dimensions of the Nonprofit Sector*, ed. Lester M. Salamon et al. (Bloomfield, CT: Kumerian Press), 3–60.

14 Scholte, "Civil Society and Democracy."

15 Hiba Raouf Ezzat, "Beyond Methodological Modernism: Towards a Multicultural Paradigm Shift in the Social Sciences," in *Global Civil Society 2004/5*, 40–60.

16 Ibid., 45.

17 Abdel Samad, "Civil Society in the Arab Region."

18 A group of Lebanese and Tunisian NGOs organized a regional preparatory meeting for the Social Summit on Social Development in Lebanon in July 1994. The meeting nominated a regional follow-up committee representing twelve Arab countries. The Arab caucus, during the summit in March 1995 in Copenhagen,

established the preparatory committee of the Arab network, which organized the first founding general assembly of the network in Beirut in July 1997.

19 "Liberals and humanists saw the rise of global civil society as a promise of liberation from the suffocating domestic environment and external pressures." Sayed-Said, "An Arab Perspective," 60.

20 The Barcelona process is the initiative launched during the Summit of the European and Mediterranean countries, held in November 1995. The aim of the Summit was to create a zone of peace and security, prosperity and free trade. The countries participating in the summit issued the "Barcelona Declaration" calling for the Euro-Mediterranean Partnership. The Southern Mediterranean partners in the process include Morocco, Tunisia, Algerian, Egypt, Jordan, Israel, Palestine, Syria, and Lebanon. The process included negotiations between the EU and the partner countries on bilateral association agreement, leading to a free trade area by the year 2010. All the involved countries signed these association agreements except Syria, which is still negotiating.

21 Raouf Ezzat, "Beyond Methodological Modernism," 56.

7

A Case of NGO Participation

International Criminal Court Negotiations

Gina E. Hill

INTRODUCTION

Non-governmental organizations (NGOs) are a growing force in the global dynamic. Several recent instances have demonstrated the power NGOs have to influence the course of events and the value of their contributions to multilateral treaty negotiations. The negotiations for an International Criminal Court is one such case. This chapter examines how NGOs came to collaborate on the matter of the ICC, and how the Coalition for an International Criminal Court came to be. It then examines the four main categories in which NGOs made contributions to the course of the negotiations: advocacy, education and information-sharing, logistics organization, and media and public outreach. The chapter concludes with an overview of the innovative collaboration between NGOs themselves, and between NGOs and states, that took place during the ICC talks.

The International Criminal Court (ICC or the Court) was a long time in coming—it had first been proposed by the founders of the International Committee of the Red Cross in 1872, but the concept did not have enough international support to become a reality. After the First and Second World Wars, a number of international criminal tribunals and commissions were formed, but all were ad hoc, situation-specific fora.

In 1993 the International Criminal Tribunal for the Former Yugoslavia was established to deal with international humanitarian law violations that took place in Yugoslavia after 1991. A similar tribunal, the International Criminal Tribunal for Rwanda, was established in 1994. The atrocities happening in Yugoslavia and Rwanda, as well as the relative success of these two tribunals, led to a renewed interest in the idea of an international criminal court to deal with such crimes. The fact that the Cold War was over allowed states to step away from previously overarching ideological constraints, thereby contributing to a new vision of accountability for violations of international criminal law and humanitarian law.

International talks began with a draft statute for the ICC prepared by the International Law Commission (ILC) at the request of the United Nations General Assembly.[1] Following this draft, the Ad Hoc Committee on the Establishment of an International Criminal Court was established and met twice in 1995, allowing government delegations to become familiar with the issues, and to discuss substantive and administrative aspects of the proposed court.[2] The General Assembly followed up the Ad Hoc Committee's work by convening the Preparatory Committee on the Establishment of an International Criminal Court (PrepCom) to begin refining the draft for the statute presented by the ILC, and to finalize a consolidated draft that could be brought to a diplomatic conference, ready for signature and ratification by states.

PrepCom met for a total of twelve weeks of working sessions between 1996 and 1998. Between Ad Hoc Committee meetings and PrepCom sessions, informal intersessional meetings were held to further the discussions and progress being made at the formal PrepCom sessions. Two additional preparatory meetings were held prior to the Rome Diplomatic Conference, which took place over five weeks from June 15 to July 17, 1998.[3]

NGOS AS PARTICIPANTS

NGOs played a significant role in the ICC negotiations, along with the usual participants in international multilateral negotiations—the United Nations and states.

The Court was conceived and promoted at the United Nations, and it is through the UN that states were able to come together to negotiate a strategy for dealing with the most horrendous crimes. The ICC incorporates—and serves—some of the most important objectives of the UN Charter.[4] Several UN agencies were involved in the development of the ICC Statute, and the UN Secretariat was responsible for running the PrepCom and the Rome Conference.[5] The UN wanted the negotiations to succeed and did what was within its purview to ensure that they did.

States were, of course, the key participants in the development of the ICC. Over the course of the negotiations the positions states took regarding crucial elements of the negotiations fell into certain patterns. Based on those patterns, states formed groupings in order to strengthen their negotiating positions. None of the groups were fixed, and in many cases states moved in and out of negotiating blocs depending on the issue in question. Three broad negotiating groups emerged: the "like-minded group" (LMG),[6] the P-5,[7] and the "non-aligned movement."[8]

In addition to states and the United Nations, non-governmental organizations were instrumental in the creation and development of the ICC Statute. Throughout the process, starting with the Ad Hoc Committee, through the PrepCom, and at the Rome Conference, NGOs maintained a high level of involvement. Among the leading non-governmental organizations working on this issue were Amnesty International, Human Rights Watch, Lawyers Committee for Human Rights, the International Commission of Jurists, the International Institute of Higher Studies in Criminal Sciences, the Women's Caucus, and No Peace Without Justice.[9] These eventually joined with others to become the NGO Coalition for an International Criminal Court (CICC or Coalition). Most NGO contributions to the ICC process were made under the umbrella of this coalition.[10]

Coalition for an International Criminal Court

Creation of CICC

A handful of non-governmental organizations first started to work together on the issue of the International Criminal Court in 1994, at the instigation of the World Federalist Movement.[11] NGOs observing the progress of talks worried that movement toward a permanent court would be slowed down by eternal negotiations.[12] The CICC's objectives were stated as follows: "The main purpose of the NGO Coalition for an International Criminal Court is to advocate the creation of an effective and just International Criminal Court."[13] The NGOs involved wanted to be in a position to influence the negotiations, and in particular wanted to provide assistance to the group of like-minded states that supported the establishment of an ICC. Non-governmental organizations were encouraged by the successes of previous NGO coalitions working on issues of environment, disarmament, women's issues, and, in particular, the recent International Campaign to Ban Landmines.[14]

As details about the Coalition's mandate and methods of working together were finalized, Amnesty International took on the role of approaching other non-governmental organizations to encourage them to participate.[15] The Coalition for an International Criminal Court was formalized on February 25, 1995. Several of the original NGOs became members of the self-selected steering committee of the CICC,[16] with the World Federalist Movement serving as secretariat of the Coalition.[17]

The number of NGOs affiliated with the CICC grew steadily: at the first PrepCom session there were forty-six NGOs in the CICC; by the fifth session there were over 300 NGOs; and by the opening of the Rome Conference over 800 organizations were part of the Coalition.[18] As a result, the participating NGOs were able to increase their efforts at the site of the negotiations, as well as regionally and nationally, in significant ways.

NGOs Generally

Non-governmental organizations with radically different backgrounds came together as members of the Coalition. These included women's organizations, peace and conflict resolution organizations, global governance and UN-oriented groups, and members of religious organizations. Despite this variety, organizations of legal professionals and human rights-focused groups constituted almost half the organizations registered at the Rome Conference.[19] Some organizations were large international organizations, such as Amnesty International and Human Rights Watch, while others were smaller—regional or local groups such as the Aotearoa/New Zealand Foundation for Peace Studies and the Stavropol Association of Women Lawyers.[20]

Naturally, NGOs with varying areas of interest did not always agree on the best way forward for the ICC. This was particularly challenging when talks came to the specifics related to broad principles. Some NGOs came to the negotiations with extremely detailed and specific positions on "literally hundreds of issues."[21] On the matter of gender issues within the statute, for example, there were very heated debates among state delegates arguing from different religious and cultural backgrounds. Positions were similarly divergent among NGOs. Amnesty International, for instance, took a strong pro-gender stance, supporting the full integration of a gender perspective into the statute of the ICC, including with regard to issues of forced abortion and enforced pregnancy.[22] Other organizations, like REAL Women of Canada, lobbied strenuously against the inclusion of the term "gender" in the statute, arguing that it may have impacts beyond the context of the ICC.[23]

Fergus Watt, convenor for the Canadian Network for an International Criminal Court, explains that in fact there were few areas where NGOs had strong disagreement; more often there would be a shared view of a larger question with differences only as to the degree.[24] Despite differing opinions on some of the details, by and large NGOs working together under the CICC umbrella were able to focus on the main points required to ensure an independent and effective Court—a Court with automatic jurisdiction and an independent prosecutor. Indeed, there was an interesting tension at Rome, since the Coalition itself resisted taking positions on the issues. Instead it preferred "to maintain both the plurality of ideas and objectives represented by the coalition and the solidarity among its members."[25] In any case, despite disagreement on some specifics, the strong NGO support for an ICC demonstrated the massive popular backing for the initiative.

Because NGOs had been such strong contributors during the preparatory stages, they were given unprecedented access to meetings at the Rome Conference.[26] In its resolution for the Rome Conference the General Assembly included guidelines for the participation of non-governmental organizations.[27] NGOs were entitled to address the opening and closing sessions. They were also entitled to attend plenary meetings and most subsidiary meetings. The general rule was that NGOs were free to attend as observers. If a country objected, the chair of the working group would ask the NGOs to leave. It helped that most chairs of working groups were from like-minded countries and favourably disposed to NGOs.[28]

The fact that NGOs could participate as observers meant that their presence was felt in the room. They could receive copies of official documents and distribute their materials to delegates. Once a session ended, NGO members could immediately approach—and be approached by—key delegates. In addition, informal working group meetings were also opened to NGO attendance. As a result, NGOs had official access to many of the negotiating sessions. CICC members also held regular meetings with the bureau of the Preparatory Committee where they distributed materials. A total of 236 NGOs were accredited to participate in the Rome Conference, and they were represented by an estimated 450 individuals.[29]

CNICC

In Canada, a coalition of non-governmental organizations came together to work in support of the creation of the ICC. The first call for participation went out in 1995, when the World Federalists of Canada announced that they would provide administrative support for the network, to be called the Canadian Network for an International Criminal Court (CNICC). The CNICC, which worked closely with the New York–based Coalition for an International Criminal Court, was not intended as a location for political activities of individual members, but was envisioned primarily as an information-sharing network.[30]

While regular government–NGO briefings were the primary focus for CNICC efforts, the network also organized roundtable discussions on the ICC, regularly published the "ICC Update" newsletter, lobbied key parliamentarians, participated in the work organized by the CICC in New York, and made key documents available to all those interested in the proceedings. These activities ensured an open flow of communication and sharing of strategies between the Canadian government and NGOs interested in the creation of the ICC.

Women's Caucus

Of particular note among NGOs working together to promote human rights in the ICC negotiations is the group that came together as the Women's Caucus for Gender Justice in the ICC. The Women's Caucus, a sub-section of the CICC group, came into being in February 1997[31] when NGOs concerned with women's rights realized that women's issues were not being incorporated into the discussions[32] and were not reflected in the draft Statute. The Women's Caucus successfully pressed for gender perspectives to be integrated into all aspects of the ICC's jurisdiction, structure, and operation.[33] This sub-grouping of NGOs was remarkable in that it demonstrated the ability of NGOs to negotiate two layers of joint work concurrently: the broader goal of the establishment of an ICC and the integration of gender issues in the Court.

One of the more controversial positions taken by the Women's Caucus was that of promoting use of the term *gender* as differentiated from *sex*. Those lobbying for this inclusion saw the concept *sex* as restricted to biological differences, whereas the term *gender* takes into account perceived differences between women and men because of their socially constructed roles.[34] They succeeded in having gender crimes and sex crimes specifically listed as war crimes and crimes against humanity, as well as the inclusion of special measures for victims of sexual violence. Valerie Oosterveld, an NGO delegate on the Canadian negotiating team with a particular responsibility for gender issues, notes that the Women's Caucus worked closely with the like-minded group. As a result it was successful in having virtually all of its recommendations included in the ICC Statute, and in convincing most delegations that gender references needed to be included in the Statute.[35]

By the time of the final session of PrepCom, the Women's Caucus included approximately 300 supporters, women's organizations, and legal and gender experts, representing all regions of the globe.[36] These organizations actively lobbied their own governments at home and delegations in Rome. The Women's Caucus is well-recognized for its ability to maintain focus in principles and cohesion of members despite the pressures of the negotiations. As two commentators put it, "The Women's Caucus demonstrated a remarkable capacity for keeping its diverse and talented delegation of women from around the world focused on the inclusion of the gender-related crimes in the Statute, even in the face of sustained opposition from a number of States."[37]

ACTIVITIES OF NGOS

NGOs made significant contributions to the negotiations during the talks leading up to the diplomatic conference and in Rome itself. While there is overlap between these categories, NGO activities during the ICC negotiations can generally be broken down into four streams: (1) advocacy, (2) education and information-sharing, (3) logistics organization, and (4) media and public outreach.

Advocacy

NGOs have a long and established track record of arguing that governments should take a certain position on any given subject. In acting as advocates, NGOs used their skills and experience and the various avenues open to them, including consulting, holding strategy sessions, lobbying, and contributing NGO representatives to government delegations.

Consulting

During the two meetings of the Ad Hoc Committee in 1995, NGOs began to forge co-operative working relations with the growing number of like-minded states. The Ad Hoc meetings provided an open and collaborative environment in which it was easy for state delegates to share the experience of the process with the NGOs that were present. While the CICC was initially small— around thirty NGOs were observing the Ad Hoc Committee work—and in the course of developing its own processes, the NGO presence at the Ad Hoc Committee allowed for governments and NGOs to begin to consult with one another and to develop ways of working together that would carry through to the Rome Conference.[38] During PrepCom and at Rome, NGOs continued to create opportunities to hold consultations with governments.

Strategy

NGOs began holding strategy sessions with national delegations at the Ad Hoc Committee meetings and stayed in contact with like-minded delegations between meetings. As PrepCom progressed, like-minded governments began to rely on NGO input in preparation for plenary debates and for the development of technical issues in the draft Statute. The Coalition used this reliance to encourage LMG countries to be strategic in their role in drafting the treaty, including considering the strength they would have working as a bloc. Indeed, the fact that the LMG adopted a list of six principles to guide their efforts was largely a result of their interaction with NGOs.[39]

Lobbying

From the beginning of the first talks, NGOs lobbied governments in order to promote the creation of the Court. Coalition members approached governments in national capitals—including departments of justice, foreign affairs, and defence—to encourage them to become involved in the process of negotiating the ICC.[40] In addition, NGOs used other opportunities to raise the issues with government officials, such as intergovernmental conferences like the American Heads of State summit in Santiago de Chile in 1998. NGOs also benefited from the more relaxed atmosphere of the informal meetings between PrepCom sessions, where NGO and government delegates were seen as equals and many of the usual diplomatic restrictions were lifted.[41]

Unsympathetic delegations felt direct pressure through public shaming by NGOs,[42] while governments that supported the establishment of an ICC had both practical and philosophical support of Coalition members. During Prep-Com sessions the LMG and the CICC began to confer closely and regularly on issues such as strategies for debates and specific technical elements, and this relationship continued as the draft Statute evolved.[43]

Regular meetings between the Coalition and the like-minded countries contributed to the development of principled approaches to key issues.[44] NGO representatives, at PrepCom sessions and at the Rome Conference, used every opportunity before and after working party meetings, plenary sessions, and corridor encounters to press friendly governments to promote a strong court.[45] Indeed, it has been pointed out that lobbying was such a core activity of NGOs at the Conference, that there was no separate NGO forum at the Rome Conference as there had been at previous international conferences.[46]

Participation on Government Delegations

In the lead-up to the Rome diplomatic conference, some states came to rec-ognize the unique contribution to be made by non-governmental organizations and invited select NGOs to participate as part of government delegations.[47] The Canadian delegation, for example, included two NGO members, David Matas and Valerie Oosterveld, representing Amnesty International and the International Centre for Human Rights and Democratic Development (now Rights and Democracy) respectively. While these members were expected to participate as full members of the government delegation, and to publicly take the positions the government was taking, they were nevertheless in a position to share the views of NGOs on an informal basis. Matas relates that when he was not in official meetings, he spent most of his time in the NGO lounge area, thereby creating a valuable link between the Canadian delegation and NGOs.[48] This was a very direct avenue for NGOs to advocate their positions, as they had the ear of members of their own delegation as well as participants on other delegations.

Education and Information Sharing

Another role NGOs have traditionally been effective in carrying out is provid-ing education and information-sharing. In the context of the ICC negotiations, NGOs did this by offering subject matter expertise, by promoting national and regional education on the ICC, by facilitating caucus strategy meetings, and by providing coverage of all the meetings taking place at the Conference.

NGO Expertise

NGOs supported their advocacy work with governments by providing education on matters where NGOs had more expertise. Throughout the negotiations, NGOs produced papers offering expert analysis of issues under consideration and made these available to government delegates and UN secretariat officials.[49] The CICC published expert papers on key issues, which usually took one of two forms: journal articles, or NGO reports. In both cases the intention was to inform and influence the readers.[50]

These expert papers assisted delegates in gaining a deeper understanding of the various facets of the issues in debate. Position papers were designed as easy-to-use manuals and covered the relevant international law, standards, and practice of the topics under consideration. They also identified strengths and weaknesses of the current proposals under each chapter of the Statute. Expert papers also provided options for the negotiation of specific items. CICC member NGOs examined the ramifications of the different positions on various issues and proposed options to government delegations.[51] Such papers were particularly valuable as discussions shifted from philosophical approaches to technical details as PrepCom meetings progressed.[52]

NGOs also made available the substantial legal and technical expertise they had accumulated over the years, in the form of briefings and legal memoranda. Indeed, because NGOs were usually permitted to attend discussions as observers, they were occasionally called upon to contribute to discussions in areas where they had expertise. NGO expertise was also called upon when text was being drafted.[53]

NGOs also facilitated formal sessions and informal conversations between NGO experts and delegates, which stimulated creative thinking, and allowed for the sharing of perspectives and advice.[54] The CICC Secretariat shared articles by NGOs and governments on various issues through the *International Criminal Court Monitor,* a regular newsletter. The value of these analyses became so appreciated that they were soon expected and sought out by delegates.[55]

National and Regional Education

Coalition NGOs participated in national- and regional-level work to raise the profile of the ICC discussions taking place and to build popular support through civil society networks. Coalition members campaigned actively in their home countries[56] through events such "as public seminars and debates, book fairs, meetings with embassy officials,... and letters to governments."[57] These activities took place in over eighty countries and resulted in publications in languages as diverse as Arabic, Hindi, Romanian, and Turkish.[58]

Conferences and similar gatherings contributed to increased civil society participation. Expert meetings, public debates, seminars, symposia, and workshops were generally organized by NGOs alone or in co-operation with academic institutions and brought in speakers and resources from a range of societal groupings interested in the ICC.[59] Coalition members also made efforts to include the participation of civil society groups at the negotiations. During PrepCom, CICC NGOs met with civil society representatives from their own countries and broader regions to share different viewpoints and to enhance their understanding of various positions.[60]

Caucuses and Strategy Meetings

NGOs were well placed to acts as hubs for information sharing between governments and between governments and experts, including NGOs. At PrepCom, and continuing in Rome, the CICC convened regional caucuses to contribute to ongoing discussions.[61] The Coalition convened sectoral caucuses, such as those in the areas of gender justice, victims' rights, and children's rights.[62] There were also daily general strategy meetings for NGOs, weekly meetings with conference chairs and coordinators, and regular meetings with governments, all organized by the CICC.[63] Informal dialogue was fostered by the numerous regionally-focused meetings, convened by the CICC, between governments and NGOs.[64] In addition to national level efforts, CICC members met regularly with state delegates at the negotiation venues to exchange information and clarify positions.

Meeting Reports

Because the negotiations were so large, with often ten or more meetings going on at once, only the largest delegations could cover all the meetings with their own members. To assist with this challenge the CICC instituted thirteen teams to cover negotiations on the specific parts of the Statute.[65] Team members sat in on meetings as observers and spoke with delegates between meetings. The teams provided daily reports on negotiations, both written one-pagers and verbal reports, to NGOs as well as to governments. By making information readily available in this way, the Coalition ensured that NGO members, as well as government delegates, could get a quick overview of what was going on in all aspects of the negotiations.[66]

Logistics Organization

In order to contribute effectively during the talks, the Coalition had to be well organized, both in terms of NGO participation and the way Coalition members dialogued with governments. Initially this was relatively easy, when both the negotiations and the numbers of CICC members were small. The Coalition's skills in organization grew along with its membership and general interest in the ICC negotiations, as it provided logistical support to NGOs, coordinated experts volunteering their time, and provided support to Coalition members trying to influence home governments.

Secretariat Work

By the time of the Rome Conference the CICC was recognized as a reputable organization, and as a result the Coalition Secretariat[67] was given the task of developing and maintaining a system for accreditation of NGOs.[68] The result was one less duty for the UN Secretariat and an established position as key participant for the CICC.[69] The CICC provided staff to conduct on-site registration of NGO delegates, provided hospitality and communications services to NGOs, and hosted a reception for NGOs to improve interaction between government and NGO delegates. Hundreds of volunteers contributed to the work of the CICC Secretariat.

Expert Volunteers

In addition to practical logistical support, the CICC sponsored experts and students to attend the conference and assist delegations from developing countries. The CICC translated documents and reports and provided interpretation services for NGOs and, in some cases, for countries. Indeed, the majority of the Coalition Secretariat's work during the Rome Conference revolved primarily around supplying support services for Coalition members as well as to government delegations and the UN.[70]

National Networks

When it was felt that a state delegation was compromising on key principles, the CICC provided informal reinforcement to relevant NGOs by using its national networks to contact ministers, parliamentarians, and the media in the capital of the country in question.[71] The CICC also offered more direct assistance to governments by sponsoring interns and legal experts who could become members of government delegations as interns.[72]

Media and Public Outreach

NGOs took on the role of primary contact for the media by making information easily accessible, by issuing press releases, and by conducting interviews. In addition, CICC members facilitated public engagement by organizing demonstrations.

Electronic Information

From early in the negotiations, the CICC was the main source of information for what was happening in the ICC negotiations. As early as 1995 the Coalition created a listserv to quickly disseminate information to NGOs and governments, and a year later the CICC established a website on the ICC negotiations. As it was able, the Coalition extended these services in key languages other than English. In addition, individual membership organizations, like Amnesty International and some churches, disseminated information on the development of the Court to their members.[73]

Publications

At the Rome Conference, the CICC arranged for two daily publications and an online bulletin; *Terra Viva, On-the-Record,* and the *ICC Monitor* were the only sources of print and electronic coverage of the proceedings.[74] The daily *Terra Viva* was well regarded and had a wide readership. As two participants put it, the paper "discussed problems of principle, reported on regional or national situations or positions, and reviewed developments at the conference itself."[75]

Press Releases and Interviews

Prior to the Rome Conference, the CICC facilitated awareness-raising efforts undertaken by NGOs and other interested parties by providing background information, synopses, and other materials to work from. This made it easier for NGOs to use their in-house media infrastructures to inform sectors of the public with whom they were in communication.

Although PrepCom meetings were open to NGOs, media were barred from the sessions and therefore relied on NGO reports of the negotiations. The CICC cooperated with the UN Correspondents Association to hold news conferences at PrepComs. Once the Rome Conference got under way, local and international media were anxious for information but continued to get very little from governments. As a result, they again looked to NGOs for information about what was happening during the talks. The Coalition provided regular briefings for international and regional press representatives. The CICC organized one-on-one sessions for members of the press with Coalition experts. In addition, NGOs provided information to national media in their home countries thereby allowing information to be disseminated to audiences around the world.[76]

Demonstrations

Some Coalition members, such as Amnesty International, organized marches by candlelight and other demonstrations to promote their advocacy.[77] At least one powerful demonstration took place inside the facilities. On the third day of the conference the Mothers of Plaza de Mayo protested the disappearance of political prisoners in Argentina while the Justice Minister of Argentina was speaking. They were forcibly removed, and security measures were put in place to avoid future incidents.[78] Nevertheless, public demonstrations continued outside the Food and Agriculture Organization (FAO) building. As one participant reported, "One evening hundreds of candles shine invitingly in front of the FAO. Another evening activists and some representatives of the world public are lying down on the hot asphalt, holding hands in silence."[79]

It has been widely recognized that the work of the NGOs was professional and productive and that the participation of NGOs in the creation of the ICC Statute "significantly contributed to the positive outcome in Rome."[80] Through the tireless activities of the CICC and NGOs, the work of non-governmental organizations sustained and strengthened the momentum of the process both in the talks leading up to Rome and during the diplomatic conference itself.

CONCLUSION: INNOVATIVE COLLABORATION

The NGO Coalition for an International Criminal Court has been recognized as a breakthrough in how NGOs co-operate to move forward an agenda.[81] In addition to working with one another in new and innovative ways, NGOs also interacted with governments and their delegations in ways that had not been common until then.

Collaboration among NGOs

As seen above, NGOs pooled resources, knowledge, skills, and energies in order to ensure that a strong, effective international court be established. This was a remarkable development in the history of NGOs, as typically NGOs prefer to work independently[82] so as to be able to pursue their own agendas. The Coalition for an International Criminal Court was well organized and efficient and had a significant impact on the talks leading up to Rome and at the Rome Conference itself. Many attribute the Coalition's success to the insight and skills of William Pace, the CICC's convenor. He brought to his role substantial political know-how, a knack for fundraising, and an ability to manage.[83] It is largely because of his abilities, and the confidence he inspired in conference organizers, that NGOs were granted such broad access to the proceedings and government delegates at Rome.[84]

Many of the NGOs in the Coalition were small—a good number from the Global South—and some were themselves umbrella organizations.[85] However, large internationally recognized NGOs were also members of the Coalition, and because of their stature their views were often sought by states and NGOs alike. Organizations such as Amnesty International, Human Rights Watch, the International Commission of Jurists, Lawyers Committee for Human Rights, the Women's Caucus, and the International Committee of the Red Cross made frequent and detailed contributions to the negotiations and contributed their not insignificant resources to the Coalition's efforts.

This constellation of diverse NGOs within the Coalition makes it all the more remarkable that the CICC worked so well together and was able to maintain cohesion throughout the negotiations. William Pace, Convenor of the CICC, has reflected:

> Historically classical divisions tear apart the solidarity: North and South divisions, ethnic and racial, competing egos and mandates of large international NGOs, the conflict between peace groups, victims groups, the conflict between the women's caucus and the right to life organizations, the conflict which arises when one group's issues are winning and another's are losing, and on and on.[86]

Yet these traditional divisions did not damage the cohesion of the CICC.[87] Despite the potential for differences between NGOs to overshadow their commonalities, Coalition members were so committed to the principle of a strong and independent court that they pulled together to make it a reality.

From the outset the CICC as a whole did not advocate any particular position on the various aspects of the Statute, though individual members of the Coalition did.[88] More important than individual positions was that the views of Coalition members converged significantly on what would constitute an acceptable treaty, namely that it be independent and effective. Some believe that it was largely because of this shared conviction that NGOs were able to maintain a high degree of organization and coordination throughout the duration of the talks.[89]

There were, or course, instances where NGOs did not share the same perspective on the desired approach to particular issues. For example, though the majority of NGOs in the Coalition supported the integration of gender perspectives in the Statute, there was a small but strong group of NGOs who opposed this development. Just as states did not always agree with one another, so did NGOs differ in their views, and there was negotiation among NGOs—as among states—in an effort to find some common ground. The Coalition's goal was not to have consensus on each and every issue, but rather to allow NGOs to work together where it would be helpful to do so. As two participants describe it, "the Coalition Secretariat worked to identify and expand areas of commonality among its members and encouraged them to develop joint positions and strategies where possible."[90] Indeed, the consistent neutrality of the Coalition contributed to the cohesiveness of its members who were free to agree or disagree with one another on each issue.[91]

Collaboration between NGOs and Governments

While the co-operation between NGOs and the LMG is not beyond critique,[92] the extent of collaboration between NGOs and governments was unusually high during the ICC negotiations. While states and non-governmental organizations are "frequently in opposition" in multilateral negotiations, this was not the case here.[93] NGOs collaborated especially well with delegates from the like-minded group, particularly once both sides recognized how they could benefit from working together. NGOs could learn what was happening behind closed doors from LMG delegates, and like-minded states could use NGOs to pressure other delegations.[94] There was also at least one issue where some NGOs worked closely with non-LMG delegations. During the discussions on gender and forced pregnancy, pro-life NGOs collaborated with Arabic states, and benefited from the support of the Holy See.[95]

The development of political sophistication of the Coalition and of the LMG seemed to parallel each other over the course of PrepCom, and to some extent each could be said to have contributed to the other's growing cohesiveness.[96] There are many examples of the growing interconnectedness of the NGOs and the LMG. For instance, during PrepCom like-minded governments secured a room at the UN in which the Coalition could meet. Later, in the last PrepCom session, NGOs persuaded the LMG to develop a set of stated guiding principles that would direct their positions and discussions with other states.[97] It is remarkable that NGOs and states worked together to promote one another's interests to such an extent.

As described above, many governments benefited from services provided by the CICC during the negotiations. In turn, NGOs made their views heard by offering written reports and position papers and by speaking directly with delegates during negotiations and on breaks. While NGOs benefited from having the ear of LMG delegates, the opposite was also true. As one participant explains, "It was not uncommon for government representatives to call on NGO lobbyists to promote a particular point of view, and for members of the CICC to urge government representatives of Like-Minded States to push for the inclusion of certain provisions in the ICC Statute."[98] Indeed, NGOs were assured that virtually any position they wanted to advance would be taken up by at least one state delegate and brought to the negotiation.[99]

The International Criminal Court that was successfully called into being on July 17, 1998, had been the focus of periodic attention for decades. It finally became a reality when international political will and the determined effort of key players combined to clear the way. UN Secretary General Kofi Annan has summarized the experience well: "No doubt, many of us would have liked a Court vested with even more far-reaching powers, but that should not lead us to minimize the breakthrough you have achieved. The establishment of the Court is still a gift of hope to future generations, and a giant step forward in the march towards universal human rights and the rule of law."[100] Though the result was not entirely to everyone's satisfaction, it did nevertheless constitute a strong and independent court.

The process also provided an opportunity for states and NGOs to work closely together. State delegations—particularly those of the like-minded nations—were open to the input of NGOs. In turn, NGOs worked in co-operation during three years of PrepCom meetings and at the Rome Conference to ensure that a strong court was founded. Over the course of talks NGOs and states developed a collaborative relationship that helped them achieve their shared goal and demonstrated that they could work together in constructive ways.

Regardless of perceived shortcomings in the partnership among NGOs, and between states and non-governmental organizations in the ICC negotiations, NGOs were particularly effective in the areas of advocacy, providing education and sharing information, contributing to logistics organization, and in communicating with media and the public. Participants and observers alike have generally agreed that the extent of collaboration witnessed in these discussions was the most advanced seen in any multilateral treaty negotiations to that point. Indeed, the negotiations for the International Criminal Court serve as the high-water mark for such collaborative efforts.

NOTES

Many thanks to Dr. David J. Leech for his helpful comments.

1 UNGA Res. 47/33, 1992.
2 M. Cherif Bassiouni, "Negotiating the Treaty of Rome on the Establishment of an International Criminal Court," *Cornell International Law Journal* 32 (1999): 444. During these meetings delegations did not discuss an actual draft, nor did they enter into negotiations as such. The issues considered included the establishment and composition of the Court; issues related to jurisdiction; types of proceedings; due process; relationship between States Parties, non-State Parties, and the ICC; and budget and administrations issues; Adriaan Bos, "From the International Law Commission to the Rome Conference (1994–1998)," in *The Rome Statute of the International Criminal Court: A Commentary,* ed. Anthonio Cassese, Paola Gaeta, and John R.W.D. Jones (Oxford: Oxford University Press, 2002), 38.
3 Rome Statute of the International Criminal Court, adopted by the United Nations Diplomatic Conference of Plenipotentiaries on the Establishment of an International Criminal Court on 17 July 1998, UN Doc. A/CONF.183/9 (1998) [hereafter ICC Statute or Rome Statute].
4 Fanny Benedetti and John L. Washburn, "Drafting the International Criminal Court Treaty: Two Years to Rome and an Afterword on the Rome Diplomatic Conference," *Global Governance* 5 (1999): 23–25. The ICC would also have the effect of legitimizing the UN at a time when nations were beginning to question its effectiveness and its very existence. The court would make the UN more relevant to the lives of human beings around the world.
5 Benedetti and Washburn, "Drafting the International Criminal Court Treaty: Two Years to Rome and an Afterword on the Rome Diplomatic Conference," 4.

6 This was the first and best organized grouping to form. Its members tended to be in favour of a strong court with an independent, powerful prosecutor. Members of this group were generally middle powers and developing countries. The like-minded group started with several European states, Argentina, Australia, Canada, New Zealand, and South Africa, and eventually grew to over sixty states; Bos, "From the International Law Commission to the Rome Conference (1994–1998)," 50; William R. Pace and Jennifer Schense, "The Role of Non-Governmental Organizations," in *The Rome Statute of the International Criminal Court: A Commentary*, 119, fn. 35.

7 This grouping of states consisted of the permanent members of the Security Council: the United States, the United Kingdom, China, France, and Russia. Their main concern was ensuring a strong role for the Security Council, and ensuring that nuclear weapons and crimes of aggression were not included in the Statute. Over the course of the negotiations, the UK joined the like-minded group, and France ultimately voted for the court; Philippe Kirsch and Darryl Robinson, "Reaching Agreement at the Rome Conference," in *The Rome Statute of the International Criminal Court: A Commentary*, 71; Benedetti and Washburn, "Drafting the International Criminal Court Treaty: Two Years to Rome and an Afterword on the Rome Diplomatic Conference," 31.

8 This grouping of states was less stable than the others. Its members were generally opposed to the very existence of an ICC, and eventually insisted that the crime of aggression be included. Among the non-aligned states were Iraq, Iran, Lebanon, Libya, Syria, and Indonesia; Philippe Kirsch and John T. Holmes, "The Birth of the International Criminal Court: The 1998 Rome Conference," *Canadian Yearbook of International Law* 36 (1998): 10; William A. Schabas, *An Introduction to the International Criminal Court* (Cambridge: Cambridge University Press, 2001), 16.

9 M. Cherif Bassiouni, "Historical Survey: 1919–1998," in *The Statute of the International Criminal Court: A Documentary History,* ed. M. Cherif Bassiouni (New York: Transnational Publishers, 1998), 26.

10 Benedetti and Washburn, "Drafting the International Criminal Court Treaty: Two Years to Rome and an Afterword on the Rome Diplomatic Conference," 21.

11 Johan D. Van Der Vyver, "Civil Society and the International Criminal Court," *Journal of Human Rights* 2 (2003): 427; Pace and Schense, "The Role of Non-Governmental Organizations," 110.

12 Pace and Schense, "The Role of Non-Governmental Organizations," 109–10.

13 "About the Coalition," *The International Criminal Court Monitor* 7 (April 1998): 8; Van Der Vyver, "Civil Society and the International Criminal Court," 427.

14 Pace and Schense, "The Role of Non-Governmental Organizations," 111. Lloyd Axworthy, Canadian Foreign Minister at the time, spoke of the partnership between NGOs and governments that contributed to the success of the Landmines Treaty negotiations, and how similar principles could be applied to the ICC discussions; "Canadian Foreign Minister on ICC," *The International Criminal Court Monitor* 8 (June 1998): 7.

15 Pace and Schense, "The Role of Non-Governmental Organizations," 111.

16 The Steering Committee consisted of Amnesty International, European Law Students Association, Fédération Internationale des Ligues des Droits de l'Homme,

Human Rights Watch, International Commission of Jurists, Lawyers Committee for Human Rights, No Peace Without Justice, Parliamentarians for Global Action, and World Federalist Movement. Coalition for an International Criminal Court, "Members of the Coalition for an International Criminal Court (CICC) State Their Support for an Effective and Credible Court and Challenge U.S. Insistence on Security Council Jurisdiction," Press Release (13 August 1997) [on file with author].

17 Pace and Schense, "The Role of Non-Governmental Organizations," 111.

18 Ibid., 115, n. 23; Bassiouni, "Historical Survey: 1919–1998," 25, n. 131; William R. Pace and Mark Thieroff, "Participation of Non-Governmental Organizations," in *The International Criminal Court: The Making of the Rome Statute, Issues, Negotiations, Results,* ed. Roy S. Lee (Boston: Kluwer Law International, 1999), 392.

19 Marlies Glasius, "Expertise in the Cause of Justice: Global Civil Society Influence on the Statute for an International Criminal Court," in *Global Civil Society 2002,* ed. Marlies Glasius, Mary Kaldor, and Helmut Anheier (Oxford: Oxford University Press, 2002), 141.

20 The latter two organizations were members of the Coalition, but were not accredited as participating NGOs at the Rome Conference.

21 Pace and Schense, "The Role of Non-Governmental Organizations," 125.

22 Amnesty International advocated that recognition be made of gender-specific crimes committed against women, that judges and staff of the court receive special training on issues of violence against women, that female victims and witnesses receive adequate security; Amnesty International, "The International Criminal Court: Ensuring Justice for Women" (March 1998).

23 REAL Women of Canada, Position paper prepared by the David M. Kennedy Center for International Studies (? 1998) [on file with author]: "If 'gender,' as used in the ICC Draft Statute, in fact means something beyond 'male' and 'female,' the ICC will drastically restructure societies throughout the world."

24 Fergus Watt, interview with author, November 24, 2005.

25 Benedetti and Washburn, "Drafting the International Criminal Court Treaty: Two Years to Rome and an Afterword on the Rome Diplomatic Conference," 23.

26 Bassiouni, "Negotiating the Treaty of Rome on the Establishment of an International Criminal Court," 455. Negotiations at the Vienna Conference on Human Rights in 1993 and the Beijing Conference on Women in 1995 set positive precedents for greater NGO participation; Benedetti and Washburn, "Drafting the International Criminal Court Treaty: Two Years to Rome and an Afterword on the Rome Diplomatic Conference," 22.

27 UNGA Res 160, UN GAOR, 52d Sess., UN Doc. A/RES/52/160 (1998); Bos, "From the International Law Commission to the Rome Conference (1994–1998)," 59. Over the course of the PrepCom sessions the CICC also developed a good working relationship with the UN Secretariat, in particular with the Office of Legal Affairs and the bureau of the Preparatory Committee. When the presence of NGOs was challenged by a few delegations in the second PrepCom session, the Office of Legal Affairs and the bureau of the Preparatory Committee met and determined that NGOs had the right to have access to the Preparatory Committee; Pace and Schense, "The Role of Non-Governmental Organizations," 120.

28 UNGA Res 160, UN GAOR, 52d Sess., UN Doc. A/RES/52/160 (1998); only a few NGOs were given this option; Bassiouni, "Historical Survey: 1919–1998," 23; Watt.

29 Benedetti and Washburn, "Drafting the International Criminal Court Treaty: Two Years to Rome and an Afterword on the Rome Diplomatic Conference" 23; Pace and Schense, "The Role of Non-Governmental Organizations," 120; Pace and Thieroff, "Participation of Non-Governmental Organizations," 392; some of the larger NGO delegations surpassed the delegation size of some nations—for example, Amnesty International and Human Rights Watch; Philip Nel, "Between Counter-Hegemony and Post-Hegemony: The Rome Statute and Normative Innovation in World Politics," in *Enhancing Global Governance: Towards a New Diplomacy?*, ed. Andrew F. Cooper, John English, and Ramesh Thakur (New York: United Nations University Press, 2002), 158. Pace and Schense point out that the number of accredited NGOs may be misleading in that it does not reflect the sub-umbrella groups that formed under the CICC, such as the Women's Caucus for Gender Justice. Indeed the true numbers are closer to 500 NGOs participating at Rome and 1000 NGOs supporting the efforts worldwide; William R. Pace and Jennifer Schense, "Coalition for the International Criminal Court at the Preparatory Commission," in *The International Criminal Court*, ed. Roy S. Lee (Ardley, NY: Transnational Publishers, 2001), 707, n. 6. For a list of participating organizations, see *Final Act of the United Nations Diplomatic Conference of Plenipotentiaries on the Establishment of an International Criminal Court*, Annex IV, "List of Non-Governmental Organizations Represented at the Conferences by an Observer" UN Doc. A/CONF.183/10 (1998).

30 Letter from Fergus Watt, August 1995 [on file with author].

31 Women's Caucus for Gender Justice in the International Criminal Court, "Gender Justice and the ICC" (Recommendations and Commentary to the United Nations Diplomatic Conference of Plenipotentiaries on the Establishment of an International Criminal Court, June 1998) [on file with author]. See also www.iccwomen .org.

32 Barbara Bedont and David Matas, "Negotiating for an International Criminal Court," *Peace Magazine* (October 1998): 1.

33 "Core Principles of the Women's Caucus" *The International Criminal Court Monitor* 8 (June 1998): 13. See generally Women's Caucus for Gender Justice in the International Criminal Court "Gender Justice and the ICC" (Recommendations and Commentary to the United Nations Diplomatic Conference of Plenipotentiaries on the Establishment of an International Criminal Court, June 1998) [on file with author].

34 Gina Hill, "Gender in the International Criminal Court Negotiations" (Master's thesis, University of Toronto [unpublished], 2001), 90.

35 Valerie Oosterveld, interview with author, May 26, 2000; Hill, "Gender in the International Criminal Court Negotiations," 89; Van Der Vyver, "Civil Society and the International Criminal Court," 431; Cate Steains, "Gender Issues," in *The International Criminal Court: The Making of the Rome Statute, Issues, Negotiations, Results*, 361.

36 "Women's Caucus Recommendations to PrepCom Sixth Session," *The International Criminal Court Monitor* 7 (April 1998): 5. The Women's Caucus also had offices with permanent staff in New York.

37 Pace and Schense, "The Role of Non-Governmental Organizations," 134. As with
    the CICC itself, the Women's Caucus continued its work after the Rome Confer-
    ence to ensure that the gender related aspects of the ICC were properly imple-
    mented; Hill, "Gender in the International Criminal Court Negotiations," 89,
    n.409.
38 Pace and Schense, "The Role of Non-Governmental Organizations," 113.
39 Ibid., 113–19. Benedetti and Washburn explain that though the principles were
    never put into writing they were discussed frequently. They were: the independ-
    ence of the Court from the Security Council, the independence of the prosecutor,
    the extension of the Court's jurisdiction to cover all core crimes, the full cooper-
    ation of states with the Court, a successful diplomatic conference, that the Court
    have the power to decide on the ability of national judicial systems to proceed on
    cases; Benedetti and Washburn, "Drafting the International Criminal Court Treaty:
    Two Years to Rome and an Afterword on the Rome Diplomatic Conference," 21.
40 Bassiouni, "Historical Survey: 1919–1998," 26; Glasius, "Expertise in the Cause of
    Justice: Global Civil Society Influence on the Statute for an International Crimi-
    nal Court," 147; Pace and Schense, "The Role of Non-Governmental Organiza-
    tions," 117. This approach included providing summaries of the negotiations that
    had taken place to date so as to facilitate joining the discussions. In Canada, this
    lobbying most often took the form of briefing sessions between government offi-
    cials and NGOs.
41 Glasius, "Expertise in the Cause of Justice: Global Civil Society Influence on the
    Statute for an International Criminal Court," 148–49.
42 Mahnoush H. Arsanjani, "The Rome Statute of the International Criminal Court,"
    American Journal of International Law 93 (1999): 23.
43 Pace and Schense, "The Role of Non-Governmental Organizations," 119.
44 Benedetti and Washburn, "Drafting the International Criminal Court Treaty: Two
    Years to Rome and an Afterword on the Rome Diplomatic Conference," 23;
    William R. Pace, "The Relationship between the International Criminal Court and
    Non-Governmental Organizations," in *Reflections on the International Criminal Court,*
    ed. Herman A.M. von Hebel, Johan G. Lammers, and Jolien Schukking (The
    Hague: T.M.C. Asser Press, 1999), 202.
45 Watt. There was always some government delegate who would be willing to pro-
    mote something on behalf of the NGOs.
46 Glasius, "Expertise in the Cause of Justice: Global Civil Society Influence on the
    Statute for an International Criminal Court," 150.
47 Pace and Schense, "The Role of Non-Governmental Organizations" 117–18; Aus-
    tralia, Canada, and Switzerland included NGOs on their delegations. Non-govern-
    mental organizations had great input even in the selection of which NGO repre-
    sentatives would serve on such delegations. The NGO representatives on the
    Canadian delegation to the Rome Conference were recommended by the CNICC;
    Letter from Alan H. Kessel, Director United Nations, Criminal and Treaty Law
    Division of the Department of Foreign Affairs and International Trade, to Fergus
    Watt (August 12, 1998) [on file with author].
48 David Matas, December 6, 2005. Matas served on the delegation of the Canadian
    government on behalf of Amnesty International.

49 Arsanjani, "The Rome Statute of the International Criminal Court," 23; Pace and
    Schense, "The Role of Non-Governmental Organizations," 117. Papers were submit-
    ted by both groups and individuals, including Amnesty International, Human
    Rights Watch, International Commission of Jurists, Lawyers Committee for Human
    Rights, World Federalist Movement, Benjamin Ferencz, and William R. Pace. These
    and other materials were also made available through an electronic listserv.
50 Glasius, "Expertise in the Cause of Justice: Global Civil Society Influence on the
    Statute for an International Criminal Court," 150.
51 Bassiouni, "Historical Survey: 1919–1998," 26. See for example Human Rights
    Watch, "Justice in the Balance—Recommendations for an Independent and Effec-
    tive International Criminal Court," June 1998, online Human Rights Watch, http://
    www.hrw.org/reports98/icc.
52 Pace and Schense, "The Role of Non-Governmental Organizations," 116.
53 Arsanjani, "The Rome Statute of the International Criminal Court," 23. See for
    example Lawyers Committee for Human Rights, "The International Criminal
    Court Trigger Mechanism and the Need for an Independent Prosecutor" (July
    1997); Watt; Philippe Kirsch and John T. Holmes, "The Rome Conference on an
    International Criminal Court: The Negotiating Process," *American Journal of Inter-
    national Law* 93 (1999): 5; Bassiouni, "Negotiating the Treaty of Rome on the
    Establishment of an International Criminal Court," 455. During the conference
    legal experts and interns were made available by the CICC to a number of govern-
    ment delegations, including many from developing countries.
54 Bassiouni, "Historical Survey: 1919–1998," 26; Pace and Schense, "The Role of
    Non-Governmental Organizations," 113.
55 Pace and Schense, "The Role of Non-Governmental Organizations," 117.
56 There was little activity of this sort in Canada beyond a Meeting of Experts hosted
    by ICHRDD (now Rights & Democracy) on March 3–4, 1998, entitled *Accountabil-
    ity for Serious International Crimes: Towards the Creation of the International Criminal
    Court;* Watt.
57 Pace and Schense, "The Role of Non-Governmental Organizations," 122.
58 Ibid., 122.
59 Glasius, "Expertise in the Cause of Justice: Global Civil Society Influence on the
    Statute for an International Criminal Court," 150.
60 Pace and Schense, "The Role of Non-Governmental Organizations," 122; this exer-
    cise also allowed civil society groups that did not feel they were being adequately
    represented at the negotiations to have a sense that their voices were being heard.
61 Nel, "Between Counter-Hegemony and Post-Hegemony: The Rome Statute and
    Normative Innovation in World Politics," 158. Regional meetings included a highly
    effective tri-continental alliance that incorporated groups from Africa, Asia, and
    Latin America; Pace and Thieroff, "Participation of Non-Governmental Organiza-
    tions," 393.
62 Pace, "The Relationship between the International Criminal Court and Non-Gov-
    ernmental Organizations," 202; Pace and Thieroff, "Participation of Non-Govern-
    mental Organizations," 392; Van Der Vyver, "Civil Society and the International
    Criminal Court," 428.
63 Pace and Thieroff, "Participation of Non-Governmental Organizations," 393.

64 The CICC also convened several sessions for francophone and Spanish-speaking countries; ibid. 394; Nel, "Between Counter-Hegemony and Post-Hegemony: The Rome Statute and Normative Innovation in World Politics," 158.

65 Pace and Thieroff, "Participation of Non-Governmental Organizations," 394. The joke at the Rome Conference was that the NGO coalition was the largest delegation in Rome; Watt. Very few country delegations, and no single NGO, could have covered all the meetings on their own; Pace and Schense, "The Role of Non-Governmental Organizations," 127; "All Roads Lead to ... Rome Treaty Conference Opens June 15," *The International Criminal Court Monitor* 8 (June 1998): 1; Pace and Schense, "The Role of Non-Governmental Organizations," 126.

66 Pace and Thieroff, "Participation of Non-Governmental Organizations," 394; Benedetti and Washburn, "Drafting the International Criminal Court Treaty: Two Years to Rome and an Afterword on the Rome Diplomatic Conference," 32; Nel, "Between Counter-Hegemony and Post-Hegemony: The Rome Statute and Normative Innovation in World Politics," 158; Pace and Schense, "The Role of Non-Governmental Organizations," 126; Van Der Vyver, "Civil Society and the International Criminal Court," 428; Watt. Government missions held their own briefing sessions, but the CICC briefings were seen to be more useful by many; Pace and Schense, "The Role of Non-Governmental Organizations," 128.

67 There is an important distinction between the CICC and the Coalition Secretariat: the former was the coalition of NGOs that took positions on issues and lobbied delegates; the latter remained neutral vis-à-vis the negotiations and existed primarily to support NGOs and others in the process; Pace and Schense, "The Role of Non-Governmental Organizations," 125.

68 *Report of the Preparatory Committee*, A/AC.249/1998/L.16, 1998, summarized in Bassiouni, "Historical Survey: 1919–1998": 22–23; Pace and Schense, "The Role of Non-Governmental Organizations," 125; Van Der Vyver, "Civil Society and the International Criminal Court," 428; Bos, "From the International Law Commission to the Rome Conference (1994–1998)," 59.

69 The point has been made that because William Pace, as convener of the CICC, kept NGOs so well organized and represented NGOs so well vis-à-vis the UN, the conference organizers remained well disposed to the NGOs participating in Rome; Van Der Vyver, "Civil Society and the International Criminal Court," 428.

70 Pace and Thieroff, "Participation of Non-Governmental Organizations," 393ff. Between fifty and eighty experts from NGOs in developing countries were supported by the CICC; Pace, "The Relationship between the International Criminal Court and Non-Governmental Organizations," 202. The NGO No Peace Without Justice sponsored many experts to sit on delegations, particularly from developing countries, through their technical assistance program; Glasius, "Expertise in the Cause of Justice: Global Civil Society Influence on the Statute for an International Criminal Court," 151; Pace, "The Relationship between the International Criminal Court and Non-Governmental Organizations," 202; Pace and Schense, "The Role of Non-Governmental Organizations," 125; Pace and Schense estimate that as much as 90 percent of the Coalition's work was providing services.

71 Glasius, "Expertise in the Cause of Justice: Global Civil Society Influence on the Statute for an International Criminal Court," 150. NGOs have tried to do this at

many previous conferences, but for the first time at Rome it was done effectively; Pace and Thieroff, "Participation of Non-Governmental Organizations," 395.

72 Nel, "Between Counter-Hegemony and Post-Hegemony: The Rome Statute and Normative Innovation in World Politics," 158; Pace, "The Relationship between the International Criminal Court and Non-Governmental Organizations," 202; Watt.

73 Pace and Schense, "The Role of Non-Governmental Organizations," 114; 129; Glasius, "Expertise in the Cause of Justice: Global Civil Society Influence on the Statute for an International Criminal Court," 151.

74 Nel, "Between Counter-Hegemony and Post-Hegemony: The Rome Statute and Normative Innovation in World Politics," 158.

75 Kirsch and Holmes, "The Birth of the International Criminal Court: The 1998 Rome Conference," 11.

76 Benedetti and Washburn, "Drafting the International Criminal Court Treaty: Two Years to Rome and an Afterword on the Rome Diplomatic Conference," 24; Pace and Thieroff, "Participation of Non-Governmental Organizations," 394; Pace, "The Relationship between the International Criminal Court and Non-Governmental Organizations," 202; "NGO Activities in Rome," *The International Criminal Court Monitor* 10 (November 1998): 11; Watt describes the series of phone interviews he gave for news shows, one after another across the Canadian time zones; Watt.

77 Pace and Schense, "The Role of Non-Governmental Organizations," 128.

78 Van Der Vyver, "Civil Society and the International Criminal Court," 429.

79 Immi Tallgren, "We Did It? The Vertigo of Law and Everyday Life at the Diplomatic Conference on the Establishment of an International Criminal Court," *Leiden Journal of International Law* 12 (1999): 688. These were a "human carpet" organized by Amnesty International to represent the victims of genocide, war crimes, and crimes against humanity, and a twenty-four-hour vigil organized by No Peace Without Justice to celebrate or mourn the final result of the conference; Glasius, "Expertise in the Cause of Justice: Global Civil Society Influence on the Statute for an International Criminal Court," 152.

80 Bassiouni, "Historical Survey: 1919–1998," 26.

81 Pace, "The Relationship between the International Criminal Court and Non-Governmental Organizations," 201.

82 Van Der Vyver, "Civil Society and the International Criminal Court," 426.

83 Benedetti and Washburn, "Drafting the International Criminal Court Treaty: Two Years to Rome and an Afterword on the Rome Diplomatic Conference," 9; Watt.

84 Van Der Vyver, "Civil Society and the International Criminal Court," 428.

85 There were two requirements for NGOs wishing to become a member of the Coalition: "(1) endorse in principle the creation of a just and effective International Criminal Court and (2) wish to be involved at some level with efforts to create an ICC." "To Join the Coalition," *The International Criminal Court Monitor* 7 (April 1998): 8.

86 Pace, "The Relationship between the International Criminal Court and Non-Governmental Organizations," 209.

87 Marlies Glasius has pointed out that though the lack of rigid structures within the Coalition contributed to its ability to function effectively within the reality of the negotiations, there was an absence of democracy within the Coalition itself, as only

self-selected steering committee members had any real say in the CICC's policies; Glasius, "Expertise in the Cause of Justice: Global Civil Society Influence on the Statute for an International Criminal Court," 147.

88 Coalition for an International Criminal Court, Press Release, "Members of the Coalition for an International Criminal Court (CICC) State Their Support for an Effective and Credible Court and Challenge U.S. Insistence on Security Council Jurisdiction" (13 August 1997).

89 Letter from Fergus Watt, Convenor, Canadian Network for an International Criminal Court, dated January 10, 1999 [on file with author].

90 Pace and Schense, "The Role of Non-Governmental Organizations," 125–26.

91 ibid., 125; Kristie Barrow, "The Role of NGOs in the Establishment of the International Criminal Court," *Dialogue* 2, no. 1 (2004): 17.

92 Matas points out that while there was a fair amount of information-sharing between NGOs and the LMG, there could have been more joint strategizing on approaches that would have decreased duplication of efforts. He also observes that while the Coalition and the like-minded states shared a high degree of commonality on many key issues, the compromises made by governments were not always seen as positive by NGOs. David Matas, "The Hard Realities of Soft Power: Canada and the International Criminal Court," unpublished version (1998): 13–14.

93 Bassiouni, "Negotiating the Treaty of Rome on the Establishment of an International Criminal Court," 455.

94 Bedont and Matas, "Negotiating for an International Criminal Court," 2.

95 These states included Syria, Qatar, Saudi Arabia, United Arab Emirates, and Iran; ibid. 4; Glasius, "Expertise in the Cause of Justice: Global Civil Society Influence on the Statute for an International Criminal Court," 157. Glasius, "Expertise in the Cause of Justice: Global Civil Society Influence on the Statute for an International Criminal Court," 157; Oosterveld.

96 Pace and Schense, "The Role of Non-Governmental Organizations," 118.

97 Ibid., 119; Pace, "The Relationship between the International Criminal Court and Non-Governmental Organizations," 206; Pace and Schense, "The Role of Non-Governmental Organizations," 119.

98 Van Der Vyver, "Civil Society and the International Criminal Court," 430.

99 Watt recounts that some individuals involved with NGOs were friendly with people on state delegations who could be relied on to funnel NGO concerns to the discussions; Watt.

100 "The Gift of Hope to Future Generations," *The International Criminal Court Monitor* 9 (August 1998): 3; the Secretary General's statement at the adoption ceremony, July 18, 1998.

Influencing the IMF

Jo Marie Griesgraber

NGOs have long reviled the International Monetary Fund (IMF or Fund). It was initially designed in 1944 at the Bretton Woods Conference to assist member countries with short-term trade imbalances, but in the 1980s that role was no longer needed by the global financial community. Its major share-holders, the wealthy countries,[1] determined to use the IMF as both their "debt collection agency" when the debt crisis broke through in the early 1980s, and as their "credit rating agency," whereby low-income countries (LIC) had to be in good standing with the IMF in order to receive foreign aid. The policies the Fund required of the debtor or borrowing countries were designed to address short-term financial hemorrhaging of foreign currency by these countries. Other problems arose and intensified because the Fund per-sisted in applying the same "tourniquet-style" policies[2] over decades, thwart-ing any hope of growth.

The series of efforts to reform the IMF presented here demonstrate the difficulties of reforming a global institution that serves the interests of status quo economic powers. The energy expended on reforming the institution is based on its central role in impeding the growth of developing countries (and hence the hope for reducing poverty). The methods employed appealed to the principles espoused by democratic decision makers and to the moral val-ues of a broad swath of citizens globally. Since the earliest case examined here (the debt crisis, beginning in 1982), much has changed in the world economy. By the time of the fifth case (2007), the question becomes: Are the major economies willing to salvage the IMF by making its governance more accountable and inclusive, or do the habits of power blind them to their own long-run self-interests, regardless of the moral arguments?

DEBT, 1982

The international development community, especially religious organizations with missionaries in the field, started to toll the alarm bells shortly after Mexico's financial collapse in 1982. Fr. Tom Burns, a Catholic priest with the Maryknoll order in Peru, recounted the new indicator for Peru's debt problems: the rising number of "emergency baptisms" he was called upon to perform in Lima's slums, i.e., the rising number of infant deaths.[3]

The efforts to reduce, even remove, the debt burden from developing countries has been ongoing since at least 1982.[4] Religious missionaries of every denomination, like Fr. Burns, warned that something was seriously wrong. The initiative for debt campaigning was therefore solidly within the religious community with partners in developing countries. These were soon joined by international development organizations such as Oxfam in the UK, and by left or progressive organizations such as the Institute for Policy Studies and the Development Group for Alternative Policies (D-Gap) in the US.[5]

My work began in 1989 at the Jesuit-related Center of Concern in Washington, DC. By that time, the first coalition of debt activists had already faded from fatigue. The options for action were limited to reducing bilateral debt, either singly between the US and a particular country, or internationally through the Paris Club (the ad hoc arrangement of Western official creditors that met to address the request of one debtor to reduce or restructure its debts). Before 1993 it was possible for the president and/or the US Congress to simply write off debt. In 1993, the Credit Reform Act (CRA) required that Congress appropriate new money to cover the loss to the US Treasury of any debt write-down. This reform in terms of US government accounting placed an additional burden on anyone wanting to reduce a foreign government's debt. Bread for the World was instrumental in getting the US Congress to reduce the debt immediately prior to the implementation of the CRA, and the White House reduced the debt of Poland, Egypt, and Guyana (among others) at the same time.

Initial international NGO efforts involved Oxfam in the UK and religious/progressive groups in the US focusing on Paris Club meetings and then increasingly on the G7 Summits where major creditors would endorse increasingly generous terms for reducing debt in the Paris Club.

The real push to cancel the debt of poor countries came from the UK with the launch of the Jubilee 2000 Campaign. In the US, at the 1997 G7 Summit in Denver, Marie Dennis of Maryknoll, head of the Religious Working Group on the World Bank and IMF, and Njoki Njehu, coordinator of 50 Years Is Enough, led religious and progressive activists in announcing the formation of Jubilee 2000 USA.[6]

The research, analysis, and high energy came from Jubilee UK, which included the Catholic Agency for Overseas Development (CAFOD), Catholic Institute for International Relations (CIIR), and Christian Aid, among many others; Oxfam UK also provided substantial research. The European Network on Debt and Development (Eurodad) coordinated efforts throughout the continent. Eurodad was also instrumental in setting up the African Forum and Network on Debt and Development (Afrodad) in Africa. Jubilee South emerged later with its own demands that paralleled those of the more radical US grassroots groups.

The work in the US involved grassroots outreach and legislative advocacy. Those groups working with grassroots tended to be smaller organizations, and their agenda more "prophetic" or utopian—100 percent immediate debt cancellation, without conditions, and sometimes with talk of reparations for colonialism. The larger organizations tended more toward reform efforts, including legislative initiatives to reduce debts even if only gradually, with conditions that ameliorated some of the costs of structural adjustment policies and allowed greater national policy space.[7]

As the campaign grew in size, the demands of the various perspectives grew in intensity. There was hope that genuine change was possible from the campaign. After all, the Pope was on record calling for debt cancellation, as were religious leaders of virtually every persuasion. And the rock star Bono was talking about it at huge rock concerts and to conservative Congress people such as Senator Jesse Helms.

Outreach efforts were enormous on the part of every organization. For example, Bread for the World had all its regional organizers setting up training sessions in church basements and halls across the country, and their letters to Congress poured in, as did those from 50 Years and later Jubilee 2000 USA itself. Lobby days brought hundreds of people to Washington, DC. Every demonstration had its debt contingent.

There was easy access to the White House and Treasury under the Clinton administration. Gene Sperling, a White House economic advisor, was especially active, giving speeches and working on details of negotiating documents with Oxfam America lobbyists. Congressional interest was bipartisan—with legislation supported by Republican Spencer Baucus of Alabama (brought on board thanks to a visit from co-religionists from Bread for the World) and Democrat Maxine Waters of California.

The result of all this action both nationally and internationally was that debts of the poorest countries were reduced substantially. But the activists were also sorely disappointed: 100 percent of bilateral debt to Paris Club members was cancelled eventually, but the debt owed to the World Bank, IMF, and regional development banks remained. The same structural adjustment conditionality continued to apply to debt work-outs. Relatively little new money could be redirected to poverty reduction. Indeed, many poor countries were paying more on debt servicing, because in order to receive official debt reduction, countries had to be current on their debt payments. And always, the amount of relief provided was determined by the creditors' willingness to pay, not by the needs of the debtor countries, not by the needs of the poor people. And there certainly was no global institutional arrangement to address future bankruptcies of sovereign debtors.

The campaign continues. In 2006 the G7 agreed to the Multilateral Debt Relief Initiative (MDRI), which provided complete cancellation of the debt to the World Bank, IMF, and African Development Bank for a fixed number of low-income countries. And there are campaigns to cancel illegitimate and odious debts.

To what extent did the Jubilee debt campaign influence the IMF? The core of the Fund remains unchanged in terms of its internal power dynamics and the requirements that accompany any loan from the IMF. Likewise the donors continue to empower the IMF to serve as their credit rating agency, determining which countries can receive foreign aid and which can not. The IMF has a new name—Poverty Reduction and Growth Facility (PRGF)—for the old Enhanced Structural Adjustment Facility (ESAF). The Independent Evaluation Office of the IMF reports that the PRGF requirements, with the standard package of conditions, continues to rank above the Poverty Reduction Strategy Paper (PRSP), regardless of what the IMF's Executive Board may have indicated once upon a time. While middle-income and emerging market countries have voted with their feet and separated themselves from the IMF and its conditions, LICs do not have that option. So global campaigning has brought debt relief to many poor countries. But power relations and decision making have been unaffected.

IMF TRANSPARENCY AND EVALUATION, 1998

If an all-out global campaign had so little impact on the core dynamics of the Fund, maybe a tiny, focused assault using a strategic cadre of insiders and outsiders might have greater effect.

In 1997, having been promised a modest sum by a foundation to develop a proposal on the IMF, I approached Professor Peter Kenen, an eminent economist at Princeton, about his best idea for reforming the IMF. The two of us eventually settled on a targeted project: reform of the Fund's transparency and evaluation policies. We organized a study group of experts from diverse points of view and institutions: IMF executive directors from developed and developing countries, including the US; academics in addition to Professor Kenen from the Overseas Development Council and American University; NGOs in addition to myself (then at the Center of Concern), including Marijke Torfs and Carol Welch from Friends of the Earth. Over approximately eighteen months the group came together every other month. Experts on evaluation described experiences and best practices at their home institutions: the World Bank, the Inter-American Development Bank, and the OECD Development Assistance Committee. The ultimate IMF insider, Dr. Jacques Polak, who designed the original formula for allocating IMF resources to countries applying for Fund loans, wrote the final report. The group agreed on a very narrow range of issues; beyond that there was virtually no common ground. It recommended that the Fund make public a specific set of documents, the list coinciding with those that Friends of the Earth had sought for years. It also set a timeline for public access to Fund archives, relying on the timeline used by the US Federal Reserve Board.

The Study Group further recommended that the Fund establish an independent evaluation office, modelled on the best practices articulated by evaluation practitioners. The evaluation unit would report directly to the Board, not to management; its agenda would be set by the unit, its funding would be secure, it would have access to all Fund documents, and its reports would be public.

All of the Study Group's recommendations were eventually implemented. Why? The study group was probably catalytic in articulating which IMF documents should be released and provided a useful and principled design for an evaluation unit. But other larger dynamics were in play. First, the Asian Financial Crisis was fresh in everyone's mind. The Fund's failure to predict the crisis and then its apparent role in worsening poverty for many Asians had created a public political context that was impatient with secrecy. Second, the US Congress, especially the House of Representatives, had long been pushing for release of Fund documents. Third, the IMF was assaulted continually by accusations of the harm its conditionality had caused in developing countries as well as in Asia. A series of evaluations had confirmed these accusations. The first evaluation was an internal evaluation, eventually made public. The Board then arranged for an independent panel of experts to do an independent evaluation. Their critique was much more hard-hitting. Fourth, the Board found the work of the external evaluators useful, but this approach to evaluation was time-consuming. The Board was directly responsible for finding

and vetting the external evaluators, for drafting and approving and monitoring their Terms of Reference. Finally, the Study Group had members who
were themselves executive directors (EDs) as well as advisors to the Fund
and to the Clinton Treasury. The Study Group was invited to present its recommendations directly to the IMF EDs at an informal meeting of the Board.
The presenters were themselves people with long years of experience at the
Fund and with strong reputations for intelligence and integrity.

In short, the Study Group's report articulated the ideas and preferences of
strong voices on the Executive Board and within the US Treasury. The recommendations were virtually cost free, beyond the modest sums for a small new
office within the Fund. They threatened no one and made the Fund look
good. It strengthened the hand of the Board vis-à-vis management. But it
did not change the fundamental purposes or operating styles of the IMF.

IMF AND LABOUR, 1994 AND 1998

IMF loan arrangements often come with recommendations that the government institute "flexible labor standards," such as allowing employers to hire
and fire workers more easily, not requiring a minimum wage, and restricting
collective bargaining.[8] With pressure from US labour unions and NGOs such
as the International Labor Rights Office and Friends of the Earth, the US
Congress in 1994 passed legislation that instructed the US Treasury Department to have the US Executive Director on the IMF Executive Board use
his/her "voice and vote" to oppose lending to countries that violated human
rights, to promote labour rights in IMF programs, and to prevent IMF funds
from bailing out private commercial banks. The language was attached to
replenishment of the Enhanced Structural Adjustment Facility (ESAF), the
IMF's long-term, low-interest-rate lending facility for LICs. The Clinton
Administration wanted the funding, the unions and NGOs wanted the conditions, and labour-friendly members of Congress led key committees.

Subsequently, on April 4, 1998, the House Banking Committee called Assistant Treasury Secretary Timothy Geithner and US Executive Director to the
IMF Karin Lissakers to testify about how this legislation had been implemented. Prolonged and persistent questioning revealed that on only twelve of
some 2,000 decisions had the US executive director cast a vote, and at no
time had she voted to comply with the legislation. Geithner and Lissakers
argued that the ED had exercised her voice responsibilities frequently, but
the US did not have the weight to carry or to block the vote, because most decisions require majority votes.[9] The members of Congress were unconvinced and
concluded that the law had not been implemented. Shortly thereafter, the
US Treasury appointed a full-time staff person to promote labour rights within

the Treasury and the international financial institutions (IFIs). Despite these actions by the US government, the IMF continued to link labour flexibility requirements with many lending packages.

Efforts to reform the IMF through congressional legislation are virtually ineffective; and, if they are not accompanied by close oversight, those congressional instructions become completely ineffective. With the change in congressional leadership from the Democrats to the Republicans in 1994, followed by the change to Republican control of the White House, congressional attention began to shift from these issues—although the acerbic hearings of 1998, as described in the preceding paragraph, are a caution against generalizations. By 2006, the Treasury no longer had a person in place to monitor labour rights within the IMF. Throughout this period, the IMF insisted on labour flexibility in its conditions on loans, a requirement that is rarely consistent with the four International Core Labor Standards.[10] Through 2003 one can locate US Treasury reports to Congress on implementing legislation relating to the IMF. However, by that time the reports had become pro forma—there were no more blistering hearings. Web searches for links between the US Treasury and labour policy requirements by the IMF show a clear shift over time from references to International Core Labor Standards to references to "property rights" (i.e., the rights of owners) and "responsible labor policies" (i.e., labour practices associated with labour flexibility).

The more effective congressional mandate is usually linked with funding as well as oversight. For this reason, most World Bank reforms have been associated with International Development Assistance (IDA) replenishment. The 1994 contribution to ESAF also saw the labour rights legislation debate. However, once the IMF's ESAF money was authorized, Congress could do little more.

Congressional attention always attracts concern within the IMF, but Congress cannot mandate changes. It is most successful when it monitors closely, even aggressively, and/or when it can withhold funds unless and until changes are enacted. Within the IMF, the United States can block actions but it cannot require positive changes.

IMF (AND WORLD BANK) LEADERSHIP SELECTION, 2004

This fourth incident of NGO pressure on the IMF initially seemed like pushing on an open door, since NGOS worldwide were supporting EDs representing the majority of the world's countries to implement a joint report of Board working groups of both the Bank and the Fund. Why was this constellation of support still not enough?

In February 2000, on behalf of the European members of the IMF, Caio Koch-Weser was nominated for managing director (MD) of the International

Monetary Fund. The leading Europeans recognized that it was Germany's turn to hold the position, previously held by French, Dutch, Swedish, or Belgian nationals. It became a public scandal when the US Treasury let it be known publicly that Koch-Weser's background was not adequate for the position. Koch-Weser had the public decency to withdraw his name from nomination, and the German government next nominated Horst Köhler. So six weeks after the nomination of Koch-Weser, another German was nominated to serve as managing director, again with unanimous European support but this time with US approval.

The United States had committed a serious breach of protocol by airing its differences with the Europeans publicly and objecting after the Europeans had already reached agreement on their nominee. Subsequently the Executive Boards of the IMF and the World Bank separately organized working groups of Board Members to review the leadership selection processes. In the end, the two Committees offered a joint report in April 2001.[11] In the case of the IMF, all twenty-four members of the Executive Board "took note of the Report." Experts have yet to determine the meaning of this action. The twenty-four individuals, but not the Board, received the report.

The meaning would have to wait only a short time. In early March 2004, Köhler resigned to campaign to be president of Germany. His resignation caught the Executive Board—and the European finance ministers—by surprise. Whose turn would it be? Would the member countries feel bound by the Board Report of 2001? The European ministers seemed to feel nary a tug toward the 2001 agreement but immediately set about deciding among themselves who was entitled to head the European Bank for Reconstruction and Development (EBRD), the European Central Bank (ECB), the IMF, and be permanent members of ECB permanent committees. In the end, the IMF was one more European bureaucratic plum assignment to award, and it was Spain's turn. Rodrigo de Rato would be sworn in as the IMF Managing Director in April 2004. De Rato was regarded as a successful and conservative Minister of Economy for Spain.

Between Köhler's resignation in early March 2004, and de Rato's election in May 2004, there was an unusual level of dissatisfaction and even political activity from the Fund's Board and Staff. It seems many members of the Executive Board fully expected the European finance ministers to adhere to the process spelled out in the Joint Report. That is, the Executive Board would appoint a committee of experts to identify and then interview candidates, based solely on merit and not nationality. The Executive Board would then interview the finalists and elect one of them. In consternation at the activity among the Europeans, the developing country EDs agreed that in light of the unexpected resignation by Köhler, any ED could nominate any person so long as the individual and that person's home country agreed; all nominees were to be submitted to the Dean of the Board.

A. Shakour Shalaan, the ED from Egypt, nominated three candidates: Andrew Crockett of the UK, then head of the Financial Stability Forum and former head of the Bank for International Settlement; Mohamed El Erian, who held dual citizenship in Egypt and the United States and was a former staff member of the Fund and a successful private financial manager; and Stanley Fischer, originally of Zimbabwe but a US citizen, then Senior Deputy Managing Director of the Fund.[12] Eventually Crockett and Fischer declined the honour, since their governments did not support their nominations, but El Erian— together with the European nominee, Rodrigo de Rato—were interviewed by the Board.

Between March and May, NGOs in the US and Europe lobbied their EDs, the media, and members of Congress/Parliament to open the process.[13] During the meeting of the European finance ministers in Ireland, UK and European NGOs, led by the Bretton Woods Project, staged a one-horse race to publicize and deride the process: the single European nominee had only to submit to the "competition" of an election, with no one else in the running. NGOs collaborated with the G24 secretariat (the caucus of developing countries in the IMF and World Bank) to learn the positions of developing-country representatives. Press conferences were organized that included staff from mainstream think tanks (Brookings Institute and the Institute for International Economics), NGOs, the G24, and a former US executive director. The Financial Policy Forum, a think tank and member of the New Rules for Global Finance Coalition, organized a website for "one-stop shopping" on this debate.[14]

In the midst of these efforts the NGOs had a surprise—they learned of another "G" among the IMF EDs: the G11. The G11 was the group of eleven constituencies composed entirely of developing-country governments. They constituted by far the largest number of countries and represented most of the world's population. Not only did they go public to the NGO-world, they actually issued two press releases, which was a bold action for a group composed entirely of borrowing countries. As if this were not sufficient excitement, a senior staff member—the Director of PDR (Policy Development and Review), Jack Boorman—issued a statement to all staff that he would collect any of their views regarding the MD selection process and present them to the Board and senior management.

In short, this endeavour had the inside support of developing countries, senior staff, civil society, a Joint Report by IMF and World Bank Board Working Groups, and extensive media coverage. What happened? Nothing different. The European candidate was "elected unanimously."

Why did such a seemingly winning confluence of pressure not succeed? When it comes to the exercise, and the symbols, of power, status quo powers do not surrender them willingly. Arguments about principle were not persuasive. As one US Treasury official "explained": the Africans have the presidency of the African Development Bank, the Asians (the Japanese) the Asian Development Bank, the Latin Americans the Inter-American Development Bank, and the Europeans the IMF. Why should the Americans give up the World Bank? Further, he argued, the G7 countries cannot, by custom, be Secretary General of the UN. Presumably, the European finance ministers shared this official's perspective.[15]

When it was time for the World Bank to replace President James D. Wolfensohn, the US again stepped into its traditional role of naming his successor. The Europeans made loud noises about their distaste for Paul Wolfowitz because of his role in leading the US into the Iraq war. But they had no room to complain, since they had just used the old tools to select their man for the Fund. The Washington NGOs ran another one-horse race, this one in front of the World Bank. Just as Wolfowitz had no competition, so too there was no surprise winner of the NGOs' one-horse race.[16]

To the surprise of many but the disappointment of few, Paul Wolfowitz was forced out of office for a combination of corruption and incompetence, due in no small part to the open rebellion of World Bank staff.[17] With his exit came considerable hope and speculation that the selection of the next World Bank president would be an open, merit-based process. The Board of the World Bank did invite all member states to nominate candidates through their EDs, but only the US nominated. That candidate, Robert Zoellick, made campaign tours of many parts of the world and not surprisingly was approved unanimously by the Board. The widespread speculation was that the Europeans were so eager to get rid of Wolfowitz, as well as to protect their prerogative to name the next IMF Managing Director, that they allowed the US to name Wolfowitz's successor.[18]

The four examples so far have shown that little genuine reform has happened at the IMF. True, some debts have been reduced, additional documents have been released, and new allies have been identified within the IMF. But the status quo remains entrenched. The same policies are applied, even if the "short-term" crises the Fund was designed to address stretch on for well over a decade.[19] The 1944 military victors added Japan and Germany to their ruling clique. For sixty-three years and counting, the Fund has been led by a European, with the First Deputy Managing Director an American. Over the same period the World Bank has been headed by an American. Is change possible?

IMF BOARD ACCOUNTABILITY, 2007

Arguments based on altruism and equity have failed to change the IMF. Global campaigns, dicta from the US Congress, targeted working groups, and even its own Board's recommendations have failed to change the IMF's core functions and style. But maybe, just maybe, the IMF has become so vulnerable as to be susceptible to change.[20]

The current state of the Fund is severely weakened. Its "customers," the borrowing countries, are fleeing. Middle income countries (MIC), such as Argentina, Brazil, and Indonesia, that once held large loans have repaid them early. Only Turkey continues to have a large loan outstanding from the Fund, and hence it is the only customer providing significant interest earnings. The interest from loans has long been the sole source of income to pay the ballooning administrative costs, now near $900 million annually. Because MICs no longer want or need Fund money, its profits are down dramatically. An eminent persons panel[21] suggested several ways for the Fund to stay in business: by investing its reserves, charging for services, and even selling a portion of its gold to invest.[22]

The Fund's only stable "customers" are the low-income countries, which borrow from the Poverty Reduction and Growth Facility (PRGF), a special facility built on donations from major shareholder countries that charges only a small administrative fee. PRGF fees are too small to cover the full costs of managing the facility.

In short, the IMF is in a precarious state in terms of its internal profitability, the legitimacy of its Board, and the efficacy of its ability to address global financial problems.[23] Will the IMF—its Board of Governors and its Executive Board—have the integrity, wisdom, and generosity to undergo radical transformation? Such a development is rare indeed in the life of any individual and rarer still in the life of an institution. Given this weakened state of the IMF, what are CSO agendas vis-à-vis the IMF? Many CSOs in developed and developing countries alike are participating in the "Shrink or Sink" campaign headed by Focus on the Global South, based in Malaysia. Others, including Bretton Woods Project, UK, are focusing on IMF Governance, including voting formulas and a proposal for double majorities to give greater weight to developing countries.[24]

New Rules for Global Finance Coalition has organized a High-Level Panel on IMF Board Accountability. The project is modelled on the 1997–98 Study Group on IMF Transparency and Evaluation described above. The idea grew out of a conversation between Abbas Mirakhor, Dean of the Board and Chair of the Iran, Pakistan, Morocco, and Ghana constituency. The core issue was to ensure that reforms such as reallocation of votes and expanding the voice of low-income countries would actually change the policies and culture of the institution. The missing ingredient was accountability, especially on the part of the Executive Board.

The Panel comprises "insiders" and "outsiders," with Mirakhor suggesting a list of the former and I a list of the latter. "Insiders" included three former Executive Directors—Marc-Antoine Autheman of France, Daniel Kaeser of Switzerland, and Karin Lissakers of the United States. "Outsiders" included Jeff Powell of the Bretton Woods Project, UK, Binny Buchori of Prakarsa, Indonesia, and Patrick Watt of Action Aid International, UK. All invitees are characterized by knowledge of the IMF and a commitment to principles of accountability.[25] The Panel considered first the Articles of Agreement: What are the Board's responsibilities, and to whom are they responsible? It then considered the evolving standards of accountability as applied to international organizations. One World Trust, a UK NGO that has worked about eight years on articulating these standards, is an advisor and a participant in the Panel.

A review of the Articles, especially Article XII, revealed significant gaps in accountability. The Board of Governors is responsible for choosing the Executive Directors but is not charged with monitoring or evaluating their performance as a corporate entity. The Executive Board has no formal obligation in the Articles to conduct self-evaluations or to solicit external evaluations. The Executive Board is formally responsible for selection of the Managing Director, but the Articles are silent on evaluating the performance of the MD. The MD has never undergone a performance evaluation; nor does the MD conduct performance-based evaluations of his three Deputy Managing Directors.

Evolving standards of accountability encompass four essential characteristics: (1) transparency, (2) evaluation, (3) participation, and (4) external complaint mechanism. Combining the identification of gaps in the Articles with these four criteria shaped the Panel's recommendations. The Panel expressed strong support for the selection of the Managing Director through an open, merit-based process, and for Executive Board transparency, with Board decisions and transcripts to be made public under an ever shorter timeline.

As with all recommendations, the question is implementation. The hope is that by having both insiders and outsiders on the Panel, both inside and outside pressure can be brought to bear to ensure implementation. Similarly, the Panel deliberately chose to keep its recommendations within the parameters of the Articles so the need to amend the Articles would provide neither an excuse nor a genuine obstacle to implementation. The Executive Directors invited the Panel to present their recommendations prior to the public release of the report. Panelists raised all the key issues, in polite but direct language; EDs spoke clearly about their concerns. The EDs felt powerless to change

Board behaviour. Even some G8 EDs expressed powerlessness. Given that the EDs are usually mid-level bureaucrats within their own national finance ministries, their reaction may be reasonable.

If the EDs are not able—or perhaps willing—to reform the IMF from within, change will need to come from external political pressure on leading powers. Finance ministries need to see a global financial institution such as the IMF as useful to their own interests. They also need to see that continuing the current internal Fund governance will weaken the institution beyond repair. If the status quo powers, the G8, do not see the IMF as critically injured, and the emerging powers (China, India, South Korea, Brazil) see the IMF as more harmful than useful, the accountability reform proposals will not be implemented and the new quota formula agreement will ensure the entrenched powers remain in place. Without reform, the IMF would probably be too weak to respond and its efforts possibly counterproductive. If IMF member countries that are not part of the status quo power arrangement do not find the IMF useful, they will vote with their feet, as many have already done.

In sum, if CSOs are to influence the IMF in its core functions, they will have to bring along the major status quo powers, by persuading them that acting on altruistic motives and relaxing their hold on power could earn them significant political capital in any new arrangements, as well as renew an institution that should be of service to the global community. The fluid dynamics of shifting relative financial powers suggests that emergent powers could be enlisted as allies. Deciding who makes the decisions within the international financial institutions is a high-stakes game. If those institutions become irrelevant actors on the sidelines, their governance could become fairly easy to modify, but it would then be irrelevant.

NOTES

1 Votes on the IMF's Executive Board are determined mainly by the size of the economy. The size of the gross domestic product (GDP) is measured in market-level exchange rates, thereby favouring the hard-currency countries (US, UK, Eurozone, Japan). For more information, read any of several papers by Ariel Buira on the G24 website: http://www.g24.org.

2 Called variously stabilization policies, neo-liberal policies, or the Washington Consensus. See the websites of Jubilee USA Network (http://www.jubileeusa.org) and 50 Years Is Enough (http://50years.org) for material describing these policies. For a description of the "post-Washington consensus," refer to the websites of New Rules for Global Finance Coalition (http://www.new-rules.org) and the Center for Global Development (http://www.cgdev.org).

3 I started working on debt issues at the Center of Concern in Washington, DC, in spring 1989. During the next eleven years I worked on debt, including as chair of

the Executive Committee of Jubilee 2000 USA. Analyses of the causes of the debt can be found at the Center of Concern website (http://www.coc.org) as well as Jubilee USA Network (www.jubileeusa.org).

4 For earlier debt problems in the Americas, see works by Oscar Ugarteche, notably *El estado deudor: Economia politica de la deuda, Peru y Bolivia, 1968–1984; El falso dilema: América Latina en la economía global* (Lima: Fundación Friedrich Ebert, 1996); and *Adios Estado, Bienvenido Merca*do (Lima: Fundación Friedrich Ebert, 2004), in Spanish.

5 My knowledge base/experience is in the progressive US Catholic community. Others will have different experience, hence different emphasis.

6 The Moral Imperatives Statement was written and disseminated in May 1997 by the Religious Working Group (RWG) on World Bank and IMF: http://www.sedos .org/english/maryknol.htm. RWG was chaired by Marie Dennis, Director, Maryknoll Office for Global Concerns in Washington, DC, which was the lead organization in starting what was originally called Jubilee 2000 USA and is now called Jubilee USA Network (www.jubileeusa.org). RWG members Marie Dennis, Carol Welch of Friends of the Earth, Njoki Njehu of 50 Years Is Enough, and Rev. Douglas Hunt of the United Church of Christ went to the G7 Summit in Denver 1997 and there announced the formation of the new Jubilee 2000 USA. 50 Years Is Enough, a campaigning organization to shut down the World Bank, was started in 1994 by a coalition of US environmental and social and economic justice NGOs, led by Development-GAP.

7 The Heavily Indebted Poor Country Initiative (HIPC), announced at the 1999 G7 Summit in Cologne, in part insisted that savings from debt payments be directed toward health and education; the Poverty Reduction Strategy Papers (PRSP) were to provide space for local people to participate in shaping government policies toward poverty reduction.

8 Unlike the other case studies presented in this chapter, I was not directly involved in the one about the IMF and labour.

9 The US, with just over 17 percent of the total votes on the IMF Executive Board, can veto key decisions requiring 85 percent majority. But most votes, including approval of lending packages, require only majority support to pass.

10 Apparently the IMF is very solicitous of its own labour force, which is stable, well paid, and enjoys rich benefits and pension plans that were once the norm throughout the developed world but are now abandoned in the name of competition and labour flexibility. "Beyond the IMF," Devesh Kapur and Richard Webb, http:// www.cgdev.org/content/publications/detail/10246/.

11 The Bank Working Group to Review the Process for Selection of the President and the Fund Working Group to Review the Process for Selection of the Managing Director, April 25, 2001. http://www.imf.org/external/spring/2001/imfc/select.htm.

12 "IMF Executive Director Shaalan Nominates Three Candidates for the Post of Managing Director of the IMF," IMF Press Release no. 04/65, March 31, 2004. http://www.imf.org/external/np/sec/pr/2004/pr0465.htm.

13 The Financial Policy Forum website (http://www.financialpolicy.org) documents many of these activities. See also the IMF website on leadership selection process. http://www.imf.org/external/np/ed/md/2000/index.htm.

14 The website was reactivated when Paul Wolfowitz was nominated by the US to be World Bank president. It remains the single most useful site for documentation on the de Rato selection. http://www.financialpolicy.org.

15 Conversation between the author and a US Treasury official on the occasion of the Brookings Global Seminar Series dinner on April 25, 2007, with Nouriel Roubini, Professor of Economics at the Stern School of Business, New York University.

16 See photo in 2006 Annual Report of the one horse that "raced" in front of the World Bank in 2005 at the time of Paul Wolfowitz's selection as World Bank President. http://www.actionaidusa.org/pdf/actionaid_intl_2006_annual_report.pdf.

17 The entire drama was captured by *The New York Times* and the London *Financial Times*, with significant help from Beatrice "B" Edwards of the Government Accountability Project (GAP), a US whistleblower protection organization.

18 http://www.nytimes.com/2007/05/18/washington/18wolfowitz.html?ei=5088&en=d403cde0a64042d9&ex=1337140800&adxnnl=1&partner=&adxnnlx=1186412857-lCP3fQhjATkDyp+Vduhe7A. The old process persists. At the IMF, following the unexpected resignation of Rodrigo de Rato as Managing Director, the Board set out a clear process and criteria for the selection of the next MD. Only the Europeans have nominated a candidate. "Press Release: IMF Executive Board Moves Ahead with Process of Selecting the Fund's Next Managing Director," http://www.imf.org/external/np/sec/pr/2007/pr07159.htm.

19 Independent Evaluation Office, International Monetary Fund, "Evaluation of the Prolonged Use of Fund Resources," September 25, 2002, http://www.ieo-imf.org/eval/complete/eval_09252002.html.

20 The single best public source for information about the "Shrink or Sink" campaign against the IMF is the 50 Years Is Enough website. See for example: http://www.50years.org/cms/updates/story/325.

21 See the Crockett Report on the IMF's website. www.imf.org/external/np/tr/2007/tr070131.htm.

22 When severely indebted poor countries sought debt relief, those reserves and the gold were regarded as essential for the financial integrity of the institution and therefore untouchable.

23 For a fuller discussion of the troubles ailing the IMF and options for dealing with them, see Jo Marie Griesgraber and Oscar Ugarteche, "The IMF Today and Tomorrow: Some Civil Society Perspectives," *Global Governance* 12 (2006): 351–59.

24 "Bridging the democratic deficit. Double majority decision making and the IMF," Peter Chowla, Jeffrey Oatham and Claire Wren., Bretton Woods Project, UK, 2 February 2007. http://www.brettonwoodsproject.org/art.shtml?x=549743.

25 Report with recommendations and list of Panel Members can be found at www.new-rules.org/docs/imfreform/imfaccountability041007.htm.

9

Civil Society, Corporate Social Responsibility, and Conflict Prevention

Virginia Haufler

In 2000, three prominent NGOs published a ground-breaking report on *The Business of Peace: The Private Sector as a Partner in Conflict Prevention*. It laid out the case for business to be more interested and engaged in promoting peaceful resolution of violent conflict in their areas of operation. This report brought to the fore of the international agenda a growing interest in engaging the private sector in zones of conflict. This came after a number of high-profile investigative reports detailed the detrimental impact of particular industries on long-running conflicts in Africa, such as the role of oil and banking in financing the Angolan civil war, or of diamonds in Sierra Leone.[1] In the ensuing years, a new "business and conflict" agenda has been established, supported by particular NGOs, the United Nations Global Compact, and select donor governments. It is part of a larger effort to hold corporations accountable and to demand socially responsible action from actors that are profit-oriented. And it is unexpected—for all the evidence that corporations are often a contributor to instability, corruption, and conflict, there is now a set of policymakers and activists who insist that conflict prevention can only be undertaken in partnership with the private sector.

This agenda emerged out of the activism of NGOs concerned about the inability or unwillingness of governments to intervene and end long-running bloody conflicts that were devastating parts of the developing world. It reflects an increasing reliance on civil society and the private sector to resolve difficult international issues, even war and peace—the traditional responsibility of sovereign governments. Increasingly open and competitive markets have led investors into every corner of the world, no matter how remote, undeveloped, or poorly governed.[2] The lack of stable and capable governance is at the heart of the political, economic, and social problems they find, and unfortunately, in many cases the corporation is the most effective institution in the country. While there may be a business interest in peace, there are limits to what they can do to promote it. Recent initiatives, which will be described below, are innovative methods of providing a governance framework in unstable areas. At the same time, the limits of these private efforts point to the continuing need—perhaps even a stronger need than ever—for capable national governments.

In this chapter, I examine the general evolution of corporate social responsibility as a counterpart to increasing globalization, and rising concerns within civil society over the role of corporations as the main beneficiaries of increased economic integration. Then, I will survey the literature, both popular and scholarly, linking foreign investors to the creation or exacerbation of conflict in the developing world. Increased transnational activism against corporate misbehaviour has combined with the emerging empirical and anecdotal evidence linking conflict and investment to produce the "business and conflict" or "corporate conflict prevention" agenda. This is made up of a variety of disparate proposals and initiatives that reflect a wide variety of governance mechanisms in this arena. After describing some of these efforts, I will conclude with some thoughts about what we have learned so far, and where this agenda will go in future.

CORPORATE SOCIAL RESPONSIBILITY

We can say with some justification that we are now in the era of corporate social responsibility (CSR). Across a wide range of issues, civil society increasingly demands that business act "responsibly." Within the business community, the discourse today is all about CSR. Some of the elements of what we think of now as CSR were in place a long time ago, viewed alternately as philanthropy or paternalism toward employees.[3] But the politicization of CSR that accompanied globalization dates back approximately forty years.

In the 1960s and 1970s, critics first raised modern concerns about the impact of multinational corporations on foreign cultures. In France—by no means a weak or developing state—Serban-Schreiber decried *Le Défi Américain* as US multinational corporations expanded their presence in Europe.[4] In the developing world, newly independent states created in the wake of decolonization strove to establish the sovereignty and legitimacy of their governments by criticizing foreign investors. A number of them chose to nationalize or expropriate the assets of foreign investors, and declared all natural resources to be the property of the state.[5]

A number of countries in the developing world called on the United Nations to sponsor negotiations over the rights and responsibilities of foreign corporations. The UN launched negotiations for a Corporate Code of Conduct for Transnational Corporations in the 1970s. The demands of the developing nations during this time ranged widely, but centred on concerns regarding the sovereignty of the newly independent states. Economists and sociologists at this time hypothesized that over-reliance on foreign investment could lead to dependency and underdevelopment, reinforcing concerns about the intrusion of foreign capital.[6] Some scholars analyzed the close relationship between the foreign policy of the US and the interests and activities of US-based multinationals.[7] During the UN negotiations, the companies and their government backers expressed concern for property rights, and just compensation and dispute resolution in cases of expropriation or nationalization. In the end, one observer commented that all sides agreed on about 80 percent of what was being negotiated, but the last 20 percent proved a major stumbling block.[8]

The Code of Conduct died a slow death over the course of the 1980s, as dramatic changes in the world economy and ideological and policy shifts reduced the demand for it. The Reagan and Thatcher governments were not interested in pursuing further negotiations. During this time, any developing countries that had previously been leery of foreign investment began to open their doors and compete to attract it. The 1970s had been a high point for expropriation and nationalizations of foreign assets. In the succeeding decade, government leaders across the developing world rushed to liberalize their markets.[9] The failure of the UN Code of Conduct set the stage for the next step in the evolution of corporate social responsibility.

During the 1980s, one of the most significant early transnational movements emerged in the fight against apartheid in South Africa. While the anti-apartheid movement itself had been in existence for about forty years, it took on a higher profile in the 1970s. Two strategies emerged that had significant ramifications for business: a campaign to boycott South African products and services and disinvest from all operations in South Africa; and a movement for remaining companies to adopt a code of conduct establishing the principle of equal treatment of employees. The latter move was originated by the Reverend Leon Sullivan, a US-based minister who served on the board of General Motors. The "Sullivan Principles," as they were called, were premised on the idea that it would be possible to undermine apartheid from the inside by changing major economic organizations. Sullivan eventually came to doubt the efficacy of this strategy and threw his support behind the international divestment campaign. In the end, it was through internal political change that apartheid was eventually overthrown, in combination with a global campaign against the system.[10] But the targeting of the private sector as an instrument for system change had some impact on the outcomes. If nothing else, the use of anti-corporate campaigns as part of a larger issue-based struggle became a common practice afterwards, particularly among environmentalists.[11]

The "take-off" in corporate campaigning and corporate social responsibility probably can be dated to the 1992 UN Conference on Environment and Development. This global meeting tying together the environment and development agendas was marked by the huge participation of non-governmental organizations (NGOs) in the planning and preparation for the conference. Corporate leaders began to recognize that they would have to be involved too and not just as opponents of every initiative. The final results of the UNCED included many references and expectations for corporate social responsibility, industry self-regulation, and public–private partnerships with business. In the years since, there have been numerous anti-corporate campaigns, such as the highly visible one against Nike for sweatshop conditions in the factories where its products were made. Across a range of issues, these campaigns have combined with political and legal action to put pressure on companies to go "beyond compliance" with the law, as some put it, and adopt a more progressive and socially aware stance. Almost every company now has an independent code of conduct, and particular industries have adopted standards on issues of concern to them. There now exist a range of monitoring and certification standards and systems and various partnerships between business, NGOs, and governments.[12] It is not an exaggeration to refer today to a CSR "industry."

TRADE, INVESTMENT, AND CONFLICT

After the end of the Cold War, with the fraught tension between the US and USSR at an end, it seemed as if civil conflict exploded in the developing world. There was increasing concern over conflict and instability and frustration over the humanitarian disasters spawned by seemingly intractable conflicts. Humanitarian groups such as Global Witness and Partnership Africa Canada pointed to oil, banking, and diamonds as financial resources that had been appropriated by warring groups to prosecute violence without end.[13] "Conflict" or "blood" diamonds in particular caught the attention of the public. This brought out the economic factors involved in modern war and pointed the finger at industry as being complicit in the violence. Trade and investment were seen as contributing to the outbreak and continuation of bloody conflict in a number of developing countries.

Donor governments, particularly those of the US and UK, invested in research on failed and fragile states to explore the determinants of instability and violence in the developing world. International institutions such as the World Bank established new research units devoted to teasing out the links between conflict and development, spurring further attention to economic factors. Think tanks such as the International Peace Academy launched prominent programs exploring economic agendas in civil wars, producing policy-oriented scholarship that stimulated debate over greed versus grievance as causes of violent conflict.[14] Debates ensued over the so-called "resource curse," since the countries richest in natural resources were often the poorest in terms of their development and often mired in conflict.

The research and activism identify four general mechanisms by which economic transactions can create or exacerbate conflict, corruption, and criminality in weakly governed states.[15] The *honey pot effect* occurs when a very valuable resource located in a specific area becomes the bone of contention between competing groups who seek to control that resource and its revenues. Governing elites may compete for it through institutional means, such as by establishing government-owned corporations that funnel resources to the favoured group, or by more extreme measures that eventually destabilize the system, as happens often with agricultural exports in Africa. People at the other end of the income and status scale may also compete for access to the resource, for instance, by moving into the area where a resource is being developed in order to find employment, housing, and government services. When a new mining operation is established, local groups may find themselves in competition with newcomers flooding the area, leading to new fault lines in the relations among different groups. Outsiders may also be attracted to the area, as when both Uganda and Rwanda intervened in the conflict in the Democratic Republic of the Congo.

Economic factors can also be a source of conflict when they have a significant *distributional impact*. Any development in a poor country will affect the distribution of wealth and income, and this inequality often reinforces existing grievances. In Nigeria and Sudan, the violence is partly due to the way in which the central government distributes the revenues it receives from oil development, favouring some groups and regions over others. Foreign investors often inadvertently widen the gap between the haves and have-nots by their decisions about where to locate investment and whom to employ. In cases of major resource development, particularly oil, the contract between the central government and the investors is secret, and the revenue streams from the oil company to government coffers is hidden.

Economic transactions have been implicated in the *financing* of rebellion and secession in numerous conflicts. If a secessionist movement or rebel group has—or potentially has—control over land where valuable natural resources are located, then they may gain international credibility. They will have access to a steady source of revenue for continuing to fight, making them reluctant to come to the bargaining table. In the case of fixed assets such as oil development rights, foreign investors have been known to sign contracts for "booty futures," in which the investor essentially bets on which side will win the war. In the case of movable or "lootable" assets, it can be easy for rebels to obtain resources that can be sold for cash to pay soldiers and buy weapons.[16] In Sierra Leone, alluvial diamonds became a significant resource for the rebels to support their violent habits. Companies were accused of funding such conflict indirectly and directly through their participation in the market for tainted diamonds.

Government revenues from national efforts to develop natural resource wealth are clearly a huge windfall for governing elites. The funds can be used to repress their opposition and support a lavish lifestyle. In many cases, companies are accused of complicity in government abuses for their willingness to sign development contracts with corrupt and repressive regimes. In some cases, government military or paramilitary forces become the security police for natural gas pipelines and oil platforms, further implicating the foreign investors in human rights violations. In fact, the arrangements for security that companies make have often become the focus of accusations against the companies.[17]

This brief overview gives some idea of the various ways in which trade and investment were seen as contributors to violence in the developing world. Even as civil conflict declined throughout the 1990s, the concerns remained.[18] The business community, especially the extractive sector, was targeted by activists and humanitarian groups determined to reduce the suffering they witnessed. The combination of long-running conflicts, high visibility, and the growing interest of donor governments and international organizations eventually would merge into a new business and conflict agenda that sought to encourage proactive conflict-prevention measures by companies operating in conflict zones.

A NEW AGENDA

The recognition of links between economic activities and local instabilities— by both activists and researchers—helped feed into the emergence of a larger agenda in which business would become not just the problem but also the solution. The public has been horrified by the negative impact of natural-resource development in many countries—environmental degradation, corruption and repression, and a host of ills. Many have argued that corporations should divest entirely from operating in zones of conflict or in countries where government corruption runs deep, on the premise that there is simply no way for a company to conduct business in a legitimate manner in such an environment. Otherwise, the company becomes complicit in violence, repression, criminality and bloodshed.

A number of proposals emerged over the course of the last ten years. One of the leaders in defining this agenda was the United Nations Global Compact, which was created at about the same time that the issue of business complicity in war began to be raised. The UN Global Compact was founded out of the rising concern of UN policy-makers and business leaders about the anti-globalization sentiment that was beginning to gain force. Kofi Annan, the UN secretary general at that time, argued that, given the rights and benefits provided to business by globalization, they must equally take on more social responsibility for their negative effects. The Global Compact is a voluntary agreement between business and the UN system, in which participating businesses agree to promote and uphold nine (now ten) major principles drawn from UN conventions (they address issues of labour, human rights, environment, and corruption). The UN Global Compact launched its first Public Policy Dialogue on the topic Business in Zones of Conflict. The participants were drawn from the private sector, different UN agencies, the World Bank, a variety of NGOs, and other observers.

The various conflict-sensitive practices that were highlighted at this Dialogue summed up the various approaches being considered at that time and established an initial agenda for debate. Many observers argued, first, that businesses should undertake a conflict-impact assessment prior to a major investment, in order to determine how its own operations would be likely to affect local and national political and social values.[19] Management is often so focused on looking at political risk, or how the local situation might affect their trade or investment, that they ignore how that economic activity might affect the local society. Second, the participants highlighted the importance of encouraging more transparency and reporting of revenue payments by companies, making both the companies and the governments more accountable to civil society. Third, the discussion pointed to the need to develop revenue management programs to address the negative effects of large resource revenue windfalls. Finally, the Dialogue participants promoted the creation of multi-stakeholder initiatives that would include representatives from business, NGOs, international organizations, and governments. These would address particularly difficult issues through negotiations among all affected groups.

One of the first initiatives to attempt to cut the link between trade and conflict resulted in the Kimberly Process for the Certification of Diamonds. In the 1990s, a number of activist NGOs began publicizing the way in which diamonds financed war in Sierra Leone, a horrific conflict in which child soldiers and bodily mutilation symbolized the brutality of the warmongers. The activists effectively relabelled the precious stones as "blood diamonds," raising the possibility that potential customers would turn away from buying diamonds in disgust at what their sale finances.[20] The diamond industry, which is very culturally conservative and dominated by the company DeBeers, was reluctant to accept the need to respond to this campaign and initially ignored it. But they eventually became convinced that this campaign posed a threat to their reputation and to their consumer markets. In response, the industry proposed a means of identifying raw diamonds from conflict-affected regions, and developed a "chain of custody" process to ensure the conflict diamonds did not enter legitimate markets. The United Nations convened a meeting in Kimberly, South Africa, to establish a broader global regime regulating the export and especially the import of diamonds under this certification system. The system has not operated perfectly, in part due to the weakness of governance in many diamond-rich countries. Nevertheless, the Kimberly Process is a unique effort to address the particular way in which trade and conflict intersect in failed states such as Sierra Leone. Similar systems have been proposed for other "conflict commodities," such as timber, coltan, and gold, but there has been no effective action on them.

Another issue that has come to international attention, but with a less successful outcome so far, is the problem of providing security to the people and facilities at risk in conflict-affected regions—without at the same time endangering local communities and individuals. Headlines have pointed to the complicity of corporations in abuses by government police and military forces that were supposed to protect the corporations' people and assets but did so by violating the security of their own citizenry. They have used corporate equipment in order to launch attacks on communities, as has happened in Nigeria. Some companies have attempted to protect their interests by paying off local paramilitary and rebel groups, as Chiquita Brands did in Colombia, potentially prolonging the violence there. Other companies have tried to avoid complicity with government forces by hiring private security companies, but these companies have been accused of corruption and human rights abuses.[21] In the final year of the Clinton administration, foreign policy leaders in the US and the UK began to address the intersection of security and human rights. They convened a multi-stakeholder forum, including the two governments, a number of major international human rights organizations, and a handful of companies. They developed what came to be called the Voluntary Principles on Human Rights and Security, a set of principles for companies to adopt when contracting for protection. The principles provide guidance on working with both public and private security providers, and they are intended to be included in company contracts with host governments.

In the past few years, actors have struggled for the Principles to become more institutionalized, with a wider array of participants and an international mechanism for promotion and expansion. Some companies and governments have adopted the Principles, but they have not so far had a significant impact. Dialogue and negotiations continue, both within the structure of the Voluntary Principles and within other arenas. There has been an ongoing search for some way to reduce the complicity of companies in abuses by governments and to regulate the behaviour of the private security companies, which have become all too ubiquitous in Afghanistan and Iraq.[22]

One of the most interesting and innovative initiatives that attempts to ensure that investment benefits a society instead of undermining it is the revenue-management plan established for the Chad–Cameroon Natural Gas Pipeline project.[23] In this case, a consortium of oil and gas producers, led by ExxonMobil, realized that instability and pervasive corruption in these countries, particularly Chad, mixed with extreme poverty, were likely to make any major infrastructure project like this one risky. They asked the World Bank to participate, which proposed and negotiated an extensive revenue-management system. Under this plan, the majority of the revenues the companies would pay to the government—80 percent—were placed in an offshore account in London, governed by a board of eminent persons. These funds would be used for development, health, and education projects. Another percentage would be for a fund for future generations, essentially a savings account for when the gas was depleted. The rest would go to the government. As a requirement for the project to go forward, the Chadian government passed legislation incorporating the plan into domestic law. The plan was an innovative attempt to establish a system similar to ones that exist in Norway and Alaska, but imposed on a reluctant government. The corrupt regime in Chad has done everything it can to undermine the system, passing new legislation mandating that a larger portion of revenue go directly to the government, primarily for weapons purchases. The World Bank suspended its relations with the government for a time, trying to negotiate a better outcome. The plan has come under heavy criticism for weaknesses on the implementation side.[24]

The final example has to do with the transparency issue—the fact that companies and governments do not make public the terms of their agreements: How much money is generated by a project? How much is paid by the companies to the government? What do the governments spend the money on? Many people see this secrecy as a barrier to accountability and more productive and equitable use of the revenues. In response, the UK government under Prime Minister Tony Blair launched the Extractive Industries Transparency Initiative (EITI), to persuade governments to come clean and publicize their revenues and their budgets. At the same time, a coalition of NGOs, now numbering in the hundreds and underwritten in part by the financier George Soros, launched the Publish What You Pay campaign. The PWYP is targeted specifically at companies and urges them to publicize their payments regardless of any confidentiality clauses in their agreements with host governments. The EITI has now been adopted by a number of countries, including Nigeria, which now publishes revenue data in the local newspapers. Companies have not been eager to adopt transparency provisions, although they are indicating more willingness to consider doing so as long as other companies do it too. The EITI and efforts to promote corporate transparency of revenues are both relatively new initiatives, with more potential than actual impact at the moment.

These are the major international initiatives to promote what some call "conflict-sensitive business practices." In addition, there are literally hundreds of smaller projects involving small and medium-sized enterprises operating at the local level.[25] They all involve new forms of partnership between the private sector and governments, international organizations, and NGOs. All are viewed as new models designed to limit the degree to which investment, particularly in the natural resource sector, contributes to conflict and corruption. But, as is obvious, none has been completely successful.

STUMBLING DOWN A NEW PATH, OR TAKING THE WRONG ROAD?

The initiatives described above all suffer from a lack of political commitment and weak institutionalization. None of them provides a clear-cut model for the business and conflict-prevention agenda. It may be that the problems we see are simply a reflection of the fact that these are entirely new sorts of governance mechanisms, with all the faults we would expect in an experimental phase. Or it may be that the business and conflict agenda rests upon incorrect assumptions about conflict prevention and the degree to which it is possible to reduce conflict and corruption by targeting private sector activity.

The significant intervening variable in this equation is the role of the host governments. This is the weakest link in conflict prevention. In some cases, the government is a participant in or instigator of violent conflict. In other cases, leaders are conflicted over their willingness or capacity to act upon these new initiatives. Too often, government leaders have no incentive to support the kinds of initiatives described above. Many are unwilling or unable to find the right formula to distribute wealth and economic activity or to shield the vulnerable from the effects of change. Many developing countries suffer from weak institutions in general, with unresponsive and unaccountable governments. Without the will to reform internally, or even if there *is* internal pressure for reform but too many obstacles to overcome, then sustainable development with peace will be difficult to achieve.

Companies themselves face competing incentives to act against violence, human rights abuses, and corruption. On the one hand, there may be a long-term business case to be made for action in the present to prevent losses in the future.[26] But often, short-term interest dictates that companies maintain the status quo. Individual action can undercut the competitiveness of a company in important markets, and collective action is undermined by the temptation to cheat. We particularly see this in the case of diamonds and transparency.

The international community could do more to facilitate constructive action by the private sector and foster better governance in host countries. Donor governments and international agencies such as the World Bank can provide incentives for transparency and better revenue management by making access to aid, export credits, and trade benefits conditional on steps in this direction. The Chad–Cameroon project, despite its weaknesses, demonstrates one way in which an international organization can provide the framework and incentives to organize action on the part of companies, governments, and civil society representatives. In exceptional cases, donors should consider imposing sanctions on companies or governments in response to violations of emerging norms. Certainly, at a very basic level, the international community can do much more to provide information and expertise that would facilitate more conflict-sensitive practices by firms, as the UN Global Compact has tried to do with its Dialogue on Companies in Zones of Conflict and its extensive knowledge network. The international community as a whole should facilitate further negotiations to expand and institutionalize existing initiatives. They should promote further efforts, such as certification systems for other commodities similar to diamonds, and ensure that revenue management systems are established in new oil-producing states in particular.

When it comes to the role of companies in weakly governed countries, all involved do need to grapple with the one issue that has not been settled—are there places so ripe for breakdown and abuse that corporate investors should avoid them entirely? Is the pressure or need for development in poor countries so great that investment should be encouraged no matter the consequences? And should corporations be making this decision? To date, we have no effective international regulatory mechanism for global corporations, despite decades of half-hearted efforts in this direction. Nevertheless, there are some who believe this next step is inevitable—and too long delayed.

NOTES

Acknowledgement: This chapter is based on a talk given at the Centre for International Governance Innovation on May 29, 2006. It is based in part on a report for the United Nations Global Compact, *Enabling Economics of Peace: Public Policy for Conflict-Sensitive*

Business (2005), co-authored with Karen Ballentine. The author would like to thank John English and Patricia Goff for their invitation to CIGI, and Denise O'Brien and Melissa Powell of the UN Global Compact for the opportunity to work with them on an important project. The research for this chapter was supported in part by a grant from the United States Institute of Peace. The opinions, findings, and conclusions or recommendations expressed in this chapter are those of the author and do not necessarily reflect the views of the United States Institute of Peace.

1 Ian Smillie, Lansana Gberie, and Ralph Hazleton "The Heart of the Matter: Sierra Leone, Diamonds, and Human Security," Ottawa: Partnership Africa Canada, 2000; see also Global Witness, "A Crude Awakening: The Role of Oil and Banking Industries in Angolan Civil War and the Plunder of State Assets," 1999. http://www.global witness.org/media_library_detail.php/93/en/a_crude_awakening.

2 Despite their expansion internationally, most investment is in the "triad" of North America, EU, and Japan. However, in recent years there has been a surge of investment into the developing countries.

3 Litvin's book, *Empires of Profit,* provides a historical context for CSR by examining the similarities in the difficult encounters between foreign companies and local societies ranging from the British East India Company to Nike today. See Daniel Litvin, *Empires of Profit: Commerce, Conquest, and Corporate Responsibility* (New York and London: Texere, 2003).

4 Jean-Jacques Serban-Schreiber, *The American Challenge*, translated by R. Steel (New York: Avon Books, 1969).

5 Charles Lipson, *Standing Guard: Protecting Foreign Capital in the Nineteenth and Twentieth Centuries* (Berkeley and Los Angeles: University of California Press, 1985).

6 Fernando Henrique Cardoso and Enzo Faletto, *Dependency and Development* (Berkeley: University of California Press, 1979).

7 Robert Gilpin, *U.S. Power and the Multinational Corporation* (New York: Basic Books, 1975). See also Stephen Krasner, *Defending the National Interest: Raw Materials Investments and U.S. Foreign Policy* (Princeton: Princeton University Press, 1978).

8 John Kline, *International Codes and Multinational Business: Setting Guidelines for International Business Operations* (Westport, CT: Greenwood Press, 1985).

9 Beth Simmons, Frank Dobbin, and Geoffrey Garret, "Introduction: The International Diffusion of Liberalism," *International Organization* 60 (Fall 2006): 781–810.

10 Audio Klotz, *Norms in International Relations: The Struggle against Apartheid* (Ithaca, NY: Cornell University Press, 1995).

11 For an excellent overview of the corporate accountability "movement," see Robin Broad and John Cavanagh, "The Corporate Accountability Movement: Lessons and Opportunities" (Washington, DC: World Resources Institute, 1998); and Jem Bendell, "Barricades and Boardrooms: A Contemporary History of the Corporate Accountability Movement" (Geneva: UN Research Institute for Social Development, 2004).

12 Virginia Haufler, *A Public Role for the Private Sector: Industry Self-Regulation in the Global Economy* (Washington, DC: Carnegie Endowment for International Peace, 2001).

13 Global Witness, "Rough Trade: The Role of Companies and Governments in the Angolan Conflict," 1998; see also Global Witness 1999, and Smillie at el., "The Heart of the Matter." The report can be downloaded at: http://blooddiamond.pacweb .org/docs/heart_of_the_matter.doc.

14 Karen Ballentine and Jake Sherman, eds. *The Political Economy of Armed Conflict: Beyond Greed and Grievance* (Boulder, CO: Lynne Rienner Publishers, 2003); Mats Berdal and David M. Malone, eds. *Greed and Grievance: Economic Agendas in Civil Wars* (Boulder, CO: Lynne Rienner Publishers, 2000).

15 Macartan Humphreys, "Economics and Violent Conflict," Harvard University, 2003; Macartan Humphreys, "Natural Resources, Conflict, and Conflict Resolution," *Journal of Conflict Resolution* 49, no. 4: 508–37.

16 Michael L. Ross, "Oil, Drugs, and Diamonds: How Do Natural Resources Vary in their Impact on Civil War?" Produced for the International Peace Academy project on Economic Agendas in Civil Wars, 2002. In *The Political Economy of Armed Conflict: Beyond Greed and Grievance*, ed. Karen Ballentine and Jake Sherman (Boulder, CO: Lynne Rienner Publishers, 2003).

17 Governments often require companies to utilize government security forces, but even when a company hires private security, these forces are often equally unaccountable and corrupt. See Deborah Avant, *The Market for Force* (Cambridge: Cambridge University Press, 2005); Anna Leander, "Private Agency and the Definition of Public Security Concerns: The Role of Private Military Companies," in *The Politics of Protection, Sites of Insecurity and Political Agency*, ed. Jef Huysmans, Andrew Dobson, and Raia Prokhovnik (London: Routledge, 2006).

18 Ted Robert Gurr and Monty Marshall, "Peace and Conflict 2005" (College Park: Center for International Development and Conflict Management, 2006); Human Security Centre, "Human Security Brief 2006," Andrew Mack, ed. (Vancouver: University of British Columbia, 2006).

19 Foreign investors typically undertake some form of political risk assessment prior to investing, but this evaluates how the local and international environment will affect the company. A conflict impact assessment is the reverse—essentially, it is a political risk assessment for the local population that would be affected by the new investment.

20 Smillie et al., "The Heart of the Matter"; Alex Vines, "Oil, Diamonds and Death," *World Today* 58, no. 3 (March 2002): 19–20.

21 For a detailed examination of the evolution of private security companies and the issues they raise, see Deborah Avant, *The Market for Force* (Cambridge: Cambridge University Press, 2005).

22 Bennett Freeman, "Statement, Corporate Social Responsibility—Confusion or Multi-Pronged Approach?" Paper read at Congressional Human Rights Caucus Members' Briefing, September 28, 2005, at Washington, DC.

23 Donald R. Norland, "Innovations of the Chad–Cameroon Pipeline Project: Thinking Outside the Box," *Mediterranean Quarterly* 14, no. 2 (2003): 46–59.

24 Amnesty International, "Contracting Out of Human Rights: The Chad–Cameroon Pipeline Project" (London: Amnesty International UK, 2005).

25 Jessica Banfield, Canan Gunduz, and Nick Killick, eds. *Local Business, Local Peace: The Peacebuilding Potential of the Domestic Private Sector* (London: International Alert, 2006).

26 Jane Nelson, *The Business of Peace: The Private Sector as a Partner in Conflict Prevention and Resolution* (London: Prince of Wales Business Leaders Forum, 2000).

10

The FIM G8 Project, 2002–2006

*A Case Analysis of a Project to Initiate
Civil Society Engagement with the G8*

Nigel T. Martin

THE MONTREAL INTERNATIONAL FORUM (FIM)

The Montreal International Forum (FIM) was established in 1998 in Montreal
as a global alliance of individuals and organizations with the goal of improving the influence of international civil society on the United Nations and the
multilateral system. FIM believes that the stated goals of the UN are beyond
reasonable reproach and that the challenge of the FIM alliance is to assist
meaningfully in bringing them to fruition.[1]

FIM provides a neutral setting for an annual forum for reflection and
active learning about the interaction between international civil society and
the multilateral system. In so doing, the forum draws lessons from experiences
in different sectors, regions, and multilateral institutions that can strengthen
the voice and participation of civil society actors in the multilateral system.

BEGINNINGS OF THE FIM G8 PROJECT

This project is an excellent example of collaboration between a private funding foundation and a global civil society organization. The spark of the idea
began within the Ford Foundation. Ford was concerned about the lack of
public accountability of the G8 and inquired whether FIM, with its interest in
multilateral democracy, would be interested in trying to open up a direct dialogue with the G8.

A memo was prepared for the FIM board of directors and the board discussed the proposal via teleconference. It was agreed that the proposal fell within the mission of FIM. The G8 is multilateral, even though it has no permanent secretariat and no institutional home. It was deemed essential that the voice of Southern civil society be heard within the G8. Although the G8 is almost a virtual structure, it does make real decisions that, when applied, have an important impact upon the South and upon those multilateral agencies whose policies and programs directly impact upon the South. Also, FIM could bring its neutral convening powers to the process. There were, however, substantial risks to embarking on this project.

Identifying and Managing Risks

Several risks were identified from the outset. The greatest concern was that FIM would isolate itself from the broader civil society community by appearing to be a spokesgroup for a broad CS constituency. This concern was twofold. First, there was a concern that, by our actions, we would appear to be a representative body. A second concern was that some of the G8 authorities would use FIM discussions to claim that broad-based consultation had taken place with international civil society.

There were additional risks. It was unclear whether sufficient consensus as to the value of the exercise could be achieved within civil society networks, including within FIM itself. There was also serious concern that, by beginning a formal dialogue with the G8, FIM would confer a greater legitimacy upon the G8 than was intended. Time constraints posed an additional risk. At the time of the FIM board discussions and ensuing decision to proceed, less than six months remained before the Kananaskis meetings. Given these time pressures, FIM might not have been able to achieve the required quality of analysis and discussion. It was also recognized that any proposal would have to satisfy the wishes of the Ford Foundation. Ford was the sole source of funding readily apparent at the time, and it was understood that changing the consultative patterns between civil society and the G8 would be a long-term process. Last but not least, it was recognized of course that the G8 authorities might reject the idea of such a dialogue outright.

To manage these risks it was essential that responsibility for approval of the process, for selection of the participants, and for strategic options be with the FIM board of directors. While concern was expressed within the board about the risks involved in proceeding, it was agreed that the G8 was perhaps the paramount multilateral body of global influence and that some form of dialogue with international civil society was essential. The board decided to approve the project subject to four important conditions:

1. FIM would not present itself as a gatekeeper of global civil society.
2. FIM would concentrate on the means of improving the process of dialogue between civil society and the G8. (It was recognized that other bodies are better equipped to discuss the content of a G8 meeting.)
3. FIM would deal only with global issues affecting civil society and the G8 and would not deal with issues specific to Canada, the host G8 country in 2002.
4. In opening up dialogue with the G8, FIM did not wish, in any manner, to confer legitimacy upon the G8 as a global governance mechanism.

CS/G8 2002: KANANASKIS, CANADA

Context

The choice of site, agenda, content, and process of each G8 meeting is almost entirely the prerogative of the host head of state. The host sherpa plays the major role in administering all arrangements, but in a very real way the G8 remains personal to the head of state, and informal. The sherpa may or may not be a senior professional civil servant. In some cases, the sherpa is a trusted friend of the head of state. The same sherpa may be in place for several years or may be changed yearly. From a negotiating perspective this makes the G8 a moving target. In 2002 there were no precedents to be observed, nor was there any institutional memory that could give a legitimate series of benchmarks. Given this rather ephemeral structure, the accumulated experience within the FIM network of dealings with multilateral organizations had limited value.

All negotiations with host authorities were conducted with a secretariat set up within the Canadian Ministry of Foreign Affairs. This secretariat, although having some semblance of permanence, was in reality shored up considerably to assume Canada's hosting responsibilities.

At the outset, expectations by FIM were high, if not downright naive. FIM hoped to be part of the G8 formal discussions, similar to the position that civil society actors play in other multilateral fora. Our original objective of meeting with the heads of state themselves was rejected out of hand. Senior bureaucrats pointed out somewhat petulantly that not even ministers of the host country had access to G8 discussions. Thus FIM embarked on a steep learning curve as it began to develop a strategy for engagement.

Orienting and Developing a Strategy for Engagement

Part of this learning curve was the realization that, while meeting heads of state was impossible, even a meeting with all the sherpas was highly unlikely.

For the Kananaskis meeting, the major hurdle in bringing together all sherpas was lack of time. Given the increasingly late date, this was an understandable limitation. As expectations quickly became more realistic, the FIM strategy for engagement took on a clearer focus.

FIM staff began to understand the G8 context through observation of some of the consultative sessions with representatives of Canadian civil society organized by the Canadian host sherpa. It was apparent from these observations that these were consultations in name only. The real exercise appeared to be to inform civil society about the G8 and its priorities and to sell the proposed Canadian agenda. Any embarrassing and/or critical questions were readily deflected. No real dialogue emerged, and the meetings were not structured to allow civil society participants to present any kind of coherent counter-agenda.

Given these observations FIM became convinced that it was essential that the host sherpa not be designated as host or chair of the proposed meeting. It was suggested, and accepted, that a mutually acceptable neutral chair be identified. It was also apparent that the selection by FIM of the civil society participants would be key to the meeting's success. Unfortunately, since agreement on the principle of the meeting itself occurred so late in the process, it was impossible to present names of participants to the G8 authorities until late in the process.

Choosing Civil Society Participants

FIM identified several basic principles and qualities for choosing civil society participants. First, it was important that participants attend in their individual capacity. However, it was also imperative that participants have strong networking experience and diplomatic skills. FIM felt that it was essential that the meeting be discreet in nature, that it be "behind closed doors," and that embarrassment on either side be avoided. Both parties had to leave the meeting judging that it had been a success and that it would be worthwhile to continue the exercise in the future.

It was inevitable that not all participants would have known each other in advance nor have collaborated together. Participants would have a relatively short period of time together. They would have to quickly agree upon the immediate and long-term objectives, identify and prioritize an agenda, and identify spokespeople. Thus it was essential to choose people with a well-developed capacity for teamwork.

FIM invited fifteen participants from around the world. The majority of participants came from the South, and there was strong gender and regional balance, although because of the attention being given to Africa, this continent was slightly overrepresented. Participants were invited in their personal capacity and on the basis of their knowledge of and experience with international civil society dealings with multilateral bodies. In spite of a tight time-frame and the delicate nature of the project, the response from invitees was enthusiastic.

Negotiating Agreements with the Host Country

Canada agreed early on in the negotiations that the host sherpa would participate in the meeting, and from there a convenient date was established. FIM strongly requested that, irrespective of the lateness of the date, senior representatives from the other G8 members be invited and this was agreed to. The agreements were in fact tripartite, among FIM, the host government, and Ford Foundation. Contact with potential participants had to be developed before a final agreement was in place.

Within FIM it was agreed that there were several precedents in multi-stakeholder dialogues that could provide important lessons for any form of consultation between civil society and the G8. It was agreed that no long-term objectives by FIM, and/or other possible organizations, could be identified until the first meeting was concluded.

It was recognized that the planning process for Kananaskis was well advanced, and that civil society input could be more viable and effective leading into the 2003 meeting in France. Nevertheless, it was agreed to ask that African civil society representatives be invited by the G8 and/or the host government to meet with the five African heads of state invited to Kananaskis.

Preparatory Meeting in Montreal

In preparation for the meeting with the G8 representatives, the fifteen civil society participants met in Montreal on May 21–22 for two full days of planning. Presentations were given by both participants and outside experts on the history of multi-stakeholder dialogues, an insider's view of the G8 from a former sherpa, and African perspectives on the NEPAD (New Partnership for Africa's Development) experience. Special attention was given to the role of African civil society, and how that might influence NEPAD.

In the ensuing discussion, considerable attention was paid to the danger of allowing the G8 to use meetings with civil society as a means of establishing a long-term G8/civil society agenda and, therefore, strengthening their own (G8) legitimacy.

It was agreed that process and content are both part of the same spectrum, and that while process was the priority, it could not be totally divorced from content. In this regard, it was agreed that NEPAD was an important example of how the quality of the content could be adversely affected by a poor process of consultation beforehand. Ultimately, therefore it was decided to discuss the NEPAD experience with the G8 representatives. The group was ready.

Ottawa 2002: The First Civil Society Engagement
with G8 Officials

The first FIM-facilitated meeting was held in Ottawa on the afternoon of May 23, 2002. The G8 was represented by the Canadian host sherpa to the G8, the French ambassador to Canada and a colleague, the British High Commissioner to Canada and two representatives from the Japanese embassy to Canada. Betty Plewes, an independent Canadian consultant, chaired the meeting.

The meeting lasted three hours. Following general introductory comments, civil society participants made the three following presentations, each of which was followed by one half-hour discussion:

1. The global democratic deficit and civil society engagements: the G8 is seen as an informal club with little accountability. This leads to public apathy, cynicism, and a widening credibility gap between global governance structures and those being governed. The G8 consultative process is recent and inadequate.
2. The NEPAD consultative process: Although there was some satisfaction that the G8 was responding to NEPAD, there was concern that NEPAD was a top-down process that did not include inputs from African civil society. Participants felt that NEPAD did not have wide African support. It was not a one-time opportunity. It was seriously flawed, with a total lack of gender analysis, its underlying macroeconomic framework has been put into question, and its resource mobilization strategy may well be unworkable. The NEPAD process needed to be opened up.
3. Future G8/CS dialogue, building upon multi-stakeholder experiences: The underlying principles must be good governance, transparency, and legitimacy. G8 cannot continue to hide from its constituents. There is a wealth of experience of dialogue between civil society and multilateral bodies. Several examples of previous engagement between civil society, the G7/8 and different multilateral organizations were presented.

Finally, the CS group requested that the G8 host facilitate a meeting between African civil society representatives and the five African heads of state invited to Kananaskis.

Outcomes: CS/G8 2002

While the Canadian G8 host made no concrete commitments, there were several requests and agreements resulting from this first engagement. Some of these were followed through and some were not. The request to meet with the African leaders was deemed to be best arranged directly between African civil society and the African leaders, but the request for facilitation by Canada was not denied outright. (FIM wrote a letter to the Canadian host sherpa requesting official Canadian support in arranging a meeting between African civil society representatives and the invited African Heads of State. No meeting occurred.)

The Canadian host sherpa requested that all African civil society critiques of NEPAD be forwarded to his office to inform their own work for the G8 Action Plan for Africa.

There was a mutual agreement to have a Kananaskis post-mortem meeting with civil society. (Although FIM and the Canadian authorities agreed upon the value of a post-mortem, this never occurred. Immediately following Kananaskis there were significant changes within the Foreign Affairs' secretariat. This halted all momentum and made continuity difficult.)

Another outcome of this meeting was a checklist of considerations in establishing an effective CS/G8 consultation process. This was presented to, and accepted by, the French delegates. The French expressed their interest in consulting with civil society leading up to the 2003 G8. (Once the 2003 host sherpa was named and the new team well ensconced, Canada was very helpful in supporting FIM's efforts to organize a 2003 consultation, to be held in France shortly before the Evian G8. Similar support was also received from the UK and France itself, two of the participants of the 2002 meeting.)

Lessons Learned from CS/G8 2002

In spite of its fluid structure, the G8 is, for civil society activists, an unavoidable multilateral body. Global civil society is a major actor in global governance and had by 2002 developed sufficient diplomatic experience to exert influence. The time had come for collaborative initiatives, and these would take time and effective strategies. It was evident that a growing number of G8 countries (perhaps even then a majority) favoured improved dialogue with civil society. It was also confirmed that reaching an agreement on an improved and consistent model of CS/G8 dialogue would be a lengthy process.

Civil society efforts must be proactive in nature, and strategies must be applied throughout the year, beginning long before the official hosting responsibilities are transferred. (Host countries change officially on each January 1.) Civil society must try to influence the agenda setting well in advance of the meeting. Although the agenda is entirely the prerogative of the host head of state, it is inevitably influenced by the ongoing meetings of G8 Ministers, world events, perceived priorities of the host country, and carry-over issues.

While, in general, civil society expertise and political clout are highly appreciated, receptivity for ongoing dialogue is not universal and continues to vary depending upon the sentiments of both civil society representatives and governments of the host countries. Civil society leaders in the host country must see the FIM dialogue as complementary, not contrary, to other civil society initiatives being undertaken globally and/or within the host country.

As preparations began for the 2003 G8 in Evian, France, it was agreed that civil society actions had to be coordinated with the G8 schedule. Civil society coordination had to be in place early enough to attempt to influence the setting of the agenda, normally completed less than six months prior to the actual meeting. From the outset, close co-operation between French and global civil society would be essential. A strategy began to form.

Once identified, all G8 sherpas must be contacted individually and collectively by civil society within and outside of the G8 countries. With the finalization of the agenda, global coordination by civil society would concentrate on two converging priorities: bringing their expertise to bear upon the content of the meeting and ensuring that there is a viable system of democratic consultation. Most important, and certainly a difficult challenge, was ensuring that all of this was accomplished in a way that did not further legitimize the G8 as a governance body. Given the divisive attitudes within CS as to the very existence of the G8, let alone its legitimacy on governance issues, any slippage on this objective would split civil society into weakened camps.

With this in mind, the Global Governance Conference (GO2) held in Montreal from October 13 to 16, 2002, entitled Civil Society and the Democratization of Global Governance, included a special session on the G8. This session served as an important occasion to bring together those civil society participants from France who were actively planning an engagement for 2003 and their global counterparts.

CS/G8 2003: EVIAN, FRANCE

Preparations

Preparations with the French government officials for the 2003 G8 went smoothly. The French had arrived in Ottawa in 2002 with a somewhat skeptical attitude but had rapidly seen the value of the direct and forthright dialogue between civil society actors and G8 officials within the office of the President of France.

There were two minor issues to be resolved before a meeting could be finalized. The French government wanted formal assurance from French CS organizers that this meeting would receive their support and, since they wanted to host the meeting at the Elysée (the official residence of the French president), they were opposed to the appointment of a neutral chair. On the first point, FIM undertook discussions with representatives of the two major French coalitions of NGO networks preparing for the G8, CRID (Centre de recherche et d'information pour le développement) and Coordination-Sud, to ensure that the FIM project would complement any national civil society efforts within France leading up to the G8. As a result of these discussions, when asked by the French officials whether our initiative would cause them any difficulties with their own civil society, FIM was able to confirm that we had their "official support." On the second point both parties agreed that there would be no designated chair.

Coincidentally with FIM's preparation for the 2003 meeting in Paris, the French coalition of international NGOs, Coordination-Sud, convened a meeting with some of its counterparts from the other G8 countries. This first meeting of what was known as The Platform Group included representatives from the Canadian Council for International Cooperation (CCIC), InterAction of the USA, and BOND of the UK. Because of their broad-based membership, this grouping of umbrella NGOs brings a certain capacity to claim representivity of the NGO community within the G8 countries.

Elysée 2003: The Second CS/G8 Meeting

The 2003 CS/G8 meeting was held in the Elysée in May 2003, in a special global context. The war in Iraq had begun and relations between France and the USA were strained. The Americans had attempted to isolate the French in their opposition to the war. Perhaps as a result of this ambiance, French government officials indicated to FIM that France wanted to collaborate increasingly with global civil society.

For the second year running the only sherpa present was the host sherpa. In addition, there were senior ambassadorial representatives from the UK, Canada, Germany, Italy, and Russia. The Japanese ambassador to France attended, and there was no American representative.

At this meeting many substantive issues were discussed. CS participants raised issues based on a commitment to principles of democratic global governance and a strong belief in the need for G8 accountability to universal multilateral bodies, as well as to a wider grouping of nations and peoples, particularly in the South. Largely due to the Iraq war, global security was addressed as a major topic. Participants argued that: "A human security approach is needed because the 'war on terrorism' increases social and economic instability, impacts negatively on human rights, exacerbates local conflicts and monopolizes enormous resources that could otherwise be spent on human security priorities."

Participants asserted that human security was best addressed through existing frameworks such as the Millennium Development Goals (MDGs). The MDGs address critical G8 agenda issues such as poverty, AIDS, and water. Responsibility of G8 countries supporting MDGs is critical, although the credibility of their commitments is still lacking. Urgent progress is needed on funding different mechanisms simultaneously, such as: Official Development Assistance (ODA) levels, debt reduction, and a new international taxation scheme (they are meant to be additional to the MDGs). Economic and financial stability can be secured through opening G8 markets to products from the South (agriculture, notably), elimination of dumping, and reform of macroeconomic rules of the International Monetary Fund (IMF) that limit social spending.

This was the second year of NEPAD discussions, and many pressing issues were raised. Participants observed that the NEPAD process is diffuse and that transparency is needed with respect to implementation steps, levels of disbursements, and interface mechanisms with civil society both at the regional and country levels. Peer review process should work both ways.

The African CSO participatants observed that the responsive approach of G8 countries to NEPAD should also be applied to African demands with, among many areas mentioned, agriculture, where there is an urgent need to move beyond the moratorium on biotechnology (which is a good first step) to agreement on commodity prices, eliminating dumping, and opening G8 markets to Africa; HIV/AIDS, where there is a need for immediate and adequate commitments for the special fund; access to medicine, with, at a minimum, no backsliding on the Doha agreement; and ODA, which should not be used as a negotiation card by G8 countries in trade talks in Cancun.

Outcomes of Elysée Meeting: CS/G8 2003

As in Ottawa, participants continued to advance the advantages of democratic multilateralism and of "democratizing" the G8 process. In response to the crisis, and the systemic undermining of the multilateral system, G8 countries need to renew a clear commitment to a multipolar world and put its weight behind the UN system to reinforce multilateralism. On "democratizing" the G8 process and facilitating engagement with civil society, the following recommendations were made:

1. Make decisions more transparent through the use of communiqués;
2. Institute more informal and formal exchanges and timely releases throughout the year;
3. Approach demonstrations as a key democratic right of citizens, not as a security concern;
4. Make public the follow-up and implementation status of past G8 decisions;
5. Make public all steps in the twelve-month G8 cycle including the transition process;
6. Use and build on precedents and experiences for facilitating CS dialogue in other multilateral systems; and
7. Create space for briefing (before) and debriefing (after) with civil society.

Lessons Learned from CS/G8 2003

During preparations for the French meeting, it became obvious that the FIM initiative required support from the host civil society and, in particular, those elements of national French CS who were responsible for organizing parallel events. In fact the office of the French president insisted that such support be confirmed. This realization influenced future planning and has been an important component of planning since.

In some ways the 2003 dialogue was a love-in between the civil society participants and the host government. Given that the Americans were not present and that both CS and the French government were seriously opposed to the war in Iraq, the discussions were amicable and geared unexpectedly toward the war. Also, for the first time, it became apparent that the host government saw political advantage in being in solidarity (on selected issues) with key elements of international civil society. This tendency has since been maintained and, in some cases, intensified. The absence of American officials, however, brought a sense of unreality to the dialogue. CS participants realized that any serious agreement with G8 officials would require American buy-in.

CS/G8 2004: SEA ISLAND, THE UNITED STATES

2003 marked the second straight year that the USA had not participated in the dialogue with civil society. FIM entered into planning with American officials with a realistic assessment that the possibility of achieving their commitment was low. The FIM secretariat explored closely with senior American officials the possibility of a civil society dialogue prior to the 2004 G8 meetings in Sea Island. Since the FIM board was concerned from the outset that the Americans would not agree to a meeting, parallel negotiations with the British, the 2005 hosts, were also conducted.

Following several phone conversations, a face-to-face meeting was held in Washington with a career foreign affairs diplomat who had been seconded to the National Security Council (NSC). The NSC oversaw the 2004 G8, and this official reported directly to Condoleeza Rice, then head of the NSC. FIM received a sympathetic hearing to our proposal, but eventually the Americans recommended that we put all of our efforts into the UK G8. This was received as realistic, friendly, and helpful advice. Months later we learned that the American administration had decided that in 2004, there would be no "outreach," because if there were, they would have to deal with the NGOs. Thus, with the G8 Project stalled, a backup plan and funding was needed to keep the project alive to 2005.

Backup Plan Rejected

Following the notification that there would be no dialogue with G8 officials, FIM submitted a backup plan for financial support to the Ford Foundation. This alternative plan had been in the original submission to Ford, included due to the possibility that a formal US meeting might not occur.

In lieu of a direct dialogue with G8 officials, FIM proposed a two-day meeting that would have two main objectives. First, the event would be a serious brainstorming occasion to finalize the concept of a permanent civil society mechanism of dialogue after the 2005 UK G8. This would be done with the intent of ensuring agreement with the UK to have this model agreed to by all G8 countries during their 2005 meeting. The second objective was to use the US 2004 meeting to ensure high-level media understanding of civil society's interest in the G8 process. In order to achieve these two objectives we aimed to convene a meeting close to the dates of the 2004 G8 and close to the G8 site. Ford rejected this proposal, convinced, they told us, that the clearly recalcitrant attitude of the American administration had irreparably damaged the process.

Although FIM had wanted to proceed with the standard G8 meeting in the US in 2004, we were not really disappointed about the US reaction. Given their absence from the first two meetings, it was doubtful that we could have begun to negotiate any kind of a permanent mechanism with them as hosts. This freed us up to begin negotiating with the British much sooner than would otherwise have been the case.

Of Special Note in 2004

Although American CS and international civil society activities were low-key in the 2004 G8 at Sea Island, there was an important CS initiative out of Africa. This led to the arrival of a delegation of African CS participants in the USA at the time of the G8 that concentrated on sensitizing the American public and media to the issue of NEPAD. Additionally, a second meeting of the Platform Group (first convened in France in 2003) was held in Washington in early 2004, and coalitions were present from all G8 countries with the exception of Russia. A similar meeting was planned for the UK at some time prior to the 2005 G8.

REFLECTIONS: FIM'S GROWING UNDERSTANDING OF THE G8

Up to 2004 the FIM experience had been very much a learning-on-the-job process. Some of the key factors that influenced our capacity to negotiate, as well as the means by which we do so, were learned through trial and error. Each G8 is the personal affair of the host head of state. He or she determines the agenda. The official G8 meeting is very private and is a meeting to which normally powerful ministers seldom have direct access. The host head of state takes over the process on January 1 of the hosting year.

There is no permanent G8 secretariat. Every head of state names a sherpa as their official representative in the planning process. Each sherpa will have a small secretariat support team. Typically all eight sherpas meet several times a year. When it is time for a head of state to host the meeting, the secretariat in the host country can typically grow in size for a period of about eighteen to twenty-four months, this occurring therefore every eight years.

There are no automatically recurring agenda items. This was somewhat changed with the 2002 introduction of NEPAD and the subsequent naming of ongoing African personal representatives (APRs), who are still in place. Non-host heads of state are very sensitive about pressuring the host head of state regarding any perceived agenda priorities. However, the agenda is often altered at the last moment due to world events and/or the unavoidable influence of the US head of state. Nevertheless, it remains entirely the prerogative of the host head of state to decide whether any issue will continue to be on the agenda.

Time constraints remain a challenge. A host country assumes responsibility for the G8 in January. The host sherpa may be named at a still later date. The G8 meeting is in June. The final agenda is often decided upon close to the June date. This typical tight schedule increases the challenge for civil society to plan and react with care and knowledge.

Reality Check: Reflecting on the Original Expected Outcomes

The original intent of the Ford Foundation and FIM was to establish a permanent dialogue mechanism between international civil society and the G8. Following the Genoa tragedy at the 2001 G8, wherein an Italian protester was killed by Italian police, G8 governments acknowledged that there had to be some form of dialogue with civil society. In that respect, the FIM proposal was judged to be timely. It was an unspoken understanding that G8 governments wanted to diminish the perceived need for costly and often dangerous civil society demonstrations and that the FIM dialogue might help in that objective.

FIM's intent was to build an atmosphere where constructive and respectful dialogue would occur. Indeed, international civil society had within its ranks the knowledge, experience, and diplomatic skills required to contribute meaningfully to the G8 exercise. It was hoped that FIM would create a selection process of the CS participants that was transparent and included some form of accountability back to a broad CS constituency. It was assumed that, given the variety of issues that are dealt with by the G8, different areas of CS expertise would be tapped each year, according to the host agenda. One important objective had also been to engage the Americans early enough so as to ensure a successful meeting in the US in 2004. With a permanent dialogue mechanism in place, FIM planned to retreat from the process after the 2005 meetings in the UK.

By the end of 2004, FIM had achieved only some of these objectives. It was generally agreed that we had generated constructive dialogue. On that basis, we were in a position to possibly have some increasing influence on G8 agendas and their content. We were however no closer to a permanent dialogue mechanism than when we started, nor had we implemented, nor even identified, a more transparent and accountable process. Furthermore, we had not succeeded in engaging the American administration. Given the 2004 political climate of the United States, it was difficult, if not impossible, to identify American civil society partners who supported strong multilateralism and at the same time had access and influence with the American administration. This had hampered our ability to engage the US in this project.

The G8 Platform Groups (which can claim some degree of representivity within their respective G8 countries) were still at an embryonic stage. The differences in institutional culture between the various coalitions are large and they were still getting to know each other. It was, and remains, clear that it will be a long time before they are able to implement any kind of significant joint efforts on the G8. Progress had been made however. The two host governments that, up to 2004, had collaborated with FIM were positive about their experience and had indicated their satisfaction with FIM and with the project methodology. A strong majority of G8 members were willing to support the FIM effort.

At the end of 2004, it appeared that the objective of creating a permanent dialogue mechanism was faulty. It appeared highly unlikely to occur. The principle of the host head of state being free to set the agenda is sacrosanct. It was not felt to be in the best interests of civil society to encourage any "institutionalization" of the G8. As difficult as it was to deal with such a "moving target," the possibility of encouraging, even indirectly, a permanent and inevitably powerful secretariat, was considered to be fraught with danger. FIM, or a replacement coordinating body, could aim for more transparency and broader involvement. It was not feasible however, to try to identify an organization or structure that represented, and was legally accountable to, international civil society. The potential of the Platform Groups to bring concentrated CS influence from within the G8 national constituencies would take several more years to come to fruition.

It was also critical to remember that the voice of Southern civil society is an important component for effective G8 agenda planning. It remained essential that this voice be channelled directly, rather than via Northern-based representatives. Following the difficulties of 2004 and given the above reality check, the FIM board made the following recommendations in September 2004.

Board Recommendations for FIM

That FIM:

1. Maintain its commitment to the G8 project beyond 2005 and that this commitment respect the conditions as originally outlined by the FIM Board;
2. Seek alternate sources of funding for the project and in particular that FIM encourage the G8 governments themselves (or, if necessary, the host country) to finance the project annually;
3. Move the annual date of the joint meeting up to January of each year;
4. Try to ensure that the G8 participants are all at the sherpa level;
5. Broaden involvement from within Southern civil society;
6. Be more transparent and participatory in the selection process of CS participants;
7. Ensure expert-level input from civil society into specific agenda items that are judged as being of special import to Southern civil society; and
8. Continue to encourage official American participation in the project.

CS/G8 2005: GLENEAGLES, UK

Preparations

Discussions with senior G8 officials in the UK began in mid-2004. FIM had several preparatory talks with the key British officials responsible for organizing the 2005 G8. From the outset, the UK indicated a strong openness to dialogue with civil society. They had verified with the Canadian and French authorities the merit of the FIM approach and indicated that their commitment was solid. This was clearly the case from the outset and all the way though 2004–2005. They also made it clear from the beginning that no final decision regarding our proposal would be made until January 2005. In no manner did they want to appear to be sending a critical signal to the Americans during 2004, while the US was still the official G8 host. At the end of 2004, FIM also had several meetings with British Overseas NGOs for Development (BOND), the umbrella body of UK NGOs and CS coordinator of G8 activities in 2005. The purpose of these meetings was to ensure a complementarity between the FIM approach and that of UK civil society.

UK authorities were much more advanced in their planning and identification of agenda issues than were the 2002–2004 hosts at a comparable point in time. In general, the UK authorities seemed to be prepared to continue with the basic model that we had used beforehand. However, they recommended strongly that we advance our sherpa meeting to January, in order to increase our capacity to influence the final agenda.

In discussions with UK officials during the final planning meeting in 2004, they suggested that a representative from Chatham House join us at the meeting. Chatham House is an independent London-based think tank, with strong connections to the UK government. They had an interesting G8 project that the British proposed could integrate well with the FIM initiative. In that meeting it was agreed that FIM would retain responsibility for planning the sherpa meeting while Chatham House would be responsible for organizing some prepatory expert meetings on the two 2005 agenda topics, Africa and Global Warming. The UK government agreed to finance the dialogue. This was the first time that financing had come from within G8 circles. FIM had discussed the possibility of the dialogues being financed within G8 budgets and had some reservations about CS losing control of the process. In discussions with UK officials, we did examine the advantages of the dialogue being funded from a common G8 pot to be funded by all G8 members. This idea was rejected as being too unwieldy and contentious.

In a final phone call between FIM and UK officials, just before the financial allocation was finalized, the UK official suggested that their funds be transferred directly to Chatham House, since they were already receiving monies allocated to other G8 civil society preparations and that a single grant would simplify administrative procedures.

2004 was the first year in which FIM began to work in collaboration with other networks. Chatham House, in partnership with FIM and also the Green Globe Network, Climate Action Network, and LEAD International, convened a series of planning meetings. Both CSOs and G8 officials agreed to a neutral chair, Simon Upton, Chair, Sustainable Development Roundtable, OECD.

Preparatory Meetings: Africa and Climate Change

A series of meetings in preparation for the sherpa consultation was arranged in the days before 23 March. On 21 March two expert meetings were held, focusing on the Gleneagles Summit themes—Climate Change and Africa. These meetings allowed for broader stakeholder input into the sherpa meeting.

Sherpa Consultation CS/G8 2005: London, UK

In London on March 23, 2005, all G8 governments including five sherpas and the European Commission attended the CS/G8 meeting. This was an unprecedented turnout. Following is a brief resumé of the rich and comprehensive discussions that focused on our global interdependency, Africa, and climate change.

The Global Context

There was a sense of urgency in 2005. Important gatherings that year included Copenhagen and Beijing conferences, the MDGs, the Millennium summit, and the WTO. Leaders of G8 were expected to exercise leadership and to contribute to solutions of problems facing humanity as a whole, not just within the G8 countries. There was a growing interdependence of causes and of consequences of problems, demanding global actions based on strong multilateralism. Although civil society had participated in a growing number of commitments made in previous decades through treaties, conventions, and agreements, there was a sense of disillusionment with global leadership because of the lack of resources and political support required to deliver these commitments. Attention to issues of growth, development, poverty, environment, and security was fragmented, and there was a lack of comprehensive, integrated strategies and actions to address them.

Civil society participants expected the G8 individually and collectively to use its offices to move forward through local, national and global institutions and deliver existing and new commitments in response to these pressing issues. Strengthening consultations with civil society and stakeholder groups locally, nationally and globally can contribute to the delivery of commitments.

Africa

Concerns regarding Africa and NEPAD remained critical. NEPAD and G8's Action Plan for Africa was premised on mutual accountability. (The Action Plan for Africa was presented by the UK as a separate initiative from NEPAD, with the similar objective of supporting African development. With time, it was increasingly integrated with NEPAD.) African progress included the African Union's (AU) adoption of NEPAD as a development program, and the G8's progress included commitment to, and the monitoring and evaluation of, progress on G8's Action Plan for Africa. The Commission for Africa's Report was an indicator of how far both sides still had to go.[2]

Addressing the mutual accountability of CS and the G8 in recognizing the contribution of the arms trade to conflict in Africa, members of the G8 were asked to commit to a legally binding treaty on arms proliferation within the appropriate multilateral fora and increase the transparency of their extractive industry transnational corporations beyond voluntary codes of conduct.

CS representatives reiterated existing civil society recommendations for Africa including: 100 percent debt cancellation; delivery of existing debt relief measures without conditionalities beyond the promotion of inclusive democracy; reaching agreement on modalities for enhanced debt relief measures pre-G8 2005 summit to enable progress on aid at the summit in Gleneagles. They welcomed the recommendations in the report of the Commission for Africa on increasing aid to Africa and proposed the immediate doubling of aid to Africa by all members of the G8 and the establishment of a date for meeting the Official Development Assistance (ODA) target of 0.7 percent GDP.

In addition, representatives requested that ODA be untied and that economic conditionality be dropped. It was also suggested that, within the appropriate multilateral fora, G8 members commit to an end to agricultural subsidies, an end to pushing for WTO compliance within the context of bilateral and other trade agreements, and an end to tariff escalation on African exports. Finally, CS urged a review of the functioning of the current link between the NEPAD leadership and the G8 African personal representatives (APRs) through the Africa Partners' Forum, with particular respect to the ability of civil society from Africa and the G8 to contribute to its deliberations (and, for example, through opening up reporting under the UN Economic Commission for Africa and the OECD directorate).

Climate Change

CS participants requested that the G8 members accept the outcome of the Hadley Centre conference Avoiding Dangerous Climate Change.[3] This conference showed that the scale and urgency of climate change is much greater than previously thought. G8 countries committed to a multilateral approach to preventing climate change must move ahead toward strengthening the Kyoto protocol, with or without unanimous participation. It was recommended that domestic targets be set for renewable energy sources and that, within the G8 countries, a network of the agencies financing energy efficiency and renewable energy projects be created. CS views energy efficiency as the least-cost response to climate change, and the G8 members were urged to strengthen standards on vehicles, buildings, appliances, and equipment.

Finally it was recommended that G8 members mainstream climate change into development planning.

Lessons Learned: CS/G8 2005

The 2005 UK meetings marked an important watershed for this dialogue. For the first time, all G8 members participated. For the first time, the G8 host country financed the dialogue with CS. The CS approach moved considerably from its previous emphasis on process to dealing with the specific content proposed by the host head of state. For the first time, there was sufficient planning time available for CS, including the necessary time to convene experts. Also for the first time, most of the preparation work was done by host civil society organizations (led by Chatham House) and the role of FIM was directly complementary to national CS initiatives. FIM expenses were covered within the general budget, which was administered by Chatham House.

Importantly however, Southern CS provided less leadership than before. In the African expert meeting, for example, only about five participants out of close to sixty were from Africa. At the same time, Northern participants dominated the preparations for climate change.

For the first time the CS participants used a divide-and-conquer strategy. When it became clear that there was agreement among seven G8 countries on the importance of global warming, the participants asked whether those seven countries would be prepared to act in unity without the engagement of the lone dissenting country. The host sherpa indicated with no ambiguity that such a choice was indeed possible.

CS/G8 2006: ST. PETERSBURG, RUSSIA

The 2006 meetings between civil society and the G8 were handled quite differently than in previous years. From the outset, Russian president Vladimir Putin named a former parliamentarian and current human rights spokesperson, Ella Pamfilova, as chair of an NGO coalition. This coalition became responsible for what became known as Civil G8. A National Advisory Council and an International Advisory Council guided Civil G8. This latter body seemed to change in composition regularly, but included several Russian members. Two FIM board members were on this body.

From the outset, the Russian process was heavily financed by Russian private and governmental sources. Civil G8 covered all FIM out-of-pocket expenses. FIM was regularly consulted throughout the process, but communications remained fuzzy, perhaps in part due to language difficulties.

Preparation Meetings in Moscow

Following an unsuccessful effort by Civil G8 to formalize a common position on eight G8-related topics, including the three G8 official agenda items, a closed meeting was held in May between nineteen CS participants and all sherpas. Unlike in previous years, the CS participants spent very little time planning together (a total of about two hours in lieu of two days). As a result, the CS positions were not focused, and, for the first time, there was open disagreement among CS representatives in front of the sherpas. Without the required time to prepare, the quality and professionalism of the CS presenters varied considerably.

Following this meeting under the leadership of the National Advisory Council and benefiting from written comments from the international advisors, the CS participants continued to hone their position papers in preparation for a large July meeting in Moscow.

The July meeting involved about six hundred CS participants, including nearly five hundred from Russia. Southern involvement was scattered, but the African delegation was relatively strong. Sessions followed a format that was similar to all previous Civil G8 meetings. Participants were divided into eight working groups, each of which had the mandate to finalize a position paper in time for a meeting with Russian president Putin. The eight topics, including the three G8 agenda items (global energy security, education, and infectious diseases) as well as sustainable development, human rights, global security and CS, ecology and genetically modified organisms (GMOs), and business and society.

Meeting with the Russian President

Prior to meeting with Vladimir Putin, a full day was set aside for CS planning meetings. During these meetings the International Advisory Council met formally on two occasions. FIM and others fought hard and successfully to ensure that presentations to Mr. Putin were limited to three minutes each. We also insisted that each working group nominate its presenter, who would then rehearse the three-minute presentation in front of us. This was resisted at first (it was seen as somewhat paternalistic by the Russian members of the council), but after successfully airing different "cultural perspectives" on this approach it was adopted and utilized. Many participants expressed the view that this led to a successful and historic occasion.

The plenary with President Putin lasted about two hours. After each three-minute presentation, he responded at length. The thorny issue of impending legislation defining the legal context of Russian civil society was raised within the human rights presentation. Putin committed himself to ensuring that the legislation would not be abusive toward Russian civil society. His main concern was the intrusion of foreign NGOs into internal Russian politics. He expressed sympathy to the CS anti-nuclear position but indicated unequivocally that Russia would go nuclear. In other words, when Putin disagreed, he did so unambiguously. When he agreed, which he often did (especially on GMOs), it appeared to most participants that he was being equally straightforward.

The fact that a meeting with the host head of state took place prior to the actual G8 meeting encouraged participants to believe that some impact on the agenda content had been achieved.

Passing the Torch: Russia to Germany

In November 2006 there was a meeting designed to pass the Civil G8 torch on to Germany, the 2007 G8 host. A preliminary plan from the Germans had already been approved by the 2006 International Advisory Council. At this meeting it became clear that the German sherpa and G8 secretariat would come from the German Ministry of Economics. Historically this ministry was not favourably disposed to civil society, so the gains of 2002–2006 remained far from assured.

Reflections on CS/G8 2006

Civil G8 was an impressive process (lengthy as it was) of work over several months, through several drafts of position papers, which concluded in highly focused presentations to Putin. In an exciting and often frustrating way, this was democracy in action. Each issue was thoroughly and openly discussed. Some debates were hot and irreconcilable. However, out of this came some clear consensus on each issue, which could be shared with Putin (and/or other G8 leaders and their sherpas).[4] Each was a hard-fought consensus, which had to be seriously considered by G8 organizers.

Lessons Learned CS/G8 2006

In many ways, Russia 2006 continued two important changes begun in the UK. Each change is a sign of success, but they have brought with them a new set of issues.

The first change is that the G8 host governments are increasingly committed to and engaged in this dialogue. This also means that they are committing funds, and to some extent, influencing the agenda and the process. In 2005, the UK government contributed about £250,000 and in 2006 Russian sources, including the government, probably contributed several million US. In each case the money was granted to a host national coordinating body and the CS process, including international engagement, became effectively the responsibility of this national mechanism, which also in each case, continued to consult with FIM.

In these two years it also meant that the host country's priorities strongly influenced, if not dominated, the CS debate and agenda. In 2005, British CS was working in a pre-election context and knew that the G8 would have an impact on whether Labour or the Conservatives were elected. This influenced the entire working relationship with the host government. 2006 was even more dramatic in some ways. Clearly, with the eyes of the world on the host country, the G8 was an occasion to consolidate and ensure the gains of Russian civil society within a newly emerging democracy. It is reasonable to conclude that this was, in fact, the major intent of Russian CS.

The second change is the increased national CS involvement. The increased interest of host G8 governments in formally dialoguing with CS is a clear indication that, on one important level, the FIM initiative has been a success. This is leading in turn to a rapidly increasing interest by a growing number of NGOs to become part of this process and/or to initiate parallel processes. We can only expect this trend to continue.

In 2006, for example, there was a parallel engagement by the IANGO (International Advocacy NGOs) group. This includes some of the larger international NGOs such as Greenpeace (the initiator), CIVICUS, and the World Wildlife Federation (WWF). Most of them are Northern based, although Social Watch is also an active participant in this informal grouping. They succeeded, with no prior discussion with the Civil G8 Advisory Council, in having their own meeting of twelve participants with Putin. Originally they had requested to meet with all G8 heads of state, but this was refused out of hand.

The broader engagement of CS with the G8 can only be welcomed. We can expect this type of interest to grow, not only among international NGOs but also among national NGOs within the G8 countries and especially within each year's host country. This progress however has brought a new set of issues related to the diminishing role of Southern CS.

From the outset of this project in 2002, FIM saw this exercise as an occasion for spokespersons from Southern Civil Society to bring their concerns directly to senior G8 officials. FIM has always felt that G8 governments have ample occasion for meeting CS representatives from within their own country. As well, it is relatively easy for host sherpas to visit with CS participants from other G8 countries at the same time as they visit their counterpart sherpas throughout the planning phase. The missing component in the growing G8 dialogues was Southern CS.

As G8 governments and host country NGOs have become more engaged, however, the numbers of Southern participants has decreased substantially. It is worth mentioning that of the sixty or so people at the year's final Civil G8 meeting in Russia in November, there was not one participant from the South. The closest was the representative from the London-based African Diaspora movement.

LOOKING FORWARD: FUTURE CS/G8 ENGAGEMENTS

FIM has now reached a point where it is possible to think of implementing a multi-functional process. The first function would be to try to influence the G8 agenda before it is finalized. Ideally, this would include a proactive position by CS in addition to reacting to topics proposed by the host government.

This would require some form of internal CS dialogue early in the calendar year.

Once the agenda is finalized, the second function would be to influence the content of the agenda. This would require expert analysis, keeping in mind that the primary agenda topics will probably change each year. It would also involve, similarly to this year's Civil G8 process, achieving some level of consensus throughout a growing portion of international CS.

A third function is a highly focused meeting with the sherpas. This could continue to be the prime responsibility of FIM and would be an occasion to ensure that the voice of Southern CS dominates. However, this is being increasingly encroached upon by civil society from within G8 countries, and we can expect increasing pressure from a growing number of INGOs.

FIM is well placed to continue to try to ensure strong Southern CS involvement. In some cases this will be an uphill battle, as many NGOs based in G8 countries believe themselves to be sufficiently empathetic and knowledgeable to play an effective intermediate role.

A fourth function is the systematic monitoring of G8 commitments. In 2006 the director of the G8 Research Group at the University of Toronto was actively involved with the CS process. The Munk Centre at the University of Toronto has been monitoring G8 decisions for years and is considered to be the leading school of knowledge and intelligence on G8 matters. They are prepared to collaborate actively with CS in the future.[5]

FINAL ANALYSIS: REVISITING THE QUESTIONS OF LEGITIMACY AND REPRESENTIVITY

When FIM began its dialogue with G8 planning officials in 2002, our intention was to shepherd the process until a more representative body from within civil society could take over. The initial assumption was that the process would not be viewed as legitimate unless and until this happened. But how was this to happen? One of the tenets of representative democracy is that it must be the product of universal suffrage, but there is no civil society electorate. How could any organization bring to the table delegates representing the vastness and diversity of civil society around the world? The answer, we decided eventually, is that it can't, nor should it pretend to do so. In spite of this, FIM believes that the FIM/G8 dialogue still has legitimacy.

In retrospect it appears that there were three major constraints to this process of becoming representative and claiming legitimacy. One was very practical in nature; one was strategic. The third, a conceptual one, developed later out of the other two.

Practical Considerations

Due to financial constraints and also because we wanted to ensure a fully participatory dialogue, we were faced with an immediate practical constraint of how to achieve broad-based representation. We therefore decided, both internally and with G8 officials, to limit civil society participants to fifteen. FIM took great care to ensure regional and gender balance in these fifteen slots, while always respecting the FIM mandate to ensure that Southern participation dominated. But this of course was merely scratching the surface of the representation question. Even within these limits, there was no "suffrage"—these people were nominated by FIM, not selected by their own groups. Indeed it would have been impossible to ensure that every minority linguistic, lifestyle, religious, ethnic, and/or disadvantaged group was involved.

Given these inevitable constraints, and while never actually using the term, we sought other means of ensuring some degree of legitimacy. In addition to the two group selection criteria used, we also drew up a short list of individual selection criteria. We felt that we needed individuals who brought, through their experience and reputation, wide-scale credibility. We also sought people who had extensive experience in multilateral negotiations. Because of the delicate nature of the dialogue (the 2002 G8 came on the heels of the Genoa tragedy, and no one could predict whether Kananaskis would also be subject to large-scale violence), we looked for people who worked well in a team and who had proven diplomatic skills.

FIM's niche is in civil society/multilateral relations and, as with all professional communities, the major players are by and large known to each other. We were reasonably confident from the outset that we could bring together a team that would have the required skills and also receive broad external moral support.

Strategic Considerations

While recognizing the importance of this dialogue, FIM was concerned that our entering into it could have two consequences we were anxious to avoid. First, it could imply that we recognized the G8 as a legitimate global governance mechanism. Secondly, the G8 might confer on us the status of representating international civil society, and as a result feel justified in claiming they had consulted with civil society. We therefore stated at the outset, in writing, that FIM was in no way a gatehouse for international civil society and that our entering into this dialogue did not mean that FIM recognized the G8 as a legitimate global governance mechanism. The G8 organizers accepted these terms.

Conceptual Evolution

We had both practical and strategic reasons for disclaiming representative status. But were the factors underlying these reasons specific to our situation or systemic? It began to seem to us that our particular difficulty was part of a larger whole. The more we disclaimed representivity and the less we aspired to be representative, the more we questioned the premise that representivity is an essential component of legitimacy, especially for a civil society organization. Legitimacy does not necessarily come from representivity.

In view of our concerns over representivity and legitimacy, this manoeuvre may seem odd, but since there was in any case no practical possibility that we could *be* truly representative, we were anxious that representative status should not be ascribed to us for purposes we disapproved of. But if the legitimacy of the FIM project was not rooted in any claim that we represented international civil society, what *was* it rooted in? A partial response is that it comes from "goodwill," embodied in the tacit acceptance of the FIM G8 Project by civil society and G8 officials.

Tacit Acceptance, Representivity, Accountability, and Legitimacy

The French were sufficiently satisfied with the results of our discussions prior to Kananaskis in 2002 to decide to continue the process in 2003, and the British and Russians both strengthened the process. It became clear that by some means we had established credibility and, by extension, some degree of "legitimacy." Although the Americans did not attend the 2002 and 2003 meetings, they participated with vigour in 2005 and 2006.

In our internal reviews after each meeting, the FIM Board also reiterated its commitment to continuing this difficult project, which we knew would take time to produce measurable results. For the first two years FIM limited its public reporting to a short resumé of proceedings on its website.[6] In 2005 FIM collaborated with Chatham House in London, and the process was more visible than it had been previously. It also included a greater degree of outside consultation than before. This growing transparency reflected a greater security in the overall credibility of the exercise and a corresponding easing of tensions between civil society and G8 organizers. In Russia the process gathered even more visibility and inclusiveness.

If this process is not representative, how then *is* the process credible and how accountable are we? There is a parallel with the profit-making part of the private sector here. We are, in a very real way, dealing with market forces. "Goodwill" depends upon the nature and quality of the product or service in a way that is similar to that of a business enterprise. We provide a service and we have stakeholders. If we fail to deliver a service that is acceptable to our peers (our civil society stakeholders), we will be forced to abandon the project. It wouldn't take long for G8 organizers to realize that our colleagues did not respect us and that they are not receiving credible advice and/or opinions.

Our view has changed, therefore, over the course of this initiative. At the outset, we assumed that it would be legitimate in the long term only if it became the responsibility of a representative civil society organization which, for the reasons outlined above, FIM could not and would not claim to be. But it became increasingly clear to us that any existing organization would have similar difficulties in making and substantiating such a claim. Does this fact limit the potential of civil society to play a vital role in global governance? We did not and do not believe so. Instead, and gradually, FIM has found other means to develop credibility and legitimacy for the process. The mutual agreement, by G8 organizers and FIM and its partners, to continue the process conveys credibility and legitimacy.

One of the many reasons civil society is participating more directly in governance issues is because of a growing frustration with current practices of representative democracy (the democratic deficit). It would be ironic if civil society strove in its turn to fill the representative vacuum. The FIM experience with the G8 suggests that this is neither practical nor strategic, nor based on sound thinking.

We expected criticism from within civil society. We have received some, the most vocal being from colleagues who held positions of responsibility within "representative bodies," usually umbrella groupings of NGOs. The criticisms were (and are) largely conceptual in nature, centring on our right to enter into a dialogue on behalf of civil society.

Surprisingly, there has been relatively little criticism about our decision to actually undertake dialogue with the G8. This seems to reflect a mature understanding and acceptance of the diversity of civil society, and the prevailing attitude might be summed up as: "We prefer to deal with the root problem and to protest the existence of the G8, but in the meantime hopefully you can mitigate the damage." To the best of our knowledge, no participants have been personally criticized for taking part in this exercise.

We receive suggestions for agenda priorities and we are sometimes seen as naive if we seriously expect to achieve any concrete results. At this stage, however, our objective remains basic: to demonstrate to G8 organizers the value of open and frank dialogue with international civil society. Every time the new host country decides to continue the exercise, we achieve that objective.

NOTES

1 This Mission Statement, as well as most of the references that follow in this text, are taken from internal FIM documents, most of which are accessible on the FIM website. In some cases I have referred to Board notes, which although not confidential are not public documents, and on other occasions I have referred to briefing notes that I prepared for either the FIM Board or the FIM Executive Committee. On occasion I also refer to the content of discussions (as I best recall and/or noted them) with various senior G8 officials from different G8 member states. In most cases these officials were not speaking in their personal capacity but officially on behalf of their government, either on or off the record.

2 The Commission for Africa's Report is available at www.commissionforafrica.org.

3 See www.stabilisation2005.com.

4 See "International NGOs' Address to President Vladimir Putin," http://en.g8russia/ ru/page_work/21.html.

5 See www.g7.utoronto.ca.

6 See www.fimcivilsociety.org.

iii

Problems and Prospects

11

Laying the Groundwork

Considerations for a Charter for a Proposed
Global Civil Society Forum

Andrew S. Thompson

INTRODUCTION

Since the end of the Cold War, "global civil society" has become increasingly engaged in issues of international governance. To many observers, including some government officials, the very presence of literally thousands of non-governmental organizations (NGOs) and civil society organizations (CSOs), all vying to have their voices heard on the international stage, has diversified the international system yet has simultaneously made it more cumbersome and difficult to manage. Moreover, although the number of these voluntary organizations at international fora has risen dramatically over the last fifteen years, it is not clear that their ability to influence agendas and outcomes has kept pace. State officials and international civil servants are faced with the dilemma of having to decide which of these many voices they will listen to. One danger is that only the loudest (i.e., best resourced) will be heard; a second is that officials will only listen to voices with which they are in agreement; a third is that they will use competing voices to cancel each other out, yet claim to have consulted with global civil society.

Suppose for a moment that global civil society were to organize itself into a Global Civil Society Forum (GCSF) for the purpose of enhancing its collective voices on the international stage, ultimately leading to greater influence in the decision-making process. Granted, given the sheer number of actors making up global civil society, such a proposition requires a certain leap of faith and perhaps a temporary suspension of disbelief. Even so, suppose there was both a need and a desire for such an entity that could act as a nexus between global civil society and states and international governmental organizations (IGOs). Others in this volume have considered the structural features that this entity might adopt in order to ensure that it is governed equitably and transparently. The purpose of this chapter is to consider the possible values and principles such an entity might espouse in order to gain legitimacy in the eyes of its members, states, international governmental organizations, and the publics it purports to serve.

In order to make the leap from idea to reality, one of the first tasks confronting the architects of any new GCSF would be to draft a charter that outlines the purposes and functions of the assembly. Although the charter would not necessarily have to be a complicated document, it would have to be comprehensive enough to include the following features: a mandate, criteria for determining the size and makeup of the membership, guidelines for funding, and, last but not least, a clear statement outlining the entity's place and role within the existing international system. Fortunately, architects would not have to reinvent the wheel, as there are existing models to which they can turn for guidance. Perhaps the most notable is the 6 June 2006 International Non-Governmental Organisations' Accountability Charter (see Appendix, page 224), a document that could act a useful blueprint or beginning point for a GCSF charter.[1] Focusing on the categories listed above, the remainder of this chapter will assess the applicability of the 2006 Accountability Charter to a GCSF, and in the process consider some of the possible directions that organizers might pursue when drafting a GCSF charter, as well as some of the thorny questions that might arise when determining its content and scope. Indeed, setting the parameters for this new entity would be an inherently political act, one that would ultimately determine both its legitimacy, and whether it is as beneficial to the needs of global civil society as it is to those of states and international governmental organizations.

WHERE TO BEGIN? ASSESSING THE APPLICABILITY OF THE 2006 INTERNATIONAL NON-GOVERNMENTAL ORGANISATIONS' ACCOUNTABILITY CHARTER

Described as the "first global accountability charter for the non-profit sector," the 2006 International Non-Governmental Organisations' Accountability Charter is an agreement between eleven of the world's pre-eminent NGOs in the fields of international human rights, the environment, and social development. Its immediate purpose: to strengthen public confidence in these organizations. Indeed, the Accountability Charter is both timely and innovative in design. It consists of broad statements concerning ethical behaviour, codes of conduct, and best practices, as well as fairly detailed provisions about ethical fundraising and financial responsibility and accountability. The Accountability Charter is, at least in part, a product of a global environment in which there appears to be a growing mistrust and even disillusionment with the practices of both state and non-state actors—actors who many believe are failing the public good. Moreover, the Accountability Charter is a reflection of the larger view that poor governance and corruption represent serious impediments to the fulfillment of human development and sustainability, the equitable protection of rule of law and human rights for all, and the overall health and well-being of democratic institutions.[2] Of course, none of the NGOs that agreed to the Accountability Charter is likely committing to anything that it was not already doing in practice. Even so, the Charter is an important affirmation of the values and principles that CSOs and NGOs seek to uphold in the international governmental system. After all, both are in the business of "moral entrepreneurship," or raising "the barrier of the morally permissible";[3] they risk being accused of hypocrisy if they themselves choose not to practise what they preach and open themselves up to the same level of scrutiny and transparency that they expect—even demand—of public institutions.

For this reason, the Accountability Charter offers a useful beginning point for a discussion of the GCSF. But it is just that: a beginning point. While the Accountability Charter performs a particular function for the organizations that have signed on to it, its applicability to a new GCSF may depend, at least in part, on how stringent the architects wished to make the criteria for inclusion.

WHAT'S THE POINT? SETTING THE MANDATE

At first glance, crafting a mandate for the GCSF should not be a terribly big hurdle to surmount—again, depending on how rigid the organizers wished it to be. As mentioned above, the architects of this new entity would not have to start from scratch but could instead look at the mission statements of existing NGO networks and coalitions, such as the International Council on Voluntary Agencies (ICVA), InterAction, and the World Alliance for Citizen Participation (CIVICUS), all of which could serve as a rough blueprint for a GCSF.[4]

On this question, the Accountability Charter may be particularly useful. One of the strengths of the document is that it captures the essence of the concept of a "non-governmental organization," which is found in the opening lines of the document under the heading "Who we are," as well as in the middle of text under the heading "Respect for Universal Principles." The international

NGOs that have signed on to the Charter have defined themselves as a group of "independent non-profit organisations that work globally to advance human rights, sustainable development, environmental protection, humanitarian response and other public goods" whose activities have a global reach. Their legitimacy stems from a combination of the values they seek to uphold and advance, the quality of their work, and the degree to which they are accountable to both their stakeholders and the public at large.[5] The attraction of the definition found in the Charter is its simplicity. Appealing only to the broadest of principles, it explains in a few clear, short sentences what NGOs do, why they do what they do, and how they do what they do. Moreover, it is inclusive enough that it accommodates organizations from a variety of different sectors, something that would be necessary for a GCSF if it is to avoid criticisms that it and its members are engaging in parochial or "interest group politics."[6]

Still, it is not entirely clear whether a mandate of this nature would be appropriate for a larger CSO/NGO entity whose membership would surely consist of more than eleven of the largest international non-governmental organizations. Of course, any mandate or mission that the GCSF adopts would undoubtedly provide for a degree of self-selection for the membership. This is definitely the case with the Accountability Charter. Although it spans a wide range of related but independent sectors, what unites the organizations that have signed onto it is an ideological like-mindedness. At a base level, all can be found on either the centre or left-of-centre of the political spectrum, the thread that links them being a common emphasis on social justice, human security, and greater state regulation aimed at engineering a progressive international system that favours morality over power.[7]

One of the political hurdles facing the architects of the GCSF is that they would have to decide whether this would be a forum that could accommodate ideological diversity and still function effectively. Put more bluntly, they would have to determine whether the forum would be a "tent" that houses both the left and the right. The chances of this happening are unlikely. To be effective, the entity would in all likelihood have to take ideological stands on specific issues. This could prove highly divisive, as examples of potential conflict are not difficult to imagine. If discussing global poverty and the current state of the international economic order, could such an entity accommodate the interests of development groups that are social democratic in orientation, favouring protectionist measures, greater labour and environmental standards, and more foreign aid with neo-liberal organizations that believe that the solution lies in more open trade, greater private investment, and the wisdom of the marketplace? On the issue of the proliferation of small arms and light weapons and their effect on conflict situations, could such a venue accommodate both the views of civil libertarian organizations that see guns as a symbol of individual liberty with those of groups that favour increased regulation of the international system through arms control treaties and Disarmament, Demobilization and Reintegration (DDR) programs? In confronting the problem of HIV/AIDS, could the forum accommodate the views of groups that favour greater family-planning programs versus those that preach abstinence? Potentially more problematic are the fissures that exist along North–South and East–West lines. For much of the latter half of the twentieth century, human rights groups in the North and South disagreed on the question of whether poverty was a human rights issue, the former tending to see human rights almost exclusively through a political and civil rights lens while the latter viewed them in terms of economic and social rights.[8] Similarly, NGOs and CSOs in the West tend to be exporters of liberal norms, whereas in the Islamic world many organizations exist in order to buffer against the incursion of these very same values.[9] Depending on the issue being debated, similar divides are by no means out of the realm of possibility.

The point here is that the list of potential philosophical conflicts within the GCSF could be tremendous, so much so that, depending on the agenda and the individuals and organizations involved, any initial meeting could quite conceivably be overwhelmed by deep divisions among the membership, ultimately leading to paralysis. As such, any mandate would likely have to be broad enough that it draws a wide range of civil society groups, yet specific enough that there is some common denominator between members so as to permit at least a degree of focus and even consensus. Finding this happy medium would be no simple task.

WHO'S IN AND WHO'S OUT? DETERMINING THE SIZE AND NATURE OF THE MEMBERSHIP

A GCSF's legitimacy would depend, in part, on both the size and nature of the organizations seeking membership. There may be a temptation to favour greater numbers over selection based on best practices, particularly if the purpose of this organization is to represent "global civil society" at various international fora. But bigger is not necessarily better. Networks with large memberships can claim representative legitimacy, but with expanded ranks come added organizational challenges, potential strains on efficiency, and the possibility of relaxed standards. Compounding the problem is that the appropriate number of member organizations for GCSF is by no means obvious. Surely ten is far too small; yet one thousand would be unwieldy. Somewhere in between lies an appropriate balance between representativeness and efficiency, but where is not clear.

The Accountability Charter stresses best practices of good governance as criteria for membership. The eleven organizations that have signed on to it have all committed themselves to democratic forms of governance that include, among other things, elected decision-making bodies that have the authority to oversee executives and ensure that financial resources are used responsibly; clear procedures for choosing members to these bodies that include conflict of interest guidelines; and a periodic general meeting in which stakeholders can select these officials.

For a variety of reasons, many NGOs and CSOs do not engage in these practices. Unfortunately, this has had the undesired effect of fostering the perception that civil society is largely unaccountable to the publics they purport to be aiding. Ian Smillie has downplayed the extent to which this criticism holds any weight, countering that NGOs and CSOs are in fact quite accountable to their boards and members, the media, and beneficiaries whom they serve. Nonetheless, even he concedes that NGO and CSO operations need to be more transparent.[10] So too have other scholars who are equally sympathetic to greater inclusion of civil society in global governance. Along this same vein, Jan Aart Scholte has argued that many NGOs could do more to practice the democratic values that they claim to be promoting, that they "need to look inside, at their own operations, as well as outside."[11] Of course, operational mechanisms are not cheap; many NGOs and CSOs simply cannot afford elaborate governance structures. For a GCSF, the pitfall associated with insisting on high standards of accountability and transparency for members is that it would risk becoming an exclusive club of the richest NGOs, a prospect that would surely foster a legitimacy deficit.

WHO WILL PAY FOR THE GCSF? SOURCES OF FUNDING

The issue of who would pay for the GCSF is another potentially tricky one, as the source of funding (as well as the amount it receives or is able to generate on its own) would undoubtedly have a considerable impact on its effectiveness and autonomy. The vast majority of NGOs and CSOs receive at least a portion of their funding from governments; indeed, many are so completely dependent on state funding that they would cease to operate without it.[12] The architects of the GCSF would need to give a great deal of consideration to potential sources of revenue. Their challenge would be to adopt policies that ensure that the forum has the capacity to raise sufficient resources that permit it to conduct its advocacy in a timely manner, while simultaneously guaranteeing that its independence is not compromised by any of the funding that it receives.

True independence could occur only if the GCSF had complete control over its finances. Another common bond between the groups that have signed on to the Accountability Charter is that all have agreed to raise funds without assistance from governments. But this type of autonomy is far from the norm; rather, it is a luxury that is generally reserved for only the largest, most well-established international NGOs with extensive and elaborate fund-raising departments and strategies.

A common charge against NGOs and CSOs that receive public sector funding is that their ability to criticize state policy is tempered by their dependence on the state; stated another way, these groups must be careful not to bite the hand that feeds them. The same would hold true for the GCSF. If its funding comes from governments, then the possibility exists that its executive might choose to exercise restraint when given the opportunity to criticize state practices for fear that future funding would be withheld. Similarly, if the GCSF is overly critical of state practices, governments might question why they are supporting such an entity in the first place.

Ideally, it would be the member organizations that would pay for the infrastructure and overhead costs involved in running such an entity. But is this feasible? Operating such an organization could cost upwards of several millions of dollars per year, particularly if its headquarters is located in the North, as so many of them are. As non-profit entities, finding extra funds might be difficult for some NGOs and CSOs (particularly those in the South) and may even have the undesired effect of limiting both the number of organizations that are able to participate and the GCSF's ability to perform its duties. Consequently, some sort of state funding may be necessary, despite the obvious drawbacks.

WOULD IT HAVE A SEAT AT THE TABLE? DETERMINING THE GCSF'S RELATIONSHIP TO EXISTING INSTITUTIONS

The standing that the GCSF would have with international governmental organizations would go a long way toward determining whether it would ultimately be successful. As noted in the introduction, one of the rationales for establishing a GCSF is that it could streamline some of the inefficiencies of the international system while still allowing global civil society to do what it does best, namely to shape agendas, influence normative discourse, modify the behaviour of states, act as catalysts for accountability and transparency, give voice to the voiceless, and confer legitimacy on policy directives that in turn civil society helps to implement.[13]

Determining GCSF's place in relation to other international bodies is by no means obvious. Most of all, NGOs and CSOs could not be co-opted through

220   *Andrew S. Thompson*

this entity. In the context of the United Nations, Tom Weiss and Leon Gordenker have argued that NGOs that work with the UN often wind up being associated with decisions that are highly politicized.[14] To work, GCSF participation at an international gathering could not be seen as an endorsement—implicit or explicit—of state or IGO policies and practices. Rather, the GCSF and all of its members would have to be permitted the autonomy to divorce themselves from any outcomes with which they disagree. One solution might be to adopt the language found in the Accountability Charter, which indicates that these groups seek to "complement," not "replace" states and international organizations by raising "problems and issues that governments and others are unable or unwilling to address on their own," using "constructive challenge" to "promote good governance and foster progress towards [their] goals." Of course, the key phrases are "complement" and "constructive challenge." If NGOs and CSOs believe the GCSF provides them the opportunity to enhance governance in a constructive manner while still permitting them to retain their independence, then an entity of this nature might stand a reasonable chance of being accepted.

CONCLUSION: FOR WHOSE BENEFIT?

For a GCSF to get off the ground, NGOs and CSOs would first have to embrace the idea. For this to happen, it would have to be seen as a true partnership among actors; the beneficiaries could not be states and IGOs alone. But this raises a difficult question, namely "Who is calling for the creation of this entity?" If the call for a global civil society entity is coming from national governments and IGOs, and not the individuals and organizations that would make up its membership, it cannot and would not succeed. Undoubtedly, the presence and proliferation of NGOs and CSOs has complicated the international system. But issues of capacity are insufficient grounds for creating a forum whose purpose is to channel global civil society's voices. Governing is by its very nature difficult, particularly when done through democratic structures. Complexity and diversity should be seen not as detriments or impediments to action, but rather as signs of true vibrancy within the international system. While efforts should be made to make the international system more efficient, it is not the responsibility of NGOs and CSOs to make the jobs of states and IGOs any easier.

Unless there would be a tangible value added for the groups involved, an entity of this kind would in all likelihood fail. The reason is that it is not clear who stands to benefit the most from such an entity, global civil society or states and IGOs. To succeed, the GSCF cannot be a place for exploiting divisions within civil society. Nor can it be a tool for co-opting civil society by using their presence to bestow legitimacy on a particular meeting, gathering or decision. Last, a GCSF cannot be an instrument for censoring civil society voices. The idea of a GCSF that would house and facilitate a great number of NGOs and CSOs while simultaneously relieving IGOs of the added encumbrances that have come with being more inclusive is appealing—and possibly quite innovative—could only work if it augments and enhances the existing work its potential members are already doing, and if all parties—NGOs, CSOs, states and IGOs, and the global public at large—see it as a useful vehicle for constructive and complementary engagement.

NOTES

Acknowledgement: Special thanks go to Gina Hill for her feedback on this paper.

1 The NGOs that agreed to the Charter are ActionAid International, Amnesty International, CIVICUS World Alliance for Citizen Participation, Consumers International, Greenpeace International, Oxfam International, the International Save the Children Alliance, Survival International, International Federation Terre des Hommes, Transparency International and World YWCA. These NGOs have endorsed the first international, cross-sectoral code of conduct for NGOs. See Amnesty International Press Release, "NGOs lead by example: World's international NGOs endorse accountability charter," London, England, June 6, 2006. http://www.amnesty.ca/resource_centre/news/view.php?load=arcview&article =3504&c=Resource+Centre+News. Accessed June 20, 2006.

2 In December 2003, the United Nations General Assembly adopted the UN Convention Against Corruption, the purposes of which are: "a) To promote and strengthen measures to prevent and combat corruption more efficiently and effectively; b) To promote, facilitate and support international cooperation and technical assistance in the prevention of and fight against corruption, including in asset recovery; c) To promote integrity, accountability and proper management of public affairs and public property."

The impetus for the treaty can be found in the preamble, which states that Member States are: "*Concerned* about the seriousness of the problems and threats posed by corruption to the stability and security of societies, undermining the institutions and values of democracy, ethical values and justice and jeopardizing sustainable development and the rule of law; *Concerned also* about the links between corruption and other forms of crime, in particular organized crime and economic crime, including money-laundering; *Concerned further* about the cases of corruption that involve vast quantities of assets, which may constitute a substantial proportion of the resources of States, and that threaten the political stability and sustainable development of those states." See UN Convention Against Corruption, adopted on October 31, 2003, at the fifty-eighth session of the General Assembly by resolution, A/RES/58/4.

In its 2004 Annual Report, Transparency International reported that more than two-thirds of the nearly 150 countries it examined were perceived by "business people and country analysts" to have high levels of corruption, sixty of which had "rampant" levels of corruption. See Transparency International, *Annual Report* (Berlin: Transparency International, 2004), 8.

3 Michael Ignatieff, *The Lesser Evil: Political Ethics in an Age of Terror* (Princeton: Princeton University Press, 2004), 23.

4 The ICVA's mission statement is: "The International Council of Voluntary Agencies (ICVA) is a non-profit global association of non-governmental organisations that works as a collective body, to promote, and advocate for, human rights and a humanitarian perspective in global debates and responses. The heart of the ICVA mission is to support NGOs to protect and assist people in need, to address the causes of their plight, and to act as a channel for translating patterns and trends into advocacy." See http://www.icva.ch/cgi-bin/browse.pl?doc=doc00000923. Accessed August 4, 2006.

Similarly, InterAction's mission states: "InterAction exists to enhance the effectiveness and professional capacities of its members engaged in international humanitarian efforts. InterAction seeks to foster partnership, collaboration and leadership among its members as they strive to achieve a world of self-reliance, justice and peace. To realize this mission, InterAction works to: Enhance the identity, autonomy, credibility and diverse perspectives of each member agency; provide a broadly based participatory forum for professional consultation, coordination and concerted action; foster the effectiveness and recognition of the PVO [private voluntary organization] community, both professionally and publicly; set a standard of the highest ethics in carrying out its mission." See http://www.interaction.org/about/mission.html. Accessed August 4, 2006.

Finally, CIVICUS's mission is: "CIVICUS is an international alliance dedicated to strengthening citizen action and civil society throughout the world." See http://www.civicus.org/new/default.asp. Accessed August 4, 2006.

5 The stakeholders listed include: "Peoples, including future generations, whose rights we seek to protect and advance; Ecosystems, which cannot speak for or defend themselves; Our members and supporters; Our staff and volunteers; Organisations and individuals that contribute finance, goods or services; Partner organisations, both governmental and non-governmental, with whom we work; Regulatory bodies whose agreement is required for our establishment and operations; Those whose policies, programmes or behaviour we wish to influence; The media; and The general public," Accountability Charter, 352.

6 See P.J. Simmons, "Learning to Live with NGOs," *Foreign Policy* 112 (Fall 1998): 83.

7 The aims of the NGOs that have signed on to the Accountability Charter are quite explicit: "We seek to advance international and national laws that promote human rights, ecosystem protection, sustainable development and other public goods. Where such laws do not exist, are not fully implemented, or abused, we will highlight these issues for public debate and advocate appropriate remedial action," Accountability Charter, 353.

8 For instance, only in August 2001 did Amnesty International expand its mandate to include a greater focus on economic and social rights; prior to this shift, the organization had focused its efforts almost exclusively on political and civil rights.

See also Henry J. Steiner, *Diverse Partners: Non-Governmental Organizations in the Human Rights Movement* (Cambridge, MA: Harvard Law School Human Rights Program; Ottawa: Human Rights Internet, c1991): 28–29.

9 Quintan Wiktorowicz and Suha Taji Farouki have argued that Islamists use NGOs in order to "combat the intrusion of Western values and cultural codes." Quintan Wiktorowicz and Suha Taji Farouki, "Islamic NGOs and Muslim Politics: A Case for Jordan," *Third World Quarterly* 21, no. 4 (2000): 685.

Similarly, Alan Fowler has noted that NGOs fulfill different functions in different societies, some of which are less than honourable. For example, in Russia, NGOs are often "seen as a cover for organized crime," whereas in places such as Pakistan and Bangladesh NGOs are often the principal drivers behind "fundamentalist causes." Similarly, for much of the latter half of the twentieth century, many development NGOs in the West were allies in the struggle to "win the Cold War." See Alan Fowler, "NGO Futures: Beyond Aid: NGDO Values and the Fourth Position," *Third World Quarterly* 21, no. 4 (2000): 592.

10 Ian Smillie, "NGOs and Development Assistance: A Change in Mind-Set?" *Third World Quarterly* 18, no. 3 (1997): 575.

11 Jan Aart Scholte, *Democratizing the Global Economy* (Warwick: Centre for the Study of Globalisation and Regionalisation, University of Warwick, June 2004), 64.

12 For example, in the case of civil society organizations in Canada, Les Pal has revealed that, in the 1980s and 1990s, many of the "equality-seeking groups"— again, women's, ethnic and language groups—received the bulk of their funding from the Canadian government through the Department of Secretary of State of Canada, a department that was established in order to fund groups whose mandates were consistent with the federal government's ambitions to foster within the Canadian psyche support for federalism and national unity based on a sense of common citizenship. Many of these groups, most of which were on the left of the political spectrum and were highly critical of Canadian state practices, could not have survived without the federal funds. Leslie A. Pal, *Interests of State: The Politics of Language, Multiculturalism, and Feminism in Canada* (Montreal & Kingston: McGill-Queen's University Press, 1993).

13 See Margaret Keck and Kathryn Sikkink, *Activists without Borders* (Ithaca and London: Cornell University Press, 1998), 25; Peter Willetts, "From 'Consultative Arrangements' to 'Partnerships': The Changing Status of NGOs in Diplomacy at the United Nations," *Global Governance* 6 (2000): 191–212. See also Kofi Annan, "The Quiet Revolution," *Global Governance* 4 (1998): 123–38; and Vikram K. Chand, "Democratization from the Outside In: NGO and International Efforts to Promote Open Elections," *Third World Quarterly* 18, no. 3 (1997): 543–61; and Tim Draimin and Betty Plewes, "Civil Society and the Democratization of Foreign Policy," in *Democracy and Foreign Policy: Canada among Nations 1995*, ed. Maxwell A. Cameron and Maureen Appel Molot (Ottawa: Carleton University Press, 1995), 63–82.

14 Leon Gordenker and Thomas G. Weiss, "Devolving Responsibilities: A Framework for Analyzing NGOs and Services," *Third World Quarterly* 18, no. 3 (1997): 447.

International Non Governmental Organisations' Accountability Charter, 6 June 2006

WHO WE ARE

We, international non-government organisations (INGOs) signatory to this Charter, are independent non-profit organisations that work globally to advance human rights, sustainable development, environmental protection, humanitarian response and other public goods.

Our organisations are proud and privileged to work across a wide range of countries and cultures, with a diverse range of peoples and in varied eco- and social and political systems.

Our right to act is based on universally-recognised freedoms of speech, assembly and association, on our contribution to democratic processes, and on the values we seek to promote.

Our legitimacy is also derived from the quality of our work, and the recognition and support of the people with and for whom we work and our members, our donors, the wider public, and governmental and other organisations around the world. We seek to uphold our legitimacy by responding to inter-generational considerations, public and scientific concerns, and through accountability for our work and achievements.

By signing this Charter we seek to promote further the values of transparency and accountability that we stand for, and commit our INGO to respecting its provisions.

HOW WE WORK

INGOs can complement but not replace the over-arching role and primary responsibility of governments to promote equitable human development and wellbeing, to uphold human rights and to protect ecosystems.

We also seek to promote the role and responsibilities of the private sector to advance human rights and sustainable development, and protect the environment.

We can often address problems and issues that governments and others are unable or unwilling to address on their own. Through constructive challenge, we seek to promote good governance and foster progress towards our goals.

We seek to advance our mission through research, advocacy and programmes. It is common for our work to be at the international, national, regional and local levels, either directly or with partners.

We work with other organisations where this is the best way to advance our individual missions.

THE CHARTER'S PURPOSE

This Charter outlines our common commitment to excellence, transparency and accountability. To demonstrate and build on these commitments, we seek to:

- identify and define shared principles, policies and practices;
- enhance transparency and accountability, both internally and externally;
- encourage communication with stakeholders; and
- improve our performance and effectiveness as organisations.

We recognise that transparency and accountability are essential to good governance, whether by governments, businesses or non-profit organisations.

Wherever we operate, we seek to ensure that the high standards which we demand of others are also respected in our own organisations.

The Charter complements and supplements existing laws. It is a voluntary charter, and draws on a range of existing codes, norms, standards and guidelines.

We agree to apply the Charter progressively to all our policies, activities and operations. The Charter does not replace existing codes or practices to which signatories may also be party, except as specified by them. Its adoption does not prevent signatories from supporting or using other tools to promote transparency and accountability.

We will refine the Charter through experience, taking into account future developments, particularly those that improve accountability and transparency.

OUR STAKEHOLDERS

Our first responsibility is to achieve our stated mission effectively and transparently, consistent with our values. In this, we are accountable to our stakeholders.

Our stakeholders include:

- Peoples, including future generations, whose rights we seek to protect and advance;
- Ecosystems, which cannot speak for or defend themselves;
- Our members and supporters;
- Our staff and volunteers;
- Organisations and individuals that contribute finance, goods or services;
- Partner organisations, both governmental and non-governmental, with whom we work;
- Regulatory bodies whose agreement is required for our establishment and operations;
- Those whose policies, programmes or behaviour we wish to influence;
- The media; and
- The general public.

In balancing the different views of our stakeholders, we will be guided by our mission and the principles of this Charter.

PRINCIPLES

Respect for Universal Principles

INGOs are founded on the rights to freedom of speech, assembly and association in the Universal Declaration of Human Rights. We seek to advance international and national laws that promote human rights, ecosystem protection, sustainable development and other public goods.

Where such laws do not exist, are not fully implemented, or abused, we will highlight these issues for public debate and advocate appropriate remedial action.

In so doing, we will respect the equal rights and dignity of all human beings.

Independence

We aim to be both politically and financially independent. Our governance, programmes and policies will be non-partisan, independent of specific governments, political parties and the business sector.

Responsible advocacy

We will ensure that our advocacy is consistent with our mission, grounded in our work and advances defined public interests. We will have clear processes for adopting public policy positions (including for partners where appropriate), explicit ethical policies that guide our choices of advocacy strategy, and ways of identifying and managing potential conflicts of interest among various stakeholders.

Effective Programmes

We seek to work in genuine partnership with local communities, NGOs and other organisations aiming at sustainable development responding to local needs.

Non-Discrimination

We value, respect and seek to encourage diversity, and seek to be impartial and nondiscriminatory in all our activities. To this end, each organisation will have policies that promote diversity, gender equity and balance, impartiality and non-discrimination in all our activities, both internal and external.

Transparency

We are committed to openness, transparency and honesty about our structures, mission, policies and activities. We will communicate actively to stakeholders about ourselves, and make information publicly available.

Reporting

We seek to comply with relevant governance, financial accounting and reporting requirements in the countries where we are based and operate.

We report at least once a year on our activities and achievements. Reports will describe each organisation's:

- Mission and values;
- Objectives and outcomes achieved in programme and advocacy;
- Environmental impact;
- Governance structure and processes, and main office bearers;
- Main sources of funding from corporations, foundations, governments, and individuals;
- Financial performance;
- Compliance with this Charter; and
- Contact details.

Audit

The annual financial report will conform to relevant laws and practices and be audited by a qualified independent public accountant whose statement will accompany the report.

Accuracy of information

We will adhere to generally-accepted standards of technical accuracy and honesty in presenting and interpreting data and research, using and referencing independent research.

Good Governance

We should be held responsible for our actions and achievements. We will do this by: having a clear mission, organisational structure and decision-making processes; by acting in accordance with stated values and agreed procedures; by ensuring that our programmes achieve outcomes that are consistent with our mission; and by reporting on these outcomes in an open and accurate manner.

The governance structure of each organisation will conform to relevant laws and be transparent. We seek to follow principles of best practice in governance. Each organisation will have at least:

- A governing body which supervises and evaluates the chief executive, and oversees programme and budgetary matters. It will define overall strategy, consistent with the organisational mission, ensure that resources are used efficiently and appropriately, that performance is measured, that financial integrity is assured and that public trust is maintained;
- Written procedures covering the appointment, responsibilities and terms of members of the governing body, and preventing and managing conflicts of interest;
- A regular general meeting with authority to appoint and replace members of the governing body.

We will listen to stakeholders' suggestions on how we can improve our work and will encourage inputs by people whose interests may be directly affected. We will also make it easy for the public to comment on our programmes and policies.

Ethical Fundraising

Donors

We respect the rights of donors: to be informed about causes for which we are fundraising; to be informed about how their donation is being used; to have their names deleted from mailing lists; to be informed of the status and authority of fundraisers; and to anonymity except in cases where the size of their donation is such that it might be relevant to our independence.

Use of Donations

In raising funds, we will accurately describe our activities and needs. Our policies and practices will ensure that donations further our organisation's mission. Where donations are made for a specific purpose, the donor's request is honoured. If we invite the general public to donate to a specific cause, each organisation will have a plan for handling any shortfall or excess, and will make this known as part of its appeal.

Gifts in Kind

Some donations may be given as goods or services. To retain our effectiveness and independence, we will: record and publish details of all major institutional gifts and gifts-in-kind; clearly describe the valuation and auditing methods used; and ensure that these gifts contribute towards our mission.

Agents

We seek to ensure that donations sought indirectly, such as through third parties, are solicited and received in full conformity with our own practices. This will normally be the subject of written agreement between the parties.

Professional Management

We manage our organisations in a professional and effective manner. Our policies and procedures seek to promote excellence in all respects.

Financial Controls

Internal financial control procedures will ensure that all funds are effectively used and minimise the risk of funds being misused. We will follow principles of best practice in financial management.

Evaluation

We seek continuously to improve our effectiveness. We will have defined evaluation procedures for our boards, staff, programmes and projects on the basis of mutual accountability.

Public Criticism

We will be responsible in our public criticisms of individuals and organisations, ensuring such criticism amounts to fair public comment.

Partners

We recognise that our organisational integrity extends to ensuring that our partners also meet the highest standards of probity and accountability, and will take all possible steps to ensure that there are no links with organisations, or persons involved in illegal or unethical practices.

Human Resources

We recognise that our performance and success reflect the quality of our staff and volunteers and management practices, and are committed to investing in human resource development.

Remuneration and benefits should strike a balance between public expectations of voluntary-based, not-for-profit organisations and the need to attract and retain the staff we need to fulfil our mission. Our human resources policies seek to conform fully with relevant international and national labour regulations and apply the best voluntary sector practices in terms of employee and volunteer rights and health and safety at work. Human resources policies will include procedures for evaluating the performance of all staff on a regular basis.

Bribery and Corruption

Human resources policies will specifically prohibit acts of bribery or corruption by staff or other persons working for, or on behalf of, the organisation.

Respect for Sexual Integrity

We condemn sexual exploitation, abuse and discrimination in all its forms. Our policies will respect sexual integrity in all our programmes and activities, and prohibit gender harassment, sexual exploitation and discrimination.

Whistle-blowers

Staff will be enabled and encouraged to draw management's attention to activities that may not comply with the law or our mission and commitments, including the provisions in this Code.

Looking to the Future
A Global Civil Society Forum?

Jan Aart Scholte

INTRODUCTION

Preceding chapters in this book have richly described and interrogated the emergence of a global civil society. Citizen action groups that seek, from outside political parties, to shape the rules governing society have over the past half-century acquired far more pronounced global qualities.[1] To extents not previously witnessed in history, civil society associations now address global issues, engage global governance institutions, adopt global organizational structures, use global infrastructure, tap global finance, and draw on (as well as bolster) global solidarities among people. This expansion of global dimensions does not mean that civil society in the twenty-first century has lost local, national, and regional features, which on the contrary remain as significant as ever. Yet, like contemporary society at large, civil society today also manifests a marked degree of globality alongside (and in complex interrelations with) regional, national, and local aspects.

Civil society always engages a governance apparatus, that is, an amalgam of sites where rules for social life are formulated, implemented, adjusted, and enforced. In the past, when societal regulation occurred predominantly if not exclusively through the state, civil society mobilizations correspondingly focused almost entirely on national and local governments. In today's more global world, however, governance emanates from multiple types of institutions, including many agencies with global jurisdictions and constituencies.

Not surprisingly, this expanding global governance has also attracted growing civil society attention.

Contemporary global governance involves multiple actors and diffuse activities.[2] The most familiar type of planet-spanning regulatory agency is the formal intergovernmental agency. These traditional multilateral institutions
include the United Nations (UN) and the World Trade Organization (WTO),
as well as other planet-spanning bodies like the Commonwealth and la Fran-
cophonie that do not aspire to universal state membership. In addition to
old-style multilateralism, recent decades have witnessed major growth of
planetary-scale regulation through transgovernmental networks. In these
cases senior officials from multiple states jointly pursue governance of common concerns with informal collaboration through conferences, memoranda
of understanding, and day-to-day communication. Instances of transgovernmental regulation include the Competition Policy Network, the Group of
Eight (G8), and the Nuclear Suppliers Group. Other new kinds of global governance arrangements interlink regulatory authorities on substate and supras-
tate scales. In this vein one finds global translocal collaborations like United
Cities and Local Governments (UCLG) and interregional arrangements like the
Asia–Europe Meeting (ASEM). Meanwhile other rules with planetary reach
have emerged from regulatory arrangements based in the private sector.
Examples of private global governance include the Forestry Stewardship
Council (FSC, to promote ecologically sustainable logging) and the Global
Reporting Initiative (GRI, to advance corporate social responsibility). Finally,
over the past decade other global governance has come to transpire through
public–private hybrids that combine elements from official, market, and civil
society circles. Examples include the Internet Corporation for Assigned Names
and Numbers (ICANN) and the Global Fund to Fight AIDS, Tuberculosis and
Malaria.

Thus global governance as it is currently unfolding shows little sign of
being or becoming a global state, in the sense of a modern nation-state
expanded to a planetary scale. Emergent global regimes decidedly lack attributes of centralized coordination, exclusive resort to legal means of violence,
and sovereignty. Instead, transplanetary regulation is dispersed across various
kinds of agencies that co-exist not only with one another but also in complex
relations with other institutions operating on local, national, and regional
scales. Analysts have variously referred to the emergent mode of governance
as being "plurilateral," "polycentric," "networked," "neo-medieval," and "dis-
aggregated."[3]

As the extent and influence of global governance in these multiple guises
has grown, so has pressure for greater citizen participation in and control
over global policy processes. Yet how can this citizen involvement be achieved?

Global regulatory bodies are unlikely in the foreseeable future to obtain directly elected representative legislative assemblies. Moreover, nationally based political parties and parliaments have largely ignored global governance issues, albeit that they arguably could and should do much more in this area.[4] In these circumstances large numbers of citizens, policy-makers, and political theorists have turned for an answer to global civil society.

Civil society mobilization in respect of global governance institutions activities has indeed become substantial since the 1980s.[5] This citizen activism has encompassed all manner of groups, including animal rights activists, anti-poverty movements, business forums, caste solidarity groups, clan and kinship mobilizations, consumer advocates, democracy promoters, development co-operation initiatives, disabled persons alliances, environmental campaigns, ethnic lobbies, faith-based associations, human rights advocates, labour unions, local community groups, peace drives, peasant movements, philanthropic foundations, professional bodies, relief organizations, sexual minorities associations, think tanks, women's networks, youth groups, and more. No global policy maker can now ignore the insistent presence—and influence—of civil society in global affairs.

Yet the cup is also partly if not substantially empty. Arguably civil society activities on global regulation have so far realized only a fraction of their total possible fruits. Thus, looking to the future, global governance requires more civil society engagement at the heart of policy processes, in respect of the full range of regulatory institutions, and involving all quarters of society. In addition, civil society mobilization vis-à-vis global governance generally needs to be more systematic, more sustainable, more competent, more strategic, more energetic, and more accountable.[6]

Indeed, all too often past civil society campaigns on global governance problems have suffered from severe shortfalls of coordination and consolidation. As a result, limited civil society resources have been dissipated through fragmentation, duplication of efforts, and internecine competition. Moreover, most global policy makers have been reluctant to engage with what seems in their eyes to be a diffuse swarm of often ill-defined and poorly accountable civil society activities. These officials have preferred to focus their relations with citizen associations on a restricted circle of well-known quantities, particularly major business lobbies and high-profile non-governmental organizations (NGOs). Yet these better connected civil society bodies tend to draw on a narrow and privileged social base.

What might be done concretely to enhance future civil society contributions to more effective and just global governance? All manner of initiatives could be considered: some geared to individual civil society associations and global governance institutions; and others aiming more generally at the overall sector. In the latter vein, for example, a "global civil society university" could be developed for enhanced training in the engagement of global governance institutions. In addition, a "global civil society resource centre" could provide services such as assembling records of previous campaigns on global governance questions, mapping networks of regulation and power in relation to different global issues, and translating important civil society and global governance documents into relevant languages. A "global civil society think tank" could serve as an incubator for ideas and programs on collective citizen engagement of global governance agencies.

Taking another tack, the present forward-looking chapter explores another speculative idea, namely, the construction of an imagined "Global Civil Society Forum" (GCSF) that would improve the coordination of and broaden the participation in civil society inputs to global governance.[7] Such a mechanism for assembling civil society at large could advance both the technical performance and the democratic foundations of transplanetary regimes. At the same time a framework of this kind could also enhance the competence and democratic credentials of the civil society associations that participated in it.

The general idea to assemble civil society voices vis-à-vis global governance is not new, of course. For example, the Conference of Non-Governmental Organizations (CONGO), the Montreal International Forum (FIM), and Social Watch have provided venues for civil society to congregate in relation to the UN system. The Bridge Initiative and the World Forum of Civil Society Networks-UBUNTU have sought to facilitate civil society exchanges with a wider range of multilateral institutions. CIVICUS-Worldwide Alliance for Citizen Participation, the State of the World Forum, the World Economic Forum (WEF), and the World Social Forum (WSF) have also constructed broad tents for civil society, albeit without seeking specifically to engage global governance agencies. For their part certain global regulatory bodies have convened so-called "multi-stakeholder dialogues" as a mode of civil society input to policy.

However, these past initiatives have arguably been limited in several important respects. First, the exercises have tended, with the notable exceptions of the WEF and the WSF, to limit coverage of "global civil society" to NGOs. Thus large swathes of global citizen action in social movements and business forums have been marginalized. Second, previous attempts at more collective civil society engagement of global governance have tended to limit "global governance" to the most visible intergovernmental organizations. Thus transgovernmental networks (apart from the G8), translocal arrangements, interregional mechanisms, private global governance, and public–private hybrid institutions have almost never figured in the picture. Third, existing instruments for civil society engagement of global governance have usually focused on the macro-level of major conferences or the micro-level of service delivery, with far less attention to the meso-level of day-to-day policy-making processes. Fourth, multi-stakeholder dialogues—when they have existed at all—have tended to be ad hoc exercises with the reins of control held firmly in official quarters.

As elaborated in the first section below, a GCSF would seek to address such shortcomings. It would be more inclusive both in the sense of encompassing a fuller range of civil society actors and in the sense of addressing a fuller range of global governance agencies. A GCSF would also provide an instrument for ongoing inputs into all stages of global policy processes. In addition, a GCSF would better balance initiative and power between civil society associations on the one hand and global governance authorities on the other.

In addition to contemplating the shape of a GCSF process, the discussion that follows assesses the conditions that would need to exist in order to put such a new instrument into place. After all, however appealing a vision might be, it will not progress beyond a vision if the inspiration is not linked to a course of practicable politics. Thus the second section of this chapter reflects on key historical circumstances that could enable the construction of a GCSF during the coming years.

It should be stressed that the general tenor of this discussion is cautious if not ambivalent. This is not an advocacy paper designed to promote a GCSF in the particular guise imagined here. Rather, it is a thought experiment meant to stimulate further debate on how civil society engagement of global governance might be taken forward given currently prevailing historical circumstances.

THE SHAPE OF A GCSF

The first part of this exercise in futurology sets out the general attributes of a Global Civil Society Forum. A succession of six subsections below cover in turn: the aim and purpose of the instrument; its constituencies; its organizational arrangements; its modus operandi; its accountabilities; and its sources of legitimacy.

Aim

The designation of this prospective framework of civil society engagement as a "forum" is quite deliberate. In other words, the venue would serve as a site for assembly, exchange, and debate. A GCSF would not be an instrument to formulate singular policy positions for the whole length and breadth of global civil society. Deliberations through a GCSF would certainly influence the policies of both the citizen associations and the governance institutions who participate in it. However, a GCSF as such would not formulate or advocate specific policy prescriptions.

In this respect the present GCSF concept takes inspiration from the WEF and the WSF that predate it. Both initiatives have succeeded in engaging large and diverse civil society constituencies over a number of years. This accomplishment has arisen precisely because these venues have not, in hosting deliberations on global problems, imposed a specific policy agenda on participants. Like the WEF and the WSF, a GCSF would function as a facilitator of dialogue rather than as a campaign machine. It would be a meeting place for other associations and not a mega-organization that encompasses and ultimately swallows its constituents.

In fact, a GCSF should probably have still fewer partisan hues than even the broadly based WEF and WSF. This newer forum would endorse neither the WEF mantra of "entrepreneurship in the global public interest" nor the WSF slogan of "another world is possible." Instead, a pithy GCSF mission statement could merely extol the virtues for global politics of informed civil society activism on the one hand and responsive global regulation on the other. A GCSF manifesto would advance no other vision than a fairly anodyne assertion of the reciprocal benefits to be gained through contacts between global civil society associations and global governance institutions.

A GCSF would also differ from the WEF and the WSF by having an explicit and specific function to provide channels of dialogue between citizens and global authorities. A GCSF would meet a need—affirmed widely in both civil society and global governance circles—for more systematic and inclusive mutual engagement. Hence when civil society actors would assemble in a GCSF, they would do so for the particular purpose of relating to one or several global regulatory mechanisms. Likewise, global governance institutions would turn to a GCSF with the precise aim of disseminating information to and collecting input from civil society groups.

Participation

A GCSF would not have a fixed membership roll. Subject to two conditions elaborated below, such a forum would in principle be available to any civil society association and any global governance agency that wished to make use of it. Participants in GCSF activities would thus constantly vary depending on the policy questions under discussion.

From the side of official circles, a GCSF would be accessed at one or another moment by all of the different types of global regulatory bodies described earlier. At one juncture the official user might be a traditional multilateral institution like the UN or the WTO. At the next juncture it might be a newer form of global authority like the G8 or ICANN. As it is envisioned here, a GCSF would not be attached to any particular global governance agency. The forum staff would work closely with civil society liaison units in the various global regulatory bodies, but a GCSF itself would be strictly independent—both constitutionally and in practice—from any of the governance organizations that used it.

From the side of civil society, a GCSF would be open to a broad spectrum of citizen associations, covering all manner of issues, objectives, ideologies, cultural styles, organizational forms, tactics, and competences. This point must be stressed: the label "Global Civil Society Forum" most decidedly does not designate "International NGO Forum." A GCSF would be deliberately designed to widen citizen access to global governance beyond an elite of (mainly North-based, professionally staffed, and male-led) international NGOs. Such a forum would offer space to all types of civil society initiatives on global affairs, including by business associations and by social movements as well as by NGOs.

This openness of civil society participation in a GCSF would be qualified by two important conditions. The first qualification would be that all associations who participated in a GCSF would need to endorse and respect a code of conduct erected for the forum. Building on earlier exercises like the 2006 INGO Accountability Charter, this statement of principles and practices would be formulated through a broad consultation during the process of creating a GCSF. Compliance with the standards (whose provisions would be subject to periodic review) would be monitored by a dedicated evaluation unit within a GCSF secretariat.

Application of a code of conduct might at first appear restrictive. However, the effect in the case of a GCSF would in fact be to broaden civil society participation in, and increase its impact on, global governance. The standards set would involve baseline norms (e.g., against racism and armed violence) rather than compliance with ambitious "best practices" that only the most highly resourced organizations could hope to attain. The code would therefore serve to identify, expose, and weed out ill intent and malpractice, so that global regulators could be assured of the bona fides of the civil society interlocutors that they meet through a GCSF. As a result, those authorities would feel confident to give a serious hearing to a much wider range of civil society groups than the high-profile and professionally more adept actors that have in the past had disproportionate access to global governance circles.

The second qualification to open civil society participation in a GCSF follows on from the preceding remark, namely, that the forum would take proactive steps to ensure a hearing for voices that tend otherwise to be excluded. After all, in civil society as elsewhere, purportedly "free" markets invariably favour the strong. All too often global civil society engagement of global governance has manifested arbitrary hierarchies of opportunity that mirror structural inequalities within society at large, *inter alia* along lines of dominant and dominated regions, cultures, classes, genders, races, (dis)abilities, sexualities, ages, castes, and urban/rural divisions. In recognition of these tendencies toward skewed access, another unit within a GCSF secretariat would keep the contours of civil society participation in forum activities under continual systematic review. If this monitoring revealed that certain constituencies were consistently absent from or peripheral to a given dialogue where they have a prima facie stake, GCSF offices would deliberately encourage greater involvement of the marginalized circles.

All of the above said, a GCSF would not claim or seek to be either exhaustive in its coverage of civil society or exclusive in its access to global regulatory institutions. Both the creators and the subsequent organizers of such a forum would need to recognize and respect that some citizen groups prefer to pursue their relations (or indeed non-engagement) with global authorities through other venues. Likewise, global governance agencies might wish also or instead to connect with global civil society outside a GCSF framework. A GCSF would therefore complement rather than replace other initiatives. It would rise or fall on its track record of delivery for the parties who chose to use it. The better a GCSF performed, the more participation it would attract.

Institutional Structure

In keeping with a premium on openness and flexibility, a GCSF would not have a highly prescriptive constitution. In addition to a short statement of purpose, such a Forum would have a limited organizational structure. The arrangement suggested here comprises three channels of engagement (respectively for business associations, NGOs, and social movements), a modest secretariat, and an overseeing board.

Channels

A GCSF would structure its dialogues between civil society and global governance agencies through three streams, related respectively to business, NGOs, and social movements. The business channel would assemble institutions such as chambers of commerce, industrial organizations, forums of small and medium enterprises (SMEs), associations of co-operatives, and other bodies that group market actors. The NGO channel would encompass consumer unions, development promotion bodies, environmental lobbies, human rights campaigners, humanitarian relief organizations, and other professional advocacy associations. The social movement channel would provide a venue for popular mobilizations around issues such as peace and disarmament, employment conditions, land tenure, racial equality, poverty eradication, religious faith, animal rights, and so on.

A GCSF would adopt this three-pronged approach in recognition of the highly diverse agendas and modus operandi that distinguish different sectors of civil society. It would be artificial and impractical to compress the full range of civil society initiatives onto a single platform that simultaneously included the International Organization of Employers (IOE), the World Wide Fund for Nature (WWF), and the Assembly of the Poor in Thailand. Better that each of the broad categories of business forums, NGOs, and social movements be accorded its own venue, so that all groups feel that they have a place that is more appropriate to their styles and aspirations.

Given that lines separating the three headings are not always clear cut, participating civil society associations would self-select their preferred channel of engagement. So long as the group in question complied with the GCSF code of conduct, other civil society participants and the forum staff could not deny an association entry to its chosen channel.

When accessing a GCSF as envisioned here, a global governance agency would undertake to engage all three channels in serious dialogue. A GCSF would thereby seek to counter past tendencies on the part of many global policy makers to focus their interchanges on a limited area of civil society, usually a sector with which they felt most comfortable. The structure of a GCSF would seek to ensure that global authorities hear a wider range of voices. At the same time, by bringing business, NGOs, and social movements to the same venue, a GCSF could help the different sectors of civil society become more acquainted with, and learn more from, one another.

Indeed, engagement with a GCSF apparatus could inspire the creation of cross-sectoral working groups, for example, regarding climate change and concerning intellectual property. Such informal self-generating consultative processes could emerge as business, NGO, and social movement associations saw benefit in learning more about and from each other over a given issue. However, such ad hoc gatherings would convene outside the GCSF framework itself, which would be committed to remaining a tightly focused facilitating mechanism and would resist moves toward bureaucratic expansion.

Secretariat

The preparation, execution, and review of civil society–global governance interchanges through a GCSF would be coordinated through a secretariat. These offices would suitably be substantially decentralized, with most of the day-to-day work of facilitating the dialogues occurring through regional bureaus. Separate branch offices could exist for Africa, Asia-1 (East and South East), Asia-2 (Central, South, and South West), Australasia and Pacific,

Europe, Latin America and the Caribbean, and North America. A devolved structure of this kind would promote the inclusion of more diverse, more locally rooted, and less amply resourced voices alongside those of the major transnational civil society players. Each regional office would be headed by a coordinator. Ideally, at any one time at least two regional coordinators would be drawn from each of the respective constituencies of business associations, NGOs, and social movements.

A small central office of the secretariat would house the bureau of a general coordinator for a GCSF. The regional coordinators would assemble together with the general coordinator to form a GCSF executive committee, which would operate on a consensus principle. Ideally, the location of the central office would periodically rotate among the seven regions, although in practice a fixed presence at the principal sites of global governance would probably be more likely. In any case, the GCSF governing board would select a new general coordinator from a different region at intervals of approximately five years.

The central office of a GCSF would also contain certain global departments. These units would include the previously mentioned divisions to promote inclusion and to oversee the code of conduct. In addition, the central office would require an adept information and communications team that publicized the GCSF and its work through print, broadcast, and internet media. Each regional office would also require an information and communications officer with rich experience in civil society activism. Meanwhile an expert advisers unit in the central secretariat would maintain a thematically organized register of academics, consultants, and witnesses who would be prepared to assist GCSF-sponsored dialogues, normally on a pro bono basis. A finance unit would administer GCSF incomes and expenditures.

Board

A governing board of a GCSF would set and review general policy guidelines for the forum. The board would also appoint the general and regional coordinators. The coordinators, through the executive committee, would submit an annual report of GCSF activities to the board for its approval.

The members of the GCSF board would be drawn in equal measure from business, NGOs, and social movements. For example, each of the seven regions could elect one member from each of the three principal GCSF constituencies, creating a total of twenty-one seats. To ensure turnover and renewal, board members would serve a three-year term, with the possibility of one successive renewal, although return to the board after a period off might be permitted.

Elections for all GCSF board seats would be held simultaneously and conducted online. The electorate would be composed of civil society associations who had participated in GCSF dialogues during the preceding three-year period. Each association would have one vote within a given regional election. An association that had been active in GCSF proceedings across more than one region could vote in all of the relevant board elections. The coexistence of the three channels, together with the multiple regional constituencies and the term limits, would ensure that the board of a GCSF does not become a narrowly based clique.

Operations

As indicated earlier, a GCSF mechanism would be demand-driven. Thus parties would come to the forum as and when they saw advantage in doing so, rather than on any predetermined schedule. With time certain interchanges would probably become fairly predictable in the yearly calendar, such as dialogues around the G8 summit, the UN General Assembly, and the Annual and Spring Meetings of the Bretton Woods institutions. Other GCSF-sponsored exchanges would occur on an ad hoc basis, for example, around a special conference or a key policy consultation. In general this demand-driven approach would generate fairly even levels of GCSF activity throughout the year.

GCSF-sponsored dialogues would frequently take place at the offices or other meeting venue of the global governance agency in question. However, a GCSF would also encourage global authorities to venture to its regional offices for encounters with civil society associations. This practice would enable more citizen groups to assemble, including those with fewer resources for travel. In addition, consultations in the regions would bring officials closer to the contexts of the civil society perspectives that were being articulated.

Along with in-person dialogues between civil society practitioners and global governance officials, a GCSF would also make considerable use of the internet. Comments and proposals would be invited at online discussion points on a GCSF website in advance of the face-to-face meetings. In addition, a GCSF website would maintain ongoing discussions, open to any civil society groups and citizens at large, in respect of particular global governance institutions and particular global policy issues. GCSF communications officers would monitor these conversations and prepare short summaries as part of the briefings for the in-person exchanges. However, web traffic would always supplement rather than replace the direct conversations between civil society associations and global regulatory institutions. As countless contexts have shown, the internet cannot substitute for face-to-face communications.

While sensitive to the problematic cultural politics involved, a GCSF would for practical purposes use English as its principal lingua franca. However, GCSF operations in several of the regions would also be conducted in other major languages of that region. Thus, for example, French and Portuguese would be employed alongside English in Africa. In Europe proceedings would be conducted in French and Russian as well as English. Portuguese and Spanish would serve as additional working languages for Latin America and the Caribbean. Arabic would also be used in South and South West Asia.

A GCSF would have an operational budget to cover secretariat activities, including substantial interpreting and translation costs. In addition, a trust fund would be available to enable participation in GCSF dialogues by poorly resourced civil society associations who would not otherwise be able to attend. Global governance agencies and better resourced civil society bodies would finance their own participation in GCSF activities.

Contributions to the budget of a GCSF would come from three main sources. Particularly in the early years, the bulk of funds would come from institutional donors, mainly philanthropic foundations and official bilateral and regional agencies. To promote diversity in and autonomy of a GCSF, no single institutional donor would be permitted to contribute more than 10 percent of the total budget. Modest user fees charged to participating global governance agencies would provide a supplementary share of the budget. The remainder would come from individual citizen contributions. It would be hoped that in time the institutional contributions would be replaced by larger citizen contributions and/or allocations from global taxation (e.g., on airline tickets, carbon trading, currency transactions, and Internet use).

Accountability

As well as being a venue for the exchange of information and perspectives, a GCSF could in practice serve as a mechanism to enhance the public accountability of the parties who participated in its proceedings. In respect of global governance agencies, for example, GCSF dialogues would provide a context in which civil society associations could hold global authorities answerable for their actions and omissions. Citizen groups could use GCSF-sponsored meetings both to applaud good work of global governance bodies and to lay charges and pursue compensations for mistakes. In this way a GCSF could enhance the legitimacy of global regulatory processes.

In addition, a GCSF through its code of conduct could contribute to greater public accountability of civil society involvement in global governance. Compliance with the code, as monitored through the GCSF secretariat, would give the citizen associations in question an important badge of credibility. Conversely, exclusion from a GCSF owing to transgressions of the code would tend to push offending organizations to the margins of global politics and encourage them to correct malpractices.

Yet, given that a GCSF would have these important powers of legitimation and delegitimation vis-à-vis both global governance institutions and civil society associations, it would be crucial also to ensure the accountability of the forum itself. A GCSF, too, would need to be answerable for the errors that it might commit and the damages that it might cause. A GCSF, too, would need to redress its mistakes with appropriate apologies, policy changes, resignations, and/or reparations.

To whom would a GCSF be accountable? Four broad sets of external stakeholders might be distinguished: civil society clients, global governance clients, funders, and the wider publics who are meant ultimately to benefit from interchanges through the forum between civil society and global governance. In addition, a GCSF would also owe accountability internally to its staff. Needless to say it would be no small challenge to achieve these various accountabilities simultaneously and in a suitably balanced fashion.

The accountability of a GCSF to participating civil society associations would mainly be achieved through the board that these constituents elect. The board would hire, fire, and otherwise amend the employment contracts of GCSF coordinators. The board would also accept or reject the annual report submitted by the executive committee. If civil society users of a prospective GCSF were unhappy with the board's performance they could unseat its members in the triennial elections. Civil society clients could also hold a GCSF accountable by voting with their feet. That is, the associations would signal endorsement by joining forum dialogues and rejection by eschewing the venue.

The accountability of a GCSF to participating global governance institutions would principally be achieved by the principle of use or avoidance. Thus if the forum did not operate to the satisfaction of the client regulators, then they would stay away. GCSF accountability to global authorities would also have a financial dimension through the user fees that those clients would pay. Hence global governance institutions could "punish" poor GCSF performance with a loss of revenues through non-use of the venue.

The accountability of a GCSF to its donors would chiefly be realized through the financial and other reporting procedures that those funders would prescribe. Even more than in the case of global governance agencies, the power of the purse would enable these stakeholders to signal displeasure with the forum by withdrawing funds. However, as noted earlier, special care would be taken to ensure that a GCSF did not operate at the behest of donors, as no single source of monies would be permitted to contribute more than 10 percent of the operating budget.

The accountability of a GCSF to wider publics would be obtained largely through mass communications. The forum would open itself to scrutiny by citizens at large with a published annual report, a detailed and continually updated website, regular press releases, and other public communications such as talks to interested groups by GCSF coordinators. As noted earlier, professional information and communications officers would form a significant component of GCSF staff. Socially responsible mass media, including active investigative journalists, would play an important role in keeping wider publics critically informed of GCSF operations. When presented in accessible forms, academic research would likewise document the strengths and shortcomings of a GCSF for the general public. Citizens at large would enhance the public answerability of a GCSF by providing or withholding individual sponsorships, albeit that this channel of accountability would obviously be more open to wealthier individuals and would probably amount to only a small proportion of total revenue.

Legitimacy

Next to—and tied up with—obtaining requisite funds and quality staff, the main challenge facing a new Global Civil Society Forum of the kind sketched here would be to build up its legitimacy. That is, such a venue would need to acquire the kind of credibility that made civil society associations and global governance agencies alike feel obliged to use it. Certainly eventual funding of a GCSF through global taxation could not arise in the absence of building up substantial trust and respect among users and the general public. The legitimacy of a GCSF could derive from several sources: efficacy, democracy, morality, legality, and personality.

With regard to efficacy a GCSF would need to be widely seen to provide value and achieve objectives. The mechanism would need generally to promote productive exchanges between civil society associations and global governance agencies. The parties would by no means always agree with or persuade one another, but even amid disagreement there would be helpful exchange of information and perspectives, and participants would gain valuable insight into the political realities that surround a given issue. The knowledge so obtained would be useful: for global governance agencies in constructing technically sound, culturally sensitive, and politically viable policies; and for civil society associations in pursuing adept and influential campaigns. The costs of a GCSF operation would be relatively modest, certainly in relation to the very substantial prospective benefits.

With regard to democracy a GCSF would need to be viewed by most as offering a venue where affected publics had opportunities to participate in and demand answers from given global governance institutions. In particular, a GCSF would need to enhance voice and accountability in global governance for marginalized circles such as disabled persons, indigenous peoples, landless peasants, urban poor, disaffected youth, and outcastes. A GCSF could thereby mark an important and innovative advance in global democracy, particularly in circumstances where directly elected global parliaments and a comprehensive global judiciary system remained impracticable for the foreseeable future.

With regard to morality a GCSF would need to obtain substantial legitimacy by facilitating the progress of just causes in global governance. A GCSF would need to contribute to improved global regulation of matters such as labour abuses, pandemics, natural resource depletion, and other public policy challenges. Moreover, GCSF measures to counter arbitrary hierarchies of access to global governance would be widely applauded as a contribution to global social justice.

With regard to legality a GCSF would gain wide respect and authority as more and more global governance institutions accorded it formal status in their official operational guidelines. Perhaps certain global regulatory bodies might even amend their constitutional document in order legally to enshrine the role of a GCSF in their policy-making processes.

With regard to personality a GCSF would no doubt gain some legitimacy from the popular appeal of certain leading figures who played pivotal roles in its creation and subsequent operation. The commitment and inspiration of such activists would figure importantly in generating and sustaining media and wider public interest in a GCSF. Charismatic leadership would also help to draw civil society and global governance participants to a GCSF and attract and retain high-quality GCSF staff.

With these diverse sources of legitimacy a GCSF would acquire firm political foundations to support its activities. That said, the status of a GCSF would probably not become fully secure for several decades. The reinforcement and growth of legitimacy for a GCSF would be a continuing struggle for its proponents in both civil society and global governance circles.

CONDITIONS FOR CONSTRUCTION

A Global Civil Society Forum on the lines sketched above would be a marked innovation in global governance processes. True, even on the modest proportions envisioned here, skeptics might doubt that a GCSF-like entity could emerge in the short- or even medium-term future. Yet history has repeatedly shown that rapid and far-reaching shifts in regulatory processes are possible if the conditions favour such change. For example, few commentators imagined in the 1920s that comprehensive welfare states would emerge in the subsequent decades. Likewise, few observers in the 1930s anticipated that wide-ranging multilateralism would develop in the 1940s, and few analysts in the late 1970s foresaw the collapse of communist-ruled governments a decade later. If the general political climate is auspicious and astute actors grasp the opportunities, major institutional (re)construction is possible in relatively short order. Are contextual circumstances in place or in prospect that could favour the creation of a GCSF? If so, what tactics might proponents of a GCSF adopt to exploit these potentials to maximum effect?

Perhaps the greatest circumstance that could favour the development of a GCSF in the next decade would be a widely felt and growing need in both civil society and official circles for such a venue. Certainly the demand for a GCSF-like apparatus is already greater today than it was a decade ago. The early twenty-first century is experiencing substantial and increasing levels of public awareness of many global problems and significant public desires to influence the rules and regulatory institutions that govern global issues. Witness the World Economic Forum, the World Social Forum, the Jubilee 2000 initiative, the Global Call to Action against Poverty, expanding fair trade schemes, etc. Likewise, emergent talk of "global citizenship," "global civil society," and "global democracy"—terminology that now also circulates beyond the pages of academic political theory—speaks of an atmosphere that is conducive to a GCSF initiative. Large and growing circles of people see their interests on a wide range of questions to be served (at least partly) by global public policies. These citizens wish to have input into global governance processes and often turn to civil society associations to provide it. Thus, while the contemporary context offers little prospect of creating directly elected global legislatures, the situation is reasonably ripe for innovation in respect of civil society instruments in global governance.

That said, a GCSF project would need to advance at a modest and cautious pace. Any scheme to assemble civil society voices could easily fall foul of the associations' laudable insistence on their diversity and autonomy. Most of these citizen groups will (rightly) resist any project that construes aggregation to entail centralization and amalgamation, particularly if such a strategy is seen to be encouraged by official circles. The initiative to develop something akin to a GCSF would therefore need to be treated as a cautious experiment whose pace and evolution were determined by the civil society participants themselves.

Another shift in the contemporary political climate that bodes well for the development of a GCSF is the general turn in discourses of global governance away from the scarcely qualified neoliberalism that prevailed until the mid-1990s. The political centre of global governance has in the early twenty-first century moved toward "Post-Washington Consensus" ideas that prescribe what might be termed a "global social market." This policy paradigm of "socially responsible globalization" shows considerable sympathy toward civil society involvement in governance processes. No longer does the dominant discourse suggest that globalization can proceed to best effect through unregulated market forces. Rather, prevailing arguments maintain that global markets need strong institutional frameworks and proactive public policy interventions to prevent or correct the harmful social and environmental consequences of untrammelled capitalism. In a global social market approach, civil society serves important functions of both service delivery and input to policy consultation. The latter role is expressed in various developments such as the Poverty Reduction Strategy Paper (PRSP) process, civil society seats on the board of the Global Fund, and a proliferation of civil society liaison offices in global governance institutions. A GCSF would represent an extension of such initiatives.

One significant omission in global social market approaches that the developers of a successful GCSF would need to repair concerns intercultural relations. Although the Post-Washington Consensus is amenable to civil society engagement of global governance, the paradigm tends to assume that civil society activity is ipso facto modern and Western-oriented in character. Yet plainly much collective action on global issues arises in and from a host of diverse cultural contexts. If a GCSF were to be available to all voices in an emergent global polity that meet the forum's baseline code of conduct, then the board, coordinators, staff, and participants in a GCSF would need to give high priority to cultivating intercultural recognition, communication, and negotiation.

The turn from neoliberalism to a global social market model of regulating global affairs has not come without political struggle. Moreover, governing elites remain under sustained pressure from a host of quarters to raise the benefits and reduce the damages of globalization and/or to distribute the gains and harms more equitably. Currently prevailing arrangements to govern global relations generally suffer from severe legitimacy deficits, derived in good part from very shaky democratic credentials. The upsurge of so-called "anti-globalization" resistance after 1999 has made elites more amenable to initiatives that could quiet citizen unrest. Promoters of a GCSF could therefore play on crisis sentiments in governing circles, arguing that a major new mechanism for civil society consultation could provide an important political safety valve and a boost to the legitimacy of global governance. At the same time, official circles would need to understand that the mere creation of a GCSF-like instrument would be insufficient to reduce the political pressure. GCSF-sponsored dialogues would need to be seen also to deliver substantive policy outputs. Civil society organizations would need to regard a GCSF as offering meaningful influence in global governance. A GCSF that failed to generate responses could in fact backfire on official circles and increase citizen discontents.

Even if prevailing public policy discourses have shifted over the past decade in favour of civil society interchanges with global governance institutions, some in official circles will likely remain reluctant to promote such dialogues. For example, one might anticipate considerable skepticism about, if not out-right opposition to, a GCSF from governments who regard direct engagement of global governance by citizen groups in their countries as an infringement of state sovereignty. Promoters of a GCSF would need to take care not to alienate states, in particular powerful states that could scupper the project. Moreover, a GCSF could fail in its ambition to increase the voices of marginalized regions in global politics if promoters of the forum did not carefully cultivate the support of governments in those countries.

It would also be important to keep major global commercial actors on board—or at least neutral toward—a GCSF project. Corporate endorsement of the initiative would be broadly in keeping with the currently popular ethos of corporate social responsibility. However, as with powerful states, those constructing a GCSF would need to take considerable care not to alienate big capital. Opposition from major global companies would not only weaken a GCSF project in general, but it would also undermine the forum's important potential to advance cross-sectoral dialogue between business associations and other parts of civil society.

Alongside governments and corporations it would be important for the success of a GCSF to nurture substantial, sympathetic, and non-sensationalized mass media coverage of forum operations. Widespread engaging and serious reporting of a GCSF in press and broadcast organs would be crucial if the forum were to realize its potential contributions to public education about and public debate on global governance. Low levels of media coverage or high levels of bad press could deeply undermine the construction of a GCSF. For this reason the institutional structure of a GCSF described earlier included a dedicated, talented, and well-resourced communications team.

Another crucial aspect of the general political climate that GCSF creators would need to address is the availability of philanthropic foundations and official donors that might substantially finance the early development of the project. Unlike several decades ago, considerable grants are today available for civil society engagement of global governance questions. These funds could be tapped until a GCSF accumulated sufficient experience and confidence to secure eventual majority funding from direct taxation. Given the sometimes fickle character of donor priorities, a particular challenge would be to sustain the interest of sponsors over the first fifteen to twenty years that would be required for a GCSF to acquire firm roots and independent funding.

Needless to say, none of the contemporary historical circumstances that favour the creation of a GCSF can be effectively tapped in the absence of dedicated and visionary leadership for the initiative. To be successful such a forum would require a committed board whose members actively promoted the project and recruited top-quality coordinators. It would be disastrous for a nascent GCSF to have a passive board of eminent persons who treated membership as no more than an honorific position. Likewise, the early coordinators of a GCSF would need to be hard-working inspirational leaders with a deep commitment to develop an important institution for the long term.

In sum, successful development of something like a GCSF would require a combination of:

- careful identification and encouragement of civil society demand for such a venue;
- further strengthening of the currently prevailing global social market paradigm;
- careful attention to the development of positive interculturality in the project;
- cultivation of support in official circles, both national and multilateral;
- cultivation of support from commercial circles, especially global capital;
- systematic pursuit of a substantial quantity and good quality of media coverage;
- committed, generous funders who respect the autonomy of the project; and
- dedicated and dynamic organizational leadership.

All of these conditions are in principle available in ample measure today. The further requirement is initiative that combines this mix of ingredients and ignites the current considerable potential for innovation.

NOTES

Acknowledgement: This chapter was written during study leave as Olof Palme Guest Professor at the School of Global Studies, Gothenburg University. I am grateful to "The Voice of Global Civil Society" conference at Waterloo, Ontario, in October 2006 for feedback on an earlier draft and to Barry Carin for encouraging some reckless futurology.

1 Michael Edwards and John Gaventa, eds, *Global Citizen Action* (Boulder, CO: Rienner, 2001); Jan Aart Scholte, "Civil Society and Governance in the Global Polity," in *Towards a Global Polity*, ed. Morten Ougaard and Richard A. Higgott (London: Routledge, 2002), 145–65; Mary Kaldor, *Global Civil Society: An Answer to War* (Cambridge: Polity, 2003).

2 See Barry Carin, Richard Higgott, Jan Aart Scholte, Gordon Smith, and Diane Stone, "Global Governance: Looking Ahead, 2006–2010," *Global Governance* 12, no. 1 (January–March 2006): 1–6.

3 Philip G. Cerny, "Plurilateralism: Structural Differentiation and Functional Conflict in the Post–Cold War World Order," *Millennium* 22, no. 1 (Spring 1993): 27–51; Jan Aart Scholte, *Globalization: A Critical Introduction* (Basingstoke: Palgrave, 2000);

Wolfgang H. Reinicke, "The Other World Wide Web: Global Public Policy Networks," *Foreign Policy* 117 (Winter 1999–2000): 44–57; Jörg Friedrichs, "The Meaning of New Medievalism," *European Journal of International Relations* 7, no. 4 (December 2001): 475–502; Anne-Marie Slaughter, *A New World Order* (Princeton: Princeton University Press, 2004).

4 Jan Aart Scholte, "Political Parties and the Democratisation of Globalisation," in *Globalising Democracy: Party Politics in Emerging Democracies*, ed. Peter Burnell (London: Routledge, 2006): 46–68.

5 See, for example, Peter Willetts, ed., *"The Conscience of the World": The Influence of Non-Governmental Organisations in the UN System* (Washington, DC: Brookings Institution, 1996); Robert O'Brien, Anne Marie Goetz, Jan Aart Scholte, and Marc Williams, *Contesting Global Governance: Multilateral Economic Institutions and Global Social Movements* (Cambridge: Cambridge University Press, 2000).

6 Jan Aart Scholte, "Civil Society and the Legitimation of Global Governance," *Journal of Civil Society* 3, no. 3 (December 2007).

7 After drafting this chapter the author learned that the United Nations Environment Programme (UNEP) has also used this nomenclature, convening a "Global Civil Society Forum" since 2000 ahead of meetings of its Governing Council/Global Ministerial Environment Forum. The present reflection does not draw specifically on the UNEP experience.

Democratizing Global Governance

*Achieving Goals while Aspiring to Free
and Equal Communication*

Martin Albrow and
Fiona Holland

In the 1990s after the collapse of the Soviet system, in the triumphalism of a "new world order" and of the "end of history," there was widespread confidence that there could be a universally applicable set of economic policies. Open frontiers, low government deficits, low tariffs, and privatization were regarded as equally appropriate to post-Soviet societies, Latin America, or the Far East. This "Washington Consensus," as these policies were dubbed, made it easy for the international financial institutions to dismiss critics of global governance as radicals and utopians.

In this climate of opinion, and in the absence of a global representative forum, advocates of the new democratic theory, based in ideas of free and full communication, came into outright confrontation with the institutions of global governance. But since Seattle in 1999, the World Social Forum movement, the increasing efforts of the United Nations to co-opt civil society, and the convergence of dominant and oppositional forces around a debate on the Millennium Development Goals, has created a communication space well suited to a debate on the nature and prospects of global democracy.

The sharing of these goals, to which so many agencies, both governmental and non-governmental, subscribe creates a situation that approximates a decentred global state, held together by communication rather than authority bonds. At the same time success in achieving those goals is very much in the balance, and consequently the demand for a stronger global central executive power increases.

The struggle between these contending forces, the extension of communicative democracy versus the increase of central control, lends current global political substance to Habermas's original theoretical intervention in pitting communicative against Weberian technical rationality.[1] The likely outcome remains uncertain, and if the argument of this chapter is valid, is permanently in the balance.

The more global governance approximates to the centralized global state the more readily it falls foul of the tendencies to plutocracy, technocracy, and institutional sclerosis that create disillusion with representative democracy. The classic statement from 1911 by Robert Michels,[2] much admired by Max Weber,[3] whereby a democratic party that aims to establish democracy succumbs to the iron law of oligarchy, applies to global governance as much as it did to national politics a century ago.

This chapter is devoted to an examination of the chances of establishing global democracy when there is widespread support for global goals and of whether the ideal of free and full communication can contribute to their achievement. Governance without government would appear to bring the Habermasian ideal closer to realization for the globe than has been possible hitherto in nation-state institutions.[4] But the issue remains whether civil society by means of its advocacy of communicative democracy as it signs up to global goals is able to avoid the Michels trap.

That this is very much a live issue is apparent from the chapters in this book. Jan Aart Scholte promotes the case for a global civil society forum that will be "more systematic, more sustainable, more competent, more strategic and more accountable."[5] Andrew Thompson examines the nuts and bolts of securing the legitimacy of such a forum.[6] Institutional developments proceed in parallel to those ideas. Three hundred non-governmental organizations from seventy-five countries met in Geneva on June 28–30, as the Civil Society Development Forum 2007, under the auspices of the Conference of NGOs in Consultative Relationship with the United Nations (CONGO). In their final statement they said, "We urge governments and the UN system to put an end to the democracy deficit of international organizations and to abide by their own principles of good governance."[7]

Yet their advocacy of a more authoritative voice for global civil society also betrays the constant anxiety of the democrat to avoid co-option to governing bodies.[8] Thompson is at pains to emphasize "complementarity" and "constructive challenge." Scholte tells how "citizen groups (rightly) resist any project that construes aggregation to entail centralization and amalgamation."[9] In calling for a voice, a forum, they are advocating a deliberative democratic initiative and yet insist on an ambivalent relationship toward existing governance institutions.

It was an ambivalence exhibited at the conference called The Voice of Global Civil Society attended by Scholte, Thompson, and ourselves, in Waterloo, Ontario, October 2006, where we urged and secured unanimous agreement that "democratizing global governance" was congruent with the aims of the conference. But a proposition to take this further into engaging with national parliaments received little support. "No dissent" did not translate into a program, project, or action plan. One can suspect this may be the fate of unnumbered conferences on democracy: consensus without consequences.

Civil society in national settings thrives on the withdrawal of governments from delivery of services and the growth of the strategic state—setting rules and shaping institutions, encouraging business, mutual, voluntary, community-based, and philanthropic organizations to step forward into what the governing authorities prefer to call the "third sector." The contemporary concern for governance is the necessary accompaniment of a change where responsibility for public goods is devolved on non-governmental agencies.

But the lack of a global democratic centre produces a disabling ambivalence of global civil society toward global governance. Since governance for the globe as a set of rules and institutions exists already, advocating a program for democratizing global governance can appear to suggest not just an assembly, but the assembling of a centre, the return to an old nation-state template, but this time for the globe. The top-down nature of the multilateral institutions sits uneasily with the preferred grassroots orientation of so many civil society organizations. They want top-down accountability, where the global agencies are sensitive to everyday needs as well as to international accounting standards. The tension between globalism and localism is ever present.

Moreover civil society itself can be the subject of governance concerns. Arising in societies where free association and speech are possible, it asks more of governments than it asks of itself in terms of democracy. Indeed the organizational impulses of civil society are often oligarchical, with charismatic leaders and few membership rights. "Who elected you?" is still the question that probably most inhibits full engagement between civil society and parliaments.

Uncomfortable with democratic control from the centre, equally civil society is always seeking to find non-centralizing ways of fulfilling its own goals in the full appreciation of the fact that democracy as an end can inspire us all. But questions of means are technical and not best resolved by majorities or lay consensus. Decentralized goal attainment is therefore an unwritten mission for civil society.

If one thinks of what a single goal-oriented project to democratize global governance would mean, that in itself is explanation enough for reluctance to take it forward; for the grand project would need to curtail debate in order to adopt an operational definition of "democratizing global governance." There would have to be a project design template even without consensus, an organizing agent, a plan, a time line, a set of targets, resources, a budget, and so on. The signature projects of modernity are strong on achievement and weak on consultation and participation. The democratic project then is close to an oxymoron.[10]

For the establishment of democratic global governance is not just a goal in its own right. Once established it should set and regulate goals so that they might have the new democratic legitimacy. Enabling the capacity to deliver is an essential component of governance. Yet in turning our backs on centrism and managerialism we appear then to have arrived at an impasse, or to use another metaphor, are immobilized in a double bind.[11] We are determined to avoid Michels' traps but we are inspired by Habermasian universalism. We want the power that enables us to meet global challenges, yet we aspire to global democratic communication.

What we aim to show through a sequence of examples is that we can defy the disabling features of the double bind if we acknowledge that democracy is always an imperfect achievement and that democratization is an ongoing process that is never complete. Democracy based in a communication ideal involves the constant auto-critique of both institutions and goals. The necessity for this is not just based in the reflexive nature of communication. Advances in communication technology, the means of communication, always unsettle the prevailing accommodations between media and democracy.

Habermas' advocacy of a communication ideal is in permanent tension with the realities of media ownership and technical control, the problematic that preoccupied Harold Innis, who insisted all communication involved bias.[12] We need the ideal because it highlights how far the existing conditions in which communication operates fall short of it.

But we need it not just for democratic checks on media control. Even more fundamentally, as an ideal it promotes the ongoing review of the idea of democracy itself and beyond that a recognition of ideas as a protean factor in human life, not simply a limited resource. When we move beyond technical rationality we engage with the purposes of communication and the realization of the aspirations we share with our fellow human beings.

COMMUNITY RADIO

We begin with an example of the aspiration to create community as well as to reflect it in the voices of its members. Community radio is not only about broadcasting, it is a social movement, actualized by legions of local volunteer producers and reporters, and international umbrella institutions, such as the World Association of Community Radio Broadcasters (AMARC), which are dedicated to supporting its development around the world.

Many principles of operation and ownership distinguish community radio from commercial and public service broadcasting; the overarching ethos is best encapsulated by the phrase "radio *by* the people *for* the people."[13] Embracing the right to communicate, community radio is committed to providing access to minority groups, is owned by the local community, maintains editorial independence from state or corporate interests, values the contribution of volunteers whom it commits to train, and operates on a non-profit basis.

Community radio has had different origins, influence, and trajectories in various regions, depending on political and social contexts and intellectual ideas. In Western Europe and North America it evolved in the 1960s and 1970s. In the US, the KPFA station, established at Berkeley by the Pacifica Foundation and dubbed "listener-sponsored radio,"[14] debated issues such as drugs, homosexuality, and communist ideas—areas of discussion shunned by commercial radio of the time. Interestingly in Canada, the Canadian Broadcasting Corporation encouraged local programming as a bulwark against America's commercial programming that flowed easily across the border.

Elsewhere, such as in Latin America, community radio emerged out of opposition to military rule and authoritarianism and developed different forms and acquired different labels. Indeed, the feel-good nature of "community" has encouraged widespread application of the term and an elasticity that can confuse and blur the distinctions between community radio and its commercial and public cousins.[15] The BBC and commercial stations may broadcast "for the community," but such programming is still planned, produced, and presented by professionals. This is diametrically opposed to the "voice to the voiceless" ethos of community radio, which exists to express the views of social groups marginalized in mainstream media (unless they are heard via "vox pops" edited by professionals to fit a particular discourse).[16]

This terminological tangle may explain a preference for the phrase "participatory communication," embodying the idea of transformative power, which was inspired by Paolo Freire's ideas about education.[17] In *Making Waves: Stories of Participatory Communication for Social Change,* Alfonso Gumucio Dagron details many examples of community radio in Africa, Asia, and Latin America, where the end of authoritarianism has led to a blossoming of participatory communication. Much can be learned from the evolution of alternative media in Latin America, particularly by academics and development organizations in the North, which have often overlooked the significance, or misunderstood the essence, of this history, argues Gumucio Dagron.[18]

A celebrated example is Radio Mineras, the Bolivian miners' radio that began in 1949 and during its 1970s heyday encompassed a network of twenty-six stations in the highlands of Potosi and Oruro. Gumucio Dagron describes how, in times of peace, Radio Mineras was fully integrated into community life, often replacing the role of post and phone in this remote highland area. During political upheavals, the stations were the only source. of trustworthy information. The network continued broadcasting, despite military coups and the shutdown of the mainstream media, until the 1980s, when mining and the power of the unions was in decline.

But Radio Mineras did not go without a fight. Gumucio Dagron describes how the "Miners' Chain" continued broadcasting, each station handing over transmission to its neighbour as the military approached. One of the last to fall under military control was Radio Animas, and during its last moments gunshots could be heard on air. Those that defended their right to communicate were killed.[19]

On the other side of the globe and thirty years later, gunshots may not ring out on air, but in the wake of a string of fatal shootings in London in Spring 2007, debate about gun crime does. Sound Radio,[20] a community radio station based in Hackney, embraces the social and economic diversity of this North London borough.[21] For station manager and CEO of Sound Vision Trust, Lol Gellor, the uniqueness of Sound Radio lies in the diversity of perspectives expressed via a range of programs broadcast by and for the various communities living in the borough. Whether they are Jewish, Kurdish, Afro-Caribbean, Bangladeshi, Turkish, or English, "the key thing is being prepared to listen to views you don't like," says Gellor.[22]

Interestingly, Sound Radio does not stipulate what can and cannot be broadcast—there are no rules relating to on-air discussions that may be perceived as homophobic, racist, or sexist, for example. Instead, the station's mission statement suggests that either listeners switch off if they don't like what they hear—or come in and make a program themselves. Few commitments or expectations are placed upon program makers. Gellor argues that the point of community radio is to engage people who are socially excluded by just those sorts of barriers in the mainstream media. That said, Sound Radio seeks to encourage vibrant discussion rather than polarization through programming that includes a variety of perspectives, in which consensus may or may not be reached.[23]

What community radio demonstrates is that it is possible to democratize the voice of a community through rules of access to a medium that has long been controlled by government or business. Although it does not prescribe a concern for global issues, its worldwide replicability facilitates the formation of global public opinion. It can therefore raise levels of accountability for global governance while remaining very much a forum for debate and dissemination of information and ideas.

INDYMEDIA

Community radio is democratic voice without global collective agency. Its scope is limited both by the local community base and reliance on a single old and trusted medium of communication. Indymedia breaks from those constraints and seeks to create a dynamic news and communication network where the users are also engaged in the ongoing transformation of the media. The network, active in more than a hundred countries, uses custom-made software that enables the rapid upload and download of audio, text, video, and photos for instant and global circulation.

Technical characteristics aside, it is much more than a global communications network. Comprising more than a hundred local Independent Media Centers, Indymedia is an "experiment in media democracy" according to co-founder Jeff Perlstein,[24] and its ethos is perhaps best encapsulated in the slogan, "be the media."[25]

The effect of this philosophy—that everyone who wishes to should have access to the production of "news" and telling of stories—is to amplify voices of marginalized groups and underrepresented peoples. Its do-it-yourself model of reporting, which originated in Seattle during the 1999 protests against the World Trade Organization,[26] focuses on protests, events, and issues relevant to the global anti-capitalist, and peace and social justice movements. During the Seattle protests, volunteer news crews reported from a grassroots perspective, producing documentaries circulated via satellite, a newspaper, and hundreds of audio segments transmitted via the internet. Consulted two million times during the demonstration,[27] Indymedia website remains a flagship virtual resource, and for Seattle-based activists, a physical meeting space.

Indymedia follows a long tradition of mediated opposition for expressing cultural and political dissent outside of the mainstream or corporate media. According to Jankowski and Jansen,[28] what distinguishes Indymedia from previous alternative media initiatives is its capacity to operate globally. "In a way never before realised, this alternative medium is able to connect voices of dissent across continents. At the same time, Indymedia are grounded in the specific contexts—political, cultural, and geographic—of those engaged in such dissent."[29]

The global–local character of Indymedia is highlighted by Dorothy Kidd, who suggests that in lessening the focus on demonstrations and mobilizations around multilateral summits and other meetings of global governance institutions, and increasing coverage of locally important issues, Indymedia is evolving from an alternative media initiative to a model of "networked autonomous communications."

The Network has begun to move away from the reactive mode of much "alternative media" which focuses only on countering hegemonic messages of the corporate and state media. Instead IMC's emphasis on the direct witness of "open publishing," and on the self-rule of local sites, begins to prefigure autonomous communication centred in the dreams, realities and communications needs of each locale.[30]

A brief examination of various Indymedia sites, randomly selected, indicates that local, national, and/or regional concerns are prioritized over international stories. According to Jankowski and Jansen's content analysis of five Indymedia sites, postings contain information and opinion, which is often emotional and reflective. They suggest that although discourse may be voluminous, it is frequently limited in qualitative substance, "short reactions of support as opposed to extended contributions of argument."[31] There is also the challenge of maintaining a global collective network, staffed by volunteers. North American and European Indymedia websites are numerous compared to the four or five in Africa (Nigeria Indymedia may no longer be operational).[32]

However, the significance of Indymedia may lie less in what it reports than how it does so. In line with Tim O'Sullivan's characteristics of alternative media, Indymedia seeks a democratic/collectivist process of production and a commitment to innovation or experimentation in form and/or content.[33] Open source software allows anyone with a modem to upload or download information to or from the Indymedia sites.

The philosophy of the network, based on values of inclusivity, plurality, diversity, transparency, and accountability, operates on the basis of consensus with regard to day-to-day editorial policy and strategic decision making. This "radical democracy" is Indymedia's most important innovation according to Victor Pickard, who says: "Indymedia's radical democratic practice entails an active renegotiation of all power relationships by democratizing the media (exemplified by an interactive web-based interface), levelling power hierarchies (exemplified by consensus-based decision making), and countering proprietary logic (exemplified by open-source software)."[34]

The challenges of maintaining consensus decision making globally, the issue of long term sustainability, and maintaining the principle of a bottom-up, participatory collective are carefully explored by Pickard, who concludes that notwithstanding these tensions Indymedia is "extending radical democratic practice to unprecedented levels.[35]

In multiple respects Indymedia is an anticipatory form of collective decision making for global governance. More than the voice of democracy, it democratizes the media that carry the voice and in doing so takes democracy beyond community boundaries. It is driven by the urgent sense that media technology itself needs to hardwire democratic principles.[36] Its concern for the media as such provides tools of immense potential for global governance while remaining relatively disengaged from its more specific tasks. As such, Indymedia is part of the global struggle, a mobilization of counter-hegemonic power.

THE GLOBAL CALL TO ACTION AGAINST POVERTY

In the 2005 Global Call to Action against Poverty (GCAP)[37] we can see how democratic voices and globally networked media can be brought into alliance with powerful agencies capable of delivering global goals.

Billed as the world's largest anti-poverty alliance, involving 150 million people made up of trade unions, faith groups, NGOs, and community organizations, GCAP enabled ninety-five national coalitions to maintain independence and diversity while working toward an agreed set of goals. GCAP supported the Millennium Development Goals (MDGs)[38] as a first step toward eliminating poverty. And, like the UN-initiated Millennium Campaign,[39] GCAP used the "White Band" symbol and White Band days of action to mobilize a significant number and range of individuals and civil society groups around the world.

During 2005, led by CIVICUS secretary general, Kumi Naidoo, GCAP employed a variety of communications tools that exploited new marketing techniques and responded to the needs of the mainstream media in order to progress the key campaign targets of trade justice, debt cancellation, and more and better aid. The innovative use of such techniques reflects the breadth of perspectives, expertise, and contacts of coalition participants—in particular, of the UK campaign, Make Poverty History (MPH).[40] Thus, the mobilizations and communication strategies devised by GCAP and national coalitions such as MPH, cannot be analyzed without considering the web of relationships among senior campaign figures, politicians, celebrities, scholars, and media professionals.

GCAP campaigning coalesced around mobilizations such as the First International White Band Day, July 1, 2005, when demonstrators around the world wore white bands and buildings were wrapped in them. In the North, campaigning climaxed at key events in the calendar of global institutions, in particular the G8 meeting in Gleneagles, Scotland, on July 6. Targeting the G8 summit, which attracted a variety of civil society activity in different locales, may not seem unusual given the demonstrations that have become common around multilateral summits and meetings of heads of state. But six years after Seattle, when thousands demonstrated against the World Trade Organization and "global civil society" entered the lexicon of leader writers, politicians, and government officials had learned much about the influence of ordinary citizens' voices.

In 2005, the UK government played host to the G8 and held the EU presidency, and British politicians and civil servants were open about the need for popular support at home to combat poverty in developing countries, particularly in Africa. One of the ways they sought to catalyze this support was via leading non-governmental organizations, celebrities, and media professionals. It can be assumed that the web of relationships spun between senior NGO leaders, politicians, and celebrities from the film, fashion, and music worlds, was mutually beneficial. Thus MPH supported the report of the Commission for Africa,[41] an entity set up by UK Prime Minister Tony Blair, with seventeen commissioners. A few weeks prior to the G8 meeting, Bob Geldof was persuaded to stage Live 8—ten concerts beamed around the world on July 2, when 225,000 marched through Edinburgh in support of the anti-poverty initiative, four days before the Gleneagles summit.

Prior to the July events, MPH had, with the help of a host of celebrities recruited by Richard Curtis,[42] filmmaker and friend of then Chancellor Gordon Brown, created a series of television, print, and billboard advertisements—the "click films," which were matched in Africa by "Africa Snaps." Capturing the attention of a young audience was clearly important to GCAP and the national coalitions; MPH member Oxfam encouraged people to sign up online to receive updates—and even buy "pants to poverty."[43]

MPH's campaign succeeded in increasing coverage of Africa in the mainstream media significantly.[44] However, evidence from public opinion polls suggests that increased media coverage may not, in the long term, maintain concern about poverty in Africa. According to Andrew Darnton, who worked on Public Perceptions of Poverty, a quantitative research program funded by Britain's Department for International Development, levels of awareness and involvement in anti-poverty initiatives peaked in July 2005 and have steadily, if only slightly, declined since then.[45]

Within GCAP there were significant disagreements about the role of celebrities, the relationship between civil society groups in the North and South, the nature of campaign goals, and the process by which these were selected. Some groups refused to sign up to GCAP, such as Focus on the Global South and Jubilee South, which argued that it was a Northern-dominated campaign that failed to work for those it purported to represent.[46]

Since the hiatus of 2005, GCAP has reflected on such issues. The "White Band Book: a review of people and events in 2005" is candid in its assessment: "Once celebrities are placed at the forefront of campaigns like GCAP, it can be difficult to maintain control of statements they make to the media. Bob Geldof's endorsement of the G8 outcomes was one such instance.

Although celebrities bring valued publicity to a cause, they can also be unpredictable."[47]

The role of Southern civil society in the launch of the coalition and some of the subsequent mobilizations, such as the first White Band Day, were also recognized as serious shortcomings. "The obvious lack of Southern representation and participation led to charges of a Northern- and donor-driven agenda. It appeared to some that positions taken by GCAP were not sufficiently progressive or responsive enough to champion southern issues."[48]

What GCAP and MPH illustrate is the shared understanding of numerous agents of the potential of a vast range of communicative and organizational alternatives at their disposal for the realization of an idea in the contemporary world. Organization, communication, and mobilization interlock in something that is more than movement or campaign, more a benign growth, a developing nexus of human activity inspired by shared aspirations.

COMMUNICATIVE RESISTANCE

"Call to Action" was an open-ended invitation to explore any mode of communication. It was democratic in aim and inclusive both of people and methods. The focus of GCAP's aspirations was the reduction of poverty worldwide. Arguably it was the most ambitious attempt yet to introduce participatory democracy into global governance. At the same time its methods have been insufficient in themselves to induce even democratically elected governments to match up to their pledges.

The criticisms GCAP suffered both during and after the Gleneagles summit should alert us to another persisting element in democracy, however far goals are democratically legitimated. The voice of opposition is always there. Factions are inherent in democracy, not just in representative systems. Government requires opposition. We illustrate this in our final set of examples of communicative resistance in order to highlight their potential for the pursuit of democratic global governance.

We highlight the importance of the Internet and the viral characteristics of twenty-first century communications. We point to the multiple media employed by different "communicative resisters," their overlapping interests and collaborative potential, the freedom of audiences to interpret their messages variously, and the reactions of their targets.

These media indicate something beyond government and opposition. They suggest that binary oppositions may not be adequate for grasping the transformative effects of democratized media on global governance. Techniques of communicative resistance—whether parody, satire, subversion, or simply disseminating one's first-hand experiences and discoveries to a global audience—can be exploited equally by social movements, corporations, government information campaigns, and extremists of various hues.

Because of our focus on democratic global governance, we will examine examples of blogging, culture jamming, and contemporary art practice that challenge hegemonic discourses. They take us to a critical point in contemporary controversy over the control of the means of communicating those ideologies. They bring us to the unresolved issue of whether there have to be limits to full and free communication if democratic global governance is to be a sustainable aspiration.

In 1999, the term "blog"—which conflates "web log"—was coined. Since then, blogging has burgeoned. An estimated 75.2 million blogs have been indexed by Technorati.[49] Blogging is enabled by the standard format software of the Web 2.0 user-generated content platform, which allows anyone with a computer and Internet access to create, and easily update, their personal website or diary. It is not only the number of bloggers around the world, but the nature of this new sphere of communication, that has important implications for global civil society, the mainstream media, governments of all political hues, and democracy.

One of the most beneficial and important effects of blogs must be the provision of alternative sources of information to the mainstream media, particularly in non-democratic countries where traditional print and broadcast outlets may be censored.[50] The window bloggers open on events not covered by state-controlled media is of interest to activists, journalists, and ordinary citizens alike, both within and beyond the country concerned. The fact that journalists in the mainstream media pay attention to blogs, and vice versa, and that newspapers and broadcasters are encouraging readers and listeners to respond and engage in online debates, indicates the extent to which the interactivity of the blogging phenomenon is changing how we communicate.[51]

That presidents have established blogs—however ironically in the case of Iranian president Mahmoud Ahmadinejad[52]—suggests the growing influence of this form of communication. In non-democratic contexts where blogging has proved a particularly attractive tool for dissidents and activists, the targeting of bloggers has increased in the last five years.[53] Many countries filter Internet communications (often justified in the fight against terrorism) and increasingly, some are using refined forms of Internet censorship to target blogs. Other, less subtle types of suppression are also used, including the intimidation, arrest, and trial of bloggers—which may be illegitimate. According to Ronald J. Deibert and Rafal Rohozinski, China and Iran are the primary perpetrators of threats against bloggers who are least likely to be informed of charges and most likely to face lengthy detention. Bahrain comes second to Iran in the numbers of bloggers arrested, followed by China, Malaysia, and the US.[54]

It would be easy to portray the blogger–state relationship as one of David and Goliath in the battle for freedom of expression, but the reality is more complex. Global civil society is not the preserve of progressive actors, and neither is the blogosphere; bloggers may not only be "the good guys." Extremists apart, "uncivility" is inevitable in a system that is neither regulated nor mediated. Some commentators (admittedly mainstream journalists and book authors) argue that the backbiting and lack of purpose is stalling the development of this revolution in communication. According to journalist Tim Dowling, the blogosphere is "a seemingly intemperate, foul mouthed, grotesquely misogynistic community where no one can spell and everyone is blessed with a surfeit of time."[55]

Such issues have met with two main responses. First, the creation of blog "consolidators," which select blogs from around the world, aggregate them and encourage debate that is regulated. Global Voices Online is one such initiative, founded by Harvard Law School's Berkman Center for Internet and Society in 2004, which is supported by several philanthropic organizations, and companies including Reuters. According to its website, the project seeks to "aggregate, curate, and amplify the global conversations online—shining light on places and people other media often ignore."[56] The Global Voices site welcomes comments from anyone but moderates posts to weed out spam, hate speech, and pornography.

Second and more ambitious are proposals for self-regulation of the blogosphere, most recently by Tim O'Reilly (who coined the phrase Web 2.0) and Jimmy Wales (founder of Wikipedia). They proposed a "Blogger Code of Conduct," in a bid to help "create a culture that encourages both personal expression and constructive conversation,"[57] with Kitemarks for those who comply. However, this idea met with a predictable response from those who believe the lack of regulation is a key strength of the blogosphere.[58]

With so many and varied effects, it may be too soon to evaluate definitively the impacts of this young and evolving sphere of communication. However, its rich complexities and often unexpected effects encourage us to examine a recent, much blogged about incident in the hope of better understanding some of the implications of the blogosphere—in particular for ordinary people.

From a myriad possible examples, we chose the story of "China's Last Nail House,"[59] which was first reported by bloggers in China on February 27, 2007. They relayed the story of couple Wu Ping and Wang Yu, who since 2004 had fought against the demolition of their modest house to make way for a new development in the city of Chongqing, in southwest China.[60] Bloggers differed over the history and details of the story, but there was greater consensus about one thing: Wu Ping's feisty resistance of the developer and the authorities in defence of her rights made for a compelling story. Striking photographs of the slim, ramshackle building perched atop the last unexcavated sliver of land in the midst of a huge construction site doubtless kindled people's curiosity and appeal for the media—the house, adorned variously with a protest banner and Wang Yu waving the Chinese flag, could be seen clearly from Chongqing's railway station.[61]

From Chinese blogs, the story entered the mainstream media, both local and national, print and broadcast. Even the state run *China Daily* reported the story.[62] An illustration of the seamless traverse of information between mainstream media and blogosphere was provided by blogger Matt, of the Coffee House, who translated and posted the "Peering into the Interior" post of March 8 (itself a translation of the *Southern Metropolis Daily* report), only to find the Chongqing Nail House pictured in Britain's *Daily Mirror* on March 14 (and Metro.co.uk on March 11).[63] "Amazing how news stories go from obscurity to a global audience in a relatively short time frame these days. It's the Google thing ... and now anyone can play reporter!" says Matt.[64] This was the beginning of what was dubbed "a media frenzy" over an incident that had been "frothed up like crazy on the Web," according to Chongqing Mayor Wang Hongju.[65] Newspapers and broadcasters around the world featured the story, including, to name a few, *The New York Times, The International Herald Tribune,* the BBC, CNN, *The Globe and Mail,* and *The Guardian.*[66] And in the 1,380,000 hits Google returns for "China's last nail house"[67] there must be many more media reports.

Debates in the blogosphere about this mainstream coverage ensued, not all of it complimentary. However, despite frequent disparagement from both sides, the relationship between bloggers and journalists is perhaps more mutually beneficial than they are prepared to admit—at the very least, as illustrated above, information flows rapidly between these spheres, adding to knowledge and magnifying interest. A catalyst to the "Last Nail House" story spiralling around the world was Zola Zhou,[68] a twenty-six-year-old man who arrived in Chongqing to investigate further, inspired by a self-professed sense of justice and the fear that coverage would be soon be censored. John Kennedy, of Global Voices, translated the March 23 blog of Zhou, dubbed the "nation's first citizen reporter":

> As everyone knows, some reports of news like this which involves the government will surely never be reported, and [online] stories will be deleted at the request of unknown "relevant departments." There had been a Sina blog reporting 24 hours a day on the situation, but that blog later disappeared. That's why I realised this is a one-time chance, and so from far, far away I came to Chongqing to conduct a thorough investigation, in an attempt to understand a variety of viewpoints...[69]

Indeed, the Chinese government reportedly attempted to suppress mainstream media coverage of the story and blocked online access to it via Google.[70] Zhou's thorough and insightful investigation, during which he stumbled upon an expected discovery, may have contributed to the authorities' concern about the implications of the extensive media coverage.[71] He found that people from elsewhere, as far away as Zhuhai, Chengdu, Xian, and Shanghai, had come to Chongqing in the hope of publicizing their stories of lost homes, inadequate or no compensation, and sometimes forced evictions. Among those was Mr. Chen, from Zhuhai, Guangdong, who told Zhou his home was torn down after the residents were lured out of the building and beaten; and Ms. Lui, of Chongqing, who protested against the inadequate compensation for her house in Huaxin village, Yu district.[72]

Mr. Chen heard about Chongqing's Nail House on Phoenix Television. It seems that the extensive coverage and passage of a new law guaranteeing private property rights (which Wu Ping used in her defence) galvanized others who felt similarly wronged to vent their feelings in a bid for redress. According to Yang Zhizhu, assistant professor at the China Youth University for Political Science, "It was precisely the universality across the country of this brutal eviction and demolition, of insufficient or delayed compensation, that generated such sympathy and support for the 'toughest nail house.'"[73] Struggles between residents and developers are common in China's rapidly developing cities,[74] and the implications of the agreement reached eventually over the Chongqing Nail House for citizens' rights and the public sphere were discussed widely online and in print.[75]

In addition to catalyzing ordinary citizens in China, the Chongqing saga encouraged the exchange of similar experiences over the blogosphere. For example, "Louise" describes a struggle between Brooklyn developers and residents.[76] The blogosphere is a communication space where the struggles over rights, hitherto defined as national, involve an appeal to an aspiration for transnational standards.

CULTURE JAMMING

Culture jamming is defined variously by scholars, the key elements being the use of parody, satire, and/or pranks to counter and subvert the consumption-focused messages originating from corporations and other power holders, and communicated via the media.[77] This "semiological guerilla warfare"[78] or "meme wars"[79] is rooted in "detournement," an idea articulated by the 1950s/60s art movement Situationism to describe the modification of existing text to convey a meaning different from the one intended.[80] Decades later, catalyzed by advancements in information and communications technologies, and the transformation of the public sphere, the term "culture jamming" was coined by the performance/activist group Negativland on their 1984 recording *Jam-Con84*.[81] Considered as a form of media practice or activism, Carducci suggests that "culture jamming endeavours to achieve transparency, that is, to mitigate the asymmetrical effects of power and other distortions in the communications apparatus, cutting through the clutter as it were to clarify otherwise obscured meaning."[82]

Culture jamming takes many forms: "hijacking" or "liberation" of billboards with spoof advertisements, computer "hacktivism," pirate radio, parodies of corporate and NGO websites, impersonation, and performance. Often it has been directed at the perceived exploitative labour practices and ecological damage wrought by corporations and manufacturers of consumer products. By "peeling away brand veneer" and thereby making transparent the relationship between consumption and production, culture jamming can be seen as a consumer avant-garde[83] or an ad hoc form of social marketing.[84]

Some of the most infamous and widely circulated culture jams parody the advertisements of leading brand names such as Calvin Klein, Esso, Tommy Hilfiger, and Nike, to name a few. However, many culture jammers would deny their aim was solely to ameliorate the worst effects of consumerism, asserting not only an anti-consumerist ethos but according to Adbusters Media Foundation, a desire "to topple existing power structures and forge a major shift in the way we live in the twenty-first century."[85] Thus "the Yes Men" engage in "identity correction," impersonating business and political leaders in public in order to reveal what they believe are the unacceptable effects of capitalism and the gap between corporate rhetoric and reality on environmental, health, and other issues.[86] By credibly creating fake websites and impersonating spokespeople, the Yes Men have pretended to represent the Dow Chemical Corporation on the BBC, where they announced the company's full responsibility for the Union Carbide chemical accident of 1984 in Bhopal, India. Since the "Bhopal Hoax," the Yes Men have pretended to represent Dow again, this time at a banking conference, and impersonated a WTO spokesperson to engage in a debate on Voice of America about "private stewardry of labour" in Africa, a thinly veiled attempt to promote slavery, which was taken seriously by the radio station.

Kalle Lasn is the founder of Adbusters, an online archive of advertisement parodies and a quarterly magazine, and author of *Culture Jam: The Uncooling of America*. There are countless other culture jammers as the links on Sniggle .net attest.[87] While Adbusters buys street advertising space and time on mainstream television and radio to air its "anti-spots," other masters of ad parodying, including the Billboard Liberation Front, the California Department of Corrections, and Ron English, hijack hoardings in a bid to subvert the messages of political and military institutions as well as consumer manufacturers.[88] Just as culture jammers contest the authenticity claims of big business, so too do they question the communications of political leaders via reworkings of film posters, newspaper front pages, bumper stickers, and political party advertisements.[89] In part, this may have been catalyzed by 9/11, terrorism and the "war on terror," and the increasing politicization of ethnic and religious difference.

The relationship between art and culture jamming has been alluded to; some jammers conceive their work as art, and indeed techniques of detournement are visible in some contemporary art. For example, Martha Rosler juxtaposes the consumer-driven lifestyles of Americans with the carnage of the Iraq war in her photomontages *Bringing War Home: House Beautiful, new series* (2004). The viewer is invited to gaze upon a beautiful home interior, perfect and peaceful, except for the bloody casualties of war slumped in designer chairs, and the battle raging in the garden. In this way, Rosler challenges audiences to rethink the boundaries between the social and political and the public and private.[90]

The Guerrilla Girls Inc, a group of anonymous women artists, cleverly combine art and activism in order to expose the "sexism and racism in politics, the art world, film and the culture at large."[91] Founded in 1985, their provocative posters and stickers, which were once pasted at night on the walls of Soho, are now collected by major museums and studied on art courses. When invited to speak at colleges and museums, and in the media, the Guerrilla Girls assume the names of dead women artists and wear gorilla masks in the public eye, in order to focus "on the issues, not on our personalities." These self-styled "feminist masked avengers" are committed to "fighting discrimination with facts, humor and fake fur!" according to their website.

Although scholars disagree on whether culture jamming represents a new social movement, there is some consensus on how and when jamming is most effective. Alliances between culture jammers and ecological, labour rights, or other social justice movements may "offer more viable alternatives to the global capitalist system, and result in a more comprehensive form of critical thinking that advocates a paradigm shift."[92] Indeed, by enabling ordinary citizens to voice dissent, reclaim the public sphere, and claw back some control over the means of communication, culture jamming could be seen as "politics carried on by other means."[93]

THE POWER OF THE DEMOCRATIC IDEA

The sequence we have followed through community radio, Indymedia, the Global Call to Action against Poverty, and finally communicative resistance, illustrates the ever-present potential for democratizing global governance inherent in the ideal of full and free communication. If some of this potential overreaches, and can even become self-defeating for democratic governance, it is in part because there are enduring recalcitrant factors that work against this ideal and that, unchecked, will reinforce structures of unequal power and privilege. The greater the injustice the less likely is opposition going to be satisfied with the kinds of resistance that suit an open democratic society.

The pursuit of profit arising from monopolistic control of the media endangers democracy as much as governmental control. Technocratic oligarchy is also an ever present threat. But technical rationality is an essential aspect of practice designed to meet challenges in the human environment, and a hierarchical, professionally-backed division of labour is often the best method for achieving a specific goal. There can be little doubt that, however comprehensive the system of democratic global governance, it must exercise oversight over technical systems that cannot always be organized democratically if they are to be effective. Disaster relief is a clear example of the need to have a permanent system of command and control in place. At the same time, the numerous accounts of the way it fails to achieve its results demonstrate the importance of continuous feedback and information from the maximum number of sources.[94]

The demands of a rapidly changing technical environment added to the permanent tendency of individuals and groups to exploit the advantages that accrue from ownership or strategic position are a standing challenge to democracy. But the idea of democracy shows a resilience equal to the challenge. Our examples have shown the continual reshaping of the idea, both in the development and the use of communication technology. We can distinguish three ways in which this works.

The first is an effect of the pursuit of an idea, any idea, and in this respect democratic global governance is always in tension with technical rationality, doctrines of project management, goal attainment, and economic definitions of resources. This is not to its disadvantage. Ideals, ideas pursued to realize their meaning and value, mobilize people beyond any predetermined division of labour. They encourage commitment beyond remuneration and imagination beyond codes.

Lawrence Lessig quotes American president Thomas Jefferson urging in 1813 "that ideas should freely spread for one to another over the globe" and points out that in the terms of modern economists this means they are difficult to keep from others but also they are "non-rivalrous resources," your possession does not lessen mine.[95] In fiercely defending the free exchange of ideas, Lessig at the same time calls for common control of the means to make that possible, what he terms "the creative commons."

Lessig is in the front line of democratic resistance to the increase of the power of owners of communication and information technology. He advocates the recognition both of ideas and media technology as resources that should be open to all. In his insistence that democratic ideas are involved in the very design of communication technology and systems, he combats the often unacknowledged technological determinism that is at the root of so many pessimistic accounts of the inevitable loss of freedom to technical advance.

At the same time we need to insist that ideas are more than just resources, even if they are common resources. They may harbour the non-negotiable, the sacred, and the true, which means that quality as resources will only be revealed incidentally.[96] They are antecedent to resources, proto-resources, which is why their assimilation to the idea of capital can be misleading.[97] They also can be conveyed through any medium of communication.

So if we are committed to democratizing global governance as an idea, it can be celebrated in music or represented on the stage. It can blossom as a campaign, animated by slogans, focalized in events, in rock concerts and music festivals, projected through the media, supported by philanthropists and public appeals. The public relations and advertising industries will bolster its impact and in turn exploit its potential for branding and product development of all kinds.

Ideas are never exhausted by words—they lurk behind the expressions to which they give rise—and the expressions exist too in a communicative frame that can employ words to serve very different functions. We can use Democratizing Global Governance (DGG) as headline, strapline, or even a byline, if for instance it refers to a collective author. It can be a book title, as it has been.[98] Or a lapel badge. Individuals show themselves to be expert users of all these communicative devices in their own assertions of identity and belief.

Adherents of movements make an autonomous commitment and are inherently resistant to claims either to speak for them or to own any part of the messages that circulate freely among them. To support a movement requires no more than affirmations of identity as a student, a woman, a green. But the green may disavow Greenpeace. The supporter of the peace movement may well be a skeptic about the Campaign for Nuclear Disarmament, the blogger can denounce the GCAP. Therein lies the appeal of movements: they provide both for personalized identity and affiliation with like-minded people in a constantly shifting territory of personal space.

This is the second source of the strength of the democratic idea, not in the same way as any other idea, but specifically in the vital regulative function that democracy, rule by the people, implies. It confronts the vast diversity in the expression and exchange of ideas between individuals by providing for collective decision making and control of ideas to common benefit. It is an idea that accords equal weight to consensus and diversity of opinion, and in seeking a balance between them constantly shifts our attention from procedure to substance and back again. As a result the idea of democracy incites a continuous process of reform and renewal in changed conditions. In the tension it manages between individual and community it is cognate with diversity but appeals to unity, invites alternatives but requires respect for the collective view. The main contemporary theoretical development of this source is in the idea of deliberative democracy.[99]

The third strength of the democratic idea has accrued under the contemporary conditions of a networked, knowledge society. When linked to economic activity it favours markets and unsettles hierarchies.[100] When joined with intellectual inquiry it inspires the growth and renewal of scientific communities. When applied to communication it seeks technologies that aim to give every listener a voice, to every reader a writing opportunity, to create a world of free and equal exchange of views and information.[101] Jefferson's idea of the power of ideas is joined to Habermas's view of full and free communication to become the corollary of the idea of an open global society. Communication that is full and free encourages the exchange of ideas with the other, those outside the community, and this extension of the democratic idea is inclusive rather than exclusionary.[102]

Global democracy implies an all inclusive human community.[103] Democratic governance can therefore work through all the constituent agencies of that community, from the IMF through to the local recycling group or a global anti-war network. There is an infinitely varied way in which their co-operative relations can be configured. DGG is then a set of contemporary practices, informing and inspiring people to act now in a certain way. It is an immanent tendency, not a future trend. We can see it in village councils, in accountable development aid, in the World Social Forums, in participatory research, even in consultation between G8 leaders and civil society. We have to democratize all the time, simply to keep up with the relentless pace of economic and technological development.

Our argument points to a reversal of the usual relation between consciousness of actors, social processes, entities, and cultural phenomena on the one hand and a future desired state on the other. They are not the basis of a project plan that will achieve democratic global governance at some future time. Instead DGG is an impulse animating agencies of all kinds, a medium for debate, a creative collective moment that brings humankind and the future of the globe into our everyday considerations as well into the deliberations of global governance agencies.

CONCLUSION: DEMOCRATIZING GLOBAL GOVERNANCE AS AN IMMANENT IDEAL

We have confronted the paradox—we all agree on democratizing global governance, yet have no agreed strategy for achieving it. The paradox exists however only if we work in a one-dimensional frame that insists on lines of power and authority culminating in a single apex. That is inimical, indeed directly contradictory, to democratizing global governance, which, as we hope our examples have suggested, can advance everyday through our various personal and collective contributions. We just have to be alert to the power of the democratic idea and the potential resources out there waiting to be used.

For both science and economies, a broad body of opinion holds that national policies are best that allow most freedom. We therefore have reviewed DGG in the broadest possible sense for its potential to be translated from idea into reality without central authority and without a command structure. We understand that must involve working in the world, using resources, respecting logic and circumstantial limitations alike, but we are not going to employ means that negate the very values we seek to realize. We are indeed seeking to do what Robert Michels found to be impossible with the German Social Democratic Party, namely to seek democracy without sacrificing it along the way.

We have acknowledged there is a certain credibility gap in civil society's aspiration for democratized global governance, and there is also a manifest lack of specifics about what it would look like if it were achieved. For the end itself is open to question, to democratic debate. The whole history of thinking about democracy illustrates how an appeal to the judgement of "the people" provides always for objections, for an appeal to democracy of a higher quality than the defective system of the moment. How can we get there if we can't agree on the goal? But insisting on an answer to this question imposes closure on an open concept.

Democratic global governance is an immanent ideal that can be realized on a day-to-day basis and reproduced through an immense variety of cultural practices. It is emancipatory not just in respect of encouraging free expression, it enhances the range of what is thought to be possible. It opens up, rather than closes down futures and this is why as a dynamic element in the process of reform it has no endpoint.

This is neither a pessimistic nor optimistic position. It is realistic, and we would argue importantly respectful of the past too. Community radio was not, is not simply a dated solution to the problems of global communication. Its early advocates achieved as much for democracy in their time as bloggers do in our own.[104] The challenges change and democracy in a global society will remain ever incomplete.

272 *Martin Albrow and Fiona Holland*

For instance, governance systems for one set of authorities can contain consultative, participatory, and regulatory mechanisms that relate to duties to shareholders, only for environmental impacts to require a quite different set of parties to be represented. At the moment the pressure to expand the self-appointed central committee of global governance, the G8, to add five or to expand to twenty-one, is in part dictated by its failure to represent the greater part of the world's population, but also by the shift of substantive concern to global warming.

In the reform discussions for the international financial institutions, the case for the voices of the debtors as well as of the lenders to be heard is harder to resist. Once it is recognized that the conduct of multilateral relations has an impact extending to the global collectivity, and not just to the parties to those relations, then issues of democratic legitimacy come to the fore.

These shifts toward more democratic global governance are not of course predetermined. As we have stressed, the counter factors are numerous and frequently rehearsed: huge imbalances of power and wealth between countries, the impact of market forces, ethnocentrism, and the use of violence, both by states and non-state actors. There is also the requirement to ensure global decisions are made and implemented with the best technical and professional resources available, in which democracy is not an intrinsic component.

Contemporary democratic theory, however, with its stress on free and full communication, highlights democracy as a neverending process of democratization countering the sclerotic tendencies of ruling institutions to fall under oligarchic control. We are not advancing toward some future goal of perfect democracy, we simply struggle to sustain democratic ideals under conditions that provide an ever renewed challenge to their maintenance. Knowledge society and global democracy: the future of humankind is held in the balance between the two. Civil society, poised between the powers of government and business, has a decisive role to play in maintaining that balance.

NOTES

1 Jürgen Habermas's contribution in challenging the Weberian restriction of rationality either to ends–means thinking or the logical pursuit of absolute values, and therefore according communication an equal status with them as a basic type of human action, is the seminal statement for contemporary democratic theory. See Jürgen Habermas, *The Theory of Communicative Action*, 2 vols. (Cambridge: Polity, 1984 and 1989).

2 Robert Michels, *Political Parties* (Glencoe, IL: Free Press, 1958).

3 For an account of the relation between Max Weber and Robert Michels see Wolfgang Mommsen, "Robert Michels and Max Weber: Moral Conviction versus the

Politics of Responsibility," in *Max Weber and His Contemporaries*, ed. Wolfgang Mommsen and Jürgen Osterhammel (London: Unwin Hyman, 1987), 121–38.

4 As John B. Thompson (*The Media and Modernity: A Social Theory of the Media*, Cambridge: Polity, 1995) has pointed out, Habermas's engagement with Weber and his
elaboration of the idea of the public sphere remained very much within the
notion of co-presence. Transformations of "spatial and temporal proximity has
caused to be relevant democratization of responsibility in concern for distant
others" (p. 263).

5 See chapter 12 in this volume, Jan Aart Scholte, "Looking to the Future: A Global
Civil Society Forum?"

6 See chapter 11 in this volume, Andrew S. Thompson, "Laying the Groundwork:
Considerations for a Charter for a Proposed Global Civil Society Forum."

7 The Forum met on June 28–30, 2007, in Geneva with the theme "A Platform for
Development: Countdown to 2015." http://www.ngocongo.org/files/csdf_2007_finl
_statement_english.pdf. Accessed July 26, 2007.

8 Leon Gordenker and Thomas G. Weiss, "Devolving Responsibilities: A framework
for analyzing NGOs and services," *Third World Quarterly* 18, no. 3 (1997): 447.

9 Scholte, "Looking to the Future," 11.

10 Even the wider conception of "the project" as an overall modernizing movement
such as that promoted by the "Third Way" thinking of the British Labour Party only
replaces the central authority with a professional technocratic elite. Nico Stehr, in
Knowledge Societies (London: Sage, 1994), 262, concludes that "new forms of inequality based in knowledge emerge and are firmly institutionalized, creating and
extending advantages as well as forms of deprivation." The "digital divide" comes
immediately to mind.

11 For an excellent account of the way alternative forms of organizing using the new
information and communication technology can neutralize this double bind see
the doctoral thesis on Michels iron law of oligarchy and Friends of the Earth by
Neil J. Washbourne, "Beyond Iron Laws: Information Technology and Social Transformation in the Global Environmental Movement," University of Surrey PhD,
1998.

12 Harold Innis, *The Bias of Communication* (Toronto: University of Toronto Press,
1952). For an account of Innis's work, see James W. Carey, "Space, Time and Communications: A Tribute to Harold Innis," in *Communication as Culture: Essays on
Media and Society* (New York: Routledge, 1992), 142–72.

13 Peter M. Lewis, "Community Media: Giving 'a Voice to the Voiceless,'" in *From the
Margins to the Cutting Edge: Community Media and Empowerment*, ed. Peter M. Lewis
and Susan Jones (Cresskill, NJ: Hampton Press, 2006), 13–40.

14 Ibid., 18.

15 Ibid., 26; for a fuller discussion see John D.H. Downing, *Radical Media: Rebellious
Communication and Social Movements* (London: Sage, 2001).

16 Lewis, "Community Media," 16.

17 Paolo Freire, *The Pedagogy of the Oppressed* (London: Penguin, 1972).

18 Alfonso Gumucio Dagron, *Making Waves: Stories of Participatory Communication for
Social Change: A Report to the Rockefeller Foundation* (New York: Rockefeller Foundation, 2001).

19 Ibid., 43–44.

20 See http://www.soundradio.org.uk/index.php.

21 "As a commitment to access to media Sound Radio aim to provide a multilingual and multicultural radio station that reflects, as far as is possible, the make up of the East London community to whom we broadcast on the AM/MW band." See the Sound Radio homepage for more on its profile and objectives. http://www.soundradio.org.uk/about.php.

22 Lol Gellor during a lecture on the Alternative Media course, February 26, 2007, at LSE.

23 Ibid.

24 Quoted in Dorothy Kidd, "Carnival and the Commons: the Global IMC Network" (draft), presented at Our Media III Conference, Barranguilla, Colombia, May 2003, page 2.

25 Quoted in Victor W. Pickard, "Assessing the Radical Democracy of Indymedia: Discursive, Technical, and Institutional Constructions," *Critical Studies in Media Communication* 23, no. 1 (March 2006): 19–38.

26 See www.indymedia.org for more on the founding, history, and mission statement.

27 See http://seattle.indymedia.org/en/static/about.shtml.

28 Nicholas W. Jankowski and Marieke Jansen, "Indymedia: Exploration of an Alternative Internet-based Source of Movement News," presented at Digital News, Social Change and Globalization Conference, Hong Kong Baptist University, December 2003.

29 Ibid., 2.

30 Kidd, "Carnival and the Commons," 4.

31 Jankowski and Jansen, "Indymedia," 33.

32 Although still listed on the Indymedia website, Nigeria Indymedia URL cannot be found.

33 Tim O'Sullivan, *Key Concepts in Communication and Cultural Studies* (London, New York: Routledge, 1994), quoted in *Alternative Media* by Chris Atton (London, Thousand Oaks, New Delhi: 2001), 15.

34 Pickard, "Assessing the Radical Democracy of Indymedia," 20.

35 Victor W Pickard, "United yet autonomous: Indymedia and the struggle to sustain a radical democratic network," *Media Culture & Society* 28, no. 3 (2006): 315–36, 334.

36 Compare this earlier statement on the social nature of the Net, "It is a different way of performing organizing activity. The Net is equally no more just technology than money is the economy, for we all know that money is a political artefact." Martin Albrow and Neil Washbourne, "Sociology for Postmodern Organizers: Working the Net," in *Do Organizations Have Feelings?* by Martin Albrow (London: Routledge, 1997), 135–51, 149.

37 See http://www.whiteband.org/GlobalPages/AboutGcap/en.

38 The MDGs are a series of time-bound development targets in eight areas that 189 countries signed up to in 2000 and recommitted themselves to in September 2005. The eight goals, to be achieved by 2015, are to eradicate extreme poverty and hunger; achieve universal primary education; promote gender equality and empower women; reduce child mortality; improve maternal health; combat

HIV/AIDS, malaria and other diseases; ensure environmental sustainability; and develop a global partnership for development.

39 See http://www.millenniumcampaign.org/site/pp.asp?c=grKVL2NLE&b=138312.

40 Here we focus on the activities of GCAP and MPH during 2005, when three pivotal events for anti-poverty campaigners took place: the G8 summit in Scotland (July), the UN Millennium +5 Summit in New York (September), and the WTO meeting in Hong Kong (December). Post 2005, MPH was wound down (see BOND, http://www.bond.org.uk/campaign/index.htm), but GCAP has remained operational.

41 *Our Common Future: Report of the Commission for Africa* 2005. The Commission for Africa was formed in 2004, comprising seventeen members, including Tony Blair, Gordon Brown, Sir Bob Geldof, and nine Africans drawn from business and politics. Its report contained ideas for action by the G8, EU, international institutions, and African leaders.

42 Stuart Hodkinson, "Inside the Murky World of the UK's Make Poverty History Campaign," 2005, available at www.focusweb.org/main/html/modules.php?op =modload&name=NMake Poverty Hoistoryews&file=article&sid=626.

43 Fair trade, organic, and sweatshop-free underpants. See http://www.pantstopoverty .com/.

44 See Fiona Holland, Box 1.2, "Mainstreaming Africa," in *Global Civil Society 2005/6*, ed. Marlies Glasius, Mary Kaldor, Helmut Anheier (London: Sage, 2006).

45 Andrew Darnton, "Public Perceptions of Poverty in 2005," in *The Networker*, available at http://www.bond.org.uk/networker/2006/may06/ppp.htm.

46 See Hodkinson, "Inside the Murky World," and Focus on the Global South, www .focusweb.org.

47 See http://whitebandbook.org/content/blogcategory/18/31/.

48 Ibid.

49 Tchnorati is an Internet search engine for searching blogs. See Technorati's state of the blogosphere report, April 2007, reported in Tim Dowling "Comedy of Manners," in *The Guardian*, April 14, 2007.

50 For example, see Julien Pain, "Bloggers, the New Heralds of Free Expression," in *The Handbook for Bloggers and Cyber-Dissidents*, Reporters Without Borders, September 2005. http://www.rsf.org/IMG/pdf/handbook_bloggers_cyberdissidents-GB.pdf.

51 See for example http://commentisfree.guardian.co.uk/index.html.

52 See http://www.ahmadinejad.ir/. Iran, along with China, is at the top of the list of countries that target bloggers, according to research by Rafal Rohozinsky and Ronald J. Deibert (see "Good for Liberty, Bad for Security? Global Civil Society and Securitization of the Internet," in *Access Denied* [MIT Press, forthcoming, 2007], already cited). Iran has more bloggers arrested (mostly without recourse to legal assistance and often not informed of the actual charges against them) out of eleven countries surveyed. Deibert and Rohozinski say the targeting of bloggers has increased significantly between 2001 and 2006.

53 See Ronald J. Deibert and Rafal Rohozinski, "Good for Liberty, Bad for Security? Global Civil Society and Securitization of the Internet," in *Access Denied*, ed. Ronald J. Deibert, John G. Palfrey, Rafal Rohozinski, and Jonathan Zittrain (MIT Press: forthcoming, 2007).

54 See Deibert and Rohozinksi, "Good for Liberty," 26, who say: "perhaps more alarming is the finding that 40% of those arrested face charges and sentences that are not made public. Most bloggers arrested will be detained without access to legal recourse until the state, of its own volition, chooses to release information on the blogger's sentence and occasionally release the blogger either outright or pending a trial or retrial."

55 Dowling, "Comedy of Manners"; Andrew Keen, *The Cult of the Amateur: How Today's Internet Is Killing Our Culture* (London: Nicholas Brealey, 2007), quoted in Dowling, "Comedy of Manners."

56 See http://globalvoicesonline.org/about/.

57 Quoted in Tim Dowling, "Comedy of Manners." See also blogging.wikia.com/wiki/blogger%27s_Code_of_Conduct.

58 See Jonathan Freedland, "The blogosphere risks putting off everyone but point-scoring males," *The Guardian*, April 11, 2007.

59 *Ding zi hu* literally "nail house" in Chinese, refers to a household or person who refuses to vacate their home to make way for property development. Nail houses literally stick out like nails in an otherwise modern environment, and their owners, just like nails, refuse to be beaten down, to give in. See http://www.virtual-china.org/2007/01/shanghais_stron.html. The description was also applied earlier in 2007 to "Shanghai's Strongest Nail House."

60 Many blogs, in English and Chinese, posted this story. For English-language blogs, see Peering.into.the Interior, http://venture160.wordpress.com/2007/03/08/chinas-most-incredible-holdout/, and Global Voices online, http://www.globalvoices online.org/2007/03/22/china-homeowners-hold-their-ground/.

61 See http://www.metro.co.uk/news/article.html?in_article_id=40673&in_pageid=34&expand=true.

62 See http://www.chinadaily.com.cn/china/2007-04/03/content_842221.htm.

63 There is no longer a record of the Daily Mirror coverage, but see http://www.metro.co.uk/news/article.html?in_article_id=40673&in_page_id=34&expand=true.

64 See http://environmentdebate.wordpress.com/2007/03/08/one-chinese-mans-battle-to-save-his-environment/.

65 Quoted in "Media Overexcited in 'Nail House' coverage," an editorial in the *China Youth Daily*, March 29, 2007 by Lu Gaofeng, which was translated by David Bandurski of the China Media Project at Hong Kong University at http://cmp.hku.hk/look/article.tpl?IdLanguage=1&IdPublication=1&NrIssue=1&NrSection=100&NrArticle=828.

66 See for example http://www.iht.com/articles/2007/04/03/news/house.php; http://newsvote.bbc.co.uk/go/pr/fr/-/1/hi/world/asia-pacific/6483997.stm; http://howard french.com/archives/2007/03/27/chongqing_journal_homeowner.

67 As of April 15, 2007.

68 Zhou's blog is at http://www.zuola.com/weblog/.

69 See http://www.globalvoicesonline.org/2007/03/30/china-nations-first-citizen-reporter/.

70 See http://chinadigitaltimes.net/2007/03/chinese_government_forbidden_media_reports_about_the_na.php.

71 See http://www.globalvoicesonline.org/2007/03/30/china-nations-first-citizen-reporter/. It is worth noting that such detailed reports, common to blogs, would

be extremely unlikely in newspapers where naturally space is at a premium. The same applies to the 3,644-word telephone interview with Wu Ping by Peering Into the Interior, which was posted on 22 March. See http://venture160.wordpress.com/2007/03/22/interview-with-chinas-most-incredible-holdout/.

72 For more details, including photographs of the protestors, see http://www.global voicesonline.org/2007/03/30/china-nations-first-citizen-reporter/.

73 Quoted in David Bandurski, "Chinese media and Web users discuss the winners and losers following demolition of China's 'toughest nail house,'" on the China Media Project at http://cmp.hku.hk/look/article.tpl?IdLanguage=1&IdPublication =1&NrIssue=1&NrSection=100&NrArticle=833.

74 See for example http://howardfrench.com/archives/2007/03/27/chongqing_journal _homeowner; http://www.chinadaily.com.cn/china/2007-04/03/content_842221.htm; http://blog.foreignpolicy.com/node/4211.

75 See for example http://cmp.hku.hk/look/article.tpl?IdLanguage=1&IdPublica-tion=1&NrIssue=1&NrSection=100&NrArticle=833.

76 According to "Louise," "The situation is not that different here in Brooklyn, USA. Developers want to seize six homes that residents claim are part of the Underground Railroad of the Civil War era. The City has tried all sorts of tactics to discredit the residents. It seems like the same story gets repeated over and over: 'selfish and possibly crazy holdouts preventing progress.' In Downtown Brooklyn, developers want to destroy homes using eminent domain to build an underground parking lot." See comments at http://www.virtual-china.org/2007/03/another_chinese.html.

77 See Vince Carducci, "Culture Jamming: A Sociological Perspective," in *Journal of Consumer Culture* 6, no. 1: 116–38; and J.M. Handelman and R.V. Kozinets, *Encyclopedia of Sociology*, entry on "Culture Jamming," unpublished manuscript, quoted in Carducci.

78 Umberto Eco "Towards a Semiological Guerilla Warfare," in *Travels in Hyperreality*. (San Diego: Harcourt Brace, 1986), quoted in Todd Tietchen, "Language Out of the Root: Excavating the Roots of Culture Jamming and Postmodern Activism from William S Burroughs' *Nova* Trilogy," *Discourse* 23, no. 3 (Fall 2001): 107–29.

79 Kalle Lasn, *Culture Jam: The Uncooling of America* (New York: Eagle Brook, 1999), quoted in Carducci, "Culture Jamming."

80 See Tietchen, "Language Out of the Root."

81 See Bart Cammaerts, "Jamming the Political: Beyond Counter-hegemonic Practices," in *Continuum: Journal of Media & Cultural Studies* 21, no. 1 (March 2007): 71–90.

82 See Carducci, "Culture Jamming," 118.

83 Naomi Klein, *No Logo: Taking Aim at the Brand Bullies* (New York: Picador, 2000), quoted in Carducci, "Culture Jamming," 119.

84 Philip Kotler and Eduardo L. Roberto, *Social Marketing: Strategies for Changing Public Behavior* (New York: Free Press, 1989), quoted in Carducci, "Culture Jamming," 119.

85 See http://adbusters.org/the_magazine/.

86 See http://www.theyesmen.org/.

87 See http://sniggle.net/.

88 See http://www.geocities.com/billboardcorrections/index.htm; http://www.popaganda.com/billboards/index.shtml.

89 Bart Cammaerts, "Jamming the Political."

90 *Media Burn* exhibition and leaflet, Tate Modern, London. December 16, 2006–February 18, 2007.

91 http://www.guerrillagirls.com/interview/faq.shtml.

92 Victoria Carty, "Technology and Counter-hegemonic Movements: The Case of Nike Corporation." *Social Movement Studies* 1, no. 2 (2002): 129–46.

93 D. McAdams, J.D. McCarthy, and M.N. Zald, "Social Movements" in *Handbook of Sociology*, ed. Neil J. Smelser (Newbury Park, CA: Sage, 1988), 699, quoted in Carducci, "Culture Jamming," 130.

94 James Surowiecki, *The Wisdom of Crowds* (New York: Anchor, 2005), is a brilliant popular account of evidence that the sum of informed popular opinion is more effective in decision making than the sole expert.

95 Lawrence Lessig, *The Future of Ideas: The Fate of the Commons in a Connected World* (New York: Vintage, 2002), 94.

96 Lessig comes close to recognizing this in stressing that many ideas remain taken for granted, uncritically accepted (ibid., 5). They are not then so much resources as impediments. But then neither are ideas that change the world "resources," they motivate to action.

97 As in Pierre Bourdieu and Jean-Claude Passeron, "Cultural Capital and Pedagogic Reproduction," in *Reproduction in Education, Society and Culture* (London: Sage, 1977), 71–106.

98 Eşref Aksu and Joseph A. Camillerie, eds., *Democratizing Global Governance* (London: Palgrave Macmillan), 2002.

99 See especially James Fishkin, *Democracy and Deliberation: New Directions for Democratic Reform* (New Haven: Yale University Press, 1991). David Held, *Models of Democracy,* 3rd edition (Cambridge: Polity, 2006), 231–53, provides an overview of current ideas of deliberative democracy, which seek to base decisions in both expertise and inclusiveness.

100 Note that we are not saying it is the network that diminishes inequalities of power. The thrust of Manuel Castells' *The Rise of Network Society* (Oxford: Blackwell, 1996) is that the network as the new organizational form arose from business strategies that replaced one kind of power with another. For an overview of Castells and other main theories of the relation between information and society, see Frank Webster, *Theories of Information Society* (London: Routledge, 1995).

101 The challenge for the future of a democratic media lies more in shaping the structures of ownership and control than in technological development. Peter Dahlgren argues the Net enhances the public sphere and allows new communication spheres to develop. See Peter Dahlgren, "The Public Sphere and the Net," in *Mediated Politics: Communication in the Future of Democracy*, ed. W. Lance Bennett and Robert M. Entman (Cambridge: Cambridge University Press, 2001), 33–55. Thomas Meyer and Lew Hinchman, in *Media Democracy: How the Media Colonize Politics* (Cambridge: Polity, 2002), argue that "Democratizing the rules of media selection and presentation may be the greatest single challenge that democratic politics will face in the future" (142). For further accounts of the tension between the media and democracy, see Henry Jenkins and David Thorburn, eds., *Democracy and New Media* (Cambridge, MA: MIT, 2004); Douglas Kellner, *Media Spectacle and the Crisis of Democracy* (Boulder: Paradigm, 2005).

102 See John S. Dryzeck, *Discursive Democracy: Politics, Policy and Political Science* (Cambridge: Cambridge University Press, 1990), who argues for the adaptation of Habermas's communicative rationality to take account of the reconstruction of tradition.

103 David Held, *Global Covenant: The Social Democratic Alternative to the Washington Consensus* (Cambridge: Polity, 2004), argues that the two principles of inclusiveness and subsidiarity in an interconnected world require a multi-level system of global governance with a global covenant enshrining global social democracy. Amitai Etzioni, *From Empire to Community: A New Approach to International Relations* (New York: Palgrave Macmillan, 2004), writes of the possibility of a global community in advance of democratization, arguing for security first. It is difficult to see how the difference between these two views can be resolved except through democratic debate.

104 Now it is the turn of the bloggers to be the focus of critical debate and efforts are being made to certify their responsibility with a "Civility Enforced" badge proposed by Jimmy Wales, creator of Wikipedia, and Tim O'Reilly, of Web 2.0 fame. In the words of Jonathan Freedland, "For the blogosphere represents an enormous democratic opportunity.... But this freedom has its downside." *The Guardian*, April 11, 2007, 31.

NOTES ON THE CONTRIBUTORS

Isolda Agazzi Ben Attia is Senior Program Officer for the Conference of NGOs (CONGO). Isolda holds a master's degree in international relations from the Graduate Institute of International Studies (IUHEI) of Geneva. She has worked for more than ten years in the field of development co-operation, for bi- and multilateral donor agencies, an academic research institute, and NGOs, in Switzerland and on the field, covering socio-economic development and good governance issues. She joined CONGO in 2002, and since 2004 she has also been a lecturer in international law at the University of Calabria (Italy).

Martin Albrow is a sociologist whose books include *Max Weber's Construction of Social Theory, Do Organizations Have Feelings, Sociology: The Basics*, and the prize-winning *The Global Age*. Formerly he was founding editor of the Journal *International Sociology*, president of the British Sociological Association, and chair of the Sociology Panel for the British universities' Research Assessment Exercise. Emeritus professor of the University of Wales, he is currently a Visiting Fellow in the Centre for the Study of Global Governance in London and an editor in chief of *Global Civil Society*, 2006/7.

Renate Bloem completed her studies in medicine, languages, and literature at the Universities of Bonn, Munich, and Columbia University and started her academic career by teaching at international schools and cultural institutions worldwide. Elected president of the Conference of NGOs in Consultative Relationship with the United Nations (CONGO) in November 2000 and re-elected in December 2003, she has been involved in numerous UN meetings, led CONGO delegations to the World Conference against Racism, to the World Summit on Sustainable Development. Through the CONGO Working Group on Asia she has organized the Asian Civil Society Forum 2002 and 2004 in Bangkok, Thailand, and, together with Latin American NGO networks, the NGO Seminar in Santiago, Chile. Most recently, together with Board member FEMNET, she organized the African Civil Society Forum in Addis Ababa.

Together with the CONGO Team she has been at the forefront of guiding, supporting, and coordinating civil society in the processes of the World Summit of the Information Society (WSIS) in Geneva and Tunis.

John D. Clark has worked with development NGOs, the World Bank, United Nations, universities, and as advisor to governments on development and civil society issues. His career has focused on poverty reduction, participation, civil society, globalization, and bridging the gap between grassroots organizations and official agencies.

He is currently Lead Social Development Specialist for East Asia in the World Bank. He has focused particularly on governance, poverty, and civil society issues in Cambodia and Indonesia and spent eight months in Aceh, Indonesia, working on tsunami reconstruction, especially regarding donor coordination. Before that he took a four-year absence from the World Bank, during which he worked in the United Nations Secretary-General's office (as project director for the high-level panel on UN–civil society relations), was Visiting Fellow at the London School of Economics, and served on a task force advising the British prime minister about Africa. He also wrote *Worlds Apart: Civil Society and the Battle for Ethical Globalization,* published by Kumarian in the US and Earthscan in the UK in 2003.

He joined the World Bank in 1992 to head its NGO/Civil Society Unit—leading the Bank's global strategy for collaboration and dialogue with civil society. In 1998 he moved to the East Asia region, in particular to help address the social aspects of the Asian economic crisis. Before 1992 he worked in NGOs for eighteen years, mostly with Oxfam UK, where he was head of campaigns and policy. He is the author of four other books, including *Democratizing Development: The Role of Voluntary Organizations* (1991).

Philippe Dam is the associate program officer for the Conference of NGOs (CONGO). Philippe studied administration and public law at Sciences-Po Rennes (France) and holds a master's degree in international administration from the University of Paris I Panthéon-Sorbonne. He worked for various agencies within the UN system in Turin, Paris, and Geneva and joined CONGO in December 2004 to work on human rights and WSIS programs.

John English is the executive director of the Centre for International Governance Innovation (CIGI) and University Research Professor at the University of Waterloo. He is a former president of the Canadian Institute of International Affairs, past chair of the Canadian Museum of Civilization, and served as a Canadian member of parliament.

Jo Marie Griesgraber is the executive director of the New Rules for Global Finance Coalition, a Washington-based international network of activists and researchers concerned with reforms of the international financial architecture. Previously, Dr. Griesgraber was the director of policy at Oxfam America, where she supervised advocacy programs on international trade, humanitarian response, global funding for basic education, and extractive industries. Before that, she directed the Rethinking Bretton Woods Project at the Centre of Concern, a Jesuit-related social justice research centre, where she worked on reform of the World Bank, regional development banks, and the International Monetary Fund. She has taught political science at Georgetown University, Goucher College, and American University, and was the deputy director of the Washington Office on Latin America, a human rights lobby office. She chaired Jubilee 2000/USA's executive committee and edited, with Bernhard Gunter, the five-volume Rethinking Bretton Woods series. Ms. Griesgraber received her PhD in political science from Georgetown University and her B.A. in history from the University of Dayton, Ohio.

Virginia Haufler (PhD, Cornell, 1991) is an associate professor of government and politics at the University of Maryland. She is an expert in the fields of international relations, international political economy, and business and world politics. From 1999 to 2000, Dr. Haufler was a senior associate at the Carnegie Endowment for International Peace, where she directed a program on the role of the private sector in international affairs. She serves as a board member of Women in International Security (WIIS) and is on the advisory committee of the Peace Research Institute, Frankfurt. She recently co-authored the UN Global Compact report *Enabling Economies of Peace: Public Policy for Corporate Conflict-Sensitive Practices*. Among her other publications are *A Public Role for the Private Sector: Industry Self-Regulation in a Global Economy* (2001); "Is There a Role for Business in Conflict Management?" in *Turbulent Peace* (eds. Crocker, Hampson, and Aall, 2001); *Private Authority and International Affairs* (co-edited with Cutler and Port, 1999); and *Dangerous Commerce: Insurance and the Management of International Risk* (1997).

Gina E. Hill has been a human rights activist since 1993 and was called to the Bar in 2001. Her areas of specialization are international human rights and non-governmental organizations. Currently completing her LL.D. at the University of Ottawa, Ms. Hill's research examines the cases of the Ottawa Process for a Landmines Treaty and the negotiations for the International Criminal Court. Ms. Hill is president of the board of directors of Amnesty International Canada. She has lived, studied, and worked in six countries and speaks five languages fluently.

Fiona Holland is managing editor of the *Global Civil Society Yearbook* at the London School of Economics' Centre for the Study of Global Governance.

Prior to joining LSE, where she completed a master's degree in development studies in 1999, she was editor of *Orbit,* which in 2001 won "best magazine" in the One World Media Awards, the most respected prize for international development coverage in the UK. In addition to various editing and reporting roles in Asia and the UK, Fiona has project-managed public awareness campaigns and curated photographic exhibitions on cultural exchange, Northern perceptions and portrayals of developing countries, and the notion of global risk. Currently she is working on an exhibition of political cartoons, linked to the forthcoming publication of *Global Civil Society 2007/8,* and collaborating on a multi-pronged initiative exploring sexuality and intimacy.

Mohini Kak is a practitioner scholar with the experience of working on issues of local self-governance, civil society building, and women's empowerment. She is an integral part of the Systematization of Knowledge team of the Society for Participatory Research in Asia (PRIA). She holds a master's in social work with a specialization in urban and rural community development from the Tata Institute for Social Sciences, and her first attempt at bridging the world of a practitioner and an academician came in 2006 when she presented a paper at the 4th International Conference on Citizenship and Participation in Jaipur, India, based on her experience of working on the issue of civil society and local self-governance in the State of Himachal Pradesh, India. She has also worked on issues relating to gender and development. She is co-editor of *Citizen Participation and Democratic Governance: In Our Hands*, published by Concept Publications in February 2007.

Nigel T. Martin is the founding president of the Montreal International Forum (FIM), an international NGO think tank based in Montreal. FIM is a global alliance of individuals and organizations with the goal of improving the influence of international civil society on the United Nations and the multilateral system.

A graduate of Mount Allison University, Mr. Martin has over thirty years' experience in the NGO community in Canada and elsewhere and has been the executive director of several NGOs. These include the Canadian Council for International Co-operation (CCIC) in Ottawa, Euro Action Accord in London (UK), and OCSD and Oxfam-Québec in Montreal.

He began his career with the Canadian International Development Agency (CIDA) in 1971, where he was one of the earliest staff members of the then-fledgling NGO program. Before leaving the government in 1975 for a career in the NGO sector, he was the director of Asia programming for the CIDA NGO division.

Mr. Martin was the initiator and founding co-president of the original World Bank/NGO Committee.

He has served on several boards of directors and is currently on the boards of the Carold Foundation in Toronto. He is also a founding board member of The Mothers' Trust.

Kinda Mohamadieh serves as the program manager at the Arab NGO Network for Development (ANND). ANND brings together twenty-seven NGOs and seven national networks from eleven Arab countries active in the fields of social development, human rights, gender, and the environment. The network aims to develop the capacity of Arab civil society organizations and promoting democracy, human rights, participation, and good governance within civil society and among governments. The network's programs focus on issues of development, mainly the Millennium Development Goals; democracy and human rights; and the socio-economic impact of trade liberalization in the Arab region. Miss Mohamadieh has academic training in economics at the undergraduate level and in international development and non-profit management at the graduate level. Throughout her work at ANND, she concentrated on trade and globalization issues and capacity building of civil society organizations in relation to the work being done within the scope of the World Trade Organization, Euro-Mediterranean Partnership, bilateral free trade agreements, and regional economic integration. She participated in writing several papers concerning the role and the challenges of civil society organizations in the Arab region, particularly in the above-mentioned fields of ANND's concern.

Elizabeth Riddell-Dixon is a professor of international relations and former chair of the Department of Political Science at the University of Western Ontario. Her publications include five books, *Canada and the Beijing Conference on Women: Governmental Politics and NGO Participation* (author, 2001), *The State of the United Nations, 1993: North–South Perspectives* (co-author, 1993), *International Relations in the Post–Cold War Era* (co-editor, 1993), *Canada and the International Seabed: Domestic Determinants and External Constraints* (author, 1989), and *The Domestic Mosaic: Interest Groups and Canadian Foreign Policy* (author, 1985), as well as articles in *Global Governance*, the *International Social Science Journal*, *Canadian Journal of Political Science*, *International Journal*, *Canadian Foreign Policy*, *Journal of Comparative and Commonwealth Politics*, and *Journal of Estuarine and Coastal Law*. She is currently on the board of directors of the London Museum of Ontario Archaeology. She has served on the executive board of the Canadian Political Science Association (2005–2006), board of directors of the Canadian Political Science Association (2004–2006), and the editorial board of *Canadian Foreign Policy* (1993–2005). She was co-director of the Summer Workshop Program of the Academic Council on the United Nations System (2004-2005), chair of the Academic Committee of the Board of Directors of the Lester B.

Pearson Canadian International Peacekeeping Centre (1998-2003), chair of the International Organization Section of International Studies Association (1998–2003), and vice-president of the Academic Council on the United Nations System (1991–1993).

Ziad Abdel Samad is the executive director of the Arab NGO Network for Development (ANND), based in Beirut, since 1999. ANND brings together twenty-seven NGOs and seven national networks from eleven Arab countries active in the fields of social development, human rights, gender, and the environment. The network, established in 1997, focuses on developing the capacity of Arab civil society organizations and promoting democracy, human rights, participation, and good governance in civil society and among governments. It has been an active participant in a number of United Nations conferences, WTO negotiations, and the World Social Forum. Mr. Abdel Samad is a member of the Lebanese Negotiating Committee for the accession in the WTO. He sits on the International Council of the World Social Forum and the Coordination Committee of Social Watch, an international network of citizen coalitions that monitors the implementation of the commitments made at the 1995 World Summit on Social Development in Copenhagen. Mr. Abdel Samad is a member of the board of directors of CIVICUS: World Alliance for Citizen Participation. He is a member of the UNDP CSO Advisory Committee to the Administrator. Mr. Abdel Samad is general manager of the Centre for Developmental Studies (MADA), a Lebanese centre for social and economic studies and research.

Jan Aart Scholte is professor in the Department of Politics and International Studies and co-director of the Centre for the Study of Globalisation and Regionalisation at the University of Warwick. He held previous posts at the University of Sussex, Brighton, and the Institute of Social Studies, The Hague, as well as visiting positions at Cornell University, the London School of Economics, the International Monetary Fund, the Moscow School of Economics, and Gothenburg University. He is author of *Globalization: A Critical Introduction* (Palgrave-Macmillan, 2005, 2nd edition), *Civil Society and Global Democracy* (Polity, forthcoming), and *International Relations of Social Change* (Open University Press, 1993); co-author of *Contesting Global Governance* (Cambridge University Press, 2000); editor of *Civil Society and Accountable Global Governance* (forthcoming), and *Civil Society and Global Finance* (Routledge, 2002); co-editor of *The Encyclopaedia of Globalization* (Routledge, 2006); and author of some 100 articles, chapters, and working papers. He is also an editor of the journal *Global Governance*. His current research focuses on questions of governing a more global world, with particular emphasis on questions of building global democracy.

Rajesh Tandon is president of PRIA (Society for Participatory Research in Asia). He was co-founder of PRIA in 1982 following his tenure as Fellow, Public Enterprise Centre for Continuing Education, New Delhi.

Over the last twenty-five years, Dr. Tandon has been a practitioner of participatory research and development and become an internationally acclaimed leader in the area. His work has been, over a wide variety of themes, to strengthen the capacities and institutional mechanisms of voluntary development organizations in India and other developing nations. He specializes in development management; training of trainers in participatory monitoring; networking, coalition and alliance building; participation and governance.

He is the chair on the board of many national and international civil society organizations and part of the founding board of directors of CIVICUS. He is also chair of Montreal International Forum (FIM). He has authored many books and articles on civil society and governance.

He was recently awarded a Social Justice medal by the Institute of Gender Justice and NALSA, Department of Law & Justice, Government of India, on the International Women's Day, 2007.

Andrew S. Thompson is a Special Fellow with the Centre for International Governance Innovation (CIGI) in Waterloo, Canada. He holds a PhD in history from the University of Waterloo, and his areas of specialization include human rights and international governance. He has written a number of book chapters and is co-editor of *Haiti: Hope for a Fragile State* (Wilfrid Laurier University Press, 2006). He has also written reports for the Canadian Department of Foreign Affairs, the United Nations University Press, the Canadian International Council, and the Centre for Foreign Policy and Federalism. Prior to pursuing his doctoral studies, he worked for Amnesty International's Canadian Section in Ottawa, and in 2004 he represented the organization as a member of a human rights lobbying and fact-finding mission to Haiti.

Paul van Seters studied law at Utrecht University and sociology at the University of California, Berkeley. Currently he is the director of Globus and a professor of globalization and sustainable development at TiasNimbas Business School at Tilburg University, The Netherlands. Previously he was a professor of legal sociology in the Faculty of Law at Tilburg University. He has published articles and books on socio-legal theory, public administration, and cultural sociology. His current research interests include law and communitarianism, corporate social responsibility, and the global civil society. He is co-editor of *Globalization and Its New Divides* (2003) and editor of *Communitarianism in Law and Society* (2006).

James W. St.G. Walker is a professor of history at the University of Waterloo, where he specializes in the history of human rights and race relations. In 2003–2004 he was the Bora Laskin National Fellow in Human Rights Research. His books include *The Black Loyalists* (2nd edition, 1992), and *"Race," Rights and the Law in the Supreme Court of Canada* (Osgoode Society and Wilfrid Laurier University Press, 1997), and he has published numerous articles and book chapters analyzing campaigns for human rights reform. Walker has himself been intimately involved with civil society over the years. In the 1960s he served as a CUSO volunteer in a Gandhian Ashram in the state of Orissa in India, where he participated in community development projects, and later worked on the CUSO national staff in Ottawa. He was a founder and teacher in the Transition Year Program for African-Canadian and First Nations students at Dalhousie University, and a founder and long-time board member of the Global Community Centre of Kitchener-Waterloo. He has served on the boards of several NGOs with an international focus, including CUSO and the Shastri Indo-Canadian Institute.

INDEX

A

Accountability Charter, of international non-governmental organizations: and global civil society forum, xxii–xxiii, 214–16, 218–19, 220, 237; signatories to, 215–16, 221n1; text of, 224–30

Adbusters Media Foundation, 266

Afghanistan, 56, 120, 177

Africa: civil society fora in, 55–56; and civil society/G8 meetings, 186, 187–89, 192, 194, 195, 198, 199–200, 201, 202; Commission for, 260; conflicts in, and role of corporations, xxi, 64, 169, 172–74; and Make Poverty History campaign, 259–61; and NEPAD, 187–88, 192, 194, 195, 199–200. *See also* corporate social responsibility; corporations, transnational

Ahmadinejad, Mahmoud, 262

AIDS. *See* HIV/AIDS

Alexander, Jeffrey, 30

Amnesty International, 5, 29, 33, 104; and CICC, 131, 132, 136, 140, 141

Annan, Kofi, xiv, 12, 61, 71, 143; and human rights, 61, 62, 66; and Peace-building Commission, 63–64; report by ("In Larger Freedom"), 61, 66, 69; and UN Global Compact, 175

anti-apartheid movement, 13, 171–72

anti-globalization movement, 6–7, 26–28, 29, 36–37, 62, 112, 247

Arab NGO Network for Development (ANND), xix–xx, xxiv, 121–27; about, 121–22; and CIVICUS, 122–23; and Euro-Mediterranean NGO Platform, 123–24; and forum on globalization and trade, 122, 123; and global anti-poverty campaign, 123; and MDGs, 123; and Social Watch, 122; website of, 124; and World Social Forum, 121, 123

Arab region, obstacles to civil society in, 112–121, 124–27; democratic deficit, 113–14; distrust of Western democracy, 119; emergence of strong states, 113–14, 115; international interference/double standards, 117; invasion/occupation of Iraq, 116–17; limited space, 114–15, 124–25; networking challenges of CSOs, 121; occupation/partition of Palestine, 113–14, 116, 117, 120; perceived threats to national identity, 114, 115; priority challenges, 116–17; reliance on foreign aid/agendas, 115; religion as divisive issue, 118–19; rise of Islamic regimes/movements, 114, 119; rise of terrorism, 117, 120; structural/contextual complexities, 117–18, 120

Arab states: and foreign occupation, 113–14, 116–17, 120; and International Criminal Court, 143; and perceived threats to national identity, 114, 115; and rise of Islamic regimes/movements, 114, 119; as strong, 113–14, 115

Asia: civil society in, 80–81; civil society forum in, 56–57; financial crisis in, 147

Asia–Europe Meeting (ASEM), 232

Asian South Pacific Bureau of Adult Education (ASPBAE), 77

Axworthy, Lloyd, 106–107, 145n14

B

Beijing Conference. *See* Fourth World Conference on Women

"Bhopal Hoax" (Yes Men), 266

Books in the Studies in International Governance Series

Paul Heinbecker and Patricia Goff, editors
Irrelevant or Indispensable? The United Nations in the 21st Century / 2005 / xii + 196 pp. / ISBN 0-88920-493-4

Paul Heinbecker and Bessma Momani, editors
Canada and the Middle East: In Theory and Practice / 2007 / ix + 232 pp. / ISBN-13: 978-1-55458-024-8 / ISBN-10: 1-55458-024-2

Yasmine Shamsie and Andrew S. Thompson, editors
Haiti: Hope for a Fragile State / 2006 / xvi + 131 pp. / ISBN-13: 978-0-88920-510-9 / ISBN-10: 0-88920-510-8

James W. St.G. Walker and Andrew S. Thompson, editors
Critical Mass: The Emergence of Global Civil Society / 2008 / xxviii + 302 pp. / ISBN-13: 978-1-55458-022-4 / ISBN-10: 1-55458-022-6

Jennifer Welsh and Ngaire Woods, editors
Exporting Good Governance: Temptations and Challenges in Canada's Aid Program / 2007 / xx + 343 pp. / ISBN-13: 978-1-55458-029-3 / ISBN-10: 1-55458-029-3